TREASURE-HOUSE OF THE LANGUAGE

TREASURE-HOUSE OF THE LANGUAGE

THE LIVING *OED*

CHARLOTTE BREWER

YALE UNIVERSITY PRESS
NEW HAVEN AND LONDON

For information about this and other Yale University Press publications, please contact:
U.S. Office: sales.press@yale.edu   www.yalebooks.com
Europe Office: sales@yaleup.co.uk   www.yaleup.co.uk

Set in Sabon by J&L Composition, Filey, North Yorkshire
Printed in Great Britain by St Edmundsbury Press Ltd, Bury St Edmunds

Library of Congress Cataloging-in-Publication Data

Brewer, Charlotte, 1956–
    Treasure-house of the language: the living OED/Charlotte Brewer.
      p. cm.
    Includes bibliographical references and index.
    ISBN 978–0–300–12429–3 (alk. paper)
    1. Oxford English dictionary. 2. Encylopedias and dictionaries—History and criticism. 3. English language—Lexicography. 4. English language—Etymology. I. Title
    PE1617.O94B74 2007
    423—dc22
                                                                                              2007011034

A catalogue record for this book is available from the British Library.

10 9 8 7 6 5 4 3 2 1

For Chris, Alice, Miriam and Ursula

Contents

Illustrations

Acknowledgements

All researchers on the history of *OED* owe a primary debt of gratitude to K. M. Elisabeth Murray (1909–98), whose book *Caught in the Web of Words* (1977) drew in masterly fashion on a wealth of family papers to describe her grandfather's creation of the Dictionary. These papers are now deposited in the Bodleian Library, and I thank the curators of this library for permission to quote from them. Much of the quoted matter in this book, however, comes from the *OED*'s own archives and those of its publisher, from which copyright material is here reprinted or reproduced by permission of the Secretary to the Delegates of Oxford University Press. I am most grateful to this institution and its chief archivist Martin Maw for their unfailing generosity in allowing me access to their records. The former *OED* archivist Jenny McMorris (d. 2002), a meticulous and dedicated guardian, originally introduced me to some of their riches, and I especially thank her successor Beverley Hunt, who has cheerfully, imaginatively and swiftly ferreted out many documents and resolved many queries in the past two years.

I owe another debt to Peter Gilliver, one of the editors at work on the third edition of *OED*, who has readily made available to me his wide stock of knowledge about the *OED* and its archives and given me a most helpful range of comments and criticisms. His own book on the Dictionary, a history of the entire project which is to be published in some years' time by Oxford University Press, will enlarge on the majestic antecedents to this more limited narrative, fill in its gaps, and offer a different perspective. John Simpson, chief editor of *OED3*, has also given me valuable comments and feedback on matters both directly and tangentially related to the book, acknowledged here with thanks all the warmer for his benign tolerance of our occasional differences of opinion.

Much distinctive advice and fresh information has come from E. G. Stanley; I cannot thank him enough. Thanks also to those (especially Tony Augarde and Julian Barnes) who have told me about their personal experience of *OED* and its various post-1928 stages, to Mrs K. E. Schuller for talking to me about her memories of J. M. Wyllie, to Peter Glare for further information on Wyllie and for the photo reproduced on p. 87, to the estate of the late John Chadwick for its kind permission to publish excerpts from his draft obituary of Wyllie, to Celia Sisam for writing to me about her father, commenting on a draft of the book, and sending me the photo reproduced on p. 138, to Veronica Babington Smith for permission to quote from the letter by Rose Macaulay on p. 101, and to Michael Adams, Elizabeth Baigent, Sarah Bendall, Derek Brewer, Ursula Brewer, Marace Dareau, Roy Foster, John Heilbron, Simon Horobin, Alan Kirkness, Caroline Mcafee, Iseabail Macleod, Tom McCulloch, Avner Offer, Tom Paulin, Emma Smith, Chris Stray, Edmund Weiner and Christopher Whalen for generous and ready help of various sorts.

The poem by T. S. Eliot quoted from on p. 185 is in the copyright of Faber and Faber and Harcourt Publishers; the poems of Auden quoted from on pp. 193–4 are in the copyright of The Estate of W. H. Auden. All have responded most helpfully to inquiries. Aid of a different kind has come from the Arts and Humanities Research Council, which has funded a term of research leave enabling me to complete the book. All views expressed and interpretations offered within are, needless to say, my own, and are not (except when explicitly stated) to be blamed on any of the foregoing. Finally, I am, as ever, more grateful than I can express to my husband Chris Goodall.

Abbreviations

DNB: *Dictionary of National Biography* (1st edition)
DOST: *Dictionary of the Older Scottish Tongue*
NED: *New English Dictionary* (see Appendix 2: Glossary)
ODME: Oxford Dictionary of Modern English (unpublished; formerly the 'Quarto')
ODNB: *Oxford Dictionary of National Biography* (2nd edition of *DNB*)
OED1: first edition of the *OED*
OED2: second edition of the *OED*
OED2I: Introduction to *OED2* (in volume 1)
OED3: third edition of the *OED*
OEDS1, OEDS2, OEDS3, OEDS4: the individual volumes of Burchfield's Supplement
OLD: Oxford Latin Dictionary
OUP: Oxford University Press
SPE: Society for Pure English
TLS: *Times Literary Supplement*

CHR: C. H. Roberts, Secretary to the Delegates (of OUP) 1954–1974
CTO: C. T. Onions
DMD: D. M. (Dan) Davin, Assistant Secretary to the Delegates 1948–1970; Deputy Secretary and Academic Publisher 1970–78
HB: Henry Bradley
HGLM: H. G. Le Mesurier
HM: Humphrey Milford, Printer to OUP 1913–45
HWF: H. W. Fowler
KS: Kenneth Sisam, Assistant Secretary to the Delegates 1922–42; Secretary 1942–48
MP: the Murray Papers in the Bodleian Library, Oxford, as yet uncatalogued and grouped in numbered boxes by date

OED before a reference indicates *OED* archives at Oxford University Press
OED/RF refers to the as yet uncatalogued files titled 'OED Revision' in the
    OED archives
OUP before a reference indicates Oxford University Press archives
RWB: R. W. Burchfield
RWC: R. W. Chapman, Secretary of OUP 1920–42
SOED before a reference indicates *Shorter Oxford English Dictionary*
    archives at Oxford University Press

Introduction

Completion?

The year 1928 saw an event of national and international cultural significance in Britain. The *New English Dictionary*, now more usually known as the *Oxford English Dictionary*, was finally completed, after forty-four years and 128 separately published instalments (technically termed 'fascicles').[1] Its originators and first editors – R. C. Trench, Herbert Coleridge, F. J. Furnivall, the great J. A. H. Murray, and Murray's equally intellectually powerful but more gentle co-editor Henry Bradley – were all dead, but their pupils and followers had laboured on in their wake, in turn encouraged, cajoled and lashed by their long-suffering but exacting publishers, Oxford University Press. They crossed their finishing line on 19 April 1928, nearly seventy years after the Dictionary was first conceived and forty-four years after its first instalment, covering the letters *A–Ant*, had been published in 1884. One of the Press's first actions was to present a copy to George V. The King responded promptly, writing a 'very gracious letter . . . acknowledging the gift of the specially bound copy of the last volume of the Dictionary, and congratulating the University on the completion of its work'; the University was later gratified to learn that the King 'seldom failed to point out the Oxford Dictionary to guests whom he brings into the library at Windsor'.[2] The next few months saw a virtual fanfare of public acclaim as reviewers and cultural commentators on both sides of the Atlantic – not least Oxford University Press and the lexicographers themselves – remembered and retold the triumphant, if painful, journey that had been undertaken to arrive at what was widely recognized as the Dictionary's finishing point.[3]

But language does not wait on lexicographers, and successful dictionaries of current language need to be continuously revised as new words come into being and established words gradually shift their meaning. Even a historical dictionary such as the *OED* must adjust its contents and judgements to accommodate freshly published works from previously under-explored areas of the past, as scholarship rattles up the curtains on, say, the language of female authors, or of Middle English. And any human endeavour, especially one so substantial and protracted as the *OED*, is subject to error. As one of its two surviving lexicographers put it to the publishers in 1951, this greatest of dictionaries, despite its public reputation for unimpeachable authority, had 'hosts of wrong definitions, wrong datings, and wrong crossreferences. The problem is gigantic.'[4]

This book examines how the *OED* has tackled the need to revise and update itself since the completion of the first edition in 1928. In particular, it reveals the tension between two coexisting aims: to make the Dictionary as nearly perfect as possible, and to produce succeeding supplements and editions at a viable speed and cost. Since 1928, this tension has dominated the relationship between the publishers and the lexicographers. Compromises have been made and imperfections tolerated in the cause of generating income to secure the successful fulfilment of Oxford's lexicographical aims considered in their entirety, including the production of subsidiary dictionaries like the *Shorter* and the *Concise Oxford Dictionaries*, as well as the magnificent main Dictionary itself. These trade-offs (a word that only entered *OED* in 1986, with a quotation dated 1961) have never been explored. The huge project on which the Oxford lexicographers are now embarked, a complete revision and rewriting, long overdue, of the first edition of the *OED*, is a triumphant vindication of lexicographical choices and publishing strategy executed both painfully and astutely over many years.

To many of the participants in the completion of the first edition of *OED* in 1928, its publication seemed the near-final chapter in a long-drawn-out labour. From a perspective of eighty years' distance, during which the speed of change in language appears to have increased every decade, and the discovery of new texts and new words from the past has quickened rather than declined, 1928 looks more like a punctuation point in a process that will continue as long as the language exists.

A national monument

The origins of the *OED* can be traced back to 1857 (in what were later described as 'first gropings' towards the new work): two lectures delivered to the Philological Society in London in November 1857 by R. C. Trench, then Dean of Westminster and subsequently Archbishop of Dublin, which pointed out the deficiencies of existing dictionaries and proposed a number of improvements.[5] Trench's ideas were more fully developed by several

Society members in 1859, who produced a *Proposal for a Publication of a New English Dictionary* and embarked on a programme of recording words, appointing Herbert Coleridge (grandson of the poet) as their editor. The unfortunate Coleridge died two years later, aged only 31, 'from consumption brought on by a chill caused by sitting in damp clothes during a Philological Society lecture', and the Dictionary subsequently languished for twenty years or so, despite occasional periods or pockets of productivity, under the inspirational but over-stretched and unreliable F. J. Furnivall (1825–1910).[6] Momentum was attained when Oxford University Press took over the Dictionary in 1878 and appointed J. A. H. Murray (1837–1915) as editor in 1879, leading – after some difficult organizational and scholarly hurdles had been negotiated – to a more or less steady stream of publication from 1884 onwards.[7]

From early in its history, the new Dictionary had been acknowledged as advancing the academic study of language far beyond the achievements of its predecessors. Reviewers of the first fascicle called it 'a unique and peerless specimen of English lexicography' and saw that it was 'a work of the utmost importance to the scientific study of the English language'.[8] By 1898 it had only got up to the letter H, but the *Academy* spoke of it as '*the* Dictionary', assuring its readers that 'a good deal of entertainment, as well as of instruction', might be got from its pages.[9] The year before, in 1897, *The Times* described the work as 'The greatest effort probably which any University, it may be any printing press, has taken in hand since the invention of printing . . .. It will be not the least of the glories of the University of Oxford to have completed this gigantic task'[10] – though Murray was never given a university appointment or salary, and Oxford University Press displayed an ambivalent attitude towards the project and its staff, often lamenting, in internal memos, their incorrigible dilatoriness and their tendency to extend the work to a greater and greater compass. The Dictionary was a heavy burden on the Press through difficult economic times, including the First World War, and cost in total some £300,000, then an enormous sum.[11] This was despite the fact that many of its contributors were unremunerated and the salaried staff and editors chronically badly paid.

But the results were clearly worth it. It was always recognized that this was an investment that would reveal its full value in future years, and it brought with it honour and glory for the publishers, for the University of Oxford, and for the English language more generally, something the Press did not hesitate to exploit at a time of national need.[12] In 1916, while many of its staff were serving in various capacities in the war, OUP published a pamphlet extolling the Dictionary's virtues as, among other things, 'An

Imperial Asset': 'It is perhaps . . . in its exhibition of the language as a living and growing thing closely connected with the history of the nation, that it will yet have its greatest value for the British Empire and the whole English-speaking race'.[13] The *Saturday Review* praised it as a 'wonderful storehouse of our native language' which advanced the cause of English-speaking culture as well as philological investigation, and the *Asiatic Review* thought the same: 'A work of such magnificent proportions . . . should be the most coveted possession of all public libraries in the United Kingdom, in the Colonies, and at least the headquarters of every district in India and at her principal Colleges. It is not so much a Dictionary as a History of English speech and thought from its infancy to the present day.'[14] This remark may well have been prompted by one of the *OED*'s most attractive features: its munificent display of quotations to illustrate the history and usage of each word, often drawn from the nation's greatest writers – Chaucer, Shakespeare, Milton, Pope and Tennyson. These turn it into a cultural treasure-house, simultaneously testifying to the longevity of the language, the glories of the English tongue, and the scholarship of the Dictionary's editors.

The price of the finished product in 1928 was expensive: 50 guineas (or 55 guineas if one chose the best binding), amounting to more than £2,000 in today's money. But the Dictionary was bought by individuals as well as institutions, since special subscription deals over its long period of publication had made it more affordable.[15] Another reviewer urged 'every Englishman who can possibly afford it . . . to do his part in forwarding this great enterprise of national interest by purchasing the parts as they appear', words echoed by the long-term supporter and contributor W. W. Skeat, who wanted 'every man who paid income-tax to take a copy'.[16] Many of them did, so that the Press could claim in 1928 that 'from the time of the publication of the first part of *A* in 1884 the Dictionary has been a daily source of enlightenment and satisfaction to an incalculable number of readers. Each section has been eagerly welcomed.' The novelist Arnold Bennett confided to the *Evening Standard* that he 'had been buying it in parts for forty years and am still buying it. The longest sensational serial ever written!'[17] And it represented an extraordinary concentration of powerful intellectual resources on a single project, of a kind we now associate only with grand scientific research. The University's Chancellor, Lord Curzon, wrote in 1909 that the team of people working together on the Dictionary under the auspices of the Press represented 'probably the largest single engine of research working anywhere at the present time'.[18]

Celebration

At the banquet at the Goldsmiths' Hall to celebrate *OED*'s completion on 6 June 1928, the Prime Minister Stanley Baldwin described the Dictionary's genesis as 'the desire to record and to safeguard and to establish for all time the manifold riches of the English tongue'.[19] Now that it was finished, it was 'unrivalled in completeness and unapproachable in authority; as near infallibility, indeed, as we can hope to get this side of Rome'. It was a work of heroic proportions, which summed up and itself embodied the glorious achievement of English language and culture.

The preparations for the banquet had been in train for some time. R. W. Chapman, the senior publisher at Oxford University Press, discussed at length with his deputy Kenneth Sisam the complex details involved. The Press archives record an increasing ferment of preparation and excitement, with numerous, sometimes agonized deliberations over the date (which turned out to clash with Derby Day), the guest list, the precise wording of the invitation, the toasts, the speakers, and the question of what was to be done with the ladies (women were not allowed by the Worshipful Company of Goldsmiths into their hall). The University Publisher, Humphrey Milford (who bore this title by virtue of his office as head of the Press's London branch), complained that one of his American acquaintances 'took my breath away by saying one day that he should certainly come over on purpose, if he were lucky enough to be asked! I did not take up the hint.'[20] A couple of days before, Chapman wrote to the Vice-Chancellor, F. W. Pember, Warden of All Souls, 'As you know, the accommodation does not permit of the invitation of ladies, but there is room in the [minstrels'] gallery (not very comfortable I am afraid) for a few people, and we are proposing to place there one or more male members of the staff who do not care to dine, and also two or three lady members of the staff, and no doubt (if they wish to be present) Mrs Craigie and Mrs Onions [wives, respectively, of the two surviving main editors of the original team, W. A. Craigie and C. T. Onions]. I do not know if it would be dangerous to suggest that Mrs Pember might like to join this merry group. Perhaps if Lady Cave or Mrs Baldwin heard of it we might get into trouble.'[21]

Lady Cave was the wife of the Chancellor of the University, while Mrs Baldwin was the wife of the Prime Minister: understandably, they might feel slighted at being uninvited, or indeed, as Chapman put it to Craigie in another letter, 'skied' in the minstrels' gallery – as might also the various female members of staff who had worked side by side with their male fellows dining in the hall below.[22] They included James Murray's daughters Rosfrith (1884–1973), who had by then put in twenty-six years as an editorial assistant and continued working on the Dictionary until 1932, and Henry Bradley's daughter Eleanor (1875–1950), who was a member of her father's and then Onions's staff from 1897 to 1932 and helped with recording new vocabulary for several years thereafter.[23]

In the event, the dinner was a great success. It boasted nine courses, starting with caviare and smoked salmon and finishing with lobster, accompanied by seven wines ranging from an 1896 Crofts Port to a 1907 Château Margaux.[24] Baldwin's speech (which can be read online) was appositely witty but also magisterial, and was broadcast live on the radio – the publishers had reckoned that 'the *longueur*' at the dinner such an arrangement would risk would be worth it, in order 'to get the P.M. round the world. After all the company will consist of talkative people, well lit. So long as they may smoke, they won't fidget.'[25] The calculation proved correct. 'High as our expectations were pitched,' Chapman wrote to Baldwin's personal secretary Patrick Duff, 'the Prime Minister surpassed them. He was superb.' To G. R. Hughes, the Goldsmiths contact through whom they had arranged the dinner, he exclaimed, 'Bravissimo! Everyone was delighted with everything.'[26]

The Goldsmiths' Banquet was the main focus of celebration, but the University held its own ceremony too. The day before, 5 June 1928, the Dictionary editors and publishers were honoured at the feast of Encaenia, a major event in the calendar of Oxford University, held at the end of the academic year, when honorary degrees are bestowed on public, academic and local luminaries. Chapman wrote in advance to the University's Public Orator, to describe the various individual achievements and characteristics of the men who were to be thus rewarded with an honorary doctorate (Craigie, Onions, the Publisher Milford, the Printer John Johnson, and Chapman himself).[27] The Orator needed this information so that he could compose his public address to them (in Latin, of course). 'We are feeling rather like Puddletown when the King comes to open a bridge and the mayor is knighted,' Chapman said, modestly underplaying his own contribution to the enterprise.[28] In another letter discussing plans for the celebrations, Falconer Madan (former head of Oxford's Bodleian Library), who had contributed many seventeenth-century quotations to the Dictionary, pleads that the University should not forget 'the minor labourers who have borne the burden and the heat of the day' – Worrall, Lewis, Sweatman, Bayliss (the last three of whom had begun their working life as Bodleian Library employees). Could they not share with the senior editorial assistant A. T. Maling, the only minor labourer to be thus distinguished along with the honorary doctors, the privilege of an honorary MA? 'That costs nothing, and would give great delight. I understand the difficulty of grading

1. Oxford University Press officers: Humphrey Milford (Publisher), R. W. Chapman (Secretary), and John Johnson (Printer) display their academic robes after receiving honorary degrees from the University of Oxford on the completion of *OED* in 1928.

these men, without exciting jealousies, but the new generation knows nothing of the old days of toil, and only you and a few others like myself appreciate the aid rendered by the lesser folk to the O.E.D. in its harder times. One <u>hopes</u> that at least they come under some contributory scheme for pensions at the Press – but that is not my affair. A few words of encouragement to the "Little People" at the Dinner would be well bestowed, and productive of much content.'[29] Madan's plea bore fruit, and Baldwin recognized 'the sub-editors, the voluntary readers, the assistants, the pressmen, and the compositors', in the same breath in which he paid tribute to 'the ancient and benevolent University of Oxford'.[30]

As we shall see in Chapter 1, the payment and pension arrangements for both 'Little People' and chief editors were bones of contention which occasioned much misery and suffering. From the start, Murray had been underpaid, and both he and Bradley proved poor negotiators. This inheritance was to dog the enterprise over the years to come, as the Press strove to force succeeding lexicographers to yield copy on time for the printers and to reduce their work's size and scale, while on their part the lexicographers determined, with commendable consistency and resolve, to maintain the highest possible scholarly standards. Starving the Dictionary workers of funds was one way of making sure they didn't dawdle. But Madan's concern for such matters was entirely exceptional for an outsider, and was often waived by the employees themselves, who seem genuinely to have rejoiced in the magnificent achievement now so gratifyingly celebrated by their own Prime Minister, by numerous public figures, and by newspapers and periodicals across the nation.

The next step?

The lavish and triumphant applause for the finished product, and the claims for comprehensiveness, authority, and the superb realization of a lexicographical ambition unparalleled in scholarship to date, were largely justified. The *New York Times* was right to call it 'The greatest work in dictionary-making ever undertaken . . . a treasure-house for scholars, and at the same time a source of instruction and delight for the ordinary reader'. No other country had yet produced a dictionary of this size or completeness (the main competitors, the Grimm brothers' dictionary in Germany, and the Dutch *Woordenboek der Nederlandsche Taal*, were in 1928 still unfinished); no other dictionary of English had even begun to approach the erudition and range of the *Oxford English Dictionary*, which was uniquely based on a collection of five million quotations from works written between 1150 and the 1850s, contributed by hundreds of readers over decades.[31]

Nevertheless, the Dictionary began to go out of date soon after the first fascicle was published in 1884. New words continued to be coined, and existing words, already recorded, continued to modify or take on new meanings. Given the length of time over which the work had appeared, the early volumes in particular looked insufficiently in touch with current usage, as witnessed by their exclusion of several hundreds of words which had special resonance for an early twentieth-century audience. The public's exposure to and interest in scientific, technological and medical terms had greatly increased, but the first volume (*A–B*) had contained no entry for *appendicitis*, a word which came to prominence when Edward VII's coronation was postponed in 1902 for this very reason. Dozens of scientific terms (the most notorious being *radium*) had escaped both this and succeeding volumes.[32] The terminology of *aviation* (*aerodrome, aerodynamic, aeroplane*) was deficient or altogether absent, as were a multitude of terms (or new uses) relating to munitions and politics which had entered the language in the wake of the First World War and other world events (*Bolshevik, Comintern, commandant, communication lines, communication trench, comrade, concentration camp, Concert of Europe, conchy, dreadnought* (type of ship), *pacifism, profiteer,* etc.), not to mention vocabulary from other fresh fields of endeavour in technology or cultural experience (as in new senses for words like *film, jazz, movies, pictures, talkie,* or coinages such as *cinema*).

The necessity for eventual supplementation of the *OED* had been recognized in the terms under which the Philological Society had handed over the Dictionary to Oxford University Press, in an Indenture of 1879 which provided that 'The Delegates [of OUP] may also at any time, and from time to time, prepare and publish a Supplement or Supplements to the principal Dictionary'.[33] As early as 1896, one of the most loyal and assiduous of the long-term volunteer contributors to the Dictionary, Fitzedward Hall, told the Press that since parts for the letter *A* had been published in 1884 and 1885, 'not only have readers supplied hundreds of thousands of quotations, but, owing to the unprecedented interest which has recently been taken in our language, we now have access, in new publications, to an immense accumulation of linguistic facts, especially as regards dialect and etymology, demanding detailed recognition'. Hall was no doubt thinking of publications such as those of the Early English Text Society, which F. J. Furnivall had set up in 1864 partly to help the Dictionary by printing works previously available only in manuscript: many of the new words it brought to light, or earlier instances of words already recorded, appeared in works published after the relevant fascicle of the Dictionary had been completed. 'During the last eleven years,' Hall continued, 'I have copied upwards of a thousand quotations under A alone for words wanting to the Dictionary. What, then, must other readers have done for it in the same period?'[34]

All this meant that by the time the last fascicle was published in 1928, 'a great body of quotations had been amassed with a view to a Supplement on a grand scale, which should not only treat the new words and new meanings that had come into being during the publication of the successive sections ... but should also correct and amplify the evidence for what was already in print'.[35] But this, the publishers thought, was too ambitious a scheme. After the agonies of the last forty-four years, it was impossible for them to contemplate a further project which would again demand research and expenditure stretching unpredictably into the future. Instead, they decided to produce a single supplementary volume restricted to new words and senses, along with a smaller number of current words which had for some reason been omitted from the main Dictionary.

Despite the many years of dictionary-making experience shared by publishers and editors, this supplementary volume again proved most painful to produce. In 1928, the Assistant Secretary to the Delegates, Kenneth Sisam, tried to estimate its probable date of publication on the basis of the copy already prepared. Apologizing for seeming 'too much like Cassandra in these troublous times', he declared himself 'wholly dissatisfied with the position of the new words and senses'. He believed 'we are working on a 10 years scale . . . . If the Supplement is to take any such number of years, it will be out of date before it is finished, and so on until we are all dead; and Onions [the youngest of the lexicographers] toiling alongside Sisyphus among the shades.'[36] Despair of this sort had been a regular feature of the relations between the lexicographers and publishers ever since Oxford University Press had taken over the project in 1878.

The end of the work or the beginning of a new?

Notwithstanding Sisam's fears, the *Oxford English Dictionary*'s first Supplement emerged only five years later, in 1933. In the same year, Chapman wrote to the Vice-Chancellor to say, 'it is not thought practicable to provide further supplements, so that we are saying *finis coronat opus* [the end crowns the work]'. 'Fortunately,' he added, 'this does not mean that the University ceases to keep pace with the growth of the language.' The Press was preparing other, smaller, dictionaries of current English, while more detailed treatment of the historical periods already covered by *OED* were to be undertaken by 'the Americans', academic lexicographers at work in the States, in specialized projects under the direction of one of *OED*'s own lexicographers, Craigie, 'in the publication of which we hope to be associated'. Chapman was however quite clear that 'the New English Dictionary on Historical Principles does necessarily come to an end, and it may be doubted if such a comprehensive work, attempting to cover the whole vocabulary from the beginnings, can ever again be attempted'.[37]

He was mistaken. After 1933, contrary to general supposition, the publishers were compelled to keep their *OED* files open in order to field a steady stream of correspondence from the public, whether academics, dictionary enthusiasts, businessmen, amateur wordsmiths, or writers, critics, and interested users of all kinds, who queried existing entries in the Dictionary, asked for more information about specific words or language in general, offered numerous corrections and quotations that ante- and post-dated the *OED*'s evidence, and in general exhibited intense engagement with and devotion to this 'monarch among books'.[38] By 1955, ten years after another world war, a torrent of new vocabulary was pouring into English, reflecting social, scientific and cultural developments of every kind, and the 1933 Supplement was looking obsolescent. But so was the rest of the work.

Now that its readers had had time to read and digest the vast original, they were turning up more and more errors and deficiencies – while at the same time, linguistic, literary and historical scholarship was shining new light on words, texts and periods insufficiently well covered in the first edition. The Press bowed to the inevitable and determined to crank the project up again, but could bring itself only to produce a further Supplement, shelving revision indefinitely. Less agonizing than its predecessors, the second Supplement was still time-consuming, and it was over thirty years before it was complete, published in four volumes between 1972 and 1986 under the editorship of R. W. Burchfield.

Almost immediately, in 1989, the publishers brought out a 'second edition' of the *OED*: no revision of the original work, which was by now badly needed, but instead a merging together of the earlier Dictionary with Burchfield's four volumes of Supplement, a move that capitalized on the *OED*'s market value (since libraries replaced their existing copies), protected its original copyright, but added little that was new. Despite its apparently unadventurous lexicographical content, however, this composite edition heralded an enormous change in Oxford dictionary-making. It had been produced by committing its separate components to electronic tape, enabling their subsequent transference first to CD-Rom and then online, a form searchable by techniques that have revolutionized users' access to the riches within. During the late 1980s, Oxford University Press continued to explore ways of developing the Dictionary and exploiting the potential of its new electronic medium, and in 1993 it announced the start of a new, third edition, which would for the first time in its history attempt a full revision and rewriting of all its previously published material, from the late decades of the nineteenth century to the present day, with the aim of producing just such a comprehensive work, covering 'the whole vocabulary from the beginnings', that Chapman had thought impossible ever to attempt again.

This bold new project, now in its second decade, is of magisterial proportions. Under the leadership of John Simpson, the current *OED* lexicographers, numbering around seventy in all, launched their new dictionary online in March 2000, starting with the letter *M*, and have to date (autumn 2006) penetrated part-way into the letter *P*. Even a cursory study of the early material reveals that they have sought out countless numbers of new quotations for the Dictionary, from a much wider range of texts than those examined by their predecessors, and have drawn deeply on the vast quantities of linguistic and lexical scholarship published during the twentieth century and since. They have transformed the record for hosts of words and senses, both major and minor, in the alphabet range to this point treated. The scale of their achievement so far, and their vision, industry and perseverance, deserve to be celebrated (as does the staunchness of their publishers), in a task as daunting and as ambitious as that originally undertaken by Murray and his fellow pioneers.

Treasure-house of the Language explores the history of the *OED* from the completion of the first edition in 1928, through both the two, rather different, twentieth-century Supplements, to the online edition now in progress. It draws on letters and documents in the Oxford University Press archives and in the Bodleian Library, and on electronic analysis of *OED*'s second and third editions, to illuminate the penalties and obligations of this living dictionary, the most authoritative in its field, as well as its triumphs and achievements. Chapters I, II and III review the antecedents of the tortured progress of the 1933 Supplement, and recount the compilation, completion and reception of the first appendage to the *OED* as well as the Press's subsequent lexicographical activities. Chapter IV halts the chronological narrative to examine the role and function of the *OED*, the relationship between the public's expectations of the cultural treasure-house it had now become and the lexicographers' own aims and achievements; this part of the book provides a basis on which to evaluate the achievement of the post-1933 incarnations of the Dictionary. The narrative is resumed in Chapter V, with an account of Oxford University Press's decision in the 1950s further to supplement rather than revise the first edition. Chapters VI and VII look at the result: the creation and character of R. W. Burchfield's four volumes (1972–86), which brought the *OED* into the second half of the twentieth century. Finally, Chapter VIII explains how the short-term stopgap, the second edition of the *OED*, paved the way for the revision now in progress, the third edition – likely to be the last only because the process of revising may now never come to an end – and makes a preliminary assessment of the nature and quality of this ambitious new enterprise.

In the Preface to the first volume of his *Deutsches Wörterbuch*, the German equivalent to the *OED* project that stretched over many more years even than the first edition of *OED* itself, Jacob Grimm described how he thought his dictionary might play a part in the life of the average household:

In the evenings, the Father might read a few entries with his sons and thus test their linguistic ability and his own knowledge. The Mother would listen with pleasure, for women, with their sound common sense, remember pithy sayings and often have a keen desire to practise their unspoilt feeling for the language and to stand in front of the treasure chest from which pure words pour forth like folded linen sheets. One word, one rhyme, then leads to another, and the family often returns and again lifts the lid of the chest.[39]

Present-day lexicographers would demur at these constructions of gender (though one way or another gender has often been a problematic matter for the *OED*).[40] All dictionary-makers hope, nevertheless, that their works will play a daily role in the lives of their readers, including the nation's poets and writers. The *OED* perhaps more than any other dictionary fulfils Grimm's vision of a well-loved and much-consulted treasure-house of the language, both past and present.[41] That this is so is due not only to the heroic dedication and resolve of its successive editors, but also to the commitment, patience and farsightedness of its Press.

I

Press and Dictionary in 1928

The main players: publishers and lexicographers

What was the state of the *Oxford English Dictionary*, its publishers, its Dictionary editors, and their lexicographical staff in 1928? This chapter sketches in some of the history of the Dictionary and of the relationships between the main players, so as to enable us to understand the problems faced by all these groups as they embarked on the initial stages of supplementation after the first edition of the *OED* had been completed in April that year. All operated under the umbrella of Oxford University Press, or simply 'the Press', as OUP was and is referred to by many in both the city and the University of Oxford. Technically a department of the University, this venerable publishing house is presided over by a chief executive who boasts the arcane title 'Secretary to the Delegates' – the 'Delegates' being a group of senior members of the University, chaired by the Vice-Chancellor, who regularly meet as a board of directors to proffer advice to the Press on both financial and editorial matters.

Successive Secretaries and their assistants had always played a far more significant role in the editorial production of *OED* than might be guessed from the title-pages and prefatory matter to its individual volumes, which listed the main editors and staff, meticulously acknowledged hundreds of volunteer readers, but made no mention of the influence of succeeding OUP staff members or the institution for which they worked.[1] *OED* is central to OUP's prestige and reputation today, but over much of the Dictionary's protracted compilation the natural interests of Press and lexicographers were at odds with each other. The Press wanted prompt publication of predictably sized fascicles at regular intervals, while the lexicographers felt compelled to give each section of the alphabet the best possible treatment, regardless of previous estimates of time and space. Both were forced to compromise. Reined in by the deeply unsympathetic Lyttelton Gell

(Secretary from 1884 to 1898), and further harried by the Delegates, the chief editor J. A. H. Murray several times offered to resign over what he saw as insufficiently informed meddling with editorial policy and practice – as when Vice-Chancellor Jowett in 1883 made a particular play for the Dictionary to confine itself to quotations only from the best literary writers, or the Delegates in 1896 tried hard to discipline what they deemed the unacceptably lavish treatment of words after the letter A.[2] Various stand-offs had threatened to smash the relationship between publishers and lexicographers since then – including a notable uproar over words beginning with M, published 1904–8 – but the project had always pulled through.[3] Once publication had begun in 1884, attracting wide recognition and plaudits – the new Dictionary's authority was invoked in Parliament (illustration 2) and *The Times*, and even parodied in *Punch* – drawing back from the enterprise

"Impertinent" in its older sense.
(Mr. McKenna explains.)

2. Cited in Parliament: Home Secretary Reginald McKenna defends his description of an Opposition MP's question as 'impertinent' by appealing to the *OED*'s definition of the word (s.v. sense 2), 'not pertaining to the subject or matter in hand'. *Punch*, 17 July 1912; cartoon by F. H. Townsend.

became virtually impossible for both sides.[4] By the time that the 1928 Secretary to the Delegates, R. W. Chapman (1881–1960), had joined the Press in 1906, the project had gathered a steadier momentum, with several fascicles appearing regularly every year under established editorial teams, and the tone of the exchanges between publishers and editors was usually less confrontational than before.[5]

The urbane and erudite Chapman was just as interested in the content of the Dictionary as in its size and cost. Commissioned in the Royal Garrison Artillery during the First World War, he prepared much scholarly work while on active service in Salonika and Macedonia, including a series of essays called *Portrait of a Scholar* (1920) and editions both of Boswell's *Tour to the Hebrides* and Johnson's *Journey to the Western Islands of Scotland*. On his return to the Press he continued this double existence, dispatching the affairs of the Press while simultaneously publishing editions of Jane Austen as well as Johnson in an authoritative series of works, still revered, that helped establish new bibliographical and editorial standards and became instant classics in their field.[6] Chapman was a man of great charm and some eccentricity; even today he is remembered for his 'stately bicycling': it is reported that he 'never rode a horse, drove a car, or rode a motor-cycle, but was seldom parted from his bicycle clips. His bicycle was famous and he indicated to other road-users with unmistakable elaboration the way he intended to go.'[7] The Press archives contain abundant evidence of his controlling influence over the Dictionary, in the form of incidental memos, letters and – more usually – scrawled laconic comments. When legible, these are often both judicious and witty. His special lexical and literary expertise is repeatedly on show, for example in his ability to quote Johnson on every conceivable occasion, or his advice on the correct date to ascribe to *Pride and Prejudice*.[8]

Chapman's second in command, Kenneth Sisam (1887–1971), was a New Zealander who had arrived at Merton College, Oxford as a Rhodes Scholar in 1910, with a BA and MA from Auckland University. While a boy, he had read the original instalments of the *OED* as they came out. At Oxford, he embarked on a B. Litt. degree, but proved so useful an assistant to Professor A. S. Napier, who held the senior chair in the English Faculty, that he began lecturing on Old and Middle English while still a student. Another Oxford medievalist and *OED* lexicographer, J. R. R. Tolkien, considered himself fortunate to have attended Sisam's lectures and later contributed a glossary to the work for which Sisam was best known, *Fourteenth Century Verse and Prose* (an anthology familiar to generations of Oxford English undergraduates who had to study it as a compulsory set text).[9] An operation for appendicitis in 1912 had left Sisam unfit for military service and in 1915 he joined the Press as a lexicographer, working on the *OED* under Murray's co-editor Henry Bradley (both Bradley and his fellow editor Craigie had examined his thesis), and combining this with the university duties that he took over at Napier's death in 1916. In 1917 he moved to London in search of a higher salary, where he began work at the Ministry of Food and seemed to have conquered his health problems; 'his fast striding-out athletic springing walk' down the long ministry corridors was remembered years afterwards. He rose swiftly at the Ministry, becoming Director of Bacon Contracts in 1919, a job he loved despite its apparent unsuitability for a man who 'throughout his mature life . . . had an aversion to food', whose 'sturdy constitution' appeared 'to have reconciled itself to a dismally meagre diet', who 'took no lunch and manoeuvred resolutely to avoid dining out'.[10]

In October 1922 he was lured back to the Press, as a publisher rather than a lexicographer, becoming assistant to John Johnson (who was himself Assistant Secretary to Chapman) at a salary of £750 per annum, an amount determined 'in view of Mr. Sisam's age and qualifications'.[11] Sisam worked harmoniously with Chapman for the next twenty years, taking over as full Secretary in 1942 when Chapman had to step down owing to illness. Over this period they exchanged a mountain of memos, now preserved in the *OED* archives, their abundance perhaps attesting to the partial truth of Sutcliffe's report that they were 'two men who never met'.[12] It is from these jottings and incidental records that the account of the progress of the *OED* given in the early parts of this book is largely constructed.

Like Chapman, Sisam took great personal as well as professional interest in the Dictionary, and the files record many discussions between him and the lexicographers on the meanings and derivations of words and their appropriate lexicographical treatment. His years at the Ministry of Food gave him special insight into words relating to pigs and meat, an area of expertise later milked for its intrinsic absurdity by Sisam when he wrote to Onions in 1928, succinctly and accurately supplying him with the correct definition of *Wiltshire*, as in bacon (which the original *OED* had got wrong), explaining that *forward* was a euphemism for bacon 'in rather advanced condition (but not bad)', and that 'in Ireland they "torment" bacon, i.e. test its soundness by pricking with an iron skewer'.[13]

Sisam's psychological make-up, so his Press protégé and compatriot D. M. Davin thought, had been crucially influenced by the experiences of his native New Zealand, much of it in the bush, during the first twenty-three years of his life. Apparently he used to say that 'the habits of Press authors with their manuscripts put him in mind of his uncle's dog who went to sleep in the bush, instead of bringing the cattle home'.[14] Certainly he took a stiff view on punctuality and the need to keep to clearly established time schedules: it was he much more than Chapman who applied the rod to the Supplement lexicographers, assuming the role of civil servant to Chapman's government minister.[15] After his retirement to the Scilly Isles in 1948, Sisam produced further distinguished academic work as well as continuing to exercise his powerful influence over the Press, whether through letters or through invitations to stay with him in his island retreat. In the case of the *OED* this influence proved crucial in determining the Press's strategy in the 1950s, as we shall see in Chapters V and VI.

The *OED* editors were an unusual brand of Press author. While Sisam's predecessors as well as Sisam himself often feared the lexicographers spent too much time asleep in the bush, the dictionary-makers' own view of their activities was very different. A project of the scale and magnitude of the *OED* could only be undertaken by erudite, committed and meticulously diligent staff, supported over many years by staunch and responsible publishers, but such an arrangement carried its own risks: if the highest scholarly standards were pursued by the lexicographers (as they were), how would the Dictionary ever achieve completion? On this matter Sisam took a robust line, believing that 'only the office can oppose single-handedly the natural dilatoriness of lexicographers . . . . It is the exception for any huge dictionary to be finished. That O.E.D. was an exception is due more to [OUP secretary] Cannan's tireless whipping than to anything else. Have you ever found a reason why a sane man should start on one of these enterprises unless he is comfortably paid and housed? Or why, if he is comfortably provided for, he should ever finish it?'[16]

Most influential of the lexicographers for much of the period preceding 1928 had been Sir James Murray, chief editor of the Dictionary from 1879 up to his death in 1915 and responsible for 'more than half of the English vocabulary, comprising all the words beginning with the letters A–D, H–K, O–P, and all but a fraction of those beginning with T'.[17] Murray's life and character were intimately bound up with the progress and achievement of the *OED*, and have been extensively explored elsewhere.[18] In many respects an autodidact, who left school in Scotland at the age of fourteen and a half (having already begun the study of four languages), he created and maintained standards of lexicographical scholarship higher than had ever previously existed, often triumphing in disputes with the Delegates, especially in the early years of the Dictionary, that secured the work's scholarly character but extended its length and wore him down. Appointed editor in 1879, he resigned his job as schoolmaster six years later and thenceforward devoted himself single-mindedly to this new project. He worked sometimes ninety hours a week, wrote on average thirty or forty letters a day to correspondents of all kinds (often in time that would have been better spent on the

Dictionary itself, as he himself recognized), and though on occasion irritably overwhelmed by the difficulties of his task, lived a life centred on the happy family domesticity provided by his wife Ada and their eleven children, all of whom were pressed into service sorting quotations slips when young ('slip' was the technical term for the pieces of paper, about 6⅝ × 4 inches, on which quotations for the Dictionary were written, illustrating the usage of words to be defined).[19]

Murray's posthumous influence was strong: succeeding lexicographers inherited not only his uncompromising scholarly standards but also his habit of entrenchment against the publishers, inevitably if reluctantly alternated with capitulation and co-operation. Murray left three co-editors to carry his work forward – Bradley, Craigie and Onions – together with a staff (each chief editor had his own staff) of well-trained and devoted workers, three of whom subsequently worked on the first Supplement (A. T. Maling, F. J. Sweatman, and his daughter Rosfrith Murray).

The senior editorship of the Dictionary passed first to Henry Bradley (1845–1923) and then, on Bradley's death eight years later, to Craigie, both of them far less well known figures. In 1915 Bradley was aged 70, a brilliant scholar in a wide range of fields and a gentle and unassuming man.[20] He had worked uncomplainingly at the Dictionary, often bullied by Murray, since 1889, having until this point never asked for or received a rise in pay, although he lived rent-free in a house in Polstead Road belonging to the Press, which he shared with his chronically invalid wife and with his daughter, Eleanor (who was also employed on the Dictionary staff).[21] Previously Bradley had been a corresponding clerk to a cutlery firm in Sheffield, a post he held for twenty years, and had filled up his spare hours with independent and imaginative literary and philological investigations. These had enabled him to move to London in 1884 and support himself by miscellaneous literary work, including reviewing the first fascicle of the Dictionary which appeared that year. Subsequent correspondence with Murray led to his working on the Dictionary straight away (within four months, to be precise, on the latter part of the letter *B*) and his position was formalized five years later, though not without reservations from Murray, on whom the appointment had been foisted willy-nilly by the Delegates (urged by Gell) who were anxious to increase the speed of production.[22] He was elected a member of Exeter College in 1896 and a fellow of Magdalen College in 1916.

There were marked differences, both of temper and scholarly method, between the first two chief editors. Their later co-editor, C. T. Onions, who had worked first for Murray and then for Bradley, described the latter as not only 'a philological genius' but also 'one of the most original minds of his time'. 'To pass from the one to the other [i.e. from Murray to Bradley] was a remarkable experience; it was to pass from the practical professional teacher to the philosophical exponent. Murray gave formal instruction; Bradley taught rather by hint, by interjectional phrase, or even a burst of laughter.'[23]

Attractive as he sounds, Bradley was ineffectual both as an organizer of the project Murray had left uncompleted and as a bulwark against the constant pressure from the publishers. Sisam later said that Bradley's mind 'moved about three times as fast as anyone else's on the staff', but he was notoriously slow, both in speech – his staff habitually finished his sentences for him, although only Craigie was able to do this correctly – and in production of lexicographical copy; Chapman's verdict was that 'there is no doubt that he did retard the Dictionary, though the extraordinary quality of his work is perhaps adequate compensation'.[24] Although technically junior to

3. W. A. Craigie.

Bradley, the person who instead took up the reins, and sometimes cudgels, on behalf of the lexicographers after Murray's death was the sentence-finisher W. A. Craigie (1867–1957). Like his three fellow senior editors, Craigie, a Lowland Scot born in Dundee, came from middle- to lower-class origins – he was the son of a jobbing gardener – and had an exceptional capacity for hard work and learning.[25] He began his career in dictionary-making, as he told his fellow diners at the Goldsmiths' banquet of 1928, in an entertaining reply to Baldwin's address, 'about the age of thirteen, by making marginal additions on a copy of Jamieson's Scottish dictionary'.[26] His fellow lexicographer (on the *Dictionary of the Older Scottish Tongue*), A. J. Aitken, described Craigie as a 'tiny Scotsman', who was 'quietly dignified, rather reserved, yet unfailingly kindly and companiable . . . with modest tastes and tidy habits'. He achieved as much as he did by 'utilizing his time to the utmost, working methodically for most of each day and evening throughout his long life'.[27] Certainly he was treated by the OUP publishers, Chapman and Sisam, with more regard and respect than his later co-editor, the less well humoured and occasionally peevish C. T. Onions.

Craigie had begun work for the Dictionary in 1897, starting off on an experimental basis at the rate of £25 a month. He was appointed co-editor in 1901 – though again at the instigation of Gell rather than Murray himself, with the consequence that his relationship with Murray was often painfully strained.[28] 'No part of my work is so onerous and unpleasant to me as that of looking through your copy, which has consumed many many hours of this year,' Murray wrote to him in schoolmasterly fashion in 1902. 'I should be infinitely glad to have done with it . . . And if you would earnestly set yourself to making my work unnecessary, it might soon be done.' Murray was in this instance particularly objecting to Craigie's inclusion of terms like *railway director* in the Dictionary since their meaning was transparent. Their mid-twentieth-century successor R. W. Burchfield, who followed Craigie's policy of including as many such combinatorial forms in the Dictionary as he could find, as an end in themselves and deserving of record rather than definition, reports that Onions described Murray's stance on these and other occasions as 'astringent'. Craigie, by contrast, was 'more flamboyant and less economical'. Conflict was therefore inevitable.[29]

Before exposing himself to strictures such as these, Craigie had spent much time in independent study of German, French, Danish and Icelandic both during and after his undergraduate degree (in classics and philosophy) at Dundee University, and by 1897 was a lecturer at the University of St Andrews. Three years after his arrival in Oxford, he was appointed to a lectureship in Scandinavian languages at the Taylorian Institute and in 1916 he became the University's Rawlinson-Bosworth Professor of Anglo-Saxon. He nevertheless managed to devote seven and a half hours daily to lexicography, at which he evidently swiftly improved, and his formidable energy and zest for work made it easy for him to publish and research alongside his Dictionary duties. In 1925 he moved to Chicago, where he continued to work on the *OED* Supplement – though his distance from Oxford slowed this project down – and produced the *Dictionary of American English* (completed in 1944) as well as the first two volumes of the *Dictionary of the Older Scottish Tongue* (1937–2002). His industry and achievement were rewarded with wide recognition and a variety of academic honours from different countries, and Aitken judges him 'the ablest and most productive lexicographer of his time . . . universally recognized as the supreme master of the art and techniques of dictionary making' – although he has sometimes been thought the least scholarly, or the least attractive, of the original four *OED* editors.[30] Craigie later fell out bitterly with two of his senior dictionary assistants (George Watson and Mitford M. Mathews) but inspired devotion in another, J. M. Wyllie, who described in a glowing encomium how 'sweet reasonableness marked all his thoughts, actions and words'.[31] Chapman and Sisam, however, valued him rather for his ability to get work done on time and to a reasonable standard.

The fourth editor, Charles Talbut Onions (1873–1965), also assumed more prominence after Bradley's death in 1923. Onions had come to work on the Dictionary in September 1895, having been invited to join the small staff by Murray after they had met in Birmingham (where Onions had been working for his external London MA, and Murray had visited to examine in the Oxford Local Examinations). He was then 22, with a not very distinguished academic record (a third-class honours degree in French had preceded the MA), and was 'unimpressive as a young man'. He used to slip away from Murray's Scriptorium, the hut in Murray's back garden at 78 Banbury Road, Oxford, where much of the Dictionary was produced, to turn a skipping rope for Murray's children, who repaid this kindness by singing 'Charlie is my darling' behind his back.[32] He was given only minor duties until 1906, when, in his own words, he 'began to be employed on the semi-independent preparation of sections of the alphabet',[33] and (taking much longer than Craigie) became a full editor in his own right in 1914, responsible for the sections *Su–Sz*, *Wh–Worling* and the volumes containing *X*, *Y* and *Z*. As his *DNB* biographer and Oxford colleague J. A. W. Bennett pointed out, he thus 'contributed the very last entry to the whole work in the form of a cross-reference – "Zyxt, obs. (Kentish) 2nd sing. ind. pres. of SEE *v.*" – which he liked to mention as it was taken, because of its position, as a brand name for a soap.' Bennett also reports Onions's 'almost personal pride in his mother tongue, which he once described as "a rum go – but jolly good"'.[34]

In 1918 he worked in the naval intelligence division of the Admiralty, taking the rank of honorary captain in the Royal Marines, and on his return to Oxford in 1920 he was made first a University lecturer in English, then in 1927 a reader in English Philology (1927–49). In 1923 he was elected to Bradley's old fellowship at Magdalen College and from 1940 to 1955 held the post of fellow librarian. It was in this role, after he had retired from Oxford University Press if not from lexicography, that he met and – with his own trademark 'astringency' – encouraged the New Zealand Rhodes Scholar of 1949, R. W. Burchfield, who came to Magdalen in that year to read for a second BA, and as Onions's protégé succeeded to the job of *OED* lexicographer in 1957 (in charge of the second Supplement).[35] Bennett, also a fellow of Magdalen at this time, tells us that 'undergraduates and others profited from [Onions's] constant presence in the dictionary bay of [Magdalen College] library' (where he 'wore a blanket round his shoulders, to stave off the cold, for fear that the heating budget should become too burdensome'), and that 'he was equally at home in the senior common room, where his astringent rejoinders to questions on etymology and English usage were much relished'.[36]

Onions's waspishness and occasional querulousness emerge clearly from the archival papers. He had the same capacity for mordant wit as Sisam but lacked his vigorous energy, while the geniality and generosity often perceptible in the writings of Bradley, Craigie and Chapman are altogether absent – possibly because he had been kept so long in a lowly position by Murray, and always felt badly treated. Bennett comments, 'There was something Johnsonian in his attitudes and character (as well as his early struggles). For much of his life he was handicapped by a stammer and he always had a fellow feeling for other stammerers; but he was undemonstrative in his likings as in his religion.'

During the lifetime that Onions worked for OUP, he produced a number of ancillary works – most importantly the 'Abridged' version of the *OED* which was eventually published (alongside the *OED*'s first Supplement) in 1933 as the *Shorter Oxford English Dictionary*, a phenomenally successful work, but also more independent books such as a *Shakespeare Glossary* in 1911 (many times reprinted) and a book on syntax. For decades he laboured on the *Oxford Dictionary of English Etymology*, a work brought to completion with the help of two other Oxford lexicographers (G. S. Friedrichsen and Burchfield) and published in 1966, the year after Onions's death. It is clear that etymology was his principal interest and strength: Bennett remembers that 'he delighted in teasing out the history of such words as syllabus or acne or Shakespeare's "dildos and fadings"'.[37]

He was capable of a good deal of ill-feeling where his colleagues were concerned. For example, when he was able to point out, possibly with some satisfaction, 'an error – rather a bad one – in the pronunciation of Natal', in a Supplement entry for which the recently appointed Wyllie was responsible, he commented to Sisam, 'No one is infallible, but there is such a thing as invincible ignorance.'[38] On another occasion, he had to be pressed hard before he would write to thank an enthusiastic contributor of dictionary slips, on the curmudgeonly grounds that they hadn't been very useful. 'The majority of his contributions have been more bother than they were worth,' he wrote crossly to Sisam, 'no quots., mere references to titles, or otherwise ramshackly.'[39]

Recent history

The dynamics between Press and lexicographers that determined post-1928 policies and publications in lexicography had evolved during the previous decades. Constant anxiety and suspicion over the rate of Dictionary production was a deeply ingrained feature of the enterprise, with the publishers' desire for prompt and predictable output always at odds with the lexicographers' insistence on its quality and their comparative indifference to schedules. Tension and distrust between Craigie and Onions, the publishers' sense that Craigie was the more substantial force to be reckoned with, not least because he had more options open to him than Onions, and the relieved delight with which Sisam took to his heart the new employee J. M. Wyllie, who arrived in 1929, can all be traced to relationships and habits of work established many years earlier.

Since 1901, Craigie and Bradley had been accommodated in office quarters in the Old Ashmolean (now the Museum of the History of Science) in Broad Street, in the centre of Oxford. Murray, on the other hand, had laboured away in his famous Scriptorium in the garden of his house at 78 Banbury Road, about a mile to the north. Such separation had had advantages and disadvantages. His biographer and granddaughter, Elisabeth Murray, notes that the two centres of work 'encouraged a friendly rivalry and competitive spirit which helped to enliven the tedium of the work', but comparisons between the output of the various editors (and their staff), sometimes recorded month by month (or under Gell, week by week), were not always uninvidious.[40] Murray's annual output was rarely less than that of Bradley and Craigie, but in the eyes of the publishers it was Craigie who shone at establishing firm rules for productivity at the Dictionary, insisting 'that a certain job should be done in a certain time' (see p. 39 below), and during the latter stages of the project he was often – but not always – more prolific than either Bradley or Onions. Thus he produced copy for twice as many eventual Dictionary pages as Onions in the first half of 1915 (128 to Onions's 64, while Bradley was responsible for 80), and even when his lead was not so advanced, it was usually maintained.[41]

Certainly it was Craigie to whom the publishers habitually turned when the reins slackened on editorial discipline. As the publishers tracked lexicographical performance, despairing at unduly sluggish progress or distressingly inflated treatment of particular alphabet ranges, and attempting to match production of copy with the availability and supply of printing labour, it must sometimes have seemed that every crisis was succeeded by another. In December 1915, just after Murray's death, Craigie pointed out – in response to pained inquiries from the Secretary Charles Cannan on the recent increase, yet again, in 'scale' of the Dictionary – that the quantity of material they needed to process was always rising and that the quality of work now being produced was much higher than at the outset, and rallied his troops with a carefully formulated joint response. Among his reassurances to the publishers, Craigie also included a set of statesmanlike admonitions to his Dictionary colleagues to remind them of their duties. These emphasized the importance of practical and commercial imperatives as well as scholarly ones, specifying for example that 'Time should not be spent on obscure quotations, or such as are difficult to verify, unless it is clear that they are important for the history of the word', that 'No investigation should be carried to a great length without considering whether the result is likely to justify the time spent on it', and concluding, 'In general it should be remembered that a steady supply of finished copy is the first essential for the progress of the Dictionary.'[42]

The term 'scale' had a special meaning for the Oxford lexicographers. Soon after Murray assumed editorship of the Dictionary in 1879, the Delegates had stipulated that he and his staff should produce copy for the printers at regular intervals, in the ratio of about five and a half pages to one of Webster's 'Unabridged' *Dictionary* of 1864. This dictionary had been settled on as a comparator (originally by Murray, it appears) without due consideration of its significantly different character: although the best dictionary then current, it listed far fewer words and senses than were to be brought to light by protracted and scholarly scrutiny in Oxford.[43] After the dispute between Murray and the Delegates in 1896 (over the increased scale in letters subsequent to *A*, in particular *F* and *H*) the original ratio had been allowed to rise to 8:1, and by 1916 the lexicographers were producing at an average rate of 12:1, though with occasional wild discrepancies.[44] Special factors kept intervening with the plans: for example, as Bradley pointed out in 1920, W, a notable culprit on parts of which the scale reached 80:1, was 'the first letter [in the alphabet] that has no Greek or Latin derivatives. It is on the classical words that space can be saved; when we have the luck to get a run of them scale goes down.' The publishers themselves reflected that W's scale might 'be defended plausibly if not soundly on the ground that Webster scamped the work as he approached the end'. ('Alphabet fatigue' is a well-observed phenomenon in dictionaries, and OED did well to avoid it, if at the expense of time and money.)[45]

Five years later, alerted by the Printer that the rate had gone up again in March 1920, Chapman wrote to Craigie to report that 'the printers allege that the scale of U is 19. Can this be possible?'[46] When the proofs were examined, it was found that instead of reducing material when correcting them, as expected, the lexicographers were inserting additional quotations, so that, as Chapman pencilled over a sheet of the Printer's calculations in a scrawled expression of disgust, 'They add more than they cut out.'[47] U, and especially the negative prefix un, was 'one of the least important sections of the alphabet, and condensed treatment is justified on the ground that it largely replicates the positives and to some extent [the negative prefix] In-'.[48] To Sir Walter Raleigh, Merton Professor of English at Oxford University and literary adviser to the Press, he described the situation as 'really serious' and the scale as 'monstrous'.[49] As he later wrote to Craigie, U was 'an instrument of ruin'; printing it at a scale of 12:1 would cost £2,650, and at 16:1 would cost £3,550, sums (well over four times Craigie's annual salary) that 'will stagger you as they have staggered me'.[50]

It was Craigie, not Bradley, who was summoned to represent the lexicographers at an 'urgent' conference. The surviving papers show how once again he swiftly took the initiative and calmed Chapman and Raleigh down, explaining the peculiar difficulties involved in U, a letter treated cursorily by Webster, and concluding that it would 'be very difficult to make any important reduction of the scale without some serious departure from the methods hitherto followed in the Dictionary'. (Craigie may have been influenced in his defence of the preservation of the un- compounds by the fact that the final sorting of these had been done by his wife – a task she apparently later referred to proudly as her 'war work'.)[51] Craigie also wrote a long letter in which he outlined the current state of play of the Dictionary and gave a detailed timetable for completion both of U and of the remaining letters.[52] This defence mollified Chapman if it did not entirely satisfy him, and he asked the Printer to continue reporting on the scale of each batch of copy as it came in, telling him that he was 'frightening the editors'.[53]

Craigie's 'Wanderlust' and plans for a Supplement

Bradley was then 73, but Craigie was more than twenty years younger and had always been more ambitious. By 1920 he was looking for a way to move on. He warned Chapman that after he had finished *U*, 'my regular work on the Dictionary might be materially diminished. I find it increasingly difficult to combine the satisfactory discharge of professional and other duties with the regular and close attention to details which the Dictionary requires, unless I sacrifice all other interests and cease to keep up correspondence with scholars in this and other countries. I also now have on hand considerable collections of material connected with my own special studies, and am desirous of setting to work on these as soon as possible.' He recognized that completion of the Dictionary was a matter of primary importance for the Delegates but hoped that the expected progress on *W* and *U* would be such as to make possible his release.[54]

This was of course welcome news. By now, the publishers were looking hopefully towards the end of the main project, and to shuffling off much of the financial burden they had carried for so long. But Craigie's letter was also an opening shot in a struggle that persisted for some years, in which, so the publishers felt, he balanced one potential project against another in the hope of emerging with maximum gain for himself. At times of difficulty, Chapman excelled in carefully worded responses which flattered while surrendering little. On this occasion he wrote back to describe Craigie's analysis as a 'masterly disquisition on the future. This is just what we want – something to exercise our minds on.'[55] Certainly it was true that Craigie's fellow lexicographers were generally much less forthcoming when asked for forecasts and timetables.

Earlier that month, the publishers had consulted Bradley as to what should be done with the staff once the main Dictionary had been completed. He suggested that work on the Supplement should start straight away, given the 'very considerable amount of material that exists, in the shape of quotations sent to us from outside, and of notes in the margin of our office copies of the Dictionary', but no systematic collection of materials had begun as yet 'and a great deal will require to be done in supplying deficiencies'. It was not possible, Bradley felt, to make any estimate of the Supplement's eventual size.[56] By contrast, Craigie produced a more precise and detailed analysis, proposing three suggestions for the possible future employment of *OED* staff. These were the 'Records of English Literature' (a bibliography of English literature, later published as the *Annals of English Literature*),[57] an 'Oxford Dictionary of Modern English' ('a work similar in character to Littré [the French dictionary], but with the historical element reduced to a minimum', on which Onions should be deployed so as to 'to keep the new work in proper contact with the old'), and the Supplement to the *OED*. This last 'should be reduced to the narrowest limits, and probably restricted to (a) corrections of actual errors or serious omissions in the Dictionary; (b) important additions to the history (especially the earlier history) of words. Mere additions to the illustrative material should be disregarded, the probability being that equally good material has already been discarded.'[58]

It seems likely that a Supplement file was set up in the second half of the 1880s, shortly after the first fascicle was published and it became impossible to add to the record of words beginning with *A*.[59] Murray himself reported to a Philological Society 'Dictionary Evening' of 1908 that 'The collection and arrangement of material for the Supplement steadily flows on', and his predecessor Furnivall (who maintained his interest in and support of the Dictionary up to the end of his long life) referred to the importance of the Supplement 'a short time before he died' in 1910, noting that it would have to include 'All the words brought into use by the motor-car industry and the new science of flying'.[60] During the war, Craigie had collected a 'pile of material' for the Supplement from Murray's Scriptorium, added it to the collections at the Ashmolean, and had the whole 'reduced to alphabetical order at small expense' by a Belgian refugee, Mr Pallemaerts.[61] More had accumulated since then, and the staff had regularly noted down corrections and additions in the margins of their office copies of the parts of the Dictionary already published (these copies still exist).

What form the Supplement should take, when work on it should begin, and how long it would take to complete, were not to be decided for a number of years, by which time the project had turned into something of a football in the dealings between the lexicographers and publishers. In the first place, this was precipitated by Craigie. From 1920 onwards, Craigie's disposition to spread his energies widely began to slow the big Dictionary down. Bursarial responsibilities at his Oxford college, Oriel, though temporary, distracted him during the winter of 1922–23 and reduced his flow of copy, as did his summer trips to Chicago, where he was shortly to take up a chair – although conversely these trips vastly improved the Supplement's treatment of US vocabulary, given Craigie's improved access to direct sources. The publishers tried to keep their nerve and also to defend themselves against external criticism of the length of years it was taking to complete the work. As Chapman put it in an internal memo to the OUP Publisher Humphrey Milford, commenting on a report in the *Daily Mail*, 'abusing the publisher won't raise Murray or Bradley, nor restrain Wanderlust in Craigie, nor reduce the extent of Onions's family [he had ten children], nor make W an easy letter ... no good will come of revolver-practise [*sic*] through the windows of the Old Ashmolean'.[62] In 1924 Craigie was disputing whether delays of copy were due to his (or his assistant George Watson's) tardiness or the Press's inefficiency, and simultaneously stiffly negotiating, without success, to raise his salary from Oxford sources;[63] in 1925 he moved to Chicago permanently, apparently motivated as much by money as by increased academic opportunity. (The professor-ship thus left vacant was competed for by Sisam, who was said to be put out when it went to the younger and more brilliant Tolkien, a decision in which Onions, one of the Electors, had played a part.)[64] Salary was a sore spot for Craigie as for his fellow editors, not least because he felt that his capacity for hard work was unjustly penalized. When the University had reviewed salaries 'round about 1920', 'account was taken of the salary which Craigie was receiving as editor [of *OED*] and the stipend of his chair was left at £600 odd'. The source of this information, Craigie's supporter J. M. Wyllie, reported that Craigie's wife felt this keenly. To her 'it was as if the university had said "your husband may do two jobs, if he so chooses, but he is only to get one salary"'.[65] Once in Chicago, Craigie continued to act as co-editor of the *OED*, but swiftly expanded his lexicographical horizons in a scheme to exploit the Dictionary's massive resources for further projects.

In these the projected Supplement played a significantly negative role. Craigie had always been struck by the wealth of material that *OED* had had to exclude from its pages, notably from Tudor and Stuart writings but from those of other periods too. He knew that the Press retained vast quantities of rejected slips detailing historical words and usages that were of ines-timable value for recording the language in more detailed ways than had been practicable for the main Dictionary. As early as 1919 he had proposed to remedy this, while simultaneously providing himself with substantial further work, by initiating a number of 'period' dictionaries – four alto-gether, treating Old English up to 1175, Middle English from 1175 to 1500, Early Modern English from 1500 to 1675, and Scots up to 1700; in 1922 he had explained to the Press that while 'within their own sphere' these diction-aries would be 'a great advance upon the O.E.D.', they would not 'enter into competition with it as a whole' but 'would ... ultimately clear the way for a new edition of the Dictionary', so that in due course, once the present work had become 'antiquated', it would be possible 'to produce a compre-hensive dictionary of Modern English, not overburdened with a dead weight from the past stages of the language'. Preparing a Supplement straight away would therefore be a waste of time.[66]

Craigie had now discussed these projects with universities in the US – principally Chicago and Cornell – and had also thought of a fifth one, a

Dictionary of American English (the notion had come to him in the summer of 1924, while reading through *OED* proofs, when he had been struck by the number of quotations from American authors and had realized the American language needed proper historical investigation in its own right).[67] The Americans had come up with significant financial backing, with an initial $10,000 from Chicago alone.[68] So in October 1925 Craigie sent the Delegates a long, carefully written letter, in which he rehearsed his plans in more detail and asked them whether they would let him have the rejected *OED* slips in order to make his new dictionaries.[69]

This proposal threw the Press into disarray. Agreeing to it would divert time and energy from completion of the main Dictionary, while refusal would create a public row and risk Craigie's desertion altogether. With some acerbity, Onions noted the practical difficulties of his absent colleague's scheme. '"To carry out the redistribution of the Oxford material would be a simple task", says Craigie. Simple, no doubt; but has any calculation been made, can any calculation be made, of the time necessary for one or two assistants to sort out and distribute among the centuries a mass of something like 5000000 slips? My own view is that all efforts on this side of the Atlantic should be directed towards the completion of the N.E.D., its Supplement, & its abridgement [what was to become the *Shorter OED*], and I rather grudge the diversion of any of my Dictionary time to the consideration of plans that do not assist towards this end.'[70] But Chapman, ever the pragmatic diplomatist, was 'opposed to a simple negative. It may well be true, as is suggested,' he wrote, 'that Craigie has got his position in America largely by hinting at the treasures of material he can bring over, and that he is now called upon to deliver the goods. But he can probably carve these Dictionaries out of the N.E.D. whatever we do . . . .'[71]

Having consulted widely, he drafted what the Publisher Milford judged an 'admirable' letter ('couldn't be better') to Craigie, reporting the Delegates' decision that a carefully defined set of slips could be sent over, with all expenses to be borne by the Americans. But he was careful to exclude 'the whole material compiled since the publication of any part of the Dictionary and designed for use in a Supplement', and warned, 'You will, I am sure, understand that it has not been altogether easy for the Delegates and their advisers to persuade themselves they ought to agree to your proposals.'[72]

Ill will and suspicion were exacerbated by continual tussles between Onions and Craigie over the speed with which they and their assistants were turning out copy, and over the payment and lexicographical competence of Craigie's assistant Watson. In addition, Watson was reputedly undermining the resolve of Onions's staff (or as Sisam put it, 'The die-hards stick well to their last trench, but the Bolshevik lexicographer Watson will soon enfilade them').[73] Milford warned Chapman that 'Craigie is going to make himself unpleasant over the "Period Dictionaries" in spite of all you can do', while Sisam cautioned that 'the main consideration was to keep Craigie sweet by any means during the next five years, during which he could do us a great deal of harm both financially and in reputation'.[74] In January 1926 Craigie wrote to claim partial ownership of the Supplement material and to object to decisions being taken on it in his absence.[75] Chapman returned a typically emollient reply, reassuring him that 'I have little doubt that we shall be able to concoct a <u>modus vivendi</u>'. Simultaneously he shot off a memo to Milford to say 'there is nothing in his grumble about the supplementary material. In the first place, if he has long periods of absence he must expect things to happen (but I shall not say so); in the second, we have done nothing with the slips except arrange them in alphabetical order, stack them in the Old Ashmolean shelves, and refer to them in the course of revising Little [the planned abridgement of *OED*]; in the third place they are visible from Craigie's own desk, and it is childish to pretend that he doesn't know what is going on – he ought to know.'[76]

One advantage of the fracas was that it concentrated minds on the Supplement. Less than a month after Craigie's original request for the slips, Onions produced a proper report of progress so far. All the material had been put in order and it occupied about 80 feet of shelving. 'Periodicals like <u>Notes & Queries</u>, the <u>Athenaeum</u> & the <u>Academy</u>, together with journals specially devoted to language, have been examined, but much remains to be done in this line.' Slips for *A–Aero* had been 'minutely examined and compared with the printed Dictionary, and a provisional selection has been made of what is considered necessary'.[77] But still no real decision had been taken as to what sort of a work it was to be. One possibility was, as Chapman had reviewed in 1923, that it should set out to repair the imbalance between the early and later volumes of the *OED*, given that it was 'true of A–B and in a less degree of (say) CD that they are not so nearly <u>well</u> done as the later letters'. Of this proposal, with its acknowledgement of serious defects in *OED*'s treatment of the first letters of the alphabet, he had at the time concluded, 'least said, soonest mended',[78] and as negotiations with Craigie over the slips proceeded through 1926 and 1927, the publishers seem to have become clearer that what was needed was instead an 'integrating Supplement', in other words a fairly minimal stopgap which could be applied to the existing material in the main Dictionary to make good the absence of words like *appendicitis* and *radium*. Onions nevertheless revived the earlier idea with apparently serious intent in October 1926, not as an argument for a different sort of supplement but as a proposal for an additional full-scale revision.

This was greeted with horror by Sisam. In the old days, he pointed out, Murray's Scriptorium used to produce 800 slips a week (i.e. the processed quotation slips sent in by readers, along with the 'topslips' subsequently prepared by the lexicographers on which they recorded their definitions, etymologies, etc.), while now 'Onions with 6 experienced men and a reserve of ladies' could only manage, 'under pressure', 200 slips, and 'the Craigie–Watson minority' 500.[79] Taking wages into account, 21.5 columns by Craigie cost £97, while 15 columns by Onions cost £187, 'quite apart from the value of time'. Keeping these calculations in mind, and observing also that revision could not stop short of the first two volumes but would have to continue through the alphabet, Sisam worked out (assuming a doubling of scale), that '15,000 new columns will cost (@£10–£150,000 for editing only', and 'at the present rate (which is being hurried) the preparation will take 75 years'. Staffing problems would necessarily add to the cost. 'I am not mathematician enough to draw up the equations for time and cost,' Sisam went on,

> but I guess the solution to both will be infinity. Perhaps after 20 years of revision there will be in one room of the Delegates' asylum a band of grey-haired and well-fattened lexicographers, gibbering with delight over the last refinement of their craft, whereby the scale as compared with 1 page of Webster has been reduced to nil; and in another, too worn and broken to need a padded cell, the Secretariat, moaning 'Onions, give me back my millions'.

In a note below, he added, 'I need hardly say that the moment you began issuing the revision, the sale of the existing Dictionary would fall, because people would wait for the new edition.' This killed the revision idea. As Chapman reported, Onions later explained that his letter was 'only dialectics, not intended seriously'.[80]

But the publishers' increasing clarity about what the Supplement should contain had still to be persuasively impressed upon Craigie, without whom – given Onions's extraordinary slowness – success could not be certain. By April 1927, relations with Craigie had decisively perked up and the rate of progress on the main Dictionary was such that completion could be confidently forecast for 1928. Sisam forced through their plan in a meeting with Craigie that month, turning him round from his initial position, that 'a real supplement to the main Dictionary cannot be done until all the period dictionaries are done', to accept instead 'a very short supplement of essential things, to be issued here in about three years' time'. (A later document spells out that this 'short complete Supplement' was to consist 'almost entirely of neologisms', with no attempt being made 'to correct or enlarge words already in N.E.D.'). No doubt Sisam, whom Chapman thought 'a monster of tact', had operated very skilfully, but Craigie had been malleable material. Sisam judged his other plans to be both 'nebulous and unremunerative . . . . He seemed prepared to do anything we wanted done, and it is strange that such marvellous executive efficiency should be coupled with so many vague and grandiose schemes.'[81]

The 'Little People'

As the main Dictionary edged painfully to a halt in 1928, the publishers continued to bring monthly reports on Dictionary matters to the Delegates and to worry away at problems relating to its progeny. Of these, the most important was the Supplement, now well under way but at a dangerously slow pace, along with the 'Register' – a bibliography of works cited in *OED*. The 'Oxford Dictionary of Modern English', previously mooted by Craigie, is not at this stage mentioned (it was later to resurface as the 'Quarto'), but a different project had been occupying Onions for some time: the abridgement of the *OED*, incorporating some of the Supplement material, that was later to appear as the *Shorter Oxford English Dictionary*.[82] It was essential to retain staff for these less ambitious but still demanding and time-consuming projects. Staffing issues were now at the forefront of the publishers' minds: how should employees be rewarded for their years of devotion to the Press's flagship publication, and which of them should be retained, under what arrangements, for the years that it would take to produce the Supplement and its two fellow projects? And how many years would that be?

Like the other subjects considered in this chapter – the publishers and the editors, the history of the Dictionary, and the antecedent plans for the Supplement – the 'Little People', as Falconer Madan called the staff, played an important role in determining the events immediately following completion of the *OED* in 1928. As we have seen Madan guess in his letter to Chapman (pp. 6–7 above), their payment and pension arrangements (as with those of the chief editors) had always been difficult matters, not least because a 'deferred bonus' scheme had been introduced in March 1900, regrettably tied to the already procrustean 'scale' arrangement. Staff were eligible for an annual bonus only if the editorial team of which they were a member had worked through a sufficient amount of material, as measured in Webster's 'Unabridged'. 'A portion' of the sum allotted to them was paid straight away, while the remaining portion was 'reserved for payment upon the completion of the Dictionary to every participant who shall continue to

be employed until that event, or if any participant shall die while in employment upon the Dictionary, then upon his death'.[83] The scheme notionally
took the place of a pension system, which the publishers were understandably reluctant to set up given that the Dictionary would (they trusted) be
complete long before many of the employees reached pensionable age.

But the bonus scheme was full of pitfalls. One was the inverse reward for
scholarly performance, whether adequate or outstanding. Improving in
significant ways on Webster's original meant including many more words
and explaining them in much more detail, but by doing so the lexicographers were cutting off their own noses (and those of their staff). Murray and
Bradley were far too scrupulous to condense what they believed to be
the proper lexicographical treatment of items untreated, or insufficiently
treated, by Webster. Instead, they and their staff overshot their target year
after year by completing excess copy, consequently forfeiting any bonus,
though Murray used to make up the shortfall to his staff out of his own
pocket (another irritant), and the Delegates occasionally paid *ad hoc* sums
to the staff at times of severe difficulty, for example after Murray's death in
1915.[84] The scheme was therefore discontinued in 1920, though the reserved
portion of the bonuses continued to be kept by the Press until completion in
1928.[85] Employees like Murray's daughter Elsie, who emigrated to South
Africa in 1921, and L. F. Powell, who left in the same year to become
librarian of the Taylorian Institute, forfeited their bonuses (£40 and £88 16s.
respectively) altogether. It is difficult not to regard this as unfair, though it
may have seemed less so in relation to employment practices of the time.[86]

Despite Madan's plea, none of the editorial team members, other than
Maling, received honours in 1928 such as were accorded the main editors
and publishers. The Press did however set out to make what were then
generous disbursements of cash. The female staff – Murray's daughter
Rosfrith, Bradley's daughter Eleanor, and Mrs E. R. Powell – were paid
'double the sums standing to their credit in the Bonus account, on completion of the Dictionary, as a full discharge of all claims'.[87] The figures were,
respectively, £58 5s., £19, and £61, doubled to £116 10s., £38, and £122.
Rosfrith wrote Chapman a warm, effusive, grateful letter in reply:

> My twenty-six years on the Dictionary Staff have been full of interest,
> and I always felt deeply that my Father would like one of his name to be
> 'in on the finish', since this was denied to him himself. He started me on
> to 'sorting slips' at the age of seven years, so you will understand that the
> Dictionary has played a large part in my quiet life . . . your words of
> appreciation have given great pleasure to my mother and myself.[88]

The male staff were encouraged to forgo the bonus in favour of what the publishers believed would be an ultimately more favourable pension arrangement (the Press did not consider a scheme for pensions for women until 1931, its differential treatment of women in this respect as in wages being entirely characteristic of the time).[89] Suffering ensued nevertheless. Walter Worrall, born in 1862, had joined the Dictionary staff in 1886, worked for many years as Bradley's chief assistant (suffering chronic neuralgic headaches which he ascribed to his occupation), and had now completed forty-two years of service. The publishers retired him from regular employment in January 1928 and gave him his full salary of £300 for three months (pro rata) thereafter, followed by 'a pension of £2 a week during the Delegates' pleasure, Mr. Worrall resigning his claim to deferred bonus', with the expectation that he would carry out piecework for the Dictionary after 30 April 'without deduction from pension'.[90] His subsequent work on the Supplement brought him welcome additional income, which meant that its completion in 1933 was a severe blow. In 1934 he wrote to the Press pleading for more work, referring to his '48 years of unremitting toil' for the Dictionary, and apologizing that 'the "allowance" which I receive from the Delegates is far from sufficing for my modest needs'.[91]

By comparison, Chapman's salary in the late 1920s was £1,500 and Sisam's £1,000; Rosfrith Murray's was £130 and George Watson's was £275 (prices have increased about forty-fold since the 1920s, and wages have increased many times more).[92] The difference between male and female pay may have been in part attributable to different hours worked, while such a gap between the salary of the chief executive of a company and that of more lowly members of staff was usual then as now. Identifying suitable comparators is a tricky undertaking, but the remuneration of *OED* staff looks distinctly ungenerous beside that of other lower-professional groups of the time – qualified male teachers were paid a salary of £353 in 1924, for example, while assistant librarians at the Patent Office received £463.[93] Many *OED* staff members had arrived at OUP with little experience and few or no qualifications, at or near the beginning of their working lives, so that the Press was able to exploit the fruits of its own meticulous training while relying on its employees' apparent unwillingness, or inability, to move to jobs elsewhere. But there were compensations. The Press maintained a strict but paternalistic attitude towards its staff, acknowledging a carefully weighed measure of responsibility towards them (and their families), and receiving years of loyal and committed service in return.[94]

In the years immediately following 1928, the staff's devotion to the Press's most significant scholarly project sometimes took the form, so the publishers felt, of spending unconscionably long periods of time on particular words and letters. Doubtless this was due to the lexicographers' determination to preserve the high standards of the parent Dictionary. But it seems likely that anxiety about concluding an enterprise which had supported some of them throughout their entire working lives, and which once completed might leave them with insufficient pay and prospects, also played a significant role in delaying the (supposedly) final stages of this great work.

II

'Beating the Track of the Alphabet': Work on the First Supplement

'Delenda est Carthago'

Unsurprisingly, work on the Supplement proved as taxing as had work on the original *OED*. The publishers continued to deplore the lexicographers' dilatoriness, seeking to instil discipline, resolve and punctuality in the new project. Memos flew to and fro between Chapman and Sisam on the waywardness of their tiresome charges; copies of these documents, preserved in yellowed and tattered form in the Press archives, make sorry, if sometimes sharply witty, reading. These various pieces of paper, scattered among correspondence on many other issues, provide glimpses of the administrative nuts and bolts of constructing the work and reveal the publishers' ruthless determination to drag this final part of the *OED* into existence.

In 1927–28, Oxford University Press had on its payroll a variety of Dictionary employees, most concentrated on the Supplement. Aside from the main editors, Craigie (now Sir William Craigie, having been knighted that year) and Onions, there were two old workhorses dating from many years back: Worrall, who had joined the *OED* staff in 1885 and from May 1928 was working on piecework rates, and A. T. Maling, the favoured recipient of the honorary MA, who had arrived the year after Worrall and had originally been a member of Murray's team. Seven other assistants worked alongside these men: W. J. Lewis, an *OED* employee since 1889, F. J. Sweatman (1890) and H. J. Bayliss (1891), all formerly on the Bodleian staff with many years' service to their credit, together with a more recent arrival, J. W. Birt, who had been with the Dictionary since 1906. Three women made up the remainder, Miss R. N. A. Murray (James Murray's daughter Rosfrith), Miss Bradley (Henry Bradley's daughter Eleanor) and Mrs L. F. Powell, who had joined the staff in 1901 as Miss E. R. Steane and had married the assistant who had subsequently left to become librarian of the

Taylorian Institute. (Referring to women by their titles was standard practice at the time, a convention followed in this book when reporting information from original documents.) Additionally, Miss Senior (who had been
employed in 1924 specifically to work on the Supplement)[1] and a Miss
Savage assisted Onions on his other major task, the 'Abridged', as it was still
called (soon to become the *Shorter OED*), while Sweatman and Bayliss
worked also on the bibliography of the *OED*'s quotation sources which they
called the 'Register', which was to be issued at the same time as the
Supplement.[2]

Crucially, Craigie was based in Chicago, working away on two other
dictionaries at the same time with the support of his more independent
assistant, the so-called Bolshevik, George Watson, a Dictionary employee
since 1907 who had moved to Chicago as an assistant professor to join
Craigie.[3] Craigie was protected from the publishers by both his distance
from Oxford and his professorial status, while Onions and the others
worked in the Old Ashmolean building next door to the Bodleian Library,
less than a mile away from the Press offices, and found it much harder to
escape vigilant scrutiny. The two editorial teams divided the Supplement
work between them, the first part of the alphabet, plus letters *S–T*, handled
by Onions, and the second (*L–R* and *U–Z*) by Craigie, with the Oxford
workers being set to process Chicago copy as it arrived, and Chicago taking
responsibility for the 'Americana' (words with specifically US senses or
evidence). Matching the rates of production and making appropriate
allowances for the length of time it took copy to travel over land and sea
from Chicago to Oxford was difficult, as was efficient distribution of work
between the three main projects. Bafflingly, though on past form predictably,
Craigie's team – soon to be joined by the new recruit J. M. Wyllie, initially
based in Aberdeen – proved much swifter in moving through their alphabet
range than did those working under Onions.

It had originally been planned that the Supplement would be finished two
years after the main Dictionary, in 1930–31.[4] But by the early summer of
1928, this was looking increasingly unlikely, and the publishers cast about
for new employees who might be able to speed things up. On 6 July 1928, a
month after the Goldsmiths' dinner celebrating the completion of the main
work, Sisam reported to the Publisher, Milford, that

> Craigie today thought the best hope of cutting through was to get an
> assistant trained in some business school of lexicography, Pitman's or
> Cassell's or Chambers'. . . . We would take a man on loan for one year
> or two or three, or take him over. We have plenty of scholars and
> researchers, but we want a hard worker capable of cutting through

material, and unless he can do that he is no use to us. Power to handle material and produce copy for an editor in a rapid and orderly way is more important than philological knowledge, which the editor [i.e. Onions] will supply.

Grudgingly, he allowed they might go up to £300 'for the right man', and thought 'It is just possible one of these publishers would be able to put us on to a man. It is clearly in their interests that the Supplement should be produced as rapidly as possible, so that they can steal it . . . . The great thing is a hard, steady worker, with the ability to arrange and define.'[5] This approach eventually (October 1928) yielded E. G. Ogan, from Cassell's, who helped them briefly but was later replaced by Wyllie; meanwhile Chapman and Sisam tried a variety of young women, 'rabbits' as they slightingly called them, sometimes irritatingly absent from their 'warren' (the *OED* office), who were of varying usefulness and suitability. (One of these worked for *OED* for many years to come: Jessie Senior, who under her married name Coulson was to make significant contributions in the future to the *Shorter, Little, Pocket* and *Russian* dictionaries).[6]

But the publishers continued to be intensely worried about the lexicographers' slow progress. In a Dictionary report of March 1928, Sisam had tried, as we saw in the Introduction, to compute the likely completion time of the Supplement, and had concluded that it was ten years hence. 'I do not think the present rate of progress should be allowed to continue after March without drastic steps,' he warned, 'however difficult they may be.' The solution was to tighten discipline. 'Onions will have to do as Craigie did – insist that a certain job should be done in a certain time . . . . It is quite time that all members of the staff except the regular researchers on Bo[d]ley – Bayliss Mrs Powell and Birt – should be required to work a full day in the Dictionary Room [i.e. the *OED* offices in the Old Ashmolean] so that they may get through some copy. No satisfactory progress has been made since Onions let go this sound rule which Craigie maintained to the end . . . . Delenda est Carthago!'[7]

The irresistible temptation for many of the staff was to spend time in the Bodleian Library in Oxford (the University's main research library), looking for additional examples of the words they sought to document, and checking the quotations which had been amassed for the Supplement over many years, whether by Dictionary staff or by enthusiastic contributors such as Furnivall (Murray's predecessor), who specialized in finding new examples of usage in newspaper and magazine literature long after his editorship and whose material took up 16 feet of shelf space (estimated by Craigie to amount to '35,000 slips!').[8] Browsing in Bodley got the staff out of the office, away from supervision, and was a satisfyingly scholarly activity which enhanced the quality of the Dictionary while licensing wide and exploratory reading. But the publishers found it infuriating, since it produced yet more copy while simultaneously delaying work on the copy already in place. The tendency to 'drift to Bodley' continued to be a sore spot well into R. W. Burchfield's reign in the 1960s and later, as those who worked under him attest. The unfortunate Mrs Powell was reported to Chapman by Sisam the following year, when he noted that she was 'drifting more and more into the Bodleian, instead of getting on with the rough work ahead as arranged'.[9] On the other hand, work on the Supplement could not proceed properly without extensive checking of the references they already had to hand, and this required library work.

This problem was partially solved by the lexicographers compiling lists of what they termed 'desiderata' – words for which further examples were required in good quality print sources – and publishing them in the Press's own 'organ', the quarterly journal called *The Periodical*. Onions's first list, which appeared in the issue of October 1928, included not only contemporary items of vocabulary like *A.B.C. shop* (example wanted from before 1897),[10] *ace* (airman) (before 1918), *active list* (before 1927), *airman* (before 1910), but also other terms, which one would not necessarily associate with the early part of the twentieth century, such as *Aberdeen terrier* (before 1880), *agin* (the government, etc.) (before 1904), *alley-way* (before 1882). These appeals were reported in *The Times* and other newspapers and the Dictionary files filled up with letters of response, which came, as the second Supplement editor Burchfield later said, from 'every quarter of the globe', to produce a yield of 'many thousands of quotations'.[11]

In soliciting help in this way Craigie and Onions were following in the steps of the earlier *OED* editors, for whom the public had always been a rich source of information and aid. Murray had begun his editorship in 1879 with an extraordinarily successful *Appeal* to the public, and subsequently wrote hundreds of letters a week to a wide range of correspondents, many of whom had written to ask (perhaps the favourite question) how many words there were in the English language, or to point out omissions, request definitions of a word not yet treated, offer ante- and post-datings of words already recorded, and discuss lexicographical or philological puzzles of one sort or another.[12] Onions was clearly aware that he could tap well-intentioned and well-read members of the public in this way, and knew that such appeals served a dual purpose: they both advertised the activities of the *OED* and elicited useful evidence. Rather surprisingly, given the severity of his communications with his colleagues, he was good at showing journalists round the Dictionary premises and getting a satisfactory article written in return. In the *Observer* of 26 June 1932, for example, he discoursed learnedly both on punchy colloquial phrases like 'no flies on him' (traced back to a book of 1848 on bush life in Australia, subsequently quoted in the Supplement, 'no flies about that black bull') and on recent political coinages such as that of Asquith in 1903, 'fiscalitis' (not included in the Supplement, though *fiscalism* and *fiscality* made the grade), and Lloyd George's reference in 1909 to 'robbing the henroosts' (this phrase did get in, with attribution to Lloyd George's speech, as illustrating the figurative sense of *henroost*, 'a source of plunder'). He had also slipped into the article a plug for the forthcoming abridgement of *OED*, the 'Shorter', as 'virtually a key' to the larger dictionary: 'an excellent substitute for those who have no room to house the main work. Will contain about 2,600 pages and cost 3 guineas.'

The previous year, Onions had written a letter to *The Times* to ask for help with ante-dating the word *gadget*, conjuring up an arcane and fascinating world of word exploration and suggesting that readers themselves might enter it.[13] Reporting that 'the *ad interim* Supplement of the N.E.D. had reached the word "gadget"', and that his 'investigations into its history have arrived at an interesting but puzzling stage', he went on to describe how, 'by a stroke of good fortune', the Dictionary offices had received a letter from a reader enclosing a quotation for this word from the *Bristol Times and Mirror* of 1899, noting its omission from *OED*, and claiming that the term – said to mean 'a craft equipped with mechanical gear for the discharge of ships' – had been in use for at least half a century before. The earliest other example Onions had come across had been that in a Kipling short story of 1902, which referred to 'steam gadgets'.[14] 'All the evidence,' Onions wrote,

> points to a nautical origin. I do not know how many years it is since a friend of mine recorded an encounter with a sailor for whom every person was a qualified bastard, and every thing a similarly qualified gadget. But mere recollections a lexicographer can but rarely record, because of the fallibility of human memory. We need the documented instance of the written word, and for any such evidence of 'gadget' before the year 1907 I shall be grateful.

This was picked up by the *Daily Mail* (27 May 1931) for a column called 'Phipps Solves', which announced 'THE GADGET MYSTERY: the academic bloodhounds are out, lads, and all for a household word with a hidden past . . . .'

When the Supplement was published, it was revealed that the search had thrown up an earlier quotation for *gadget* than that of the Bristol newspaper, a particularly apposite one since, in the best manner, it gave a good indication of the meaning and usage of the word (and gratifyingly confirmed Onions's intuition that the word was originally nautical). From a book published in 1886 by R. Brown, entitled *Spunyarn & Spindrift*, it read 'Then the names of all the other things on board a ship! I don't know half of them yet; even the sailors forget at times, and if the exact name of anything they want happens to slip from their memory, they call it a chicken-fixing, or a gadjet, or a gill-guy, or a timmey-noggy, or a wim-wom – just pro tem., you know.'

In another issue of *The Periodical*, published in December 1929, Onions gave a much more sober account of the agonizingly onerous nature of work on the Supplement. In a brief preface to yet another list of desiderata (accompanied, like the others, by an illustration of a properly filled in slip and strict instructions as to how to achieve this), he described

> long and arduous preliminary work (begun before the main Dictionary was concluded) on the great collection of [quotation] material which has been amassed slip by slip in the Scriptorium and other workshops of the Dictionary during the last half-century. This preparatory labour – necessary and inevitable before the word go could be given for the letter A – consisted in the organization of the whole equipment with a view to a first and experimental selection from a mass of slips which occupied some 65 feet of shelving. On the basis of this selection the editorial staff has built and is building the articles as they will appear in the Supplement.[15]

'It cannot be denied,' Craigie is reported to have said of the kind of work to which he devoted so much of his life, 'that dictionary work for the most part is very dull and boring.' Descriptions of this sort – emphasizing laborious process rather than the delights of scholarly discovery – indicate that Onions must often have felt it so. Craigie himself approved various methods of cheering the discipline up, and was 'very pleased with the now famous last quotation for the word *moron*, when he saw it in the first proof of the *Supplement*... "I have always maintained," he said, "that there is far too little of this kind of thing in the dictionary."' This quotation, subsequently excised from the Dictionary in Burchfield's second Supplement, read, 'See the happy moron. He doesn't give a damn. I wish I were a moron. My god! Perhaps I am!'[16]

Wyllie arrives

The person responsible for choosing and reporting (in an obituary of Craigie published in 1961) this example of undistinguished humour was the young Scot already mentioned, J. M. Wyllie (1907–71), whom the publishers had finally settled on in May 1929 as the best candidate to hasten editorial processing of the material which took up so much of their shelving space. Onions was not told about the appointment until a month later: in taking on a new hand independently of his approval Sisam was hoping to force up production rates and generally quicken the pace.[17] Wyllie, then aged 22, was a pupil of the distinguished patristic scholar and lexicographer Professor Alexander Souter of Aberdeen, whose offer of a second pupil Sisam had to refuse, explaining 'we can offer one man like Wyllie a career in lexicography if he does well', but not more than one. 'You see, our immediate work is the completion of the Supplement, and when that is done at the end of two years, there will be nothing for the ordinary staff to go on to.'[18] Over the next three and a half years, the publishers constantly juggled their need for man (or woman) power on the one hand, with, on the other, what they saw as the imperative to close down the *OED* project once the Supplement was completed.

Wyllie needed supervision and training, and the publishers felt this was not forthcoming from Onions. Writing to Craigie in America the following year, Sisam said, 'I am very glad that you feel able to make some sort of shaping at the Supplement as we are really pledged to the hilt. Wyllie is working hard, but gets practically no support from the others and badly needs a month or so of extra guidance.'[19] Meanwhile, since there could be no prospect of long-term employment, the turnover of temporary staff was high, and even the longest serving did not all stay to the end: Rosfrith Murray wrote to Chapman in June 1929 to announce her forthcoming resignation, after twenty-seven years, as she and her mother were selling Sunnyside, the house on Banbury Road in whose garden so much of the Dictionary had been written, to go to live in a new house built next door to her brother Harold near Haslemere. (Her mother offered the original set of fifty-four pigeonholes from the Scriptorium, those made by Herbert Coleridge in 1859 and intended to contain all the Dictionary material – although some 2,500 holes of this size would have been needed to hold the slips eventually collected. Onions responded with a surprisingly graceless memo to Chapman to say 'I will show a disposition to hospitality.')[20]

Illnesses of various sorts, possibly exacerbated by stress, beset the older members of staff throughout the five years of work on the Supplement. Bayliss became chronically ill, and like Miss Murray left before the

Supplement was completed; Sweatman was sufficiently worn down in November 1928 to be prescribed 'two months' complete rest' by his doctor and 'a course of detective story reading' by Onions, and in April 1932 needed 'at least a month's rest to repair his strained heart'. The younger members were also vulnerable, as when Miss Lee (who had been appointed in June 1930) contracted German measles in April 1932, at a critical moment in the Supplement's painfully protracted progress towards completion. New assistants took three to six months' training time, and hindered existing staff from pursuing their own work as efficiently.[21]

The constant delays on the Supplement put pressure on the 'Abridged', also moving towards its conclusion. Because of the difficulty of keeping the lexicographers to a fixed, predictable schedule, which would supply the Printer and his staff at a rate for which they could adequately plan, without under- or over-staffing, the publishers kept having to change their plans and priorities. Miscellaneous papers in the archives – memos, notes, jottings – indicate that Sisam was ceaselessly occupied on issues of staff management, reciprocal flows of supply between printers and lexicographers, and calculations as to whether the Dictionary was keeping up with projected rates of progress. Thus in 1930 he decided to divert staff to the 'Abridged', 'even at some loss to research on Supplement'. Sisam had discussed the programme with Milford, '& we agreed that it was best to clear up Abridged, rather than hold it back & have it coincide with Reissue [the reprinting of the entire run of the first edition of the *OED* that was to be released alongside the Supplement]. Does Onions know that we must [publish] Abridged in Autumn 1931 without fail?'[22] But in the event they had to revert to a modification of the original plan. The first volume of the *Shorter* appeared alongside the 'Reissue' in 1933, while volume 2 came out the following year.

As the lexicographical units toiled on, with Onions and his staff in Oxford and Craigie and Watson in Chicago, relations between them were not always good. There was a minor rupture over the inclusion of the verb *Chicago*, meaning to *skunk*, i.e. prevent an opponent scoring points, etc. in a game. Onions had derived this strange word from the meaning of the place name *Chicago*, namely 'at the place of the skunk or skunks'. Craigie, better placed than Onions to take a view, objected and the publishers (as usual) backed him, Sisam acidly commenting that 'The article of which Craigie complained was really useless, and the only evidence for it so far is American dictionaries which I should have thought had better be left to Craigie's side rather than occupy a staff sadly in arrears on their own job.'[23] Later, Chapman noted with customary witty laconicism to Sisam, 'C.T.O. met, says Delenda est Chicago.' Writing to inform Craigie of this victory, Sisam commented, 'From what I could see from the evidence collected for this strange sense, it arose from one dictionary copying another without any quotations as evidence. In any event, the American side is clearly one for you to settle.'[24]

On another occasion, Craigie complained to Sisam about the 'over-doing of *Graft* ['obtaining profit or advantage by dishonest or shady means'] and its derivatives', which was 'not my work. I actually supplied only six or seven of the quotations, and none of the long ones. Onions seems to have the same tendency as Murray had to give undue space to words of recent origin just because they have come into general notice for the time being. The whole column ought to be reduced to no more than half its present dimensions.' In this case, Onions prevailed and the entry was published with a liberal number of quotations.[25]

Onions could take the same attitude to Craigie, determined not to shoulder any blame that should properly attach to his colleague. Despite his own tardiness – Craigie pointed out it had taken him 'seven months to advance his proofs from E to Fe' – Onions complained whenever the flow of 'Americana' from Chicago dried up, and dissociated himself from his colleague's work. 'I cannot consent to be held in any way responsible for defects in the illustration or treatment of Americana in S and T' (letters for which he otherwise had responsibility), he wrote to the publishers on 1 March 1932.[26]

By contrast, Wyllie's punctuality and his appetite for hard work delighted the publishers, though these attributes exacted their own cost. When Bayliss, who was now working on the Craigie–Wyllie part of the venture, declined into ill health in December 1930, 'suffering from Glycosuria with some cardiac weakness', it looked as if he would not be able to return to the office until spring. His former colleague L. F. Powell, now librarian of the Taylorian, visited him, and wrote to Chapman at his home address on Christmas Day to warn that he should be protected from communication from Wyllie, evidently an importunate taskmaster: 'Perhaps you will send him some proofs to look at? Letters worry him . . . sympathy makes him cry. Any letters from Aberdeen [i.e. from Wyllie] should be returned.' Learning of this, Onions wrote to Chapman to protest, 'if any letters from Wyllie have reached him, it is not from here'; moreover, 'as to proof-reading, I can think of nothing more taxing to start convalescence with'.[27] Bayliss's condition did not improve, and Sisam decided to employ a Miss Marshall, one of the several women who had previously solicited work and whom he had put off, to carry out the work that Bayliss was not now fit for. Writing to tell Onions of the plan, he explained that they would 'bring down Wyllie for a month so that he can explain what they do at Aberdeen, and then leave them to fight it out under Craigie's guidance. But clearly that would still leave you the task of adjusting or persuading Craigie to adjust the American material to the Dictionary standards.'[28]

Wyllie accordingly came down from Aberdeen to supervise Miss Marshall in February 1931, and seems to have based himself in Oxford thereafter, but by June the two had badly fallen out over her hours, since Wyllie objected to the elasticity originally promised her. Sisam then had to tread carefully to support Wyllie's authority while making it impossible for him to be unreasonable. Trouble between these two members of staff persisted for the duration of the Supplement, Wyllie alleging that Miss Marshall visited Bodley and engaged in private conversations when she should have been working for him, and she was dismissed in the summer of July 1932 when the Press began the process of shedding Dictionary staff. (In apparent compensation for Wyllie's intolerance, Sisam tried hard to get her a job elsewhere.)[29]

Bayliss's health continued to decline. It was agreed that he should remain on full pay, that the Press would pay for him to go to the seaside if necessary, and that he was to be protected from letters from Craigie as well as Wyllie (since neither could be trusted to moderate their demands for more work). On 24 March 1931, Chapman discussed with Onions whether they should urge him to retire. But he was 'anxious not to do anything that might frighten him into his grave. What do you think? If he took pension and recovered, he could of course resume on a Worrallish footing' – i.e. work at piece rates while drawing his pension.[30] But in April, Sisam wrote to Craigie, he had 'had some kind of a relapse, and I think we must count him out of our plans. I very much doubt that he will ever come back to work. I am sorry, because he was a sturdy and experienced worker.'[31]

The loss of Bayliss would have been felt in several ways. Not only did he have 'really extraordinary bibliographical knowledge and aptitude for research', as Bradley had described in 1920, and 'an industry and zeal' that was 'unfailing', he also played the role of Dictionary staff jester.[32] In 1903, in a parody of reviews appearing in the Press at the time, he had produced a series of mock notices of Craigie's first fascicle (from newspapers such as the *Grocers' Record*, *Daily Squeaker* and *Birmingham Wail*), and it was in his hand that the spoof entry for *radium*, one of the items rather spectacularly omitted from the original *OED*, was written (illustration 4).[33] When Bradley and Craigie's staff moved to the Old Ashmolean in 1901, one assistant, whom it is tempting to identify as Bayliss, got so irritated by the constant interruptions from strangers knocking at the door and asking for the Ashmolean Museum that

he finally took a sheet of cardboard, printed on it in large capitals, 'This is not the Ashmolean Museum', and hung it on the inner door. As this did

radium (re^{i}d^{i}um) Forms: See Suppl. [mod.L. *radium* (B. Balius *Add. Lex.*: not in Du Cange). The orig. source is Preh. *-adami-*, *spadi-* to dig :— Antediluv. *randam-* (unconnected with PanArryan *randan*). Cognate with OHHash. *mqdrq*, OPj. *rangtum*, MHGug. *tsploshm*, MUlr. *dndrpq*; Baby. *daddums* and MPol. *rad* are unconnected.]

The unknown quantity. Math. Symbol x. Cf. EUREKA.

Aristotle *De P. Q.* li. xx says it may be obtained from the excrement of a squint-eyed rat that has died of a broken heart buried 50 feet below the highest depths of the western ocean in a well-stopped tobacco-tin; but Sir T. Browne says this is a vulgar error: he also refutes the story that it was dug in the air above Mt. Olympus by the ancients.

[Not in J., the Court Guide, or the Daily Mail Yrbk. before 1510.]

c 925 *Vesp. Ps.* xcii. 315 Sle͡ʒɛ hem wiþ by wraðiu. *c* 1386 CHAUCER *Dustm. T.* 31 Brynge. .forthe yowre waystid wrathym. **1470–85** MALORY *Arthur* XVII. 7. 935 Hauyng a swerde wiþ a blayde of rathio. **1626** BACON *Sylva* §627 Experiment extraordinary. Radiom will not washe clothes. **1669** PEPYS *Diary* 31 June, And so to bed. Found radium an excellent pick-me-up in the morning. **1678** BUNYAN *Pilgr.* 317 When I had affixed a pinch of radium to the tail of Apollyon, he went on his way and I saw him no more. **1766** GOLDSM. *Inhab. Vill.* 29 The toper still his wonted radium quaffs. **1873** *Hymns A. & M.* 2517 Thy walls are built of radium. **1905** [My son writes: I well remember introducing Radium as an illuminant into Slushton, last July.]

attrib. and *Comb.* **1600** *Hakluyt's Voy.* IV. 21 The kyng was attyred simply in an hat of silke and a radium-umbrella. *a* **1704** NEWTON *Optics* IV. 29 These rays are radium-coloured. **1747** MRS. GLASSE *Cookery* 761 Radium cutlets. **1856** KANE *Arct. Explor.* III. 57, I hurled a radium-bootjack at the beast. **1879** *Jrnl. R. Soc.* CLXX. 315 Prof. Bigass exhibited a radium-filled tooth of a cave-dweller.

4. H. J. Bayliss's spoof slip for *radium*. Reproduced by permission of the Secretary to the Delegates of Oxford University Press.

not prevent inquiry being made for other University buildings, he successively added, in alternate lines of black and red ink, 'Nor the Sheldonian Theatre', 'Nor the Bodleian Library', 'Nor the Clarendon Building', and at last 'Nor the Martyrs' Memorial – as yet'. Unsuspecting sightseers sometimes read this aloud from beginning to end and departed wondering.[34]

As Bayliss's health worsened, other of the 'old soldiers' began to fall ill also.[35] In February 1931 Onions had reported that Lewis had been absent for some weeks with lumbago, 'on which ensued influenza and general weakness', and was working from home. 'He is a devoted worker and had no particular encouragement except friendliness from Bradley (who thought highly of him) and me.' Birt, 'another devoted slave of the dictionary', was ill with 'recurrences of his gas-caused chest troubles'. He had joined the Dictionary in 1906 at the age of 16, and worked under Onions for the whole of the intervening period barring 1914–19, when he served in the army and was gassed in 1918. He was financially handicapped too in that his stipend was 'just beyond the insurable limit, so that he has to pay for his medical treatment directly out of his own pocket'. Onions urged the publishers that 'this is a case in which misericordia ["mercy"] might . . . play a part'.[36]

On the other hand, there was good news on Wyllie, now moved down from Aberdeen. As Sisam wrote to Craigie, this most promising recruit was 'showing great ability. He is always trying to devise plans for saving time, cutting down unnecessary operations, etc., and he now seems much happier in Oxford. If he will devote himself to the subject and get as much training as he can, I think he has good prospects of a career in lexicography, because the race has almost died out in this country.'[37] Particularly cheering were his regular accounts to the publishers of his work to date and his estimates for the future, which gave them a sense of where they were and how they might plan. Even if these were not always accurate – one forecast of spring 1932 as the completion date had to be replaced four months later with a more realistic reckoning of two years (as indeed proved to be the case) – Wyllie fully and credibly explained the basis for his calculations.[38] So in July 1931, Sisam and Chapman learned that the letter O would take a further six weeks, P 21 weeks, Q–R 13, S 32, T 14, and U–Z 14 weeks apiece; the delay was due to Wyllie's shouldering more and more 'secondary matters' ('fitting in American materials, making special investigations onwards, correspondence, revision generally, and proof-reading') in addition to 'the primary task of preparing copy', on which, he added darkly, he was 'receiving little real help from Miss Marshall'.[39] No such documentation seems ever to have been supplied by Onions, despite constant needling, and for this part of the alphabet, together with its staffing supply, Sisam was reduced to making all the reckonings himself.[40] Wyllie's value to the publishers was reflected in their raising his salary on 1 April 1931 to £300 p.a., and his punctilious attention to schedules, deadlines and an overall plan continued a great comfort to Sisam, who considered it 'one of his great merits'.[41]

For Onions, who despite continual efforts to goad him on was merely 'treading the path of the alphabet with sluggish resolution' (as Chapman put it several months later, in an echo of Dr Johnson, who had thus described his work on his own dictionary), there was considerably less enthusiasm.[42] For example, as work dragged agonizingly on through February 1931, Onions had cheered up at the thought that they might publish the Supplement in two parts. Writing bullishly to 'My Dear Secretaries', he argued that '256 pp. of the Supplement are now made up; that this is the equivalent of four single sections; that it makes a handsome instalment which would give the public the surprise of their lives, and bring in some money'. Sisam underlined the words from 'public' onwards and scrawled on it 'No NO – a mad thought'. Chapman was more polite and wrote back to say,

I'm afraid we mustn't think of publishing a piece. It causes a heap of trouble and expense, ragged stock, etc. etc.; and in particular we should get into difficulties with the persons entitled to a free copy (which will *not* include a binding. I hope to get something on the binding!). I am sorry, but it isn't workable. You must go on beating the path, put away vexing thoughts, and be no friend to scruples – you see there is a Johnsonian phrase for every gloomy situation of life – and look forward to 'release' at the Last Trump. I use release primarily in its modern sense [defined by Craigie in one of the new Supplement entries as 'the permitted publication or public exhibition of anything on a specified date'].[43]

But Chapman and Sisam also had reservations about Craigie's judgement. In another dispute between Craigie and Onions, they felt far less clear they should take his side – though as always seeking to manage both of the editors as skilfully as possible. When Onions found out that Craigie was proposing to leave *lesbian* and *lesbianism* out of the Supplement, falling as they did into his half of the alphabet, Onions turned it into a point of honour. On 10 April 1931 he wrote to Chapman,

> A lexicographical conscience is not so easily stifled, and when I find out that <u>Lesbian</u> and <u>Lesbianism</u> have been deliberately excluded by Craigie, I wonder what else is going to happen. <u>Lesbianism</u> is no doubt a very disagreeable thing, but the word is in regular use, & no serious Supplement to our work should omit it.
>
> <u>Lesbian vice</u>
> Is in the Concise;
>
> a fortiori must it appear in the great work.

He added the self-pitying if irritable comment, 'But any intervention of mine will probably harden hearts', indicating his accurate perception that Chapman and Sisam tended to favour Craigie over him, and observed, '*Sapphism* is in NED. But I think *Lesbianism* is now much more common.'[44] Onions's letter is initialled by both Sisam and Craigie, indicating that they had read it; Sisam additionally scribbled, in pencil, 'I should have thought it was not worth wasting time about it if Craigie has views. Not really very important.' Chapman reported his reply to Sisam, 'I have told C.T.O. (1) that I shd have thought L[*esbianism*] less important than S[*apphism*]. (2) that he had better not interfere if C. has really made up his mind. But I think it very silly to omit it. The *thing* is important enough in all conscience, if common report (in e.g. New York) is to be trusted. C. is capable of not knowing what it is!'[45] But Craigie won, as usual – in an incidental display of the culturally biassed control that the lexicographers could, if they chose, exert over the language. *Lesbian* and *lesbianism* had to wait until Burchfield's Supplement of 1976 to enter the *OED*, with quotations from 1890 onwards (see discussion at p. 205 below).

Two years to go

Wyllie's July 1931 prognosis of two years until completion was 'a gloomy prospect' for Sisam, although he agreed with Wyllie that 'we ought to face it'. At this stage he began to compare slip production between Wyllie and Onions. Working just with Miss Marshall, Wyllie had submitted 2,686 slips in little over a month – 1,100 more than the scheduled number (based on an expectation of 350 slips a week). Over the same period, Onions's much larger team, together with Onions himself (who was spending five-eighths of his time on the Supplement), had sent in 2,361 slips, which by contrast was 850 under the scheduled number (based on an expectation of 650 slips a week). This meant that 'the Printer [John Johnson] would be at a stand now but for Wyllie's excess'.[46] Sisam went on to cost Onions's production of 650 slips a week at £1,865 per annum (five-eighths of Onions's salary plus the cost of his eight staff), which compared with Wyllie's 350 slips at £360. (Craigie was supplying American material to both Onions and Wyllie, and needing to do very little on the English copy or proofs.) Sisam felt that 'the discrepancy in output' was 'serious'. It arose 'from the experienced men sticking to "proof-reading and research" instead of doing copy'. And rather than failing to keep up to 650 slips a week, Onions and his staff ought to be producing 1,000.

Things were not much better with the 'Abridged', on which Onions was spending the remaining three-eighths of his time along with three full-time (female) assistants. 'The programme has collapsed for lack of type, and with it, I fear, all chance of publication in autumn 1932, which at best hung on a slender thread.' What made things worse was that all the staff were proposing to go off on summer holiday at the same time. Meanwhile, Wyllie, 'besides new copy preparing, is reading in all stages the equivalent of 4pp. of Abridged a week'.[47]

Constant, and evidently draining, toing and froing ensued between the printers, Sisam and Onions on the speed with which copy was being delivered and processed. This was civil but not good-tempered, much like the disputes between the Dictionary staff over who was to occupy which table in the office. (Entitlement was felt to be affected by the amount of time spent at Bodley, i.e. not in occupation of a designated table).[48] Sisam determined to put more pressure on the recalcitrant Onions, and in August 1931 asked the Printer whether he could cope with 'proofs to the equivalent of 1,350 slips of copy', explaining 'my enquiry is at the moment hypothetical. I don't want to demand the slips and then find they couldn't be done. I don't in the least expect to get them, though I have a lexicographer's promise. But I shall give you good notice if it becomes a practical question.'[49] Replying to a query from the Maruzen Company of Tokyo as to when the Supplement would appear, he guessed 1933, with the qualification that 'anyone who has had to do with great dictionaries and their staffs must speak with all reserves'.[50]

By September 1931 they were in crisis again. Sisam reported to Chapman that 'The Printer is now desperately short of work, and his programme (1000 slips a week) is crashing).' Although Wyllie had been keeping to schedule, and indeed exceeding it, the main staff were now averaging 200 slips a week, including the American material. Wyllie was 'now on holiday (getting married), and cannot send in more because the American material for $\underline{O}$ has not yet arrived – it is on the way'. Onions had said it was possible to send in 1,000 a week to help the Printer's programme – and indeed, Sisam says, 'it is absolutely necessary [that he should do this] if the Supplement is to be finished'. But Sisam's 'last urgent request only produced 154 slips for the week ending 12 September, and I should be glad if you would take a hand in a desperate situation'. To Onions Sisam wrote, 'the position is desperate. Your programme of 1000 a week seems to have crashed, and all the Printer's arrangements and our publishing plans are in jeopardy. But I hope you are on the point of disgorging vast accumulations.'[51]

This was sent on 15 September 1931, but on 22 September Johnson wrote again to Chapman to say,

The irregularity with which copy is reaching me is causing the gravest embarrassment . . . . I laid my plans for [an expected '1000 "sides"', i.e. slips, 'a week, or if need be 1350'], allotting and reserving men and material for the task, but week by week my difficulties have been increased. In some weeks the quota has reached me: in others I have had only 200 or 300 sides a week. The first effect is temporary chaos: the inevitable consequence a reapportioning of men and materials to other work: and the final result may well be that I shall find it impossible to produce this work with speed just when you require speed most.[52]

Sisam commented that the Printer was 'justified in his complaint'. Craigie had told him that 'Murray at his best used to insist on a minimum of 16 columns a week (= about 800 slips of much more difficult matter)'.[53] To explain the situation to Johnson, he wrote, 'we are beating them with sticks, but one might as well beat the mist'.[54] Should they drum up reinforcements and appoint new staff, they wondered. Sisam was against. 'I am very much in favour of a piece-work threat for the old soldiers, and am against the employment of any more staff – the present staff is unwieldy and additions have not resulted in more output.'[55] The problem was simply that Onions and his staff would not keep to a 'programme', i.e. a schedule, of regular production of 800–1,000 slips a week.

The 'bottle-neck'

As the Supplement went into its final stages, a new problem is regularly referred to in the office papers. This was the 'bottle-neck'. The term had recurred constantly during the history of the original *OED*, as a way of describing what the publishers felt to be Murray's stranglehold on the process of getting copy through the editorial stage and to the printer.[56] Now, it was Onions's job to approve the work of his staff before surrendering it for transformation into print. Naturally enough, Onions could only oversee a certain number of slips a week, which he put at 450, and both he and Sisam found this unavoidable limitation irksome.

Sisam and Chapman identified three alternatives, not mutually exclusive, for dealing with this situation, a dangerous one since, so Sisam reported, 'this neck will get narrower, in my opinion, and has long been the crux'. The first was 'to cut down the quantity of matter by less research and freer omission: this is the Craigie–Wyllie policy, which gives results not merely in slips but in letters completed'. Interestingly they rejected this one, possibly out of respect for Onions's lexicographical conscience and their reluctance to lower standards. The two remaining possibilities were 'to reduce the staff to meet the bottle-neck', or 'to widen the bottle-neck by creating a new unit', in other words, to share Onions's supervisory role between more members of staff.[57] A handwritten scrawl by Sisam records Onions's grudging acquiescence in the last, in an interview of 13 October 1931: 'C.T.O. very gloomy (450 [slips] his maximum) – but will try to consider a new "bottle-neck" with O'Loughlin in charge' (O'Loughlin, a promising young man who went on to write his own dictionary at another publishing house, had just been taken on by Onions, 'to clear off A–K in the <u>printing</u> stages').[58]

Sisam was also determined to set up what he called a 'demobilization programme, so that all the staff have the longest possible notice. Otherwise they will have a grievance. I fear none of them thinks of the work as one which will be completed in space and time. Onions ought to produce this programme. It is hard that we have to produce all the programmes, and his criticism is not very constructive.' Sisam was at this stage considering a number of future possible projects – a Concise French Etymological Dictionary for Onions, sub-editorship for Wyllie on a new Latin dictionary (what was to become, many years later, the *Oxford Latin Dictionary*), and subsidiary roles for 'the only other meritorious and performing persons' on the staff, Mrs Coulson and Miss Clark, the latter a 'rabbit' who had turned out better than expected.[59]

In January 1932, Sisam reported that the 'Abridged' was making good headway. On the Supplement, however, 'the position continues to be unsatisfactory. June turns to December and December to June.' Onions had handed over *Gold–Immune* – roughly 7,600 slips in sixteen weeks, allowing for the week he had had off for Christmas, or 475 a week, whereas 'we need 700'. Craigie, too, 'has not always kept up – I don't know what the present position is – and some part of G–K has gone down without the American material, so that time will be lost in proof. (This is not C. T. O.'s fault)'. And even by O'Loughlin they had been let down. 'We do not know whether O'Loughlin has begun a section on his own,' Sisam says, despairingly, but 'if he has, no results yet . . . If he hasn't, his addition to the staff has produced no practical benefit (except to himself), and he might as well be dropped again. The staff is too big for the output, owing to the bottle-neck . . . .' Given that 'it is essential that we should finish all first proof with December 1932' (which Onions had claimed was 'not impossible'), the only means were increasing the rate of slips, or 'more elimination i.e. covering of more ground in a given number of slips', in other words, culling superfluous quotations and thus choosing (reduced) quantity over quality.[60] Years before, Murray had described to Craigie his hatred of this process, the cause of extended wrangling and dispute between fellow lexicographers as well as between editors and the Press: 'No one knows as well as I do, how it grieves one to have to do this,' he wrote in 1901, 'but I have had to steel my heart & clench my teeth to do it, for years.'[61] It is possible that 'elimination' did take place, to some degree, in the latter stages of the Supplement's coverage of the alphabet, but the apparently smaller number of quotations for this portion of the book can also be explained by its covering far fewer years, given that the relevant *OED* fascicles had appeared more recently for the end of the alphabet than for the beginning.

February of that year brought bad news. Sisam was enraged, and Chapman put out, when they heard the (true) rumour that Onions had become editor of the new medieval periodical, *Medium Aevum*. Responding to a gently probing letter, Onions wrote back with unattractive evasiveness:

I suppose I must regard your question as something more than rhetorical. The general answer is that I have always found it wise to cultivate my own particular 'lane' since I came on the N.E.D. 36 years ago . . . the new medieval society has seen fit to place me at the head of its editorial committee – a compliment which I saw some reason for accepting as graciously as I could . . . I feel as though I ought to apologise for being so much in demand – my misfortune, not my fault, though.[62]

Chapman and Onions exchanged memos the same day, Chapman inclined to defend Onions, and Sisam warning grimly 'I guess you will find that it is "editorship" [not "chairmanship"]. But CTO cannot again maintain the "non possumus" ["we can't do it"] bottleneck attitude in our discussions.' In the event, Chapman wrote back a thinly veiled warning to Onions: 'My motives, as you know, are always & necessarily mixed – but concern for yourself I believe always predominates, tho' further it might not. Rumour called you editor; I am glad to believe that chairmanship won't put any great strain on you.' He relented in a note at the bottom of the letter: 'Of course it was the obvious choice', and followed this up with another letter, undated: 'Let us talk. You <u>must not</u> let yourself be put upon.'[63] This appeared to work well with its recipient. Onions wrote back on 19 February to say, 'Yes, I know. Cannan (rest his soul) had the same solicitude.' He referred to Chapman's informant (unidentified) as 'a Lying Jade', and said that what the *Medium Aevum* committee wanted was 'that there should be some one man who had some sort of mind to make up, and had sufficient hardihood to speak it: – another way of putting it: "we must have someone to put the blame on"?!'[64]

The explanation for Sisam's constant flogging appears in a letter to G. G. Loane of 9 March 1932. If too much research was put into the Supplement it would be delayed to the extent that it would itself need a supplement, and so on *ad infinitum*. Its primary purpose was 'to make up the difference in date between A and Z'.[65] In a private memo to Chapman the next day he wrote, 'this work must be brought to an end, and Abridged must be brought to an end: both are going out of date every day they are held back. No theoretical considerations of the best order can, I think, outweigh the need of getting them on the market.'[66] This point is repeated, in different ways, time and again in the papers, as also that 'the closing of the salary list will be a great relief and will clear the way for new and less onerous enterprises, e.g. the new Lewis & Short [the Latin dictionary on which he planned Wyllie would work]'. A bonus for completing the copy for the entire Supplementary alphabet (A–Z) by 31 December 1932 was now, Sisam felt, the only way forward: 'I am afraid we have exhausted all other means'.[67]

To this end, in March 1932 they employed yet another helpful woman, a Mrs Janet Heseltine of Brunswick Square, London, who had been working in Chicago for the Chaucerian Sir William McCormick (on what was to become the Manly–Rickert edition of Chaucer). Could she 'give us 14 hours a week (say two days) in the British Museum at 29/- a week', verifying quotations? Sisam wrote to her to ask. The work 'would require plenty of wits and accuracy but no great amount of writing, and I think no particular strain. One of our expert dictionary readers [Bayliss] has had to leave through old age at a critical moment ... .'[68] Mrs Heseltine agreed. Although 'not trained to the work like Bayliss', she had 'commonsense and ability', she was to be supervised by Wyllie, and Sisam still hoped that their programme of completing copy by the end of the year was attainable.[69]

Sisam helpfully described the niceties of the job to Mrs Heseltine. It was not easy 'to initiate you into the mysteries', as 'it is so hard to foresee difficulties or to learn except by practice. But the great thing is to use commonsense: not to waste time on things obviously trifling; and not to treat all questions as of equal importance. Clearly, to find the first quotation for an important new word is worth more time than the verification of a relatively unimportant word or reference.'[70]

'I see that all things come to an end'

At last, it looked as if the end was in sight. After a 'satisfactory talk' with Onions on 19 September 1932, Sisam recorded, 'If Onions, Craigie and Wyllie can keep going for a few months more, we have come to the end of the long process of fitting jury-masts, patching sails, and splicing broken ropes.'[71] Onions was finally addressing the management problems he had long put off, in a mock-apocalyptic recognition of impending completion: '"I saw [sic] that all things come to an end", as the Psalmist says. Ought we not to talk about the Staff before the end of this month?'[72] Perhaps he was brought to this realization by the departure of Henry Bradley's daughter Eleanor, who had submitted her final account to the Dictionary three days earlier, on 23 November. She received a present of five guineas, together with a subsequent note from Chapman regretting that her 'long association' with the Dictionary (amounting to 35 years in all, or 48 if one counted the additional years of her father's involvement) had come to an end. In her thank-you letter back, she wrote 'one cannot help being a little sad at the ending up of Dictionary work but it will be a joy to see the finished Supplement'. (In fact, Bradley's association with the Dictionary was to persist for several years more, since – like others who had contributed for decades – she proved unable to banish the habit of excerpting quotations from her daily reading and sending them in to the office. But the identity and character of this long-standing servant of the Dictionary remain shadowy so far as the archival papers are concerned, evidenced by carbon copies of her payment slips and little else.)[73]

By the end of the month the publishers had agreed to let go, in various ways, all the remaining staff save Onions, Sweatman, Lewis and Birt; these men would be needed till the end of July 1933, and Onions was to be kept on indefinitely on further projects. They had also determined on the form the 'Reissue' of the *OED* would take. The parent Dictionary was to be reprinted in twelve volumes, with a newly written Introduction (including the 'Historical Introduction', an account of the Dictionary by both editors which was to serve as a preface to the whole, responsibility for which was to be split between Craigie and Onions) in the first, and the Supplement and 'Register' in the last.[74] But there was to be a different arrangement for 'subscribers', that is for those who had committed to receiving the Dictionary fascicle by fascicle since its first publication, and who would consequently not wish to buy the Reissue. For this group of people, numbering they later reckoned around 6,000, the Introduction, Supplement and Register would also be issued in a single additional volume (which they carefully refrained from calling volume 13), a procedure which 'will cause no end of difficulty because it is a different printing and paper'. Subscribers would be alerted personally (if known), or otherwise by a letter to the *Times Literary Supplement* – which eventually appeared on 21 September 1933 – that they could claim this volume free, in paper covers, although they might pay the publishers (so the Press hoped) to bind it for them.[75] Since the Supplement was an intrinsic part of the original *OED*, the publishers felt themselves bound to honour subscribers' implicit claim to the whole Dictionary. Perhaps they were also influenced by some ironic remarks of Baldwin, at the Dictionary banquet of five years previously, which might have appeared to accuse them of chasing indecorously after cash. 'If ever a dictionary were destined for eternity,' he had said, it was the *OED*, 'because no sooner have we, like myself, the second generation of subscribers, drawn our last cheque, had it cashed, and seen it honoured, and had the last volume delivered, than we are told that supplements are about to begin; and Oxford, with that sure touch of the modern generation, is appealing to us to buy this new book because there is going to be a little article in it on appendicitis . . . .'[76]

Meanwhile, Chapman was pulling strings at the Prime Minister's office, hoping there might be a chance of knighthoods or other awards for the editors and the Publisher (Milford). As he explained to Patrick Duff, who had helped with honours in 1928, the publishers had felt 'that it was rather hard on poor Onions. Murray and Craigie were knighted; nothing was ever actually done for Henry Bradley because he died too soon . . . . Nothing was done for Onions; and a very poor man with ten children is apt to feel that his social difficulties may have been a bar! They <u>would</u> be a bar, from his own point of view, to the major honour; but O.B.E. or C.V.O. doesn't send up the tradesmen's bills I imagine.' He went on to point out that 'the Supplement of 1000 pages is in itself a big achievement in which he has played the leading part; and its completion is the end of the great Dictionary as we know it. Lexicography at Oxford will go on, I trust; but it is unlikely that the Dictionary will be revived in its present form, or that more Supplements will be issued.'[77] This plea eventually yielded limited fruit: Onions was awarded a CBE in the New Year's Honours of 1934, while Milford, a richer man, was knighted in 1936.

In Oxford, Chapman solicited the University's Vice-Chancellor, recounting a more detailed history of how Onions had come to be over-looked in 1928 (he put it down in part to the sudden death of the University Chancellor, Lord Cave), and hoping for an honorary D.Litt. for him to match Craigie's. 'The great supplement', Chapman thought, would be 'the final crown of the work, for it is very unlikely that the Dictionary will ever be revived in its present form, and I doubt if further supplements are likely to be undertaken'. The Dictionary itself was 'now virtually out of print'. 'Onions has been in charge of much the most difficult part of it [i.e. the Supplement], which is of course the earlier part, some of which was 40 years old when supplementation began. Appendicitis and Aeroplane were not in the original book. It is therefore a production of importance in lexicography as well as being very learned.' He went on to explain:

> It was felt in 1928 that a knighthood would only be an embarrassment to a man of his domestic situation, but was hoped that there was nothing against a minor distinction. His part in the main work was of course much less in bulk than the parts of Murray, Bradley, Craigie, but it was substan-tial and of very high quality. Now that he is the main producer of the supplement and also mainly responsible for the two volume abridgement, which will also appear in 1933, I think myself that complete exclusion from this kind of recognition would be a rather marked omission.[78]

Chapman enlisted Craigie's help with his campaign. He hoped for rewards for both Craigie's assistant Watson and for Wyllie (now a Croom Robertson Fellow of Aberdeen engaged on a Lexicon of Sallust, which he eventually completed but never published). Craigie responded warmly, praising Watson's invaluable assistance to the *OED* over the last twenty-five years together with his wider academic attainments, and Wyllie's 'quite exceptional qualifications for lexicography'. He hoped that 'whoever presents Watson for his degree ought to mention his continued reading of the dictionary proofs while at the front'.[79] In the end, Chapman and the

Vice-Chancellor agreed to give an honorary MA to Watson and to wait where Wyllie is concerned, 'as he is younger and has the Latin Dictionary before him', while Onions duly received his D.Litt.

Final copy was at last delivered at the very end of the year, on 31 December 1932, and bonuses were paid out accordingly: £150 to Onions, £50 to Wyllie, and sums of between £10 and £22 to the remaining staff. The change that completion brought to some of their lives is scarcely imaginable. Chapman wrote to all individually to thank them for their loyalty, for example telling Mrs Powell (another Dictionary servant little remarked in the archival papers) that 'the regret which you must feel at the end of your long association with the great work will be shared by all who know anything of what you have done and the devotion you have given to it'. In her reply she wrote, 'I shall at first feel rather strange after so long a spell of work – after 31 years of one sort of life, there must needs be a complete readjustment of proceedings! No doubt I shall settle down to a home life – anyhow I must. My husband is frankly delighted to have me always at home.'[80]

The Press was anxious to secure what it considered to be decent arrangements for its long-term male staff. Sweatman and Lewis 'must look forward to pension', in the region of £2 a week – exiguous even by the standards of the time. Chapman and Sisam would try to put them in the way of piecework (for example with Craigie, who was still at work on the American and Scottish dictionaries) but this could not be counted upon. '<u>Birt</u>, being younger, must look for a job: we should tide him over'.[81] In April 1933, Chapman wrote to H. H. E. Craster, Bodley's Librarian, asking whether he (Craster) could make any use of 'our Dictionary Rump', consisting of Lewis (aged around 65), Sweatman (60) and Worrall (70). Lewis and Sweatman (both originally Bodley employees) had, he said, 'spent over 40 years on the Dictionary, and tho' slow and pernickety they are <u>very</u> accurate, and of course know their way about your library <u>and</u> its catalogue as few others can. If you have cataloguing work for which they are competent you could get them on your own terms, and as they are old and . . . already pensioned they would involve you in no liability. They are good, timid, docile creatures.'

Meanwhile, discussion had been taking place for some time with Onions as to his future. The publishers recognized their obligation to continue to employ him, and were trying to balance the cost of this against likely benefits. In December 1932 Onions was pondering an impressive range of projects: the French etymological dictionary previously mooted, a revision of Skeat's etymological dictionary (the last edition, published just before Skeat's death in 1911, had only been able to draw on the full etymological information available in the *OED* up to the letter *H*), an English dictionary 'analogous to the "Histoire-Géographie" which forms the Supplement to the Petit Larousse Illustré – a possible addition to any further edition of S. O. E. D.', and various Shakespeare books which would develop the work Onions had earlier published with the Press, his *Shakespeare Glossary* of 1911 and his completion of Sidney Lee's *Shakespeare's England* in 1916. Outlining these to Chapman, he commented, 'I suppose the first thing to determine is what is likely to pay best. It might be well to have two going at the same time.' Chapman poured cold water on any ambitious scheme,

5. C. T. Onions in 1948.

pointing out brutally, if understandably, 'The difficulty is to see how anything you produce would pay its way.'[82]

Onions was to be 60 in September 1933, by which time he would have served the Dictionary for thirty-eight years. For the latter part of his *OED* work he had been paid a salary of £600, a sum that Chapman later acknowledged to be 'meagre', but which had been supplemented by his fellowship and readership salary. As Chapman later explained, 'When the Dictionary was at an end there seemed no justifiable way of employing him on that scale, so we worked out a compromise. We gave him a pension of £300 (which in relation to salary was pretty good, since he got it at 60?) and asked him to do at his own convenience an Etymological Dictionary for £1000 (with the possibility of a bonus, naturally, at the back of our minds). He thought he <u>might</u> do this in three years . . .'; Sisam recorded at the time his own view that '3 is his minimum, & 5 more likely'. Also entering the publishers' calculations was the likelihood that Onions's Magdalen fellowship would run for four years more and that he was likely to be re-elected, while his readership 'lasts till he is 65 at least', and that he 'would be free to examine [for the University] under the pension plan', which in those days was remunerative. In fact, Onions was able to hold his stipendiary fellowship until the day of his death, over thirty years later.[83]

But his financial situation was often difficult. In 1938, he had drawn about 60 per cent of his £1,000 advance on the Etymological Dictionary, and had mentioned to Chapman that he 'found it convenient to protract the Etym. Dictionary somewhat so as to earn easier money'. Chapman took his case to the Press Finance Committee, which was 'obviously – indeed touchingly – sympathetic' to his case, and they advanced him a further increase. In 1949, Onions's readership came to an end (he was then 76), and the Press agreed, with evident good will, to raise his annual pension to £400: still a very small amount of money to live on. He was continuing to work on revision to the *Shorter* and on his Etymological Dictionary, though this was only completed after his death.

While negotiating Onions's future, the publishers were still coaxing the last shreds of material out of Craigie in Chicago. Like Onions, Craigie was finding it hard – or counter-productive – to delegate. On 13 April 1933 Sisam wrote delicately to urge him not to be held up by scruple. 'I well understand that you cannot delegate this particular job, and agree with you that the right thing to do is to do what you can over the remainder of the field quickly without any regard to counsels of perfection. The Supplement, after all, is avowedly a scratch supplement, and it is no use trying to make it complete or to make some parts complete and leave the others blank.' He concluded, 'I know you will be relieved to see the end of an enterprise which you have had to rescue so often!'[84] Craigie was still writing his share of the history of the main Dictionary, which as previously arranged was being split between him and Onions. When it came to composing the Acknowledgements, Onions was evidently reminded of ancient resentment, and this in turn fuelled current bad feelings. He told Chapman 'Harold Murray [James Murray's son, with whom he had been reviewing Craigie's draft] thought that Bradley was dealt with rather slightly, and others think that my share in the completion of the work will not be obvious to the outside reader'. He also thought that it was, as he put it, 'comical' that Craigie had put in references to Watson and another American helper, Mitford M. Mathews, in the Supplement Preface, given that they had (Onions implies) done so little.[85]

Correcting the proofs, which began to appear from spring 1933 onwards, proved as difficult as might have been expected. Sisam continued the pressure on Onions to keep to schedule, reminding him of 'our familiarity with the delays that are likely to take place in clearing the last few pages of preliminaries', and anticipating his protest a few days later that the American material from *Sk–Sp* had not been edited as normal, 'so that I shall have even more to do at it than I have hitherto had'.[86] There was a last-minute flurry of memos over items that might or might not deserve inclusion. Sisam reported to Onions that 'a reviewer in the New York <u>Nation</u> of 26th April complains that S.O.E.D. [which had just been published] omits the phrase "muscle in". My informant tells me that this phrase seems to be used in America by gangsters, and you may not wish to encourage them. But I mention it while there is still time.' Onions decided against, and this sense had to wait until 1972–86 and Burchfield's second Supplement (which filled the gap with quotations dating from 1929: 'If you think you can muscle into this joint you're off your nut').[87] They debated whether *sked* (= schedule), an example of American campus slang, should be included: probably not, as 'the trouble is that American reviewers specialise in the criticism "If this, then why not this", and [Craigie] probably thinks it not worth while to supply them with a handle for pouring out all the campus slang they know which is not in the dictionary' (*sked* was treated by Burchfield in 1986, again with quotations from 1929 onwards).[88] Onions was determined to 'squeeze in <u>body-line</u> [as in bowling] by sacrificing other things'; this term, certain, as Sisam said, 'to please the reviewers', and the Australians who coined it, had received wide attention in January that year when English cricketers had used the tactic to destroy the Australian batsman Don Bradman and thus win the Ashes. (Complaints had caused crowd disruption on the tour, and the Australian Cricket Board had cabled the Marylebone Cricket Club to threaten diplomatic action in a telegram subsequently printed in *The*

Times, from which the Supplement was able to extract its quotation.)[89] Its inclusion in so early a part of the alphabet was hailed by one of the Supplement's admirers, the President of Magdalen (and Chapman's long-standing friend) G. S. Gordon, as 'a remarkable feat', and he was 'at a loss to understand by what conspiracy of editors and printers it was performed'.[90]

Other deserving items proved less easy to insert. Chapman had noticed in December 1932 that *OED*'s first quotation for *contradiction in terms* was from 1795 and was sure it must be possible to ante-date this. 'I suppose the expression goes back to scholastic logic; but I do not remember it in Johnson where one would expect to find it.' Chapman had however spotted it in one of the letters of the poet Thomas Gray, written in 1741: 'A metaphysical poem is a contradiction in terms' (Chapman was reading the proofs for Toynbee and Whibley's edition of Gray's correspondence, whose first volume, in which this instance occurred, appeared in 1935).[91] But this ante-dating did not reach the printed pages of the 1933 Supplement, nor indeed of Burchfield's later one, and over seventy years after Chapman identified the ante-dating, 1795 remains the *OED*'s earliest quoted date for this term.[92]

Chapman also pointed out, this time in January 1933, that Onions needed to frame a careful definition of *groups, group movement*, and related terms, especially in view of the so-called Oxford group movement.[93] This was the confusing name given to the religious revivalist movement brought from America to England in 1921 by Frank Buchman, characterized by the 'sharing' of personal problems by groups, and nothing to do with the nineteenth-century Oxford Movement (the movement for the revival of Catholic doctrine and observance in the Church of England, which began at Oxford around 1833). The Oxford group movement caused what the *Daily Express* described as 'a storm of comment in the University', when that paper disclosed on 29 February 1928 that Oxford was the home of its revival. The *Express* had explained that 'The Buchmanites believe that if they conceive a sudden thought, without the exercise of a process of reasoning, this is a divine revelation, and should be acted on at once', although three months later, in May, *Isis* declared that 'Buchmanism is not widespread; probably in Oxford it never will be'.[94] But for whatever reason – possibly because it was too late to introduce the material, possibly because Onions disagreed with Chapman that the term was significant – no entry appeared in the Supplement. Instead, it was treated by Burchfield in 1972–86, who thought it important enough to merit a total of eleven quotations taken from sources dated between 1928 and 1961. Burchfield's treatment of the term forms only a small portion of his new material for *group*, which covers a wide range of applications (chemical, coding, air-force, algebraic). That he was able to illustrate most of these senses, unidentified by the 1933 Supplement, with quotations from the late nineteenth century through the 1910s to the end of the 1920s indicates how hard it was for Craigie and Onions to register much of the significant new usage of their day.

Adding new items to the proofs meant deleting others, and here too judgement was tricky. After the event, Wyllie (then working on the Latin dictionary, but also maintaining *OED* files) realized that he and Craigie had been wrong to exclude *putsch*, the word used in 1923 to refer to a crucial moment in Hitler's rise to power. In December 1933 Sisam wrote asking why it had been omitted, and Wyllie had 'had to look at the Suppl. to make sure no mistake had been made about this, but of course [Sisam was right that] it is not there. It was certainly in the first proof, but was deleted, if I remember rightly, on the grounds that it was simply a foreign word. We had several newspaper quots. for it, all referring to one or two particular events in Germany . . . .'[95]

When at last publication could be confidently forecast, in November that year, the Goldsmiths again stepped in to host a celebratory meal – though this time it was a lunch, not a dinner, with a mere five courses and five wines (held on 21 November 1933).[96] Planning the event was still a time-consuming affair, as various luminaries, both within and without the University, had to be drummed up, and Chapman had often to explain to them precisely what the Supplement was and how it was expected that dictionaries at Oxford would proceed in the future. Meanwhile, he was fending off the Goldsmiths' fear that the invited audience of 'journalists and representative booksellers' would be 'too commercial' by assuring them 'that whenever booksellers congregate they talk literature not discounts. Besides we choose the speakers and can tell them what to talk about' – for a maximum of twenty minutes.[97] But the speakers were also cause for anxiety. Sisam thought 'they look rather a gloomy lot as compared with the last occasion', and worried that 'if there are no really distinguished people speaking, the occasion will be dealt with very cursorily in the press'. He recommended trying Baldwin again, 'who is sometimes interesting', but warned that another candidate, the writer and literary scholar Logan Pearsall Smith, wasn't 'any kind of a speaker', while 'the professors are usually incapable of taking a grip of a commercial and journalistic audience'. Sisam's preferred choice was Winston Churchill, then in his 'wilderness years', whom he judged likely to be 'the liveliest man if you had room for him'.

Baldwin turned them down, signing himself 'with real regret', on the grounds that he was too busy, but asked, 'How are we to save our tongue from being ruined by the American language?'[98] But the Supplement, as its readers were shortly to discover, had gone out of its way to record America's linguistic generosity to the English tongue. As Craigie, with his specialist knowledge of 'Americana', was to put it in his speech at the lunch Baldwin could not attend, 'some of our predecessors in the science of lexicography thought it was part of their duty to improve the English language. We have got beyond that stage, and consider that if it is to be improved it is not our business to do so, but record it as it was and as it is.'[99] (The eventual main speaker, G. S. Gordon, was witty, widely reported and – by contrast with Baldwin – much taken with the newly recorded US importations (see pp. 66–7 below).

In letters to the Vice-Chancellor soliciting his advice on whom should be invited to the lunch, Chapman described how the Supplement was heavily weighted towards the letters of the front end of the alphabet, for which the Dictionary, whose first fascicle had appeared forty-four years before its last, was already out of date, or, as he put it, 'left with a ragged edge', and again emphasized his conviction that no further supplements would appear.[100]

Many years later, in 1946, he was still of this view, and confidently reporting Craigie's judgement that 'the great Oxford Dictionary was the last of its kind . . . . To attempt its like in this age, with its formidable accretions of technical terms, of colloquial variations, of deliberate journalistic perversions, of spontaneous but ephemeral slang, all to be enshrined and immortalised by the historical method, might well deter the most chalcenterous Scotsman who may hereafter seek the shelter of Oxford.'[101] In his mention of a 'Scotsman', Chapman is thinking most obviously of both Murray and Craigie, always judged by the Press to be pre-eminent among the four main OED lexicographers. OUP cognoscenti, however, would also have recognized a reference to Wyllie, who at this stage in the Press's history – as our next chapter reveals – was seen as the great hope for the future of OED lexicography, whatever form that might take.

III

After the *OED*

Reception of the first Supplement: 'the epitome of our generation'

As with the completion of the first edition in 1928, the Oxford University Press journal *The Periodical* published a special celebratory edition in which it summarized the history of the Dictionary ('this monarch among books') and advertised the new publication.[1] The Press was particularly proud of the relative price of the reissue of the first edition of the *OED*. Together with the new material – the Supplement itself, along with Craigie and Onions's 'Historical Introduction' and the 'Register' on which Bayliss and Sweatman had worked (now called simply 'Bibliography') – it came to 16,400 pages in twelve volumes. The Press was now selling each set, bound in buckram, at £21 net, which was less than half of the original price (worked out as eight-tenths of a penny per page, each of which had contained some 3,000 words).[2] The 'daughterly work', the Supplement itself, could be purchased separately, though comparatively much more expensively, for five guineas, bound in cloth; as previously promised, subscribers to the original Dictionary could claim an unbound copy free. It weighed 8¼ lb, and its two volumes contained 867 three-column pages of 'dictionary proper'. Reported as a chief item on the BBC radio news, its publication was regarded as one of the major literary publishing events of the day.

The peculiar fascination of the 1933 Supplement seems to have been the reflection in its pages of a crowded and turbulent period of social, political, cultural and intellectual history. The post-Victorian era, together with the enormous social changes wrought by the First World War, the beginnings of social democracy, and many other cultural factors – modernism, increasing exposure to American culture, the development of new sciences and industries – had thrown up vast numbers of new terms. As the main speaker at the Goldsmiths' grand lunch of 21 November 1933, the just-elected Professor of Poetry G. S. Gordon (President of Magdalen College), described to his audience, all this fresh vocabulary seemed to have found its way into the Supplement's pages. The new dictionary contained 'the whole riotous, "riproarious", linguistic wealth of the industrial, scientific, artistic, literary, and social and colloquial life, not only of England, but of all the English-speaking countries, during the last half-century'.[3] Although the later volumes of the original *OED* had had their fair share of contemporary words, these were buried among many other much older ones, so when readers browsed through a typical page of the first edition they would see a preponderance of historical material. The Supplement was a different matter altogether. It contained a smattering of nineteenth-century material and earlier, but its pages teemed with everyday, often colourfully colloquial, usages that had escaped entry to the original Dictionary.

It was clear to contemporaries that recent years had seen a 'rapid and luxuriant growth of popular idiom and phraseology'. Slang had prospered and proliferated as never before, a principal motive being 'impatience with propriety of speech, and the desire to find intentionally undignified substitutes for it'. It is probable that all ages feel the same. What may have made the first thirty-odd years of the twentieth century different from earlier periods, however, was the increasing acceptability of informal language, colloquialism and slang in printed sources, which had previously censored such usage. This meant that many more spontaneous, up-to-the minute coinages and bouncy informalities were widely published and therefore available for record in the Supplement, and they lent its pages an enchanting immediacy and social relevance. It may also be that the appetite for colloquialism had recently increased in classes previously resistant to it. 'Even among persons of riper years,' Henry Bradley had 'demurely' said, 'there are many to whom ceremonious speech is unwelcome.'[4] 'All ages and classes are in this conspiracy,' Gordon believed, and he pointed the finger at American culture, faithfully investigated and recorded for the Supplement by Craigie, as particularly influential in this respect. *The Times* agreed, quoting Mr Dooley – the fictional author of a nationally syndicated news-paper column in the USA – as saying 'When we Americans are done with the English language, it will look as if it had been run over by a musical comedy.'

It takes only a glance through the pages of the Supplement to see that Mr Dooley would have had a point. Yet, as Gordon also noted, 'when you examine the culprits, how almost irresistible at any rate the best of them are! They are so frank, so fresh, so Topsy-like, so impudently expressive and near the truth, that it is hard to deny them a place in any honest lexicon of English', even though 'Dr Johnson would doubtless have rejected them all as low, as "not yet refined from the grossness of domestic use"'. Gordon lists some of his favourite Americanisms – *graft* (which as we saw was squabbled over by the lexicographers for its too-profuse quotations), *O.K.*, *the once-over*, *dope* (the verb), *fool proof* and *step on the gas*.

Other notable Supplement inclusions, scooped by Gordon for his speech out of what he described as a 'prodigious lexicographical lucky-bag', were *apache, automobile, cubism, futurism, robot, pacifist, radium, movies, screen, talkies, sabotage, tank, hooligan, broadcasting, loud-speaker, League of Nations, lip-stick, relativity, slimming* and *psycho-analysis*. An 'odd jumble', he called them, amounting to 'a rude and crude epitome of the very strange generation we belong to or from which we are emerging'. Nevertheless, 'with their definitions and attendant quotations, their approximate birth-dates and genealogies', they were 'perhaps the most fascinating type of history there is'.

Many reviewers followed the lead of Gordon and also *The Periodical* in simply listing a selection of new terms, with attached dates, rightly seeing that they spoke for themselves (e.g. 1885 *silk, artificial*; 1886 *appendicitis, crook, damfool, gadget, zoom*). When inventoried on a dictionary page, these new words both symbolized and summed up the new age, each pointing to some striking aspect of social change.

In their Preface, Craigie and Onions made it clear that social and histor-ical relevance was what they had aimed for. The Supplement had tried to reflect the burgeoning volume of technical language relating to both arts and sciences, they say, instancing 'biochemistry, wireless telegraphy and telephony, mechanical transport, aerial locomotion, psycho-analysis, the cinema' as subjects that had been particularly prolific. They had also sought to record 'the varied development of colloquial idiom and slang, to which the United States of America have made a large contribution, but in which the British dominions and dependencies have also a conspicuous share'. On the vexed question of inclusion or omission of 'the more esoteric scien-tific terms' and of foreign words, they conceded that 'it cannot be hoped or pretended that this problem has been solved in every instance with infallible discretion'. They were more confident in their treatment of 'temporary or casual uses', which were recognized 'only in so far as they marked stages in the recent history of scientific discovery, invention, or fashion, or illustrated the progress of thought, usage, or custom during the half-century under review'. Criteria for identifying such 'stages' were not revealed, but *The Times* at any rate thought they had succeeded, reporting that the Supplement reflected 'the spirit of the modern English-speaking world – its speed, its nervousness, its inventiveness, its serious devotion to sport, its popularisation of scientific terms'.[5] 'We found this volume of absorbing interest,' said the *Notes and Queries* reviewer; and one can see why. 'There is a sense in which it may claim to be the most massive, comprehensive, enduring monument in existence of the last eventful thirty years, encompassing the very life of them, which we see, as it were, captured and pinned down in its pages.'[6]

Capturing and pinning down had been no smooth task, however, as we saw in Chapter II. And how could either editors or reviewers be sure that all suitable words had been included? Evidence of many deliberations, sometimes agonizings, over potential entries survives in the archival papers. Through a combination of variable circumstances, some worthy candidates made the grade and some did not. Of these, a number were considered by the lexicographers (for example *putsch*, or *lesbian*, as we saw earlier, and no doubt many more for which no records survive),[7] but perhaps hundreds of others seem simply to have been missed, and had to wait until Burchfield's second Supplement some decades later, when they turned out to have been regularly in use by the time of publication (for example *snide*, *snoop* (noun), *soap-box* (fig.), *social work(er)*, for all of which Burchfield was able to supply pre-1933 quotations). Conversely, many less eligible items did get into the 1933 Supplement, often linguistic ephemera (for example *sosh*, US slang for 'a person having social polish and little else'; *sourceful,* 'acting as a source'; *spadassin*, 'a swordsman'; *spalt*, 'a section of log') that no doubt looked promising to Craigie and Onions at the time but proved in the long run less durable.[8] Stunningly successful as the 1933 Supplement seemed to its contemporary public, with its cornucopia of new words and terms which summed up for them the proliferating variety and changefulness of the culture they were living through, it gradually became clear that it had fallen short of its aim to record recent significant words and senses either already well established or soon to become so.

The first Supplement's fiercest critic in this respect turned out to be the editor of the second, R. W. Burchfield, who years later (in 1977) spoke of his 'startling discovery . . . that this fine trained body of scholars, well versed in the principles of historical lexicography, were all at sea when confronted with new words'.[9] As Burchfield also recognized, such judgements are more easily made with hindsight, and it is clearly the case, despite Craigie and Onions's assurance in this respect, that it is remarkably difficult to spot which 'temporary or casual' uses will persist in the language and which will perish.

Perhaps the really surprising thing is that the first Supplement included as many appropriate items as it did. Looking back at the circumstances in which it had been compiled, Burchfield described them as of 'exceptional propitiousness', meaning that, in contrast to his own case, the earlier editors had embarked on their work with all systems still running from the previous production of *OED*. It is hard to believe that Craigie and Onions would have agreed with him. As we have seen, they were hounded every step of the way by the publishers. And although both Sisam and Chapman were learned men, with strong independent interests in words and literature, the avowedly 'scratch Supplement' produced under their auspices was necessarily uneven and defective. Given the Press's determination to complete this final appendage and clear the *OED* enterprise off their desks, it had been neither practicable nor desirable for the lexicographers to embark on reading all the publications that had appeared in the English language (however defined, whether linguistically or geographically) in the last fifty years, in a repeat of the process by which the main Dictionary had been constructed (on which see Chapter IV below). Instead, they had built their Supplement on existing files and records stored by the staff and helpers themselves, augmenting this material with the thousands of slips sent in as a result of the various public appeals. To some extent, therefore, it had been a matter of happenstance as to which words had got in. It was similarly by happenstance that defects began to be identified, as members of the public, and the lexicographers themselves, chewed over the work in more detail and at greater leisure in the months and years after its publication.[10] Indeed, some of the chewing over began at the proof stage, when copy was for the first time dispatched to outsiders.

The enthusiastic amateur: Colonel H. G. Le Mesurier

At all times in its existence, through to the present day, the Dictionary has enjoyed the services (often unpaid) of literary and logophile volunteers. The novelist Charlotte Yonge, Thomas Hardy's friend Horace Moule, Fitzedward Hall and Hucks Gibbs, Lord Aldenham (a governor of the Bank of England) were among the earliest, and they have had many loyal successors, for example Robert Bridges, Rose Macaulay, Marghanita Laski and countless others, including scores of academics, whose names are listed in the prefaces to the various volumes and editions of the work.[11] One such enthusiast was Colonel H. G. Le Mesurier (1873–1940), a retired British army officer who had spent almost all his active service years in India, where from 1914 until his retirement in 1922 he was Assistant Director-General of Military Works. While in Simla he had become devoted to a copy of the *Concise Oxford Dictionary*, initiated a correspondence with its editor H. W. Fowler, and as a result, on his return to England, read and commented on a pre-publication version of one of the most celebrated reference works of the twentieth century, Fowler's *Modern English Usage*, which was published by OUP in 1926 (Fowler had previously published another fêted volume on usage with the Press, *The King's English*, written jointly with his brother F. G. Fowler and first issued in 1906). Le Mesurier kept up the connection with Fowler and fell into regular correspondence with the OUP publishers on lexicographical and linguistic matters, often with helpful results. He assisted Fowler in his revisions of the *Concise* and *Pocket Oxford Dictionaries*, and in 1932 he published a book on crosswords with the Press, dedicated to 'my friend H. W. Fowler, Word-Fancier', in 1932. After Fowler's death in 1933 he took over both the *Concise* and the *Pocket*, along with a third project, begun by Fowler but unfinished, the so-called Quarto dictionary (discussed in the next section).

By then, the Colonel was also helping the Press by reading through Supplement proofs, and was thus one of the first skilled and practised outsiders to sift though the new dictionary. Writing in the *Times Literary Supplement* (*TLS*) some years after Le Mesurier's death, Chapman described him as 'a very remarkable man . . . . Le Mesurier used to protest that he was no scholar; and he had had no scholar's education. But he was a born lexicographer . . . . He had an amazing grasp of the vocabulary, and not the vocabulary only, of the sciences, the arts, the trades, the stage, the film [described by *The Periodical* as 'that vast field of lexicographical study'], the American language. Once a week he read the *New York Times* through.' *The Times*'s obituary (probably written by Chapman or Sisam) added, 'He was a man of the world, an amateur of all the sciences and most of the crafts, a tireless student of newspapers and technical periodicals . . . and a keen analyst of the shifting *nuances* of popular idiom.'[12] Sisam particularly valued him as one who 'understands <u>things</u> which were always rather a mystery to our O.E.D. staff'.[13]

In January 1933, Le Mesurier pointed out to Fowler that the Supplement – whose proofs he had evidently already started to read – was poor on Anglo-Indian words. 'There is a really bad example in D. The quite common memsahib's word, usually written *dai* and always pronounced dī, meaning wet-nurse, appears as *daye* pronounced dah'ī! I failed to recognize it at first. My impression is that they have been advised by someone who knows only a single Province, which is fatal' – given the degree of variation between different Indian languages. Le Mesurier wanted to have the Anglo-Indian words vetted by a committee of retired ICS (Indian Civil Service) men – one each from Bombay, Bengal, Madras, the Punjab, and the UP (Uttar Pradesh) – otherwise 'the ordinary Qui Hai [Anglo-Indian] like myself, who has knocked about in all the provinces named', will be shocked at the inaccuracies.[14] Fowler passed this on to Sisam, who noted in a memo to Onions that he was 'not very hopeful that a Committee of peppery retired Indian Servants and Colonels would agree on this very difficult subject'. To Fowler he said, 'I expect our Anglo-Indian words came from printed books and would therefore depend not so much on our advisers as on the chance of what our readers found'. Fowler sent Sisam's reply back to Le Mesurier, who returned a wise response. 'There is a good deal of danger is taking such words from books,' he observed, 'especially novels, in which a number of Madrasi words appear that are quite unknown in other parts of India', and he went on to give another example, the word *lunkah*, supported in *OED* by a single quotation from Conan Doyle dated 1889 and defined as 'A kind of strong cheroot'. 'Now I have been twenty years in India and two in Mauritius,' said the Colonel,

> I have spent over two years in Bangalore, and five months on leave in Waltair (a South-Indian tobacco-growing centre); I have a taste for words and strong cheroots; yet never did I hear of a *lunkah* until I came across it in COD! [the *Concise Oxford Dictionary*, which would have taken the word from the *OED*]. This place [i.e. Exmouth, where Le Mesurier lived] is full of ancient Qui Hais (with what someone called 'that bloodthirsty clinging to life'), and I endeavoured to trace the word. At last I found a man of 75 who had spent forty years in India; he remembered, *as a child*, having heard the word in Madras – he called it a local word.[15]

This was a valuable insight into the pitfalls of *OED*'s method, reliant as it was on a small core of lexicographers who had to have sufficient knowledge or intuition to identify mainstream as against eccentric, dubious or spurious vocabulary, and whose copy passed before a few outsiders (such as Le Mesurier himself) only at the proof stage, when it was sometimes too late to make changes.[16] Le Mesurier's far more extensive worldly experience, particularly in military and technical matters, proved its worth repeatedly over the next few years. On this occasion, Sisam replied again to say that he hoped 'you will purge Q.O.D. [i.e. the Quarto Oxford Dictionary] of the strays that have got in merely because some writer in search of local colour picked them up'.[17] The Quarto Oxford Dictionary was later aborted, but many of the Colonel's corrections did get into the *Concise Oxford Dictionary*, for which he had direct editorial responsibility. Unfortunately, owing perhaps to problems with filing and then retrieving the information he sent in to the Press, several were missed by the second *OED* Supplement produced by Burchfield in the 1970s and 1980s. Consequently they were also omitted from the second edition of *OED* in 1989, and therefore from the unrevised sections (i.e. the major part) of *OED Online* today.

Thus *daye* stayed spelt the same in both Burchfield's Supplement and *OED2* (though none of the quotations instanced this spelling), and *lunkah* remains supported with the single Doyle quotation.[18] But Sisam was right: even supposing that an army of peppery colonels had been available, would they necessarily have agreed with each other? How could OUP finance the sort of linguistic research needed to sort out all these details? Le Mesurier's sharp nose for lexicographical hooey sniffed out a number of places in the Supplement where entries should have been dropped: *gymcad*, for example, was 'quoted from Barrère and Leland's Slang Dictionary as the Shop slang term for gym instructor. It was not in use in 1890 when I was there (as was Barrère as Instructor in French), and I have never heard of it . . . . I fancy some cadet must have pulled Barrère's leg – it was not difficult.' This was on 24 February 1933, and by 8 March he was able to adduce evidence from a retired brigadier-general in support of the judgement that *gymcad* was a spurious word: 'by Cheek out of Leg-pull'. Onions commented ruefully three days later that he 'is probably right about Gymcad . . . . But how one is to know this kind of thing in advance, I don't know'; and Sisam told Le Mesurier that Onions 'may have some difficulty in touching his plates at this point. The trouble is finding something to put in or take out'. Onions evidently couldn't; Barrère and Leland's quotation for *gymcad* was printed in 1933 under *gym*, again in Burchfield's Supplement of 1972, and again in the second edition of 1989 and the online *OED*.

Le Mesurier was good at spotting omissions, too. In the same batch of E and G words, he pointed out the absence of *escapologist*, which 'has become quite common in the papers for a man who does Houdini's stunts; I saw it in the Daily Mail this week. I suppose its formation cannot be defended, but it fills a gap and seems to be used.' Onions couldn't fit that one in, and it was left to Burchfield in 1972 (who began with a quotation from 1926).

Another important term whose inclusion Le Mesurier advocated was *Fianna Fáil*, the Irish political organization founded in 1926 by Eamon de Valera which had in March 1932 formed its first government, embarking on what was to be a sixteen-year period in office. 'Surely this [term] should be in?' Le Mesurier wrote to Sisam on 12 May 1933. 'It is one of the words a correspondent of Mr. Fowler's noted as being absent from C.O.D.' Surprisingly, Sisam was not sure that it had 'claims enough', and consulted Onions, who told him that *Fianna Fáil* had previously been 'considered' for the Supplement '(along with *Fianna Eireann*, which is older), but was omitted on its supposed merits'.[19] It stayed omitted in 1933 (in what looks like an example of misjudged English parochialism) but eventually entered the *Concise* in its fourth edition of 1951, edited by Edward McIntosh, who explained that *Fianna Fáil* was 'Eamon de Valera's party, which took the oath [of allegiance] and entered the *Dáil Eireann* in August 1927'.

McIntosh (b. 1894) had perhaps forgotten the political rumpus that attended *Fianna Fáil*'s submission to the oath of allegiance – an oath that specified the British monarchy as well as the Irish Free State and was then a legal pre-condition for entry to the Dáil. Members of the party had engaged in a remarkable manoeuvre when taking up their seats: although they did indeed sign the book which contained the oath, they issued a statement beforehand explaining that they proposed 'to regard the declaration as an empty formula' (and once in power they abolished the oath altogether). The *Concise*'s definition – politically sensitive, if not clearly inaccurate – went unremarked until 1956, when it elicited a fierce complaint from de Valera himself. 'To my amazement,' he wrote disingenuously to the Press, 'I find that . . . you give gratuitous circulation to the statement that the Fianna Fáil party "took the oath" on entering *Dáil Eireann* in August 1927. No oath was taken, nor was an oath demanded by the official in charge, and many witnesses are available to prove this.' De Valera went on to 'ask for an assurance that the circulation of [*COD*'s definition] in your publications will cease, and that as far as possible you will take steps to right the wrong already done'. Ignoring the latter request, the Press promised that the definition would be changed in the next printing of the *Concise* – perhaps calculating that mention of the oath was not material to the definition, and drawing back from confrontation with a recent head of the Irish State (de Valera had been defeated in 1954 and was to be re-elected as Taoiseach in 1957).[20] The 1958 reprint of the *Concise* carried an emended entry, defining *Fianna Fáil* as the 'Irish political organization and party which was founded in 1926 and entered *Dáil Eireann* in 1927', while Burchfield's Supplement finally included the term in the *OED*, again without mention of the oath, in 1972.

In the same letter, Le Mesurier picked up the incorrect generalization of *field events* in the first proof, as 'athletic sports', rather than 'only the high, long, and pole jumps, discus, weight, and javelin'. 'He is certainly right' about this, Sisam knew, although it turned out that Onions too had noticed the error, and already corrected it.[21] Reporting to Sisam on this and other matters, Onions told him they were trying to find room for 'gold certificate' (the American term meaning 'a certificate or note certifying that gold to the amount stated on the face of the certificate has been deposited and is available for redeeming it'), as suggested by the economist Roy Harrod, 'but it wd be a tight job'. Sisam replied to advise that it should go in if possible, 'though generally I gather that gold only means gold when it suits Americans'. It proved impossible to squeeze it into an over-long entry that already covered 'gold currency, standard, and value', and it was another omission later rectified by Burchfield, who supplied two quotations, one from the *Santa Fe Weekly* of 1864 and one from *The Economist* of 1934.[22]

The Colonel detected further corrigenda for the *OED*, missed by the Supplement, when working through lexicographical material for the Quarto Dictionary several years on. In August 1938 he described to Chapman how he 'gasped' when he read the *Concise* definition for *plane-table*. 'I found that it was taken from O.E.D. [in a fascicle edited by Murray, published 1907], where we learn that it is circular in shape, is used "for measuring angles in mapping", and has a central pivoted alidade – not one of which statements is even approximately true! There is really no excuse for this, as I was using an instrument of the ordinary modern form ten years before this definition was drafted. There may have been an instrument of this kind a century or more ago, but I have never seen one, and clearly the thing described is not what a quot. given, dated 1828, refers to.'[23] The Fowler brothers had correctly defined the term in the first edition of the *Concise* (1911), in so far as was possible given that dictionary's house style, an eponymously cramped 'telegraphese' (see n. 42 below), as 'surveying instrument used for direct plotting in the field', but both this record and Le Mesurier's letter were overlooked by Burchfield in his 1972–86 Supplement, where he did not emend the original entry in *OED* (though he identified a further, verbal use of the word along with *plane-tabler and -tabling*, supplying a number of quotations for all of these forms). *OED1*'s entry was therefore reproduced without change in the second edition of 1989. Many years later, in June 2006, it was rewritten for the revised *OED* (*OED3*), but this new definition (published online) nevertheless perpetuated some of the claims so indignantly repudiated by Le Mesurier: 'a surveying instrument used for direct plotting in the field, consisting of a circular drawing board mounted horizontally on a tripod, and having an alidade pivoted over its centre'.

So who was right? *OED3*'s final quotation was from an authoritative history of geometry by Heilbron published in 1998, which helpfully reproduces an illustration of a plane-table as used in the field by Napoleon's surveyors. It does indeed include an alidade, but the drawing board on which it is mounted is unmistakably rectangular. This characteristic shape is confirmed by historical geographers and other experts in the field (circular tables would have been most inconvenient for rectangular maps!), who explain that (in the words of John Heilbron), '[a plane-table's] purpose is to make a map. Its operation is to draw lines on a piece of paper fixed to the rectangular table in the directions of prominent features X, Y, Z in the terrain to be mapped . . . . The "alidade" [an optional addition] is a rectangular rule that provides the fiducial straight edge and carries the sights. It cannot be fixed at the center of the table since the observer must be able to rotate it around the points A', B' to effect the angular measurements.'[24]

Reporting these investigations to the *OED3* lexicographers in October 2006, the present writer experienced the great advantages, not to say charms, of an online publication. The editor John Simpson replied within days, having consulted with other experts, to say that the entry for *OED3* would be immediately corrected, in line with the Colonel's original judgement, in the next batch of entries to be released (March 2007).

Lexicographical strategy: the other Oxford dictionaries

Finis coronat opus: but Oxford dictionary-making did not come to a halt in 1933; it merely assumed a different face. As we have seen, most of the Supplement staff were paid off. Unused slips, later counted as 140,000 in all, were packed away into cold storage, together with the *OED*'s extensive library of reference works, and in 1935 Sisam wrote to an inquiring correspondent (the famous critic William Empson, who was seeking elucidation on how *OED* had differentiated the senses of complex words, and hoped to be able to look through the original slips) to say that 'the reserve material for the *OED* is not now available for consultation, as the work has been closed. Part of it is warehoused in cases and is not easy to get at; some of it was lent to America for use in the new "period" dictionaries that are being undertaken there.'[25]

These '"period" dictionaries' were the ones we saw planned by Craigie many years previously, when he had speculated that 'the future of English lexicography lies in concentration upon special periods and sections of the language, so that each of these may be dealt with more fully than is possible in a comprehensive work', and hoped he might carry forward *OED*'s work (together with its spare slips) to more attractive pastures in the US.[26] Craigie had identified five separate areas poorly covered by *OED*: American English (badly in need of full independent treatment, as revealed by the Supplement's attempt, so pleasing to some of its readers, to cover recent US vocabulary that had crossed the Atlantic), Middle English, Scottish English, Early Modern English and Old English, and a number of ventures had now sprung into being to take care of all but the last of these vocabularies.[27] These prospered, or not, at varying rates. Craigie's own *Dictionary of American English*, which he co-edited with J. A. Hulbert and a large staff (including George Watson and Mitford M. Mathews), treated American vocabulary of the seventeenth, eighteenth and nineteenth centuries in four volumes and was published by Chicago and Oxford in 1936–44. The two-volume *Dictionary of Americanisms*, edited by Mathews together with a smaller team, was published (by Chicago) in 1951.[28] Both works were supported by American universities and institutions, as was the much longer running *Middle English Dictionary* (*MED*), edited by H. Kurath, S. M. Kuhn, John Reidy and Robert Lewis, which trickled out from 1952 onwards and reached a triumphant conclusion in 2001. (For a long time, it was assumed by both the Press and T. A. Knott, the *MED*'s first editor, that Oxford would publish this dictionary, but during the 1940s it gradually withdrew from the project, unsettled by its likely cost and unsure that it would actually come off.)[29] *A Dictionary of the Older Scottish Tongue*, edited by Craigie, A. J. Aitken (chief editor from 1955) and others appeared between 1931 and 2002, published by Chicago, Oxford and Aberdeen University Presses. The last project, for a dictionary of Early Modern English, had seemed the most promising to Craigie. It was enthusiastically begun by Charles C. Fries in Michigan in 1930s, but after some years fell by the wayside despite valuable work by Richard W. Bailey. (The *OED* slips which Craigie had negotiated out of OUP for the Early Modern Dictionary, greatly swelled in number by the American scholars' subsequent research, were returned to Oxford in 1997 to aid compilation of the third edition of *OED*.)[30]

One way or another, Oxford steered clear of all of these ventures in historical lexicography, some of which stretched over more even than *OED*'s forty-four years. No doubt the Delegates were recalling their predecessors' envy, decades earlier, of 'the astuteness of the American publisher mentioned by Dr Furnivall who, when the [Oxford English] Dictionary was offered to him, said he would think about it when it was completed down to the letter M'.[31] Since taking on *OED* in 1879, however, the Press had encountered a different breed of lexicographer and a different type of dictionary product. The remarkable Fowler brothers (H. W. and F. G.) appeared on the English language scene in 1906 with the publication of *The King's English*, the famous book on English usage which scourged solecisms in a manner irresistible to the public. After such formidable success, the publishers decided to ask the brothers to work on a new dictionary which they had long had in view: one that would condense the most important elements of current English in the *OED*, and fill in its gaps. In this way the Press could recoup some of its apparently endless outlay of costs on the big dictionary, and forestall (or at least compete with) the predatory forays other contemporary dictionary houses were making on the *OED* instalments as they slowly appeared.[32]

The *Concise Oxford Dictionary*, as the Fowlers' dictionary was called, confounded the Press's previous understanding of the value of lexicographers' promises, since it was published in accordance with the agreed deadline and appeared in 1911. It has been regularly reprinted and occasionally revised ever since, enabling it to fulfil its original brief of presenting 'as vivid a picture as the small dictionary could be made to give of the English that was being spoken and written at the time'.[33] As we have seen, Le Mesurier joined the Fowler brothers as a contributor in the 1930s, and supervised the dictionary's third edition in 1934 after H. W. Fowler's death the previous year.[34] It was Oxford's first step into more user-friendly dictionaries. Its unexpected popularity encouraged the publication of a second Fowler 'condensation': the *Pocket Oxford Dictionary* (first published in 1924, and subsequently also taken over by Le Mesurier), though the brothers cried off the *Little Oxford Dictionary* (1930), 'an abridgement of an abridgement of an abridgement', a task that H. W. Fowler described as 'like pulling out the hairs of one's own head one by one'.[35] No doubt the sales figures for these derived works helped hasten their existing plans for the 'Abridged' *OED* that had been begun by William Little in 1902 and was finally completed by Onions, H. W. Fowler and Jessie Coulson (formerly Miss Senior) in 1933, when it appeared in two volumes as the *Shorter Oxford English Dictionary*. This contained a judicious selection of *OED* entries, with quotations and other supporting material pruned so as to give 'a quintessence', as Onions described it, of the original at a much lower price (£3 3s.). It was again a hit with the dictionary-buying public. The Press printed 40,000 copies in its first two years, and one of Onions's tasks subsequent to 1933 was collecting Addenda for its many reprintings and further editions. It was particularly useful to those with insufficiently long shelves, or deep pockets, for the full *OED*, 'bringing something very like the parent dictionary itself' into the homes of its purchasers, as *The Times* put it, 'for it contains all the features which endear the parent to those who consult it'.[36] To many dictionary users over succeeding decades, including scholars who have (unwisely) based their work on it, it has seemed a thoroughly admirable substitute.[37]

By the mid-1930s, these Oxford dictionaries were established as leaders in their respective fields where the UK market was concerned. OUP published advertisements in which all were featured together, ordered by price and size so as to appeal to a corresponding range of scholarly and economic tastes.[38] But the most important project, one in which both Chapman and Sisam invested a good deal of personal interest and labour, was the so-called Quarto Dictionary, eventually renamed the Oxford Dictionary of Modern English (ODME) but sometimes referred to as the 'Unconcise 4to'.[39] First suggested to H. W. Fowler by Sisam in 1925, this dictionary of current English, planned at around 1,500 quarto pages, was originally intended to be 'brave enough to discard inherited obsolete matter'.[40] As Chapman later described it, in an anonymous *TLS* review of the 1946 edition of the *Shorter* which he wrote in his retirement, its difference from the *Concise* lay in its

6. 'Sprod' on the Oxford Dictionaries: *Punch*, 17 August 1959.

recognition of the importance of great works of the past to contemporary culture, and therefore language. It was to confine itself 'to modern day English: that is, to the language as it is spoken and written today'; but 'today was to include the day before yesterday, and more; for the Bible and Shakespeare, it was thought, are still modern, current in the minds and speech of educated Englishmen'.[41] In other words, while the *Concise* furnished, in its characteristic 'telegraphese', an extensive tool-kit for day-to-day pedestrian (if precise, indeed sophisticated) linguistic interaction, the Quarto hoped to do something far more ambitious: map the potential vocabulary of well-educated 'Englishmen' who had read widely in the literary classics and were hence well acquainted (perhaps wished to be better acquainted) with a huge hinterland of historical literary language.[42] After H. W. Fowler's death, his second brother and collaborator A. J. Fowler took the project over with Le Mesurier, and the Quarto soon established itself as the principal horse – now that *OED* was complete, and any revision or supplement for the time being unthinkable by the publishers – in the Oxford lexicographical stable.

The new dictionary set out to illustrate its wide literary and general vocabulary with 'liberal use of quotations', which were to be furnished with the author's name and date but with no further reference. They were to function 'not as evidence substantiating the definition (as in *O.E.D.*) but as illustration, where illustration is useful'. In this respect, Chapman felt, 'the "literary" compiler sets himself a new – I believe a high – standard. It is desired that quotations should be not merely convenient and illustrative ("short and revealing") but also, where possible, in themselves familiar, striking, edifying, informative, or entertaining.'[43] Thus it was significantly to develop the *OED*'s role, actual if not intended, of literary *vade-mecum*, and it drew extensively on existing books of quotations, on concordances, and on Oxford's own *Dictionary of Quotations* (first published in 1941). Nor was the Quarto to neglect technical vocabulary, though this was not in normal circumstances to be illustrated with quotations. Although it would not be able to compete with the chief exponent in this field, Webster's *New International Dictionary* (the second edition of which had just appeared in 1934), 'all important terms will be included, and the attempt is made to frame definitions which give some light to the amateur without sacrifice of precision'. Here, the publishers were availing themselves of Le Mesurier's 'familiarity with things', though after A. J. Fowler's death in 1939 he apparently 'showed the same sure and nice touch' when dealing with literary vocabulary as had 'distinguished his classification and definition of technical terms'. The dictionary was also to contain a decent quota of both past and up-to-the-minute US vocabulary (garnered from Craigie's American dictionary and from the Press's own *Modern American Usage*) and, an innovative measure, it used 'status-letters', or what are now called usage labels, to identify words or senses as 'general, literary, colloquial, slang, archaic and the like'.[44] When Le Mesurier himself died in 1940, the dictionary was 'three parts done', and six years later, so Chapman reported in his *TLS* review of the *Shorter*, speaking with inside knowledge, 'the machine is not quite at a standstill'. But it never issued in a publication. The dictionary had been taken over by Edward McIntosh (1894–1970), a Scottish schoolmaster who moved to Exmouth in order to work on this and other dictionaries with Le Mesurier, and who was then 'trained by Wyllie'. The *Concise* and *Pocket* dictionaries absorbed so much of McIntosh's energies, however, that in 1949 the new Assistant Secretary of the Press, Dan Davin, enlisted the additional help of Professor C. T. Carr of St Andrews University (1901–76), who also co-edited editions of the *Pocket Oxford German Dictionary*. The ODME was finally abandoned in 1958. The concept it embodied – a compendious general dictionary with a strong literary bent – was now out of date; more importantly, it had proved impossible to find an editor with sufficient psychological strength and determination to stay the course (see p. 151 below).[45]

Activity on this dictionary, dear to Chapman's and Sisam's hearts as the book was, made little impression on the Press's resources whether of time, space or money: Le Mesurier worked on it in Exmouth and the Fowlers (uninterested in remuneration) in Somerset.[46] Chapman and Sisam both contributed copiously from their own reading, but costs here were wholly incidental. Onions remained, willy-nilly, a fixture on the *OED* salary books and worked away in Magdalen or the Old Ashmolean on the *Shorter* and his *Etymological English Dictionary*. Three long-term employees continued from the old days, two of them women: Bradley's daughter Eleanor, aged 70 in 1935, who sent in slips from her general reading for which she was paid at piece-rates, and the staff member Jessie Coulson, who had worked with Onions on the later stages of the *Shorter*, had seen the first edition of the *Little Oxford Dictionary* through the press, and was now engaged both on future revision of this work and on yet another dictionary, the *Concise Encyclopaedic*, on which she was supervised by Sisam.[47] The third member was the most important: J. M. Wyllie, Sisam's blue-eyed boy, who had so pleased the publishers in the last days of the Supplement with his reliable forecasts and prompt dispatch of the alphabet, but who had harried the ailing Bayliss and found it difficult to get on with his fellow labourer Miss Marshall – significant warning signs, as it turned out.

As previously intended by Sisam, Wyllie was combining his classical training with his recently acquired lexicographical skills and was working on the Press's new Latin Dictionary (on which see further p. 86 below). But Wyllie had a second role, equally important, as keeper and maintainer of *OED* files. For Chapman, despite his conviction, many times repeated, that the *OED* 'must stand as a record of the language from the earliest times to about 1932, and cannot be further supplemented', also recognized that 'the needs of the future are uncertain'. Consequently, he was 'anxious that the collection [of new words and senses] should go on and that materials that may be useful should be preserved in a form in which they *will* be useful, e.g. that all dated and referenced slips or clippings should be kept as such'.[48]

Chapman was conducting a delicate balancing act. The Press could not contemplate another *OED*. But the value of the original investment had to be both exploited and maintained. The flotilla of new, smaller dictionaries could feed off the central store-house, the *OED* itself, and the gratifying speed with which these lesser lexicons sailed off the shelves ensured a steady stream of income. But as each day passed, the *OED*'s record of contemporary vocabulary, even that stored in the Supplement pages, became steadily less complete on the one hand, and risked obsolescence on the other. The Quarto dictionary, with its low overheads and its reliable and experienced editors, was to be a new and much cheaper powerhouse, processing fresh words and uses as they came over the linguistic horizon and releasing them as appropriate to successive editions of the *Concise*, *Pocket*, *Little* and indeed *Shorter*. Once in print, it would remind the public of Oxford's pre-eminent position in dictionary-making.

Continuous recording of new vocabulary was therefore essential to ensure the Quarto's eventual success. To this end, Chapman had by 1935 set up a reading system of current newspapers and periodicals, or what he called 'collections', described in a report to the Delegates in October that year on 'The Oxford English Dictionary and its (Oxford) Children' (partially quoted from above) in which he emphasized the centrality of the Quarto to the Press's future dictionary plans.[49] Le Mesurier read the *Daily Telegraph*, the *Sunday Times*, *Nature*, *Punch*, the *New York Times* (once a week, Wednesday's issue) and the *Atlantic Monthly*. For some years Chapman himself had been excerpting the *TLS*, published weekly, for the *Dictionary of National Biography*, another Press enterprise requiring continuous maintenance, and he was now passing on 'likely words' and references to Le Mesurier, along with cuttings from *Publishers' Weekly* and other sources. In addition, Chapman informed the Delegates, 'we all, more or less, read *The Times*', although he thought this 'a gap in our armour'. He had noticed that many of Eleanor Bradley's slips were from this newspaper, so they were 'encouraging her to cast her net wider (or use a thinner mesh) and to regard *The Times* as her special hunting ground'. All this material was filed by Le Mesurier in an index kept in an interleaved and expanded copy of the *Concise*, so that it could be used both for further revisions to that dictionary and for compiling the Quarto.

Meanwhile, in the Dictionary Room, still called that, at the Old Ashmolean, Wyllie carried out his less immediate but still important task, recording 'material corrective or supplementary of *O.E.D.*'. This was 'indexed in a copy of the Reissue', the twelve-volume copy of the *OED* published in 1933, and it was to this repository that Quarto material was sent when Le Mesurier had finished with it. On the Quarto's completion, Chapman planned that the *OED* store would receive 'large accessions'.

Slips came not just from the lexicographers and publishers themselves, but also from outsiders. Chapman clearly remembered the experience of *OED*, 'that most of the people who were solicited [for contributions to the Dictionary] produced little that was of value', while by contrast, 'a few Heaven-sent enthusiasts produced among them a great deal'. Heaven-sent enthusiasts were to emerge after Chapman's time too; meanwhile, he told the Delegates, 'we are by degrees taking opportunities of informing people of our plans and inviting their help. This at least tends to create a general impression that Oxford is still an active lexicographical machine; and some small proportion of the people we solicit may become useful contributors.' The material resulting from such approaches was various in quality, but Chapman was confident that it would not 'at any stage be very difficult to adapt . . . to any likely use' – whatever such a use might turn out to be.[50]

Wyllie and the 'OED Collections'

Wyllie seems to have thrived in his new role. The mass of correspondence in the 1930s and 1940s surviving in the *OED* archives shows that, as Chapman noted, he set up an office system in 1935 to keep track of the changes and revisions being made to *OED* and *Shorter* material by the Quarto and by the other dictionaries (this correspondence is discussed further in the next chapter).[51] But well before then, Wyllie had taken over the task of monitoring and correcting existing *OED* entries. Thus in January 1934, he was worrying over the Supplement's etymology for *plus-fours*. In 1933 there had been much speculation in the office on whether Craigie's derivation of the term, which had related it to the sartorial needs of golfers, was wrong, and that it was due instead to the use of *plus* with a numeral to indicate a golfer's handicap (the derivation favoured by Onions and printed in the *Shorter*). Sisam had been incredulous ('we can hardly believe that any golfer walked into his tailor and required his trousers to be made with as many inches of cloth as his handicap required'), and thought the term was of military origin. Now a regimental adjutant in the Coldstream Guards had written to confirm this, claiming that the garment had originated in 1912 as an imaginative adjustment to normal breeches by a Scout officer in the 1st Battalion who rode a bicycle and hence needed baggier knees – an extra four inches. Wyllie passed this engaging tale on to Sisam, troubled that a four-inch fold would actually require eight additional inches of material, and that the Guardsman's story 'savours slightly of the etymological fable'. However, 'every cyclist . . . who has worn them will appreciate the unsuitableness of knickerbockers for the bicycle, and the suitability of "plusfours", and this favours the authenticity of the account'. (Burchfield's Supplement later stuck to Craigie's version, a judgement confirmed in December 2005 by the *OED3* revisers, who explored the handicap theory – citing evidence in *The Times* of 1901 and 1902 – to decide it had to be unconnected. The Guardsman's explanation seems to have died with his letter.)[52]

Wyllie actively researched Dictionary items as well as stowing away material in the files. Thus he wrote in 1938 to the Home Secretary, asking for enlightenment as to the difference between 'imprisonment with hard labour' and 'penal servitude' in pursuit of a correspondent's claim that 'our dictionary' had not treated these terms properly. 'The distinction suggested [by Wyllie's correspondent] is that "hard labour" is only used in connection with sentences of two years or less, and "penal servitude" for longer terms.' The Home Office replied to confirm this correction: 'offenders cannot be sentenced to a period of "penal servitude" of less than three years . . . they cannot be sentenced to "imprisonment" for a period of longer than two years'.[53] Later that year Wyllie wrote, at Chapman's direction, to a hotelier to discover the meaning of *private hotel*, pursuing an inquiry by A. J. Fowler, presumably for the Quarto, and the following spring to Rolls-Royce in search of an authoritative definition of *judder*.[54] Some of these inquiries bore fruit in the later versions of the *OED* and some did not; *penal servitude* and *hard labour* were left unaltered by Burchfield, and although *penal servitude* has recently (September 2005) been treated in *OED3*, no mention is made of the Home Office's useful distinction of 1938 (the punishment was abolished ten years later).[55] One can only be grateful, on the other hand, that Burchfield showed no signs of having come across Rolls-Royce's verbose and complex views on *judder*, while he authoritatively quotes a work on hotel and catering law to explain *private hotel*.

The Quarto editors regularly turned to Wyllie as a first port of call to establish both a word list and definitions, and Wyllie in turn commented on their draft entries.[56] His letters are sometimes written on paper headed 'Oxford Latin Dictionary' (listing him as assistant editor) and sometimes 'Oxford English Dictionary', and Sisam often acted as conduit between him and the Quarto. Warmth and trust now grew swiftly between the two men. For some years, they had been 'My dear Wyllie' and 'Dear Mr Sisam'; between June and December 1935 Wyllie progressed to 'Dear Sisam', indicating what would then be regarded as a significant increase in familiarity. The relationship was cemented in out-of-office contact: Sisam's daughter

Celia remembers that Wyllie came to their house on Boars Hill quite often and that he dug a substantial bank for them in their large garden, perhaps around this time.[57] Such intimacy sheds light on the falling out that was later to come, by which both men must have felt betrayed. Sisam also passed on batch after batch of 'Dictionary slips' – additions or corrections to OED – on his own account, with accompanying memos offering comment or advice and headed 'O.E.D. Collections'.[58]

From 1935 onwards, through the 1940s and even in the early 1950s, there are records of Wyllie building up a library for OED purposes, with the full support of the Press – successive volumes of the slowly emerging Grimms' dictionary, for example, the German equivalent of OED which had begun in 1838 but was not to be completed until 1966 – and other reference books such as the 'Psychiatric Dictionary', probably the second edition of the work by Hinsie and Shatzky published by the Press in 1953. Perhaps oddly, given that Wyllie's own manifestations of mental disturbance were by this date plain, Davin (the new Assistant Secretary) sent him a copy of this dictionary on 16 July that year: 'It is full of jargon but you may find it interesting. We probably ought to have it back some time in order to add it to the O.E.D. collections that will have to be taken account of when the supplement is being revised.' Wyllie replied, on 20 July, to say that this dictionary 'certainly adds a new if somewhat lurid light on human nature. I think it would be simplest to keep it here; room 316, New Bodleian, is the O.E.D. library.' (This was the room in which Wyllie worked on the Oxford Latin Dictionary (OLD), next door to the rest of the staff in room 318; OLD transferred to the New Bodleian after this building was opened in 1940.)[59]

Wyllie's vigilant devotion to his job over this long period (with some intermissions, he looked after the interests of both OED and the subsidiary dictionaries between 1933 and 1954) appears in an article in The Times on 9 January 1949, one of the occasional flashes of publicity that the Press seems to have encouraged in order to keep alive public perception of its 'active lexicographical machine'. 'Every reader of The Times is doubtless aware that English is a living language,' reported 'our special correspondent' in January that year, 'but few are probably aware that The Times provides the lexicographer with one new word or meaning every day. This aspect of the paper's usefulness was recently mentioned by Mr. J. M. Wyllie, an Oxford lexicographer, when writing about the supply of his daily copy of The Times.' The article described how Wyllie combed the newspaper every day: 'New meanings – that is, meanings not yet recorded or quoted in the O.E.D. – occur frequently, and when Mr. Wyllie had marked with a red pencil every example he could find on a single page of The Times for a particular day the page was almost as red as it was black and white.' He had recently harvested *conurbation, Pakistan, fractionist* ('akin to *deviationist*'), *treedozer, undercover* (as in agent or man), and new usages like *disinflation* (of currency, not balloons), *absenteeism* (of workers rather than, as in *OED*'s existing quotations, landlords and their like), *freighter* (used of an aircraft, not a cargo ship), the verb *rocket* (applied to prices, not pheasants), *New look* and *low-bridge type bus*. (Both Wyllie and the reporter clearly thought these usages novel and striking, so it is interesting that when Burchfield later recorded them all, apart from *treedozer* and *low-bridge type bus*, in the second *OED* Supplement, he was able to find pre-1933 quotations for every one save *Pakistan* and *disinflation*.)[60] In addition, Wyllie had strong views on the rights and wrongs of coinages – he liked a writer 'to have courage enough to make a new word'[61] – and regularly assessed other new dictionaries on the skill and aptitude with which they defined new words (a favourite litmus test was how they tackled the word *entropy*).

The reporter concluded by reminding his readers of one of Wyllie's notorious predecessors. 'If, arriving at Oxford, one approached Mr. Wyllie with undue caution it was only because, by the merest chance, one had read in another newspaper during the train journey how, in 1872, murder was committed in the shade of the Lion Brewery, about to be demolished in preparation for the Festival of Britain [which was to take place in May 1951], and how the murderer was – a lexicographer!' Facetiously alluding to the *OED*'s task of tracking changes in the language, he wound up, 'in those distant days, having been found insane, he was locked up as a lunatic. Today he would be *detained* as a *State mental patient*'.

The murderer was the notorious Dr W. C. Minor, a former American surgeon, whose chronic mental illness was apparently triggered by his disturbing war experiences and who had indeed shot and killed an innocent brewery stoker in 1872. Imprisoned in Broadmoor for this crime, Minor had responded to Murray's public appeals of 1879–80 and had contributed many quotation slips to the *OED*.[62] A cutting of the *Times* article is carefully preserved in a bulky personal file on Wyllie in the OUP archives. No doubt it was kept because this apparently casual and innocent linking of Wyllie to the unfortunate Minor – an *OED* contributor rather than a lexicographer – was more prescient than the journalist could have guessed. Wyllie murdered no one, but he set out to slaughter *OED* and OUP reputations in a ferocious campaign of slander and libel which began in 1953 and lasted until well into the 1960s. During this time he was indeed, for a short spell, 'detained as a State mental patient'. In Minor's case, lexicography may have acted as some sort of distraction from psychological suffering (it is arguable). But in Wyllie's, it joined forces with 'war worries', domestic tragedy and thwarted ambition to exacerbate mental illness, not to relieve it, depriving the Press of one of its most promising practitioners. Wyllie's decline into madness – a narrative followed to its close in the final section of this chapter – was to create a decisive disjunction in *OED*'s history. It meant that the next main editor of the Dictionary (Burchfield) had to pick up the job when the trace had gone cold, with no direct access to *OED* traditions and methodology except what he could glean from the aged Craigie and Onions.

The *Oxford Latin Dictionary* (OLD) and Wyllie's decline

Wyllie's main job was assistant editor (under Souter, his former university supervisor, a classicist of high repute) of the projected *Oxford Latin Dictionary*, on which he had begun full-time work in 1933 after the completion of the Supplement. This dictionary, an ambitious attempt to replace the existing standard Latin Dictionary, the Press's own 'Lewis and Short' (1879), had been first proposed by Sisam in the late 1920s. It was to be based on a complete rereading of the primary sources, and in 1933 it was estimated that it would take twelve years to prepare.[63] Like most lexicographical estimates, this proved unrealistic. But the problem in the case of the *Oxford Latin Dictionary* was not just the volume of work, but the editors themselves. The Publishers' Note to the eventually completed work, whose first fascicle appeared in 1968 and whose last in 1982, reports dispassionately that 'by 1939 it was clear that progress, whether measured in terms of quality or quantity, was unsatisfactory. In that year Professor Souter retired from the editorship, and Dr Cyril Bailey [1871–1957], a delegate of the Press, and Mr Wyllie were appointed co-editors, with Dr Bailey as the senior.' Nevertheless, the Note records, 'it is to Mr Wyllie that credit for the scheme of the dictionary and organization of work in the early years is principally due'. The finished product in general followed the principles of the *OED*, with which Wyllie was by now deeply imbued, and its formal layout of articles was also similar to that of *OED*.

The archival papers make it clear that the years before 1939 had been troubled and unhappy. 'Wyllie's competence and effort were far superior to Souter's,' an internal memo records, 'but this imbalance was not foreseen'; Souter's 1939 'retirement' was in fact manoeuvred by Sisam and Chapman, who that year finally decided to move him sideways to work on a related Latin project.[64] Unsurprisingly, Souter's deficiencies had been particularly apparent to his lieutenant Wyllie, who believed that he himself was the person to assume full editorship once Souter had been nudged aside. But signs of mental instability in Wyllie had already begun to alarm his colleagues. A memo from Chapman gloomily records that Cyril Bailey, a

7. J. M. Wyllie, lexicographer, at work in the 1940s.

wise and judicious adviser, was 'decisive that W. cannot be trusted to take charge [of *OLD* on his own], being subject to delusions'. However, Bailey himself was reluctant to assume full responsibility for the project, hence the solution that he and Wyllie should divide the job between them.[65] Denied sole charge of the Latin dictionary, Wyllie was piqued and angry. In May 1939, notwithstanding – or perhaps on account of – the warmth of his previous relationship with Sisam, he wrote him a series of bitter letters, full of closely argued and somewhat manically spelt out detail (for example, on the inferences he had drawn from Sisam advising him not to sell his car, which he had interpreted as a hint that his salary was about to rise), claiming he had been misled as to his expectations. Sisam was sufficiently stung by these accusations to reply at uncharacteristic length, rebutting his charges one by one.

Months into the new joint regime at *OLD*, the publishers continued to be concerned about Wyllie. Conflict had already arisen between him and Bailey; meanwhile, in intense anxiety about the possibility of bombing in Oxford, Wyllie had moved his family to Scotland and lodged them, bizarrely, in a hayloft. Sisam wrote to Bailey on 25 April 1940 that 'owing to domestic and war worries [Wyllie] was near the verge of a breakdown'. His distress seems more than adequately explained by the information only incidentally revealed by this correspondence, that one of his children had died and another was unwell (in fact two children died while the family was staying in the hayloft, apparently from some form of cot death).[66] To calm Wyllie's 'war worries', Sisam had agreed to top up his salary to a ceiling of £700 p.a. in the event of his being called up.[67] This happened almost straight away. Leaving behind him a skeleton staff to work on the Latin dictionary in his absence, Wyllie departed to Bletchley Park for the next few years. Here he was able to put his incisive and analytic mind to good use by applying lexicographical method to break enemy codes, in addition writing a glossary of cryptographic terminology.[68] A glimpse of him at this period comes in an account by another Bletchley inmate and lexicographer, the classicist and papyrologist John Chadwick, later to become internationally famous as a decoder of the Linear B script (a third Bletchley lexicographer was C. T. Carr, the future editor of Chapman's prized Quarto dictionary).[69] Chadwick had heard that Wyllie was recruiting classicists for a job after the war and made an appointment to see him. He describes how, with 'that disconcerting gift of his for making you feel uncomfortable by putting himself at a disadvantage', Wyllie had received him 'in unmilitary fashion, seated with his legs on another chair', explaining that he had just had an operation for varicose veins. Chadwick was engaged to work on the Latin dictionary from 1946, only retrospectively realizing that Wyllie's removal to Scotland for two years after the war, where he intended to run the Latin dictionary 'by remote control', was not an indication of good relations with his colleagues or of a smooth and harmonious running of the project, and that he himself should have been warier about taking the job.[70]

On his return from the war, Wyllie's mental disturbance continued. After the two years in Scotland, he returned to Oxford and in March 1949 took over as sole editor, continuing as before to maintain OED files as well as care for the subsidiary dictionaries.[71] But it seems that relations between him and the Press began once more to deteriorate. Further light on this is shed by Chadwick, a strong supporter of Wyllie in years to come – though by his own admission he left the Latin dictionary in 1952 partly owing to irreconcilable difficulties with its new editor. Many years later, after Wyllie's death in a motor accident in 1971, Chadwick was moved by what he described as possibly 'misplaced *pietas*' to draft an obituary of Wyllie, but decided not to publish it after reading the Press's rebuttal of some of the anti-OUP judgements and views that this document contained.[72] In it, he reports that James McLeod Wyllie 'was never James to anyone I knew' (it was then customary for men of their social class, even long-standing friends, to address each other by their surnames; Chadwick presumably seeks to indicate that Wyllie had no intimate acquaintances of a more familial character). While in Oxford, Chadwick had observed the relationship between Wyllie, his previous *OLD* co-editor Bailey, and the Press, and he makes some interesting comments on the conflicting desires, aims, means and ends of the lexicographers on the one hand and the publishers on the other. Chief among the causes of these conflicts, he thought, was

> the inability of the Delegates of the Clarendon Press, or whoever then advised them, to recognize the existence of lexicography as a science in its own right.[73] The view is still widely held [i.e. in the early 1970s] that lexicography is not a task demanding any special skills or training, but something any competent scholar can do if he cares to try – in other words, it stands no higher on the scale than proof-reading or carpentry. Not until an enlightened university has founded a Chair of Lexicography will this subject receive the academic status that its true practitioners know it deserves.

Had Chadwick been stung by one of Sisam's characteristically brisk, intolerant and pragmatic observations, to the effect that industry and dispatch were more important in lexicography than time-consuming perfectionism? Whether this was so or not, he puts his finger on one of the running sores in the relations between the publishers and the lexicographers. While Sisam on occasion conceded the existence of 'high lexicographical technique', he more usually favoured 'hard-work, common sense, some learning, and the best use of time'. Craigie and Onions, on the other hand – and perhaps Chadwick and Wyllie – believed 'that the real dictionary worker is born and not made, and that no application or diligence will ever make up for the lack of natural aptitude for the work'.[74]

Chadwick further describes how Wyllie had 'been trained in the school created by the great Oxford Lexicographers – Murray, Bradley, and Craigie'. He had 'imbibed the accumulated wisdom of a great tradition'. The Oxford lexicographers 'seem to have been almost unaware of what they had invented, and their occasional errors of technique show that they worked by feel rather than by principle. It was one of Wyllie's favourite topics in later years, how he would write a book to distil this essence of lexicography preserved only in an oral tradition.'

C. H. Roberts, since 1954 the Secretary of the Delegates (and a fellow papyrologist), to whom Chadwick sent his draft obituary in 1972, responded with stalwart defence of Sisam and the impugned publishers. His letter was based on a briefing document which stated, 'The files show that K.S[isam] fully recognized the special qualities essential to lexicography. He frequently refers to dictionary projects undertaken by eminent scholars which would never be completed because of their unsuitability for the task. To the assertion that lexicography is a science in its own right I imagine that K.S., and the Delegates, would have replied that without outside planning and direction lexicography is not in itself enough to produce dictionaries and that the concern of the Press in a project like the Latin dictionary is as much to get concrete results as to further the cause of the science.' Chadwick's account was 'over-simplified', and 'does not allow for the fact that Wyllie's mental instability was already manifesting itself in 1939'.[75] Certainly the Press must have found repugnant Chadwick's clearly stated belief that it was in part responsible for the destructive pressures to which Wyllie had been subjected.

But it is hard to resist the persuasiveness of Chadwick's loyalty to and regard for Wyllie. 'I am profoundly conscious of how much Wyllie taught me in my six years on the Oxford Latin Dictionary,' he wrote.

> Lexicography is not just a matter of technique, knowing for instance how to excerpt quotations from a text, or how to improve the typography of a finished article, important as both those things are. It includes a profound knowledge of how language behaves, for there are many universal features of lexicography which are independent of the language under study. I know too, from experience, exactly how hard mental work of this kind is; no one who has not tried can appreciate the immense effort it takes to start with a bundle of slips giving bare quotations, and to end up with a neat, clear dictionary article, with careful definitions and well-chosen examples. The art is so well concealed, the uninitiated are quite unaware of the mental struggles that go into the making of a good article . . . I emphasize the mental strain this work imposes, for I think it is part of the explanation of the sequel . . . .[76]

Wyllie's role as successor to the great OED lexicographers of the past, and his tending to the correspondence on language that kept pouring in to the Press, seems to have led him to regard himself as keeper of the flame. Perhaps this was part of the problem. Answering a query as to whether the phrase 'I cannot hear me', as used by auctioneers when trying to quieten an audience, was acceptable English, he wrote (on 7 March 1936), 'There is not, so far as I am aware, an official Editor of the Oxford English Dictionary at present; and as I am in charge of the assembling and preparation of new material for this dictionary, though chiefly occupied with the Oxford Latin Dictionary, your letter came into my hands.' (His view on this example of auctioneer-speak was that 'it is not appropriate for an Auctioneer to indulge in archaic literary or poetic language. He ought to use plain and up-to-date language, unless, of course, he is trying to be funny'.) On 4 April 1936, he wrote in response to an unsolicited offer of lexico-graphical aid from a Miss Veronica Ruffer to say 'we have recently discussed the possibility of organizing a small band of volunteers to note additions to English vocabulary, idiom, etc as they appear, to avoid being far behind with our materials when we find a need for them. No appeal for help has been made publicly, because it did not seem desirable to make an appeal when we had no definite project in view; but it was decided to build up a corps of workers as opportunity offered.' He was still corresponding with her two years later, thanking her in October 1938 'for the consignment of quota-tions we received here yesterday. Your selecting of words is very good, and every further contribution is welcome.'[77]

But at that stage the publishers had no plans for financial outlay of the sort that would allow a fitting continuation of the original *OED* project. Wyllie kept on hoping, though, writing to another correspondent long after-wards, when the war was over and he had returned to Oxford after his two years' stand-off period in Scotland, that he was 'not too old to look forward to doing a major revision [of *OED*], or a bringing up to date of the OED after the Latin Dictionary is finished, and I have been trying for years to lay the foundations of such a work by keeping an eye open for new develop-ments in English'. This was on 18 May 1949 (the recipient was a Mr S. Gray, who started writing to Wyllie with his *OED* ante-datings and revisions after reading about him in a report of the *Times* article earlier that year; Wyllie ticked him off smartly in a later letter when the unfortunate Gray intimated Wyllie had made a mistake). A letter written to Assistant Secretary Davin a few days later (25 May 1949), discussing some proofs for the *Little Oxford Dictionary* which Wyllie clearly felt were lamentable, looks sharp and trou-bled and illustrates the frustration with lexicographical standards which Chadwick identified as a point of friction between him and the publishers.

> I am not sure that I fully understand your meaning, or that you under-stand mine; and I shall try to make that clearer now. It has always been my opinion that there is a certain standard of quality both of work and workmanship in what we call 'Oxford Dictionaries', and for many years I have done what I could to maintain this standard .... My efforts have not been very successful ... this L.O.D. Addenda [perhaps the work of Jessie Coulson] suggests a fresh cause of deterioration. It may well be my fault that I have never pointed out to you that competent and responsible lexicography can only be done by a lexicographer. May I do so now? And may I add that if you think work of this quality is not beneath your notice, our conceptions of lexicography must be radically different?[78]

No reply to this surely intolerable sally is preserved in the archives. And despite the evidence of many other documents in the files indicating that Wyllie was extensively consulted about all matters relating to dictionaries by Davin, and that in general he was highly responsive, authoritative and helpful, the occasionally extreme difficulty in relations meant that the publishers regretfully decided that Wyllie would not be up to the job they belatedly realized needed doing (as we shall see in Chapter V): at long last updating the 1933 Supplement. 'Nobody is more competent than Wyllie if he could be got back to the frame of mind in which he did so much for the first Supplement i.e. do what he is told to do, instead of throwing away all that others have done and starting afresh on different lines,' wrote Sisam, now retired to the Scilly Isles, in a letter to Davin of 10 October 1952.[79]

But any frame of mind approaching rationality soon proved too elusive for poor Wyllie: in October 1953 he suffered a severe mental breakdown. The loss was devastating to the Press, as Davin made clear in a letter to C. T. Carr (now editor of the Quarto): 'It is a very sad affair. We do not know when or in what state he will emerge [from the Warneford, a mental hospital] and we are trying desperately to think how we shall adjust ourselves to the loss, even temporarily, of such a brilliant lexicographer.'[80] Wyllie claimed a series of revelatory experiences which 'suddenly created in me a clean heart and renewed a right spirit within me'. Since then, as he wrote to Norrington (Sisam's successor as Secretary to the Delegates) in April 1954, 'I have continuously enjoyed a super-abundance of joy, peace, courage, energy, faith, benevolence', etc. Unfortunately, he was simultaneously penning vituperatively libellous documents which he distributed to all the Delegates, and which made it impossible for him to continue as a Press employee, given his steadfast refusal to retract them. It seems that he felt he had in some way been deceived by Sisam and Chapman in their original appointment of Souter as his superior at the Latin dictionary, in their failure to elevate him in 1939, and in their subsequent treatment of him. After another spell in the Warneford, he was dismissed at the end of this month. The Press made attempts, partly successful, to help both him and his family by delaying the payments owed them on the loan they had given him to buy his house at 42 Portland Road in Oxford, and by other forms of generous domestic support. Subsequently Wyllie 'eked out a living as a schoolmaster', moving first to a barn in his garden (in which he dispensed gin and Ribena to visitors), while his wife supported herself and family by taking in lodgers, and later to Guernsey. Over the next few years, under the pseudonym 'The Barras Seer', he issued a stream of pamphlets on such matters as sin, sex, enlightenment and the devil, printed by himself and copied on his own duplicator.[81]

These included one entitled *The Oxford Dictionary Slanders: The Greatest Scandal in the Whole History of Scholarship*, which reproduced various open letters to the Prime Minister, the Lord Chancellor, and Oxford University's Vice-Chancellor, detailing the terrible errors of his adversaries Sisam, Chapman, Souter and others.[82] Earlier, he had written a twelve-book epic poem in which Sisam figured as an Antichrist, who after pursuing Wyllie himself with fearful malice and hatred, had 'fled to Scilly's Isle' (to which Sisam retired in 1942),

> where east Atlantic rolls
> who now should oakum tease
> he Napier's logs unrolls[83]

the wholly unjust implication being that the extensive scholarship Sisam began to publish in retirement had all been plagiarized from his early mentor Napier's lecture notes.

Of this unhappy fulfilment of his early promise, Chadwick says, 'It might be kinder to draw a veil over Wyllie's last years, but it would be a kind of dishonesty he would never have countenanced.' Wyllie kept in fairly regular touch with the Press, sending them copies of his pamphlets – at one point (May 1968) prompting them to write a letter to the Post Office threatening legal action, on the grounds that the postman had delivered a letter (to Sir Roger Mynors, Professor of Latin at Corpus Christi College) with the words 'Another Oxford Slander! The Living Clarendon Press EXPOSED' prominently stamped on it in large letters, thus acting as an accessory to libel – and occasional lexicographical offerings, including the partial return in 1962 of some *OED* corrigenda and addenda slips of Craigie's (given to Wyllie on the assumption that he would be using them for a revision of the *OED* himself) and portions of a dictionary of synonyms and a Latin textbook for schools. He continued in a 'state of inspiration . . . [with] an incredible amount of energy at my disposal'.[84]

Chadwick wrote, 'There must be many who have memories of Wyllie's regular appearances at classical conferences in these later years, when he would buttonhole you with his Ancient Mariner look, and treat you to a long lecture on the iniquities of the establishment. Yet even so, it was impossible to miss the sincerity and good will behind his complaints. As always, he put himself at a disadvantage, and you had to be extremely insensitive not to feel sorry for him.'

Wyllie's contribution to *OED* remains unsung. He was given a bare mention at the foot of the first Supplement Preface, scant recognition for his role as Sisam's comforter and Craigie's UK lieutenant. The years he spent exploring and researching new words and meanings for the Dictionary, recording corrections and omissions, and generally tending the files, were recognized in neither the second Supplement of 1972–86 nor the *OED*'s second edition of 1989. The uncontrolled virulence of his repudiation of Oxford lexicography is sufficient explanation for this neglect. Many decades on, however, Chadwick's open-eyed generosity, together with the straightforwardly generous acknowledgement Wyllie receives in the *Oxford Latin Dictionary*, seems the better course.

Wyllie's supporters relinquished their hope and faith in him only after he denounced them publicly in 1954, by which time the publishers had begun the serious business of looking for an editor of a new *OED* Supplement – a post for which he had been the first, and obvious, candidate. This narrative we return to in Chapter V, picking up the threads from the mid-1940s onwards.

IV

Treasure-house of the Language: Role and Function of the *OED*

Dialogue with the public

The public did not cease its fascination with *OED* in 1933 any more than the lexicographers and publishers themselves. Over the next few decades, waves of letters on an enormous variety of words and topics were delivered to the Press in response to the publication of the reissue of the first edition and of the Supplement, often asking for rulings on meanings of words and niceties of usage, but also searching for further information, offering new uses and corrections, and querying omissions. Innocently untheoretical as they are, these letters raise a variety of questions about the role and function of the *OED* and its relation to the lexicon of the English language (however defined), providing a useful bridge to a more analytic investigation of the Dictionary's linguistic and cultural role.[1] Suspending the chronological narrative of *OED*'s institutional history, this chapter begins by looking at some characteristic correspondence between the Press and the public (and at discussions between the lexicographers and publishers themselves) before turning to the issues such exchanges raise about the role and function of the Dictionary: as objective witness to the language, but also (so many felt) its guardian; as a massive accumulation of scholarly data on language, but also a national treasure-house whose job it was to reflect, and preserve, the culture of its society. Identifying these concerns and conflicts will allow us better to assess, in the subsequent chapters of this book, the achievement and character of the *OED* in the late twentieth and early twenty-first centuries.

While Wyllie was responsible for *OED* record-keeping, the task of answering letters from the public seems often to have fallen to Sisam. As he said to one correspondent on 2 May 1939, such unsolicited communications were wholly welcome.[2] This was a typically sensible decision by the Press. The time spent pursuing linguistic inquiries and writing letters back was well worth it if it kept the *OED*'s public profile strong, for this in turn helped the sale of existing and future editions of all the Oxford dictionaries, particularly the highly profitable smaller ones. A serendipitous selection of typical correspondence yields discussion of the two words *batter* and *taper* as associated with the building of factory chimney shafts, the right and wrong pronunciation of *Raleigh* and *vitamin*, the date and origin of *toffee*, the omission of *communism* (for which the lexicographers drafted an entry), the meaning of *coronated*, a defence of the *OED*'s inclusion of the meaning 'cheat' under the word *Jew* (Sisam: 'I should like to explain that our dictionaries aim at explaining actual usage and do not attempt to form moral judgements: in other words their record that a meaning exists does not imply editorial approval of any implication of the meaning'),[3] and discussion of a myriad other terms such as *double-jointed, mass-clock, black-mass, mass-medical, match-ball* (as in cricket), *ensign, the ready, pre-election, embrangle, geir-eagle* and *house-trained* (of dogs etc.).

Why no 'batavia', meaning a variety of lettuce, a word 'to be found in most seedsmen's catalogues', one letter asked. Sisam wrote back to explain: probably 'the editors deliberately excluded this sense on the ground that they did not undertake to give the technical terms of the various special professions and crafts'.[4] It is still absent from the *OED*, which defines the word only as 'a kind of shot silk material'. Another correspondent reported surprise that the *Shorter* perpetuated *OED*'s 'popular error [s.v. glue] that hoofs and horns yield glue. Hoofs and horns consist of keratin and are always removed by the glue maker, although of course the feet of animals and the interior bony support of the horn (horn pith) yield glue or gelatin (e.g. calves' foot jelly).'[5] The *OED*'s mention of hoofs in the definition of *glue* was left unchanged by Burchfield and survives today, although the *Concise* (from 1911 onwards) specified 'hides and bones' instead. The writer assured the Press that he wrote 'in a spirit of helpfulness, and not one of carping criticism. I wonder to what extent the scientific terms in your dictionary are adequately or properly defined. This is important, since dictionaries are frequently consulted in the law.'

In June 1940, Sisam told Wyllie that an Indian correspondent had written to protest against their definition of *mango*, which claimed it had 'more or less of a turpentine flavour', insisting that on the contrary it was 'a very delicious fruit, and most of its varieties . . . have a distinctly tempting odour about them'. Sisam had turned to Sir Arthur Hill of Kew for advice, and now thought 'we should be justified in omitting the reference to "turpentine"'.[6] This was again missed by Burchfield, and the phrase survived in the *OED* to mislead potential mango-eaters until September 2003, when it was cut out of the new online version of the Dictionary. The first edition of the

Concise had also specified the 'turpentine'-like flavour, but by the third edition this had disappeared, due no doubt to Le Mesurier's watchful eye and tropical experience. It seems that Le Mesurier was also careful to correct the *Concise*'s definition of the 'fruit of the date', perhaps in response to a letter from the Director of the Botanic Garden at Cambridge which had pointed out that it was wrongly 'described as an oblong single-stoned drupe. It should be an oblong single-stoned berry.' Sisam wrote to Wyllie, 'It is wrong in O.E.D. so will you note it on your records?'[7] But *OED*'s definition continues unchanged to this day.

Many letters expressed their pleasure and delight in the great work. 'Dear Sirs,' wrote an Australian correspondent, 'I have been revelling in your Dictionary, and have enjoyed it so much that I trust you will not mind my suggesting that it might reasonably include the word "Anzac".' Naturally the editors did not. It was already in the first Supplement and Burchfield added further quotations in the second.[8] Another wrote from Essex to take 'the opportunity of saying how attractive I find this Oxford dictionary [he is referring to the *Shorter*]; the world seems spread before one and the dictionary's breadth of view seems to be commensurate with reality; in no other book I know of is such freedom from mental oppression to be found: here there is no author's arbitrary handling of the material of life to irk the reader' (he is perhaps gesturing at that complex relationship between the world of words and the world of things, much debated by philosophers of language in English from Locke onwards).[9] Others imply the same enjoyment, even as they point out a flaw, thus attesting to the view of the *TLS* in 1928, that 'if [the *OED*] has its critics, its correctors and its supplement compilers, it has itself supplied them with their standards and many of their materials . . . . It must be highly doubtful if any dictionary has received a tithe of the compliments paid to this Dictionary in the way of errata and addenda. Such offerings are really testimonials, for men do not trouble to castigate what they do not love.'[10]

It is clearly in this spirit that a correspondent from New Delhi informed 'My Dear Chapman' in 1938, that 'I was delighted to find a mistake in the Oxford Dictionary the other day. In the course of a case before the Federal Court I had occasion to refer to the word "excise" in the Dictionary and discovered that excise duties were described as being collected by the Board of Inland Revenue . . . In fact, duties of excise are collected and administered by the Commissioners of Customs and Excise' (the change-over had occurred in 1909, but the *Everybody–Ezod* fascicle had been published in 1894).[11] An earlier notice of this error appears in a letter dated 5 May 1934, with 'Noted RWB' marked on it. But there is no correcting entry in Burchfield's Supplement – although he adds a fifth sense to *excise*, implying

by this partial treatment that the rest of the entry may stand unchanged –
and the corresponding treatment in the second edition of *OED* (1989) and
in *OED Online* simply reproduces that of the first edition. As we shall see
in Chapter VII, this is one example of many where Burchfield's failure to
update *OED* material, often encyclopaedic in its scope, causes today's *OED*
to give a most peculiar impression of current social reality (up to 2004,
excise was still collected by HM Customs and Excise; since 2005 it has been
dealt with by a new department, HM Revenue and Customs). The *Concise*,
as ever more nimble-footed than the *OED*, had specified the Commissioners
of Customs and Excise from its third edition of 1934.

Another critic wrote to exclaim at a misdefinition in *OED* and the
Shorter of *baggot*. 'To my astonishment I find that the dictionary
announces that a "Baggit" is a "Salmon that has just spawned". The point
is that this is precisely what a Baggot or Baggit is NOT! A baggot is the
word used to define a salmon who has come up to spawn, but for various
reasons has not done so.' Sisam passed this 'rather important correction' on
to Wyllie: 'I see from the quotations in O.E.D. how the editors, not being
salmon fishers, were misled.'[12] Burchfield did catch this one, and his
Supplement substituted a correct definition: 'an unbroken female salmon,
one that has not shed its eggs when the spawning season is over'. Did the
correction issue from his reading of these files, or was it a response to indig-
nant anglers who wrote in later? It is impossible to tell, with this as with
many other of his additions, for example of *mariage blanc* (= 'unconsum-
mated marriage'), a term discussed with some intensity in the office in 1937.
Chapman reported that 'Sisam and Le Mesurier think it hardly qualifies for
ODME [the Quarto]. But the thing is not unimportant, and what else is it
called?' Milford replied to say, of his own staff, 'Goffin and Cumberlege had
never heard of it; Hopkins, Willert and I had . . . . A borderline case, and in
my opinion should just come in'. Chapman wrote back, 'Add Norrington
[his eventual successor as head of the Press] to the list of ignorants . . . .
Miss Withycombe was surprised at the ignorance of so many well-informed
persons; it is in the history books as well as in novels etc.'[13]

Milford was evidently a keen reader of the *OED*. Sisam wrote in
November 1938, 'My Dear Wyllie, Sir Humphrey Milford sends the
following note: – "*Oubit* [= woolly-bear] refers forward to <u>Woobut</u>, but
there is no entry under <u>Woobut</u>". Will you enter in your O.E.D. records?'[14]
This passed Burchfield by, and, even today, there is no entry for *woobut*. The
reader must guess that full information is instead to be found under the
alternative spelling *woubit*, lavishly illustrated with quotations up to 1861
but many pages further on. Milford also set off in pursuit of a phrase closer
to home, 'know your onions', reporting to Le Mesurier (who was presum-

ably researching the term for the Quarto) that although he was not himself acquainted with the phrase, he had 'found that several members of my staff are. One of them writes: "... It means 'knowing what one is talking of', 'being master of the subject', – being, in fact 'the cat's whisker' or 'head man' in this or that matter'". I have no idea of why it means what it is said to mean!' Unsurprisingly, the phrase found its home in Burchfield's Supplement, recorded from 1922 (in an issue of *Harper's Magazine*) onwards.[15]

Other discussions among the Press staff indicate a constant flow of such investigations. Of the word *higgle*, Chapman reports, 'Sisam and I are quite clear that the verb is common in commercial use. We have ourselves been talking a good deal lately on the relative merits of two systems of interdepartmental prices – standardization and higgling. The expression "the higgle of the market" is clearly earlier than 1908 when the Daily Chronicle [*OED*'s sole quotation source for the noun, added in the 1933 Supplement] put it in inverted commas. I am writing to our professor [unidentified] to ask if he can confirm our impression that it is classical.'[16] The word *higgle* was left untouched by Burchfield, though this conversation suggests that the verb was inadequately treated in the first edition of *OED* (the relevant sense is not defined, though it is indicated by a sole quotation dated 1866);[17] the word awaits the further attention of *OED3*.

Many other letters added to the hundreds of existing corrections and revisions, already stored in the files, to *OED*'s treatment of historical vocabulary, the revising of which was a task well beyond the scope of either Supplement. Thus a correspondent wrote on 24 September 1936 to point out that the Dictionary had missed Bunyan's use of the word *slithy* in *The Life and Death of Mr. Badman* (1680): 'For they are a shame to Religion, I say these slithy, rob-Shop, pick-pocket men.' As he noted, the context 'seems to give it clearly the meaning "deceitful", a meaning you do not give under either SLITY or SLEATHY'.[18]

An entertaining variation on the genre, more sparsely represented, is the group of letters seeking publicity or respectability by staking a claim to new words. In 1940, the self-styled Biosophical Institute wrote in on elaborately headed notepaper to offer a definition of *biosophy*. The word had been included in the 1940 edition of *Webster's New International Dictionary* and in 'Grosset and Dunlap' (apparently one of the reference books produced by this US publishing house), and signified 'the science and art of intelligent living based on the awareness and practice of spiritual values and ethical-social principles and character qualities essential to individual freedom and social harmony'.[19] No entry for this word is recorded in the Dictionary today. A different approach was adopted by Randall Davies Esq. of 1 Cheyne

Gardens, who submitted his laconic missive, undated save for postmark (18 January 1939), as a scrawl on a simple postcard: 'Kindly note that on the 11th inst. I invented the word BRUTALITARIAN.'[20] But Davies had been forestalled in 1904, when, as Burchfield's Supplement later recorded, *The Brutalitarian, A Journal for the Sane and Strong,* was published.

Most irritating, probably, though at the same time most reassuring, were the letters to which Sisam was able to reply, 'the evidence in the Dictionary seems to be satisfactory'. This was a well-worn response familiar to the editors from Murray onwards.[21] It meant that despite the complaint of the writer, the word or sense whose omission or misrepresentation he or she lamented was in fact perfectly appropriately dealt with in either *OED* or Supplement. He or she had simply failed to read the Dictionary properly. Thus one correspondent was made to apologize for his error, reported in *The Times,* in suggesting that 'some eminent lexicographer should be "ticked off"' for omitting the term *spine* (of a book) from the first edition of *OED.* When confronted with evidence that the usage was both recent and disputed, he acknowledged 'once again the O.E.D. (which being interpreted obviously means the Omniscient English Dictionary) [is] right and I [am] wrong. . . . It seems almost as dangerous to tilt against your massive Dictionary as it apparently was in olden times to tilt at the ring, which usually resulted in the tilter being unhorsed by a blow in the back from the sandbag.'[22]

On occasion, correspondence continued beyond an initial exchange. In February 1936, the novelist Rose Macaulay wrote to Chapman enclosing notes of ante-datings she had found of a number of words recorded in *OED*, about which she had just published a short essay called 'Improving the Dictionary', part of a collection of such musings entitled *Personal Pleasures.*[23] She describes the satisfaction to be had from doing some of the lexicographer's work for him, and trumping his findings.

> On a blank page at the beginning of the Supplementary Volume of my Dictionary, I record emendations, corrections, additions, earlier uses of words, as I come on them in reading. Ah, I say, congratulating myself, here Messrs. Murray, Bradley, Craigie and Onions are nearly a century out; here were sailors, travellers and philosophers chattering of sea turtles from the fifteen-sixties on, and the Dictionary will not have them before the sixteen-fifties. And how late they are with estancias, iguanas, anthropophagi, maize, cochineal, canoes, troglodytes, cannibals, and hammocks . . . .

She had been reading sixteenth-century works on travel and geography; her list might well have come in useful more than sixty years later when the successors of 'Messrs. Murray' et al. finally embarked on a wholesale revision of the first edition of the Dictionary. However, her sources turned out to yield far more than she herself had noticed. In the range of *m* words, for example, she listed *maize* and *manioc* from a sixteenth-century translation of a Spanish work, which had recently been published for the first time in an edition of 1932 for the Hakluyt Society.[24] But when the *OED3* revisers came to reread this work in the late 1990s they found it contained ante-datings for *marquisate, marriage-feast* and *mermaid* ('a manatee or similar animal thought to resemble a mermaid') as well.

'Had I but world enough and time,' Macaulay continued, 'I would find earlier uses of all the half a million words, I would publish another supplement of my own, I would achieve at last my early ambition to be a lexicographer. If there is a drawback to this pure pleasure of doing good to a dictionary, I have not yet found it. Except that, naturally, it takes time.' This observation struck a chord with the next editor of *OED*, Burchfield, who quoted it in the Preface to the delayed publication of the third volume of his Supplement – a four-volume work, initially projected as one volume, which took much longer than expected. Macaulay wrote again in June 1941 to ask whether the publisher still had her list, explaining that she had lost the original, 'having had my flat & all its contents [including her copy of *OED*] demolished lately by a bomb'. She feared 'it is most unlikely that all such letters [as hers] are kept; the files of the Press could not contain them if they were', but Sisam was able to return the material, having taken copies, observing 'all such papers are fairly safe with us as long as we ourselves escape your late misfortune', and gallantly offering her a replacement *OED* at a reduced price. He had been pipped to the post by another generous friend (the publisher Victor Gollancz); writing to thank him and tell him so, Macaulay said, 'It is a book which one cannot easily do without, if one has grown up with it. I still miss my and my father's notes which annotated many of the words, but that can't be helped.'[25] (Her contemporary Virginia Woolf also embarked on a 'Supplement to the Dictionary of the English Language', but gave up after two words – 'straddle-bug' and 'peeker'.)[26]

Undoubtedly the favourite question asked of the *OED* and its publishers, repeated almost endlessly, concerned the number of words in the English language. Requests for a definitive statement on this matter had constantly been made of the Dictionary's first editor Murray, and he is reported to have tried to explain the difficulty of the question (put to him as 'How many words are there in the language of Englishmen?') by replying 'Of *some* Englishmen? Or of *all* Englishmen? Is it *all* that *all* Englishmen speak, or *some* of what *some* Englishmen speak? Does it include the English of Scotland and of Ireland, the speech of British Englishmen, and American Englishmen, South African Englishmen, and of the Englishmen in India?'[27]

This answer opens up the terms of the debate and reveals the political and social assumptions which underlie it. Sisam chose a different method and style of reply. His letter to a Viennese correspondent is a typical example. 'I am afraid,' he wrote, 'it is entirely impossible for us – or indeed for anyone – to say how many words there are in the English language. It depends on how many compounds etc. are counted and what are admitted as words. In the great Oxford English Dictionary there are said to be roundly 500,000 words defined. I am sorry I cannot be more precise. Yours truly.'[28] By emphasizing the technical difficulties inherent in the question, Sisam side-steps the cultural and intellectual issues that often seem to be the reason for raising it in the first place. These are sometimes more clearly stated by a correspondent, as when an inquirer in 1940 asked for figures for (1) 'an average English working-man's vocabulary? (2) the vocabulary of a person with a secondary education: with a University education: an average business man: a statesman: a lawyer, or professional man'. Sisam replied gently to explain the difficulties involved, for example that people usually understand many more words than they actually use, so that 'vocabulary' can mean different things in different contexts, and concluded, 'your questions raise points of indefinite controversy'.[29] Another variation on the question was to inquire which language (say of English, German and French) had the greatest number of words, as a W. Lewis of Manchester asked in 1949; he enclosed a postal order for a guinea as 'appreciation of your courtesy in giving us this opinion', and suggested that it might be donated to some useful cause. The then Assistant Secretary, Dan Davin, wrote back some weeks later, apologizing for the delay but saying he had 'been rather at a loss what answer to make. Repeating Sisam's formula on the difficulty of identifying words and counting them up, he pointed out 'there is nothing to prevent someone inventing a word tomorrow that is quite legitimate'; while the OED itself had omitted many words 'for one reason or another'. He returned the guinea.[30]

Usually, the publishers' stance is that of Sisam in 1933, when asked by the Berlitz Sprachschulen in Berlin whether *asparagus* was plural or singular. 'I can assure you,' Sisam wrote back politely, 'we do not set up to be arbitrators in matters of language.'[31] But arbitrators they undoubtedly were. Well before 1933, the Dictionary was established as a final authority whose definitions were quoted in courts and even Parliament (see Introduction, pp. 15–16, and illustration 2). On occasion, the lexicographers chose to exercise that authority, and the publishers knew this perfectly well. When a correspondent sent in a newspaper cutting (not surviving) in 1939, in which occurred the 'bastard use of the word "flashpoint"', as an example of 'just the kind of misuse of a technical term which will appeal with particular force to journalists', Sisam replied to say that he would pass it on to 'our editors'. However, he thought that they 'may decide to exclude it as dangerously erroneous'.[32] Sisam was no doubt joking. But his remark acknowledges the proscriptive power inherent in a dictionary, especially one such as the *OED* which purports to record language comprehensively.

All the lexicographers were aware of their potential to legislate, as well as – paradoxically – their own impotence in the face of the irresistible force of usage. In a long letter to Sisam of 9 December 1938, Wyllie mused on the relation between usage and correctness, discussing the *OED*'s omission (still not rectified) of 'another' in the sense found in Lewis Carroll's 'The Walrus and the Carpenter': 'But four young oysters hurried up And yet another four', which had been pointed out to him by a correspondent. Pondering this apparently ungrammatical locution, which clashes a singular adjective (*another*) with a plural noun, he drew on his constant preoccupation with war on the one hand and the Latin dictionary on the other:

> How recent this development is I am not prepared to say; it may be much older than one would like to think. On the question of whether the use is right or wrong, I have no hesitation in saying that it is fundamentally illogical, or ungrammatical, and therefore in the view of some people wrong, but safely established by usage, and therefore right. Usage, I need not remind you, has the last word . . . . For a student of a living language who does not feel obliged, like Hitler, to oppose any fresh revolution vigorously while admitting the justice of past ones, this is an interesting development. My own view is that such ungrammatical innovations should be condemned and, if possible, killed when they first appear, in order to preserve what remains of the logical quality of English, and to avoid making the language which is as likely to become the universal tongue as any other even more difficult for the foreigner to learn than it is already; but it is too late to adopt this attitude to a locution when we are all using it . . . . I am quite sure that if I wanted to be impressive and did not mind not being dignified I might make a statement like 'another nineteen years and we shall have a Latin dictionary in manuscript'.[33]

In common with much of the correspondence over these years, this discussion probes the role and function of a dictionary. Was this (as Craigie had said in 1933) simply to record language 'as it was and as it is'? Or instead to set out and foster best practice (whatever that might be)? Should the *OED*, as many correspondents wished, go further and condemn ill-formed or undesirable use of language?

These questions gesture to a hinterland of assumptions and desires concerning the *OED*, widely recognized as a monument of learning about the English language and hence a symbol of the nation's culture. Over the next pages, we look at a selection of these assumptions and desires by tracing some aspects of the *OED*'s origin and early history. Why was (and is) this dictionary seen as so authoritative a record of the language, and how did it revolutionize lexicography, as its editors claimed? How were its materials accumulated and how was the Dictionary itself put together? If it could not include all words in the language – and if determining the language's extent was so difficult, as the publishers had variously explained to their correspondents – how did it decide what to put in and what to leave out? Pursuing these questions will help us contextualize the positions on inclusion and exclusion taken by the next editor of the *OED*, R. W. Burchfield, when he came to edit the second Supplement in 1957–86, as well as those in turn adopted for the first thorough-going revision of *OED* that was to start up in the 1990s.

We will begin by considering (very briefly) what earlier dictionaries of English had done in their turn, in particular the innovative feature of one of the *OED*'s most important predecessors, Dr Johnson's *Dictionary of the English Language*, which had illustrated its definitions by quoting real examples of usage from carefully selected sources. We then review the intentions and eventual practice of the first editors of the *OED*, who were inevitably forced to compromise their initial aim of chronicling every item in the language, and instead had to discriminate between words that were worthy and words that were not. In making their selection of vocabulary, the *OED* lexicographers were constrained by the cultural attitudes of their time: that it was the job of a dictionary to preserve the best words in the language rather than record the worst, and that those words were to be found primarily in the works of 'great writers' both past and present. As with Johnson's dictionary, their inclusion of extracts from such texts helped establish their work as a cultural as well as a linguistic authority, while the range of quotation sources – literature, history, philosophy, theology, politics, science – made it seem as if *OED*, in some way or other, represented not just a world of words (a popular title for dictionaries from the sixteenth century onwards), but *the* world, however conceived. This view is exemplified in the response of the Essex correspondent quoted above (p. 97), and it is widely shared: as Anatole France put it – reported in a review of the first edition of *OED* in 1928 – 'A dictionary is the universe in alphabetical order.'[34] But what exactly is the nature of the 'world' that 'seems spread before one' in *OED*? Can it really be true that this dictionary's 'breadth of view' is 'commensurate with reality', with no 'arbitrary handling' by the editors of 'the material of life' – or language – one way or another? What is the relationship between the *OED* and the lexicon of English more generally?

The *OED*'s predecessor, Dr Johnson

The most famous and influential predecessor to the *OED* was Dr Johnson's dictionary of 1755, which was enormously successful and popular during his lifetime and dominated the lexicographical landscape for many years afterwards. Well into the nineteenth century it was seen both as a maintainer of high literary standards and – more negatively – as a symbol of joyless repression and rule-giving. On the one hand, the notable prose writer Macaulay kept a much-used copy on his desk 'to keep his diction up to the classical standard, and to prevent himself from slipping into spurious modernisms'; on the other hand, as everyone knows, the independent and rule-dodging Becky Sharp, the irrepressible heroine of Thackeray's *Vanity Fair* (1847–48), tossed a copy out of the carriage window as she sped away from the great iron gate of Miss Pinkerton's academy for young ladies, the unattractive seminary at which she had been educated, sinking back in the carriage 'in an easy frame of mind, saying, – "So much for the Dixonary; and, thank God, I'm out of Chiswick."'[35]

Before Johnson, the first English monolingual dictionaries, from Robert Cawdrey's *Table Alphabeticall of Hard Wordes* (1604) and his antecedents onwards, had consisted of fairly limited lists of words, briefly defined, and on occasion supported with etymological and other sorts of information. Frequently both word and definition were borrowed, without acknowledgement, from preceding dictionaries, whether mono- or bilingual, and from glossaries to printed works. No illustrative quotations accompanied the definitions, other than the occasional cursory phrase, rarely attributed to any source. It is clear from both the title-pages and prefaces to many of these works that they were conceived as 'hard-word' dictionaries, designed to help women, boys, and less well educated men to improve their use and understanding of the English language, especially the difficult words that had recently entered the vocabulary as a result of the enormous expansion in classical scholarship. As a result, the range of words included was both restricted and uneven. By the early eighteenth century, however, dictionaries had become far more comprehensive works, vying with each other in their boasts of including vast numbers of words which were drawn from a much wider range of registers.[36] But not until Johnson did a monolingual English lexicographer substantiate definitions with quotations from (mostly) documented sources. This development, which Johnson inherited from European and bilingual dictionaries and encyclopedias, brought about a profound change in lexicographical principle and practice.[37] Reading and quoting 'great writers' as examples of how language had been or should be used often amounted to reading and quoting great thoughts, or ideas, or moments in literature, which meant that the resulting dictionary started to function not just as a book of words but as a book of ideas, a commonplace book, a book which reflected the predominant literary or political or social context of the time. This was one of the most important characteristics that the OED inherited from Johnson, and it remains a significant aspect of the OED today.

Johnson's 'chief intent', as stated in his 'Plan of a Dictionary' (1747), was to 'preserve the purity and ascertain the meaning of our English idiom' by registering the language of writers from the golden age of Elizabeth to the near-present (he hoped to avoid quoting writers who were still alive). He compiled his dictionary by ransacking vast quantities of books (often borrowed from friends since he could not afford his own copies), marking passages he thought aptly illustrated the usage of a word, and passing them to amanuenses who copied them out for printing.[38] But scrutinizing real usage for the specific purpose of recording and defining the senses of words opened Johnson's eyes to the indeterminacy both of language itself and of the way it is used. His 'Preface' to A Dictionary of the English Language (1755), written after he had completed the dictionary itself, explains how difficult it was and is to pin meaning down. 'While our language is yet living, and variable by the caprice of every one that speaks it,' he pointed out, with apparent disapproval, '. . . words are hourly shifting their relations, and can no more be ascertained in a dictionary, than a grove, in the agitation of a storm, can be accurately delineated from its picture in the water.'[39] The task he had set himself had been over-ambitious, to say the least. The capacity of human beings to use language in infinitely changeful ways means that it is impossible to capture and fix meaning either comprehensively or once and for all. Johnson had no doubt properly understood this for the first time when he scanned his quotations, and grasped the kaleidoscopic variety of senses that a word could take on according to its varying contexts. Consequently, however, he was in a much better position to distinguish between meanings and senses in individual words than any lexicographer before him, as can be seen by the sheer length of his dictionary entries and their numerous subdivisions. He identified sixty-six different senses of take, for example, together with a further fifty-odd senses of the same verb combined with a preposition or used idiomatically, while his two main rivals, Nathan Bailey's Dictionarium Britannicum (1730) and Benjamin Martin's Lingua Britannica (1749), had found only three and seventeen respectively. A hundred and fifty years later, the chief editor of the *OED*, J. A. H. Murray – himself writing a dictionary based on its quotations – fully appreciated the importance of this aspect of Johnson's dictionary, which he thought a 'marvellous piece of work', whose most important new features were its 'illustration of the use of every word by a selection of literary quotations, and the more delicate appreciation and discrimination of senses which this involved and rendered possible'.[40]

Such an understanding of the potentially inexhaustible proliferation of meaning might have seemed to demand what is now often referred to as a descriptive rather than a prescriptive attitude to language: in other words, that the lexicographer should report how language is actually used by writers and speakers, rather than attempt to discriminate in any absolute way between good and bad usage. But although Johnson said that he did not seek to 'form, but [to] register the language', and '[did] not teach men how they should think, but relate[d] how they have hitherto expressed their thoughts', his dictionary was imbued with prescriptivism.[41] He censured the usage of writers, including those he revered such as Shakespeare and Dryden, even while recording it in his dictionary, and he rigorously limited the range of sources he drew on for his quotations, confining himself, so far as he could, to a relatively small pantheon of literary giants and of writers of established stature in selected other fields (for example theology and philosophy). Just seven sources between them furnish nearly half the quotations in his dictionary: Shakespeare (15.5 per cent), Dryden (10 per cent), Milton (5.7 per cent), and Bacon, the Bible, Addison and Pope (under 4.5 per cent each), while just nineteen authors provide 67 per cent of the total number of Johnson's quotations.[42] Famously, Johnson refused to quote from the works of Hobbes and others whom he regarded as morally beyond the pale, and therefore unsuitable to supply examples of language usage, believing that 'It is not enough that a dictionary delights a critic, unless at the same time it instructs the learner.'[43] The wonderful profusion of quotations in his dictionary gave it the character of a commonplace book, full of instructive, improving, uplifting, illuminating, and in many cases delightful comments and phrases. At the same time, restricting the sources for these quotations reinforced the dictionary's function as a didactic work, one which tried to limit and restrain language and the possible views and positions language can represent.[44]

In this it met the demands of its age. During the last few decades, many writers and intellectuals had voiced their intense anxiety over the imperfections, 'abuses and absurdities' that had crept into the language as its vocabulary had rapidly expanded. Complaints like that of Jonathan Swift in his *Proposal for Correcting, Improving and Ascertaining the English Tongue*

(1712) about the unregulated circulation of these words and about the instability of the English language – whether its vocabulary or its grammar – were frequent by the 1740s, and Johnson's *Dictionary* was seen by contemporaries as an answer to the problem. As his (famously unsatisfactory) patron Lord Chesterfield put it, 'The time for discrimination seems to be now come. Toleration, adoption and naturalization have run their lengths. Good order and authority are now necessary . . . . We must have recourse to the old Roman expedient in times of confusion, and chuse a dictator.'[45]

The *OED* was also to find itself caught by crosscurrents between descriptivism (which, usually, it desiderated for itself), and prescriptivism (which its public expected of it). Paying due attention to a full range of quotation sources would seem to demand the first, but social pressures of various different kinds sometimes required the second. And although the lexicographers flung their nets far wider than Johnson, in a search for the quotations from which they were to construct their magnificent dictionary, in the event they too, like Johnson, much preferred great writers, especially those who played a significant role in the Victorian literary canon, to lesser ones. This meant that their Dictionary, superficially so different to Johnson's, in this respect resembled his closely: it is a treasure-house of the great works of the past. While this choice of quotation sources established the *OED* as a cultural icon, loved and venerated by generations of readers, it interfered with its function as an impartial historical and linguistic record.

Scientific study of language and the *OED*'s plans for inclusiveness

Language study in the eighteenth century was philosophically based, and grammarians and lexicographers started with a set of premises about the language, about how it worked and how it should be used. The didactic drive of Johnson's dictionary and his choice of quotation sources played an important part in creating the identity of the final product, however much he had to struggle with the vagaries of empirical detail. But the culture of language study changed radically over the next century. Linguists such as Jacob Grimm, Rask and Bopp studied the evidence of historical manuscripts in Sanskrit and in vernacular European languages, and based their theories about language and language change on actual data as opposed to a priori assumptions (in this respect building upon the pioneering lexicographical scholarship of Hickes, Ihre and others). As scholars amassed information about language forms of the past, philological knowledge and understanding underwent a series of transformations.[46]

In some respects, the *OED* represents the chief flowering of this attitude towards language study, since its lexicographers constructed their dictionary from a mass of empirical data – real examples of language use gathered from documents and books dated 1150 onwards – instead of relying on unscientific theories about language. This was certainly what Murray believed. In a public lecture delivered in Oxford in 1900, which he called 'The Evolution of English Lexicography', Murray described the *OED* as 'permeated . . . through and through with the scientific method of the century' and claimed that 'the scientific and historical spirit of the nineteenth century has at once called for and rendered possible the Oxford English Dictionary'.[47] Murray also used his lecture to narrate how the first father of the *OED*, the formidably well-read and lexically knowledgeable Dean Trench, had in two lectures of 1857 set out a series of criticisms of existing dictionaries – which were by then numerous, including successive versions of Johnson's dictionary on the one hand and of Noah Webster's great American dictionary (first published in 1828) on the other, along with many other (often derivative) works. Trench had anatomized the failure of these works to present a complete record of the language: they provided insufficient treatment of words now obsolete; they did not list all the possible senses of words; they did not record all the variant forms a word could take; they were one way or another partial or biassed. Taken up by the Philological Society, these criticisms in turn gave birth to the ideal of the dictionary that was to become the *OED*, one that would list every word in the language, tracing its path through history from cradle to grave, and searching out its first and last occurrence in printed texts. Enabling 'every word . . . to tell its own story' in this way would create a map of the historical development of the English language. This historical methodology was based on that of the Greek-language lexicographer Franz Passow, in his 1819 revision of J. G. Schneider's *Griechisch–Deutsches Wörterbuch*, recently translated and extended by Liddell and Scott for their own Greek–English lexicon of 1843: significantly, these dictionaries were dealing with a dead language, where there was a realistic possibility of gathering together all the relevant evidence and coming to a fixed view on it.[48] But a living language was to present different problems.

It is obvious that this project, with its assumption that words, like fossils, could be fully described by tracking their diachronic, evolutionary progress, was based on a paradigm drawn from nineteenth-century developments in the natural sciences; and the comparison between geology and historical philology (and indeed numerous other disciplines) was commonplace at the time. In both cases, incontrovertible historical evidence was to be found in the layered and linked strata of the past – deposits of rock on the one hand, successions of documents and books on the other: historical evidence which alone truly explained the function and character of present-day phenomena.[49]

Implicit in this scientific paradigm is the view that the English language comprises a set of finite data, observable and organizable, which can be impartially and objectively set down. An important corollary was the principle that all the available evidence – that is, each and every word in the language that had ever been used – was significant, and that all needed to be collected together for examination, without the operation of any form of censorship or exclusion on moral or aesthetic grounds. (As Wyllie was to say later, 'The interesting words constitute the whole of the vocabulary'.)[50] A dictionary, Trench believed, should be 'an inventory of the language', and it should describe, not prescribe. 'It is no task of the maker of it to select the *good* words of the language . . . . If he fancies that it is so, and begins to pick and choose, to leave this and to take that, he will at once go astray . . . . The business he has undertaken is to collect and arrange all the words, whether good or bad, whether they do or do not commend themselves to his judgement . . . . He is a historian of [the language], not a critic.' On this matter, Trench thought, 'there is a constant confusion here in men's minds. There are many who conceive of a Dictionary as though it had this function, to be a standard of the language . . . . It is nothing of the kind'. 'It is . . . for those who *use* [my italics] to sift the bran from the flour, to reject this or retain that.'[51]

Such claims were often repeated by the *OED* lexicographers in the years to come, and accord with standard modern notions of linguistic descriptivism, which (as we saw Wyllie trying to do earlier in this chapter) respect usage rather than grammatical rule – itself often the creation of schoolmasters and scholars trying to make the English language conform to Latin and Greek, despite the different linguistic structures of these older tongues. (It is no accident that many of the early *OED* lexicographers and contributors were fascinated by local dialects and devoted much time to describing and recording them, the product of native linguistic traditions uninfluenced by authoritarian rules and prohibitions.)[52]

Once the Philological Society had decided to take on the project which Trench's criticisms had revealed that English urgently required, they made one of their number (Herbert Coleridge) editor, and published a document in 1859 called *Proposal for a Publication of a New English Dictionary by the Philological Society*. In it, they stated the principle of unquestioning inclusion as the starting point of the Dictionary: 'the first requirement of every lexicon is, that it should contain *every word in the literature of the language it professes to illustrate*. We entirely repudiate the theory, which converts the lexicographer into an arbiter of style, and leaves it in his discretion to accept or reject words according to his private notion of their elegance or inelegance.'[53] The same notion, expressed with the nationalist and socialist conviction which motivated much of his life's work, was vigorously articulated by F. J. Furnivall (who took over as editor after Coleridge's premature death in 1861): 'We have set ourselves to form a National Portrait Gallery, not only of the worthies, but of all the members, of the race of English words which is to form the dominant speech of the world . . . . Fling our doors wide! all, all, not one, but all, must enter.'[54]

All these various remarks and statements – uttered with a confidence as yet unmediated by extensive experience of compiling and editing the new Dictionary – emphasize the paramount importance of inclusion of all known words, whatever their status, in the Dictionary. But the extent to which it was proper or acceptable for the *OED* to devote itself to linguistic descriptivism was a highly controversial issue from the start, and remained so for many years subsequently. And in practice, of course, the lexicographers experienced numerous difficulties in realizing their heroic ideal of universal inclusion. It would have been literally impossible for them to have recorded every known word in English literature (however defined), even with the help of a large band of skilled and properly paid workers: first, because of the range and number of potential sources, and secondly, because the resulting dictionary would have been unmanageably large.[55]

The inclusiveness of the Society's *Proposal* was greeted with nothing less than horror and disbelief by its contemporaries. 'What is this,' an article in the influential *Edinburgh Review* thundered, 'but to throw down all barriers and rules, and declare that every form of expression which may have been devised by the humour, the ignorance, or the affectation of any writer, is at once to take rank in the national vocabulary?' By contrast, 'one of the most laudable objects an educated man can pursue is to defend [the language] from contamination'. The writer, J. H. Marsden, an antiquary and cleric, observed that 'strange expressions and far-fetched derivations are constantly flashing on the minds of some writers; and for their own purposes authors who have got the good will of their readers may practise whatever tricks or distortions they please; but we demur to the conclusion that every one of these fancies ought to be registered for ever in the pages of a dictionary'. Marsden finished, in an echo of Lord Chesterfield (p. 108 above), by pointing out that when all the materials for this Dictionary were assembled, then 'there must somewhere lie a power of arbitration. From the moment that the building begins, the republic must give way to a dictator.'[56]

This notion – that regulation was an essential part of a dictionary's function, and that the lexicographer's job was to discriminate, not just (spinelessly) record – was picked up by Herbert Coleridge's uncle, Derwent, S. T. Coleridge's second son and an accomplished linguist. In a paper read to the Philological Society on 10 May 1860, he said he feared 'that what I conceive to be the higher functions of the Lexicographer have been to some extent disclaimed, and his office regarded as not possessing any judicial or regulative authority; – as if it were his duty to exhibit the practice of English writers, though it rest but on a single instance, but not to question its propriety: not to decide between the rival claims of varying usages . . . . Against the limitation I must enter my humble, but earnest protest.' The older man went on to say that a lexicographer 'must not merely produce authorities' – that is, evidence of usage – but 'he must adjudicate, settling each point, as it occurs, under the guidance of his own observation'.

Like Marsden, he concluded that what was needed was arbitration. 'The office of a Dictionary . . . is eminently regulative – regulative in effect, though declarative in form. It separates the spurious from the genuine . . . it is, or ought to be, zealously conservative. It sets up a continual protest against innovation: or in the rare event of some change, or addition being at once possible and desirable, it indicates the law to which the novelty must conform.'[57]

These words would have struck a strong chord with many of his contemporaries, just as they do with many dictionary users today, who turn to the dictionary for authoritative pronouncement on correct and incorrect usage rather than a neutral record of past and present practice. A major influence on this desire for regulation is the recognition that language is intimately bound up with culture, with a nation's sense of itself, and that it reflects the values – both moral and aesthetic – that the society speaking it holds dear. Consequently, it needs to be both preserved and purified. In the words of one critic of the *OED*, 'nothing is worthy of a permanent place within our walls but that which belongs to the records of our race and the creative powers of wise and far-searching minds'.[58] In the eyes of many, this was the true job of the new Dictionary: to act as gatekeeper as well as treasure-house.

Language and culture

The perceived links between language and culture lie at the heart of many reactions to and feelings about the *OED*, whether those of its critics or of the dictionary-makers themselves. The second half of the nineteenth century in Britain was a time of intense awareness of this relationship between language and national identity, not least on account of the effects on language of imperialist expansion. English was already well on its way to becoming a world language, the 'universal tongue' envisaged by Wyllie in 1938 (p. 103 above): but as it marched triumphantly across geographical and national boundaries in splendid vindication of its own virtue and power, so did it become vulnerable to corruption and contamination. The same writers who urged discrimination on the lexicographers also pointed out that 'in the extremities of this wide empire the purity and precision of the language itself are likely to be corrupted and lost', and that 'already, in the United States, in Australia, and in the Western colonies, the vernacular tongue of the people differs widely from the standard of the mother country; and the current literature of the day, being chiefly in the form of newspapers, tends rather to debase than to raise the style of diction'.[59]

The assumption that language and culture are intimately associated is accepted as a truism in late nineteenth-century discussions of language. The connection had been repeatedly made by European historians, philosophers and linguists in the eighteenth century, and was authoritatively stated by Friedrich Schlegel in a series of lectures translated into English in 1818 (by Lockhart, Sir Walter Scott's son-in-law and biographer). Schlegel also identified an important link between language and the privileged members of a society, explaining that it was the job of the ruling classes to regulate and control language.

> The care of the national language I consider as at all times a sacred trust and an important privilege of the higher orders of society. Every man of education should make it the object of his unceasing concern, to preserve his language pure and entire, to speak it, so far as is in his power, in all its beauty and perfection . . . . A nation which allows her language to go to ruin, is parting with the last of her intellectual independence, and testifies her willingness to cease to exist.[60]

These words were approvingly quoted by Trench in the first of a series of lectures originally delivered to future schoolmasters in 1854 and subsequently published as *English Past and Present*, one of his two astonishingly popular little books (the other, very similar, was called *On the Study of Words*) which appeared before the *OED* was even thought of and were reprinted many times during its long compilation.[61] By the 1860s, when the Philological Society's *Proposal* was being discussed, such ideas had trickled down to best-selling publications like *The Dean's English*, which was published by George Washington Moon in New York in 1865, as part of a ding-dong argument with Henry Alford, Dean of Canterbury, on the rights and wrongs of language usage.[62]

Trench's widely disseminated views on language are pregnant with nationalistic and moral implications, which effectively obviate the possibility of disinterested linguistic descriptivism – whatever he was to say elsewhere, in his analysis of dictionaries, about the desirability of compiling a neutral inventory of language. He believed that 'language . . . [is] a moral barometer, which indicates and permanently marks the rise or fall of a nation's life', and he delighted in exploring the (true or imagined) etymologies of words to prove his point. In the same way that fossils told us about the history of creatures, so did etymologies tell us about the history of words. 'Language may be, and indeed is, this "fossil poetry",' Trench explained, meditating on a term suggested by the essayist and poet Emerson; 'but it may be affirmed of it with exactly the same truth that it is fossil ethics, or fossil history'; 'words often contain a witness for great moral truth – God having impressed such a seal of truth upon language, that men are continually uttering deeper things than they know'. To illustrate this, Trench reports Joseph Butler's discussion of the word *pastime*, in an analysis which sits fairly and squarely in a most unscientific tradition of false etymologizing, stretching back through writers of the seventeenth and sixteenth centuries and ultimately to Plato's *Cratylus*: 'how solemn [is] the testimony which [Butler] compels the world, out of its own use of this word, to render against itself – obliging it to own that its amusements and pleasures do not really satisfy the mind and fill it with the sense of an abiding and satisfying joy . . . they serve only, as this word confesses, to *pass* away the *time*'.[63]

Trench's lectures are crammed with such examples, all to illustrate his religious thesis, and he claims that dictionaries themselves (we are in pre-*OED* days) confirm a sad and stern estimate of man's moral and spiritual condition: 'How else shall we explain this long catalogue of words, having all to do with sin, or with sorrow, or with both? . . . I open the first letter of the alphabet; what means this "Ah," this "Alas," these deep and long-drawn sighs of humanity . . . "Affliction," "Agony," "Anguish," "Assassin," "Atheist," "Avarice," and twenty more . . .' (p. 30). (It is irresistible to respond by pointing out that any reader might instead pick out 'ahead', 'ahold', 'aid', 'aim', 'akin', 'alacrity' – to choose a selection from Richardson's dictionary – and ascribe to them positive or at any rate neutral connotations).[64] Trench continues, 'And yet our dictionaries, while they tell us much, yet will not tell us all. How shamefully rich is the language of the vulgar everywhere in words and phrases which are not allowed to find their way into books, yet which live a sinful oral tradition on the lips of men, to set forth that which is unholy and impure' (p. 32). These investigations of the intrinsic morality of words and etymology are simply incompatible with the ideal of treating language impartially. Recording *all* words without discrimination, in the way Trench was later to advocate, meant including all the sinful or otherwise inappropriate ones. The 'shamefully rich . . . language of the vulgar everywhere in words and phrases' does and did find its way into print, whether in newspapers (routinely reviled by cultural commentators) or books. This ugly reality could be accommodated by the aims and methods of scientific descriptivism, but was horribly at odds with the imperative to preserve and refine one's linguistic and cultural heritage. So should quotations from these works be included in the *OED* or not?[65]

'Unsifted ore' and the indeterminate extent of the English language

Given this well-recognized connection between language and culture, and the consequent desire that a dictionary of English should defend the language's purity, why is it that Trench (in some moods, at any rate) and the other Dictionary Fathers thought that an all-inclusive dictionary was both possible and desirable? The answer is partly that they wished to gather together all the evidence, in that spirit of scientific empirical inquiry discussed above, but also that their stated aims for descriptivism were based on a flawed premise. This was enunciated near the beginning of the Philological Society's *Proposal* (p. 3), where the authors declared 'as we are unable to perceive any difference between a dead and a living language, so far as lexicographical treatment is concerned, it follows that we cannot refuse to admit words into the Dictionary which may not be sanctioned by the usage of more than one writer, or be conformable in their structure to our ideas of taste'.

The assumption that there is no 'difference between a dead and a living language, so far as lexicographical treatment is concerned', was profoundly mistaken. As Derwent Coleridge pointed out in his lecture to the Philological Society in May 1860, 'The analogy is one of contrast rather than of likeness.' He went on to describe how 'the literature of a dead language ... has been *puddled*, to use a mining phrase, in the stream of time, and though some dross has come down with the gold ... yet upon the whole we have only to deal with good stuff, and this in limited quantity, whereas in a modern language we have the unsifted ore, with perhaps but a small proportion of valuable metal, – and literally, no end of it'.[66]

Here he had put his finger on the problem, and indeed 'unsifted ore' caused the lexicographers' descriptive ideals to run on to rocky ground immediately word collection for the Dictionary began in earnest. Five months later, he could count his own nephew as a convert to his views. Herbert Coleridge also lectured to the Philological Society in an address which appeared to renege on the founding principles of the Dictionary that he himself had articulated in the *Proposal*, and to respond to his uncle's advice, by arguing that certain words should be left out. What he objected to were eccentric *hapax legomena* (such as *devilship*, found in Thomas Nashe, Shakespeare's older contemporary);[67] 'playful or "hypercoristic" terms' formed by adding on odd prefixes or suffixes (*be-* and *-kin*); usages that he called 'literary fungi' (e.g. Sydney Smith's *foolometer* or Carlyle's *whiskerage*), which he thought often correlated inversely with 'the literary rank and standing of the author'; and 'malformations' from Greek and Latin. Herbert Coleridge suggested that such words should be treated 'as probationers on trial', and printed in a separate section at the end of the Dictionary. He submitted his judgement to the democratic ruling of the Philological Society members present at the meeting, who discussed the words in turn and in general decided they should be included, suggesting at one point that: 'if an Editor did not like them, he might add some note of his dissent, but should not exclude them'. (The discussion was recorded by Furnivall, who presumably felt some socialist glee at the Society's rebuttal of Coleridge's inegalitarian plans.)[68]

But discrimination and moral evaluation had crept into the Dictionary Fathers' own writings too. In some respects their *Proposal for a New Dictionary* called for the sifting of the grain that it appeared to be arguing against. Thus, immediately following its remarks on the identical nature, for lexicographic purposes, of dead and living languages, and the consequent imperative to admit all words, the *Proposal* comments, 'However worthless they may be in themselves, they testify to a tendency of language, and on this account only, if on no other, have a distinct and appreciable value' (pp. 2–3). The suggestion that certain words may be inherently 'worthless' indicates that some sort of aesthetic, evaluative judgement has begun to operate despite avowals to the contrary. This is also apparent in Trench's mention, in his earlier lectures to the Philological Society, of 'the wrong ways into which a language has wandered, or been disposed to wander', even his claim that such wrong ways 'may be nearly as instructive as the right ones in which it has travelled', and that 'as much may be learned, or nearly as much, from its failures as from its successes, from its follies as from its wisdom'.[69] While Trench is ostensibly advocating a disinterested historical inquiry into the language, his terms of description are loaded: the language's 'failures' and 'follies' are to be set against its 'successes' and its 'wisdom'. It is a short step from here to a contrary argument, that a dictionary's job is to protect the linguistic heritage from failures and follies, not to foster further contamination.

Once serious and protracted editing of the mass of quotation material began, under Murray, editorial understanding of the complexities of registering the language became vastly more sophisticated. Murray took repeated pains to explain these both to the Philological Society and to the public (in lectures on the language and in private letters to individual correspondents).[70] As he said, 'the paramount consideration' forced upon one's attention by the process of writing the Dictionary was 'the vague and indef-inite extension of that body of sounds, with their associated ideas, which we call the *English Language*'. The English language was, he said, 'a spot of colour on a damp surface, which shades away imperceptibly into surrounding colourlessness', or, switching the metaphor, 'an illuminated area in a midnight landscape, whose beams practically [i.e. in practice] end somewhere, but no eye hath beheld the vanishing line'. The nebulousness of the language's extent was, Murray pointed out, in an echo of Derwent Coleridge, 'a phenomenon which is peculiar to a living language, as distinct from a dead one'.

This meant that a comprehensive record of it was impossible, and so was a consistent one. While 'the written remains of a dead language must be definite in quantity', so that it was 'merely a matter of time and diligence to include them all in the pages of a lexicon', this was not so with 'the language of a civilized nation', subject to ever-increasing knowledge and experience both within its own culture and without it, and as a result constantly extending the compass of its vocabulary. It was thus impossible to deter-mine its extent or to fix its boundaries. It is 'surrounded', Murray pointed out, 'by a vanishing border of special terms, scientific, technical, slang, dialectal, some of which are English to some Englishmen, and undreamt of by others'. 'At which Englishman's speech does English terminate?' he asked.[71] And in the introductory 'General Explanations' to the Dictionary, published in 1884, he drew a diagram famously resembling a compass to illustrate the indistinct and indefinable ways in which the centre of 'common' words in the language melts into more specialized areas – slang, technical vocabulary, dialect, etc. – at its periphery.

Murray's more learned and shrewd understanding of language – its inde-terminate extent, and the difficulty of drawing a line between inclusion and exclusion in the Dictionary – was not found in many of his contemporaries. He was particularly infuriated by some of the reviews which greeted the publication of the first fascicle, *A–Ant*, in 1884, which had failed to recog-nize that the Dictionary could not be a catch-all for every word ever used in the language, or simultaneously satisfy the calls for both inclusion and exclusion made by critics of different intellectual provenance. Some wanted more quotations from obscure authors, some from more illustrious ones; literary reviewers objected to the inclusion of too many technical terms, but 'a very different opinion has been expressed by various men of science, each of whom would like rather more indulgence shown to the vocabulary of his own particular department'.[72]

Murray also objected to the snobbery with which some of the language in the Dictionary had been greeted, reporting that 'considerable indignation has been expended on quotations from modern newspapers' (although those of two centuries or so ago, 'which age has since hallowed', had escaped criticism). 'Personally,' he continued, 'I think this criticism by far the silliest that the Dictionary has elicited.' Many years ahead of his time, he had often insisted on the positive value of such sources (whether or not the public thought they should be immortalized in a cultural treasure-house): 'To the philologist & historian of language – newspaper quotations are the most valuable of current instances – they show how the language grows – they make visible to us the actual steps which for earlier stages we must reconstruct by inference.' Murray himself 'never read the leaders of the daily papers without finding some word worth extracting', and he utterly repudiated the stigma attached to the claimed 'atrocities of newspaper English'.[73]

Sixty-odd years later, on the *OED*'s completion in 1928, these issues were still current. By now, *OED* was seen as the great recorder of the English language and hence the repository of its culture. But it must also, therefore, act as its guardian. As influential usage of the English language proliferated both geographically and socially – the result of imperialism on the one hand, and increasing public education and democracy on the other – it became more and more important to put a brake on change and ward off corruption. Such a stance is nicely exemplified in the *TLS*'s review of the finished product, by C. W. Brodribb, a classicist on the staff of *The Times*. Brodribb reported with comfortable approval 'the great principle that a dictionary must be a register of all words for which literary usage, good or bad, common or rare, could be cited', describing how Trench had wished to draw a 'swoop-net over the whole extent of English literature', but finished by hoping that the Dictionary would now, once completed, be regarded as arbiter and critic. Like J. H. Marsden, Derwent Coleridge and many others before and since, he felt that the *OED* had also a duty to regulate and proscribe, and in explaining this he explicitly linked privilege, class and education with the use and misuse of language:

The year of final delivery [of the *OED*] coincides with the grant of universal franchise; but at bottom the Dictionary bears the stamp of the last age of privilege. The mass of it was got together before the newly literate received their charter to treat the language as they pleased in hourly print [i.e. newspapers].[74] Some of the weakest usages quoted in the Dictionary come from Furnivall's daily newspaper; but a Furnivall of today so engaged might consume his entire life in sending neologisms from that source to the editors. Those who respect the purity of the language, who try to honour and understand its traditions and its idioms, who feel doubtful whether even so supple an instrument as English can bear without grave deterioration the incessant strain put upon it by modern democracy, will rather rejoice that the Dictionary has come into being when it has and as it has. The registration of every word and every usage they recognize to be a noble ideal; but they believe that what is now wanted is a standard of good, or at least passable, English, and a criterion to which all writers can apply as soon as education begins to turn cocksureness into diffidence. Now that the Dictionary is complete there should be ground for hoping that, although it does not set up to be an arbiter, it will nevertheless be more and more resorted to as one.[75]

English was at risk from the increased numbers of its citizens now being compulsorily educated by the state, and from the flood of new usages these scantly qualified people were pouring forth in newspapers. Consequently it was vital for the *OED*, keeper of the nation's linguistic treasure, to distinguish between verbal sheep and goats: to 'puddle' the language, retaining the ore and throwing away the dross. Brodribb's hostility to neologisms and changes in language does not recognize that English's present suppleness and richness was in part due to its previous hospitality to the same phenomena when they occurred in the past, although then too they were often seen as corruptions and malformations. His words echo those of Lord Chesterfield and other eighteenth-century language regulators as well as his immediate nineteenth-century predecessors, and convey the sense that the undifferentiating inclusiveness of the *OED*, in principle acceptable, must now cease, so that neologisms from undesirable sources are not automatically granted entrance.

Practical limits, discrimination and prudishness

So the originators of the *OED* – especially Trench and Herbert Coleridge – had begun by wanting their Dictionary to include all words, only to be thwarted by their own and others' subsequent realization that not all words were culturally acceptable. Murray and his fellow editors also recognized that limits were unavoidable, whether determined on practical grounds (that there was not enough room in the Dictionary) or theoretical ones (that it was impossible to fix the range and extent of the English language). 'Unsifted ore', needing to be jettisoned from the record, might take many forms. On the one hand, it could be the day-to-day slang and low-grade utterances Derwent Coleridge was thinking of when he used this term, language unlikely to be included in classical works of great literature. Or it could be Herbert Coleridge's 'literary fungi', once-off playful coinages by writers of greater or lesser distinction. Why should a dictionary of the English language include malapropisms, or idiosyncratic or obscure linguistic inventions, of all published authors, whatever their nature? And what about the scientific and technical words to which some critics also objected, or the obscene or slang words – Trench's 'shamefully rich . . . language of the vulgar' – together with a host of other undesirables, which were for reasons of taste, or morality, or legality, simply inadmissible to a dictionary of the late nineteenth century? Some sort of criteria had to be applied to sift out the grain from the chaff, however those two categories were to be defined, before the words got into the Dictionary, *pace* Trench (pp. 109–10). In practice, of course, such criteria were constantly appealed to, and it is not surprising if they were sometimes subjective. Thus Henry Hucks Gibbs (the businessman and man of letters who had been Governor of the Bank of England in 1875–77, and later became Lord Aldenham), a close friend and adviser to Murray, wrote to him in 1882,

> It is well – very well – to fix the first entry of a word into the language; but you must be quite sure it *has* entered . . . and is not a mere vagrant knocking at the door & who will be deservedly sent about his business. Don't allow slovenly or conceited writers to deposit their ἅπαε λεγόμενα [*hapax legomena*] in your demesne – to shoot their rubbish over land you are tilling so carefully! If you must honour such words as 'accommodated' (D[aily] T[elegraph]), 'accidented' 'accouche' and 'accoucheuse' by taking notice of them, in case they should ultimately creep into the language . . . you should have a separate limbo to which to relegate them – a hot one, I should suggest.[76]

As this indicates, even when words did get over the Dictionary's threshold, they were not all treated alike. Although Trench had insisted that a lexicographer was an historian of words, not a critic, he had not meant that he might not form a view on their value and communicate it to his readers. 'Where he counts words to be needless, affected, pedantic, ill put together, contrary to the genius of the language, there is no objection to his saying so; on the contrary, he may do real service in this way.'[77] (This is what we would now describe as being 'descriptive about prescriptivism': that is, warning the dictionary user that certain words are disapproved of by the educated classes.) And so the lexicographers who worked on the first edition of the *OED* sought, as part of their job, to characterize words by the use of 'status' labels. But such characterization could easily slide into the subjective and idiosyncratic, so that the first edition's status labels sometimes say more about the lexicographer responsible than about the usage they describe.

Different editors with different personal histories and lexical environments had, not surprisingly, differing views on the currency and obsolescence of individual words. Lynda Mugglestone has shown how the first *OED* lexicographers disagreed with each other about the register or connotations of words, how they attached derogatory labels to words found in normally acceptable print sources, and how frequency of attestation did not guarantee lexicographical approval despite the Dictionary's claims to describe rather than prescribe.[78] Murray and his fellow editors used a variety of methods to stigmatize usage, writing their disapproval into supposedly objective definitions or labels or etymologies. Saying *pants* instead of *drawers*, for example, was judged to be 'shoppy'; a new sense of *avocation* (= 'usual occupation, vocation') had, in Murray's view, been 'improperly foisted upon the word' (even though this sense was instanced by the normally unexceptionable Macaulay); the word *caucus* had been 'generally misused' in English newspapers since 1878. Certain uses or locutions (the term *ambient* if applied to the air, D. G. Rossetti's use of *gracile* to mean 'gracefully slender', *guilt* meaning 'sense of guilt') the lexicographers simply branded outright by marking them with the paragraph sign (¶), with which they identified 'catachrestic or erroneous uses'. (Any persistent and imaginative user of the electronic *OED* may easily turn up further examples of such proscription by typing suitable terms into the search engine boxes – 'misused', or 'wrongly', or 'improperly' – and sifting the results; unfortunately one cannot search electronically for the paragraph sign.)

Usage and correctness was not a theme much discussed by the reviewers of Craigie and Onions's Supplement, although some commentators routinely objected to slang and Americanisms. Nor was it one the editors themselves showed much interest in: it seems that they did not once apply the paragraph sign to any of the words they recorded (it is impossible to be sure without reading through every one of the Supplement's 867 three-column pages, which have never been transferred to an electronic medium).

However, as Wyllie's discussion with Sisam suggested, it was to loom large in the following decades, and by the time that Burchfield was writing the second Supplement in the 1970s and 1980s he thought it important enough to warrant introducing an entirely new element in the *OED*. This determined and strong-viewed man, whose early published work displays impersonal scholarly reticence, turned out to be the first, and possibly the only, editor of *OED* to bring personal, often idiosyncratic, judgements on individual words and usages openly into the Dictionary (it is no accident that he later produced a new edition of Fowler's *Modern English Usage*). Burchfield's contribution to *OED* ostensibly continued the tradition of dispassionate description, the massive accumulation of minutely observed and accurately recorded data on language, with the aim of setting down a full and impartial account, but in significant ways he departed from the objective spirit of his predecessors. 'Here and there,' he wrote of his work in volume 3 of the second Supplement, 'I have found myself adding my own opinions about the acceptability of certain words or meanings in educated use. Users of the dictionary may or may not find these editorial comments diverting: they have been added (adapting a statement by John Ray in 1691) "as oil to preserve the mucilage from inspissation".'[79] We return to his imitation of Johnsonian *ipse dixits* in Chapter VII below.

Sexual words and expressions were a different matter. As we have seen, Craigie had prevailed over Onions's 'lexicographical conscience' and put his foot down on *lesbian*, continuing the first editors' squeamishness about and avoidance of terms with which they, or some of their public, felt uncomfortable.[80] At least one reviewer of their Supplement had regretted the Dictionary's continued omission, not of the term *lesbian*, but of a sub-set of sexual words such as *cunt* and *fuck*. The author, the linguist A. S. C. Ross (later to become famous as the author of the essay on upper-class usage, 'U and non-U', which was enthusiastically endorsed by Nancy Mitford), thought it 'regrettable that the perpetuation of a Victorian prudishness (inacceptable [*sic*] in philology beyond other subjects) should have been allowed to lead to the omission of some of the commonest words in the English language' – though he made this point in a review for a Finnish periodical, and would have been unlikely to find a British publisher prepared to risk printing such words in the 1930s.[81] Careful as Burchfield was of the niceties of socially acceptable diction, he was happy to throw prudishness to the winds. The week that his first volume appeared, the *TLS* published an article by Burchfield with the title 'Four-letter Words and the *OED*'. But Burchfield's inclusion of these and a host of similar terms was no simple undertaking, not just owing to the subject matter, but because consistency of treatment, and detection of all the terms in the original Dictionary which needed updating, proved to be beyond the powers of the already overtaxed editor.

Treasure-house

In his two seminal lectures of November 1857, Trench had said, 'If . . . we count it worth while to have all words, we can only have them by reading all books; this is the price we must be content to pay.' Of course this was to be impossible, as Murray acknowledged in 1884: '*all* books have not been read, not by a long, long way'.[82] But how did the *OED* lexicographers set out in practice to achieve their *Proposal*'s aim (however unrealizable) and record '*every word in the literature of the language* [their dictionary professed] *to illustrate*'? One of the first tasks of Coleridge (confirmed as editor in 1859) and his successor, Furnivall, was to make out a list of books and assign volumes to individual readers. Volunteers were not in short supply and within two years of Trench's original lectures more than a hundred readers had offered their services. Exclusion of certain sources began straight away. The Philological Society's *Proposal* (p. 3) declared that 'all English books' were to be admitted as 'authorities' (i.e. acceptable sources) 'except such as are devoted to purely scientific subjects, as treatises on electricity, mathematics, &c., and works written subsequently to the Reformation for the purpose of illustrating provincial dialects'.[83] The criterion for such exclusion was clearly literary, and it points to an ambiguity in the word *literature*. Did this mean 'Literary productions as a whole; the body of writings produced in a particular country or period, or in the world in general', the first sense to be later distinguished by *OED* in the relevant section of its entry for this word? Or did the lexicographers instead intend the differentiated meaning given in the second part of the same section: 'Now also in a more restricted sense, applied to writing which has claim to consideration on the ground of beauty of form or emotional effect'?[84]

Almost certainly the former, although the easy slippage between the two possible senses is significant, since it allowed a welcome route to confining the range of possible sources and making the project look more intellectually respectable: a precious vessel storing the utterances of the great and the good (Derwent Coleridge's sifted 'ore') rather than a garbage bag for the uneducated diction of the 'newly literate' (Hucks Gibbs's 'rubbish'). In the words of Henry Reeve, editor of the *Edinburgh Review*, and one of the objectors to the new Dictionary's excessive hospitality to culturally unrefined sources, 'the prime duty and glory of literature is to be the storehouse and guardian of knowledge. There are thousands of readers who quench their thirst for novelty with the trifles and ephemeral productions of the hour [i.e. newspapers], which are but the surf on the edge of the rising tide; but they forget that the treasure-house of literature lies behind them.'[85]

The view that literature was in some sense the apotheosis of language was widely held. The influential American linguist William Dwight Whitney, in another series of lectures, urged the connection between the two: 'The great body of literary works of acknowledged merit and authority, in the midst of a people proud and fond of it, is an agent in the preservation and transmission of any tongue, the importance of which cannot be easily overestimated'; while one of *OED*'s early contributors, his fellow American G. P. Marsh, was clear that 'the importance of a permanent literature, of authoritative standards of expression, and, especially, of those great, lasting works of the imagination, which, in all highly-cultivated nations constitute the "*volumes paramount*" of their literature, has been too generally appreciated to require . . . argument or illustration'.[86] This takes us straight back to the connection between language – now seen as literature – and culture. It is literature, clearly, which has first claim to be preserved in a nation's Dictionary.

In this intellectual and cultural climate, the statement on the first page of the first volume of *OED*, published in 1888, that 'all the great English writers of all ages' were the first port of call for quotations, seemed perfectly natural, as did Craigie and Onions's reference, decades later, to the bibliography of sources quoted in *OED* as a 'guide to English literature'.[87] It is true that the lists of books and appeals issued and reissued over the next few years by the early lexicographers, now preserved in the *OED* archives, also record many titles from an impressive array of non-literary fields – not just theological, historical and philosophical, which might be thought to have literary claims, but also scientific, mathematical, technological, commercial, sporting, and those relating to arts and crafts of various sorts. Nevertheless, the aims and expectations of the lexicographers were in general directed at literary sources, as can be seen by their instructions to readers on nineteenth-century works. Contributors were asked to analyse carefully 'the works of any of the principal writers, extracting all remarkable words, and all passages which contain definitions or explanations . . . Wordsworth, Scott, Coleridge, Southey, Tennyson, Ruskin, Macaulay, and Froude may be mentioned as pre-eminently important'.[88] This list of names directs prospective volunteers to sources then commonly recognized by the educated classes, without defensiveness, embarrassment or anxiety, as canonical – not just for English literature, but for the English language in its entirety. No doubt they were also to the taste of the readers who were economically and intellectually in a position to be able to offer their services: men and women with sufficient income to have the time on their hands to do the reading, and sufficient education to be able to accomplish their task satisfactorily.[89]

The lists also make it clear that writers who use language in markedly idiosyncratic ways were not to be excluded. In the extract just quoted, Walter Scott is the egregious example. He turned out to be the second most cited writer in the *OED* after Shakespeare, for a strikingly varied range of words – dialect and regional usages (*cailleach*, *dinmont*), revivals from Middle English and Scots, where Scott is the only example cited for two centuries or so (e.g. *bruckle*, *dindle*), as well as archaisms (*dern*), learned or facetious *hapax legomena* (*ambagitory*) and nonce-words (*debind*), together with hosts of more 'ordinary' usages.[90] Another much-quoted nineteenth-century author, of notable linguistic eccentricity, was Carlyle, whose 5,000-odd citations liberally illustrate (as Bradley put it in 1904) 'an almost unexampled abundance of new compounds and derivatives, largely formed in imitation of German' – especially when he was translating from this language – of which 'comparatively few ... have won general acceptance' in English.[91]

Do these instructions for the original readers, and the sorts of sources that were read for the Dictionary, mean that, as Dennis Taylor has observed, 'the *OED*'s reliance on literary quotations is problematic because it skews the representative character of the sampling'?[92] The answer is unmistakably yes. The source studies now enabled by electronic searching of the *OED* confirm time and again that the language of canonical 'great writers' is given vastly more attention than that of other users. This can be plainly seen in illustration 8. Further investigation reveals that Victorian (and Edwardian) literary and cultural tastes particularly predominated: so the eighteenth century, a period not then regarded as literarily pre-eminent, is cited less than the centuries either side; William Blake received far fewer quotations than (say) Keats; female authors, even prolific ones, were cited in tiny quantities compared with male authors; and novels tended to be under-valued as quotation sources (a negative preference further militating against quotation from female authors, since so many novels were written – and read – by women).[93] As Jürgen Schäfer, the first quantitative investigator of

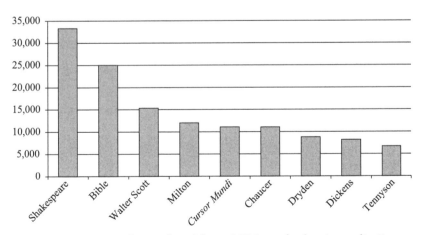

8. Top Sources in *OED* (data gathered from *OED2*; see further Appendix 1).

the *OED*, remarked in 1980, 'the *OED* was clearly conceived as an aid to reading great literature, a fact which has proved a boon for the literary scholar' (we should add, 'canonical' literary scholar). However, as he also pointed out, for the linguist, 'this policy leads to distortion and makes it necessary . . . to approach the *OED* with caution'.[94] The question is, were these writers – Shakespeare, Milton, Chaucer, Dryden, Dickens and Tennyson – the giants that most contributed to the English language, as written and spoken by men and women both yesterday and today? Or were they the sources most favoured, for a variety of reasons, by the lexicographers?

The role of the *OED* as 'treasure-house' is something that the Press has delighted in publicly embracing. In announcing the completion of the first edition in 1928, it claimed, 'it is a Dictionary not of our English, but of all English: the English of Chaucer, of the Bible, and of Shakespeare is unfolded in it with the same wealth of illustration as is devoted to the most modern authors'.[95] In one of the publicity brochures released for the second edition of 1989, the Press reproduced a series of small portraits of twelve sources for the *OED*, calling them, rather fancifully, '"Contributors" to the *OED*': Chaucer and Shakespeare, John Locke and John Wesley; Johnson and Noah Webster – these apparently included on account of their dictionaries' influence on *OED*; Austen, Charles Darwin, Mark Twain, Thomas Hardy, Virginia Woolf, James Joyce.[96] Evidently, none of these writers actively contributed; they are merely cited – in very varying proportions (around 33,300 times for Shakespeare; 227 for Woolf) – by the lexicographers; although Hardy certainly used and read the *OED*, and possibly James Joyce too (Woolf's direct use of *OED*, if it occurred, has yet to be demonstrated; she mentions only the *Concise Oxford Dictionary*).[97] Over the page, the brochure states that the *OED* is 'at once a history of thought and of our civilization'; it is 'the supreme treasure-house of the riches of the English language'. But whose 'thought', and whose 'civilization'? As with Johnson's dictionary, the *OED*'s treasures, in the form of quotation sources, were selected according to certain culturally determined tastes and values. It is a partial record, though none the less valuable, and loved by its readers, for that.

Burchfield enormously increased quotations from scientific, technical and non-literary sources in the *OED*, as we see in Chapters VI and VII below. But he still believed that recording the language of great writers was central to the Dictionary's character, and quoted liberally from writers he identified as such. This legacy of pervasive quotation from literary sources is a tricky one for the current *OED* lexicographers, engaged on the third edition, to deal with. While they will not wish to renege on this most cherished aspect of their Dictionary, it is not obviously consonant with their aim to present an impartial linguistic record (so far as such a thing is possible) of past and present usage. It is too early to be sure, as yet, what form their policy will take. They have expanded their range of sources even further than Burchfield, as we shall see in Chapter VIII; nevertheless citation from certain literary authors (e.g. Dryden and Dickens, heavily quoted in *OED1*, but also Virginia Woolf) has significantly increased rather than declined.

Quotations: 'the raw material of the Dictionary'

It is difficult to overestimate the importance for the *OED* of its quotation sources. Craigie's later pupil, A. J. Aitken (who succeeded him as editor of *DOST*), described their analysis as 'the heart of the lexicographical process', and certainly the lexicographers understood that the accumulation and scrutiny of so vast a quantity of data was the chief element that had enabled them to make their great evolutionary step forward in lexicography (see p. 109 above).[98] As Craigie and Onions wrote in their Preface to the Dictionary's 'Re-issue' of 1933, *OED*'s 'basis is a collection of some five million excerpts from English literature of every period', forming 'the only possible foundation for the historical treatment of every word and idiom which is the *raison d'être* of the work. It is a fact everywhere recognized that the consistent pursuit of this evidence has worked a revolution in the art of lexicography'. Quotations constitute the 'raw material' of the Dictionary (the phrase is often used by the editors), as it was from this primary evidence that the definitions were divined and constructed.

This is made clear by the several accounts that exist of the way the *OED* was (and still is) created, all of which emphasize the crucial significance of the provenance and selection of its sources. As Onions described in 1928, once readers had worked through thousands of texts and excerpted quotations from them illustrating how words had been used in varying senses, the editors and sub-editors studied the quotations intensively so as to arrive at an analysis of their historical and semantic relationship. 'Careful and repeated reading' of the quotations would then bring 'to [the editor's] mind definitions of senses, some well known to him, others unknown or unthought of but for the evidence now furnished by numerous examples of actual use'.[99] He would turn to other dictionaries at this stage – 'Dr. Johnson, the various editions of Webster, and the most recent supplements – gladly availing himself of any help or hint they offer in the wording of a definition, or in the record of new senses'. But 'full as the already collected material is', the editor would realize that there were gaps and absences in it, and would undertake further searches to supply these deficiencies – it was here that the 'drift to Bodley', so irritating to the publishers, would suggest itself as a welcome solution (p. 40 above). Such quests, Onions tells us, had 'always been a serious charge on the energies of the staff'.[100] He also explains that 'much of the toil of sifting and collecting fresh material consists in the examination of the Old English and Middle English dictionaries, the glossaries to early texts, and the concordances to the Bible, Shakespeare, and other poets'. Naturally, the writers for which such aids were available were the major canonical ones (already, therefore, heavily excerpted by readers and likely to be cited in the Dictionary): Shakespeare, Milton, Chaucer, Pope, Cowper, Walter Scott, Tennyson.[101] The question to what extent the editors' expectations and intuition guided, and perhaps determined, their additional and supplementary findings has yet to be properly investigated – as have also their grounds for deciding which quotations to print. Murray told the Philological Society in 1890 that the ruthless culling of quotations was 'a sorrowful necessity', required so as to keep the Dictionary's size in check. But 'as the quotations are the essence of the work, it is like shearing Samson's locks.'[102]

Murray vividly portrayed the struggles involved in wrestling with the quotations in order to elicit meanings from these examples of real usage and to clarify the connections between them. In so doing he reveals the central role played by the quotations in the creation of the OED's picture of 'thought' and 'civilization':

> Only those who have made the experiment, know the bewilderment with which editor or sub-editor, after he has apportioned the quotations for such a word as *above, against, account, allow, and, as, assize*, or *at* among

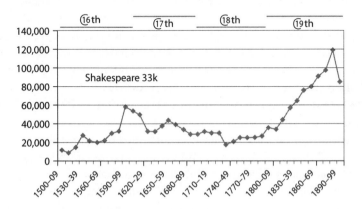

9. Quotation numbers per decade in OED (data gathered from OED2; see further Appendix 1).

20, 30 or 40 groups, and furnished each of these with a provisional definition, spreads them out on a table or on a floor, where he can obtain a
general survey of the whole, and spends hour after hour in shifting them
about like the pieces on a chess-board, striving to find in the fragmentary
evidence of an incomplete historical record, such a sequence of meanings
as may form a logical chain of development.[103]

These 'sequence[s] of meanings', together with etymologies, pronunciations
and other material were recorded on 'topslips'; appropriately arranged and
marked-up bundles of slips were then sent to the printer for the initial stages
of proof production.[104]

Quotations are therefore the bedrock of the lexicographical enterprise.
What goes in determines what comes out. Quotations dictate the definitions
that the lexicographers find and the picture of language that their
Dictionary paints. This means that when we examine the variations in the
OED's coverage of different authors and periods we must ask ourselves
whether such variations tell us about the English language itself, or about
the lexicographers and the material available to them. Illustration 8 lists
OED's favourite sources, and illustration 9 presents the *OED*'s recording of
vocabulary, in the form of quotations, decade by decade from 1500 to 1899.
To what extent is the remarkable expansion of vocabulary apparent at the
end of the sixteenth century due to the lexicographers' particular enthusiasm for Shakespeare? Or the relative dip in the documentation of the eighteenth century to the failure of the American readers to deliver the slips they
had promised, entrusted to them because it was believed British volunteers
would not enjoy reading eighteenth-century works (see further pp. 234 ff.)?
Is it really credible that these characteristics of *OED* documentation illustrate the variable ways in which the language has developed, so that, as the
Essex correspondent suggested, 'the dictionary's breadth of view' could be
in some way thought of as 'commensurate with reality'? It seems far more
likely that they are the result of the vicissitudes to which *OED* lexicography
was necessarily subject.[105] This means that one of the most important
things that *OED3* can do, as it develops its lexicographic policies and practice in the early decades of the twenty-first century, is to define and identify
both its quotation sources and its criteria for choosing them.

Coda

The features discussed in this chapter do not detract from the *OED*'s greatness as a dictionary. It is a literally incomparable record of English, essential to all scholarly study of the language, and a source of apparently

limitless pleasure to its readers. It is also the product of virtually unimaginable labour, endurance and resolve on the part of its editors and its contributors – and, to a much greater extent than is sometimes acknowledged, its publishers. Inevitably it had its imperfections and failings: no dictionary's 'breadth of view' can ever be 'commensurate with reality' (however defined); on the contrary, a dictionary creates as well as reflects the linguistic universe it records. In the 1950s, Oxford University Press decided that revision of the Dictionary remained out of the question but that further supplementation did not, and in 1957 it charged the next editor, R. W. Burchfield, with this weighty task. Burchfield strove to widen the range of sources, but at the same time to maintain *OED*'s role as what he called 'a literary instrument', one which was to illuminate the major aesthetic writings of the day. He opened up geographical boundaries, hoping to embrace 'World English', but found it impossible to record this consistently. He was determined to shuffle off 'Victorian prudishness', but also chose to act as an arbiter of good usage. He extended his admirably courageous policy on lexicographical descriptiveness to racist and other sorts of offensive usage, setting new standards for the *OED* but once more falling short of consistency. In these various ways, he carried forward many characteristics of the existing work. On the one hand, his second Supplement presented, albeit on a much smaller scale, an overwhelmingly comprehensive collection of words in English, compiled with thoroughness and scientifically disinterested objectivity. But on the other hand, the second Supplement was the product of discrimination and selection, favouring some sources at the expense of others as hunting grounds for its word-searches, and delivering (on a small proportion of its entries) opinions at odds with the demands of purely descriptive lexicography. We look at Burchfield's dictionary in some detail in Chapter VII, and in Chapter VIII we preliminarily review the reworking of the entire *OED* for its third edition, released from 2000 onwards. Meanwhile, in Chapter V, we return to the history of the *OED* in the 1940s and 1950s.

V

Supplementation or Revision?

Continuing collections

As we saw at the end of Chapter III, Wyllie was dismissed from the Press after his final explosion in 1954. One of the consequences of the disarray, distress and embarrassment in which he left Dictionary matters was a form of institutional amnesia. It was not until the early 1980s that *OED* editorial staff – with an entirely new version of the Dictionary in prospect – began the process of systematically sorting through the material he had stored away in the 'OED Collections', subsequently dispersed into different parts of the *OED* archive.[1] By then, the conventional account of *OED* lexicography between 1933 and 1957, when Burchfield was appointed to undertake a second Supplement, was that it had wholly ceased. But the documents themselves provide ample evidence of continuing collection, not enforced stoppage. Not only Wyllie and Sisam, but also Craigie and Onions, and even Chapman himself, pursued historical and current lexical research over this period, storing away notes in preparation for the revision of *OED* they all believed would have to be undertaken at some stage in the future, despite Chapman's professed inability in the 1930s to contemplate it at any near date.

In particular, Craigie found it impossible to relinquish his long-ingrained habit of word-gathering. In 1936, aged 69, he resigned his chair from Chicago and settled at Christmas Common in Watlington, in the Chiltern Hills just outside Oxford. He was now mostly occupied with his American and Scottish dictionaries, but he was held up for a period by the war, and the difficulty of posting valuable material back and forth between England and the US.[2] From 1941 onwards he was in desultory correspondence with Sisam over materials both for a revision of the standard but out-of-print Icelandic dictionary, that of Cleasby and Vigfusson, 1874 (which Oxford republished in 1957 with Craigie's 'Supplement'), and for a further *OED*

Supplement, which he seems to have been almost involuntarily compiling while engaged on his other linguistic researches.[3]

He dropped in on Sisam, not a wholly welcome visitor, on 25 June 1941 to ask, as Sisam recorded in a note for the files, 'Would we pay him a sum to put all his collections for supplementing <u>O.E.D.</u> into shape?' Sisam told him that 'the Delegates would not commit themselves to a supplement, but would, I thought, be glad to buy his collection so that he could afford the time this winter to put it into shape. Clearly, he knows exactly what is in the Dictionary, and has considerable improvements from his American dictionary.' When asked also about Craigie's proposed Icelandic materials, Sisam replied that he had 'general sympathy with the proposals <u>after the war</u>. I had to hurry him away, having several callers waiting.'[4] But Craigie would not let up. On 21 August 1941 he wrote to say, 'I have much in hand, and before long I shall show you how I propose to prepare this for another supplement in such a way that it could be printed at any time without further editing.' At this, attracted perhaps by the claim of efficiency, Sisam bit. Wyllie was away at Bletchley Park and there was no knowing how long war would last or in what state he would return. And of all the lexicographers, Craigie had always been the most organized and productive. He replied on 28 August to say, 'I should be glad to hear more about your plan of campaign. I suppose you would give six months to it?'

In October Craigie sent in a three-page plan for 'O.E.D. Supplement 2', explaining that its purpose was first 'to make more complete' the *OED*'s record of 'such words, compounds, collocations, and phrases as have been current at any time since 1600', especially those of the modern period, and secondly to bring the Dictionary up to date by adding similar terms not yet recorded.[5] He developed these ideas further in a tract published that year for the Society for Pure English (a series established by Robert Bridges and printed by OUP), called 'Completing the Record of English', where his particular interest in 'compounds, collocations and phrases' clearly appears.[6] His past co-editor Murray had been impatient with recording these forms, regarding them in many instances as examples of English syntax rather than lexis (given that they relied on word order to express 'the genitive relation', or possession).[7] But Craigie was accumulating impressive lists of examples where the *OED* record was deficient in this respect, a good number from the writings of Swift and other authors of the eighteenth century (a period neglected by the original editors): for example *book-buyer*, ante-dated from *OED*'s first citation of 1862 to 1708; *summer-boots*, post-dated from *OED*'s last cited date of 1530 to *c.* 1720; and *market-price*, for which Craigie had found a quotation of 1731 to fill *OED*'s gap between 1601 and 1880 (all these examples from Swift).[8]

By February 1942, Craigie was further augmenting and arranging his collections of new *OED* material as well as trying to process contributions sent him by an enthusiastic volunteer, St Vincent Troubridge (1895–1963). Troubridge's passions were engaged particularly by theatrical work, and Craigie was struck by the number of useful quotations he had managed to find, from play scripts, 'for earlier instances of common phrases [in the language]. It is surprising how much has still to be done in this line . . .' (he instanced the term 'seed potatoes', mentioned but not illustrated in the *OED*, for which he himself had just found two quotations of 1742).[9] In September of that year, despite the problems of petrol rationing and public transport, which made trips to Oxford difficult, and the worry of his wife's illness, he was 'going on, as time permits, with the supplementary material to the O.E.D., and Troubridge continues to send me fresh contributions almost every day'. It is clear from a casual reference by Sisam (who lived on Boars Hill, outside Oxford) to 'wrestling through various channels with the wooden petroleum officer at Reading, so that I may get to work as the buses become impossible', that each was affected on a day-to-day basis by national and international events, but these letters contain no other references to war and its tragedies or discomforts.[10] Both writers are more interested in discussing the alliterative revival of the fourteenth century, on which Craigie was planning to give a lecture to the British Academy the following month, than in either war or new words.[11] In March 1943 Craigie wrote to Sisam (now Secretary to the Delegates, having succeeded to this post following Chapman's retirement in 1942) to say that Chicago was 'bent on finishing the Dict. of Amer. English by July 1', that he was committed to producing copy for the 'Old Scottish Dict' (*DOST*) up to the end of September, but that until further funding was secured for this dictionary (from the Carnegie Trust, he hoped) he proposed to 'devote some months to the supplementary material for the O.E.D.', which he wanted 'to clear off as soon as possible'. In June, Sisam told him he was 'anxious that you should get your material into shape'.[12]

Onions, too, could not altogether abandon the daily occupation of so many years. In August 1943 Sisam heard not from Onions himself but from another Press author, J. B. Leishman (author of *The Metaphysical Poets*, published by OUP that year, and translator of Rilke), that he was preparing a list of corrections for *OED*. Sisam thought this 'a super-human task if he went beyond what he happened to have noted in his copy', and urged Leishman to call on Onions and go through with him the 'philological commentary' Leishman himself had prepared on some new words and phrases. Onions (then aged 70) had 'a great deal on hand what with [the periodical] *Medium Aevum*, a large etymological dictionary he is doing for us, some other literary projects, and his teaching here; but he has a remark-ably quick eye for new words and senses'.[13]

Craigie continued to work away in the intervals of his other employment. By 17 January 1945, as he wrote to Sisam, he had 'taken stock of the supple-mentary material for the O.E.D. which I now have in hand', and estimated there were altogether 13,000 slips by him and 4,000 by Troubridge. Perhaps, he suggested, the latter could be put into appropriate shape by the former OED staff member W. J. Lewis, one of Sisam's 'old soldiers' who had joined the dictionary in 1889; meanwhile there were more to come from his work on the Scottish and American dictionaries. Rather than wait for publication at some later uncertain date in a general Supplement, he thought, it might be worth issuing it as a separate publication now, perhaps as 'Addenda to the Oxford English Dictionary, by . . . .'

Craigie's enthusiasm for the OED work is partly explained by his enforced stoppage on DOST. As paper stocks ran low, printing had to slow down. Sisam wrote back the next day to say the same problem would affect any new OED Supplement. The printing even of 'most important books' was now being rationed, so that the Concise Oxford Dictionary, for example, was now 'priced up to 25s second hand'. At the end of the year, Sisam thought, 'C.O.D. or P.O.D. or both will disappear . . . For that reason, it isn't likely that we could give print and paper in the near future to a part-supplement.'[14] Nevertheless, Sisam encouraged Craigie to 'make the selec-tion and give it the shape you think suitable with the reasonable prospect that practically all of it will be published in the form you gave it as soon as we can deal with another supplement'. He thought they might be able to 'add more to it, e.g. from the collections for the Oxford Dictionary of Modern English [as the former Quarto was now called], which McIntosh is completing at Exmouth, or from Onions's collections, which he may be able to put into shape when he gets rid of one or two urgent commitments for us'. And the following year, in May 1946, he took up Craigie's suggestion that Lewis, then aged 78, should prepare Troubridge's cards for printing, engaging him at £2 a week for six months. (Craigie sent them to him, but with insufficient instructions. L. F. Powell wrote on 7 June 1946 to say that Lewis was in 'a pretty poor way', and 'is worried over some Dictionary material, supplementary so I gather, which you have sent him, & doesn't know what to do with it'. Lewis picked up, reporting on 28 October 1946 that he was waiting to hear Craigie's comments on the letter A and was meantime getting on with later letters.)[15]

Almost two and a half years later, in October 1948, another former OED contributor, the Revd H. E. G. Rope of Shrewsbury (1880–1978), who had been a member of the Dictionary staff in 1903–5, 1908–10, and a contributor to the 1933 Supplement, sent Sisam a bundle of new slips with 'a good many earlier, late, and additional items' to add to those already in *OED*. He had another collection in Rome, he said, which he might also be able to send, although he knew that 'the appearance of a second Supplt. is problematic and I suppose unpredictable in these crazy times'. Sisam replied straight away to say, 'I only hope that the time is not too distant when we shall be able to take advantage of them' and to encourage him to send more. This was the first of a number of such bundles, eventually to be gratefully trawled by Burchfield, along with the collections of Troubridge and Chapman, another devoted recorder of addenda and corrigenda for *OED*. (Burchfield later reported that Rope's quotations were 'mostly written on the backs of envelopes or any scrap of paper that conveniently lay to hand', and that each of these three men assembled 'several thousand quotations' in all. Although much of this material was designed for revision of the first edition of the Dictionary, a proportion was useful for his Supplement.)[16]

Public interest was again kindled by the article on Wyllie, now engaged on the *Oxford Latin Dictionary*, which appeared in *The Times* on 10 January 1949, in which were mentioned the 'number of new words and new meanings of old words he gleaned in the columns of the paper', in ways that whetted appetite for more (pp. 84–5 above). Answering a consequent inquiry, the new Assistant Secretary to the Delegates, Dan Davin (who after Sisam's retirement in 1948 took over responsibility for the Press's dictionaries), wrote in June that year to say,

> We have not as yet any fixed plan for a revision of the <u>Oxford English Dictionary</u> because it is difficult to decide whether a further supplementary volume is a satisfactory solution. Ideally, of course, a new and corrected edition of the whole is what should be produced. But this would be such a large undertaking both from an editorial and a production point of view that it is doubtful whether it is practicable in these times. Meanwhile, pending a decision, we go on collecting material as it is offered; though we have no machinery specifically designed for this collection. All this has the consequence that I am unable to give you a date of the kind you ask for.[17]

In August 1951 came new material from Rope, and in October 1951 from Craigie, the latter glad to arrange with Davin to 'clear my shelf by sending it to you'. Although he knew that Davin was 'probably not contemplating any immediate work in preparation for the new Supplement to the O.E.D.', he discusses what Supplement policy should be: the year 1600 'ought to be the back limit, if older material than the 19th c. is to be included at all'.

Earlier material would be handled by specialist publications such as Kurath's *Middle English Dictionary* (whose first fascicle was in 1951 being prepared for imminent publication). Davin wrote back to agree, welcoming the slips but making it absolutely clear that 'we have no immediate plans for the supplement'.[18]

Decision: Sisam's 'weighty memorandum'

But by May 1952, the publishers' views had changed. There seem to have been two main reasons for this. One was that the failure to update the *OED* was appearing increasingly anomalous. As Chapman had put it in 1946, 'The Oxford Press has been indeed embarrassed by the abundance of its riches: famine in the midst of plenty.' He meant that the original *OED* had stood still since 1933, while its dependent offshoots – the *Shorter*, the *Concise*, the *Pocket* and the *Little* – had proliferated in a succession of reprintings and new editions. Chapman was writing in the *TLS*, reviewing favourably – and anonymously – Onions's third edition, with addenda, of the *Shorter*, along with a rival to the Oxford dictionaries, the 1946 *Odham's Dictionary of the English Language*.[19] This latter dictionary, co-edited by the former Oxford lexicographer J. L. N. O'Loughlin (trained by Onions, as we saw in Chapter II), was a direct competitor to the *Concise*. It was becoming increasingly unrealistic for the subsidiary dictionaries to prosper in the absence of a nourishing source. While they did their best to register what Chapman called 'an Elizabethan riot of verbal invention' inspired by the war, with its proliferation of new vocabulary, it was extraordinarily difficult for dictionaries composed almost on the run to keep up with (in Chapman's words again, using terms notorious from the 1933 Supplement) 'this riproarious macédoine'.

This factor – the need to update the *OED* in order to breathe new life into the lesser dictionaries, or run the risk of the derivative dictionaries egregiously outstripping their parent source, as their editors quite properly kept up with new words and usages – was brought into sharp focus by the second main reason the publishers had to rethink the question of revision. Stocks of the 1933 reprint of *OED* along with the Supplement were running dangerously low. Chapman had originally arranged for 10,000 copies to be reprinted in 1933. When war broke out, 6,000 sheets remained ('it was thought that if the worst came to the worst they would make an excellent air-raid shelter'),[20] but by 1954 this number had fallen to below 3,000. Sales over the last few years had averaged at 400–500 per annum, which meant that existing copies would be exhausted by 1962.[21] Within a few years, therefore, the publishers would have to undertake the massive and expensive job of reprinting. But it would scarcely be feasible to market and sell a dictionary that would at that date be nearly thirty years old. Should the Press undertake a wholesale revision of the original work? Or supplement the 1933 Supplement?

In favour of the first plan was the knowledge, increasingly borne in on them as time went on, that the first *OED* had many defects: or as Onions put it to them in March 1951, 'hosts of wrong definitions, wrong datings, and wrong crossreferences. The problem is gigantic.'[22] Of all the people connected with *OED*, Onions was uniquely well placed to make this judgement. From 1897 to 1933 he had worked first on the first *OED* and then on its Supplement; now he was working through it all over again in order to revise the *Shorter*, an extraction of the most important current and historical words and phrases from the parent Dictionary. But in favour of the second plan was the knowledge that undertaking a revision on the scale required would require the Press to expend quite phenomenal quantities of time, labour and money. The dilemma exercised them considerably for several years, and it was not until 1954 that they finally made up their minds.

The decisive element in the case was the 'very important and weighty' memorandum (as A. L. P. Norrington, the new Secretary to the Delegates, described it) which Sisam produced, from retirement in the Scilly Isles, when asked for his opinion in September 1952. Sisam had surrendered his guardianship of OUP only four years previously, in 1948, and was now regarded as an *éminence grise*. Fiercely loyal to the Press, his intellectual acuity and capacity for incisive judgement were informed by decades of institutional experience. His sense of the immense financial and personal costs of the original *OED* was no doubt burnt into him, and he seems never to have seriously contemplated a complete revision of the Dictionary. His solution to the dilemma facing the Press – however lexicographically pusillanimous it may appear to us now – was driven by essentially prudential considerations of time and cost, in particular the need to maximize the value of all the Press's dictionary resources (the smaller dictionaries as well as the *OED*), and to fend off any possibility of taking on the major editorial burden, extending into unknown years, that the Press had borne in the past. Whatever the requirements of the *OED* now (or indeed of the English language itself), the economic interests of the Press had to prevail, so Sisam felt, over any pursuit of lexicographical perfection, something he anyway regarded as dangerously chimerical. In the uncertainty of the post-war years, with the mental stability of *OED*'s chief potential lexicographer (Wyllie) in question, caution was preferable to courage.

In a series of typed pages carefully preserved in the *OED* files, Sisam set out his diagnosis of Oxford lexicography's current predicament together

10. Kenneth Sisam in retirement in St Mary's, Isles of Scilly, 1959.

with his strategy for the future. Since the Supplement had been published in 1933, he observed, 'all the Dictionaries' – he meant the *Shorter, Concise, Pocket* and *Little* – 'have been maintained at incredibly low cost. As long as you can rub along in this way, profitability is at a maximum'; provided that the Press did not sell their stocks at a lower price than it would cost to replace them. This 'very economical system of renovation involves some running down in quality', he acknowledged, but this was not 'easily percep-tible to customers, and is probably less than the average deterioration of competitors'. While these rivals to Oxford dictionaries 'gain spasmodically by a rare competent revision', none except Webster (the highly successful American dictionaries published under the imprint Merriam-Webster) had a 'good . . . system of continuous revision'. Meanwhile, 'our lesser dictionaries owe their start in quality to high-class editing of the materials presented in O.E.D.' To improve this, Sisam thought, the Press would need a new stream of *OED*-type material issuing from some central source in the Press, which would assemble quotations for new words and usages from 1930 onwards and would require 'one editor with scholarship and initiative as well as industry'. However, 'there is none available within the business [Sisam means that none of the rival publishing houses had candidates strong enough to be worth luring away], and a good man will have to be paid with some regard to modern salary levels'.

Sisam was insistent that the project should have clear and narrow limits: 'I have in mind a Supplement of new words, important new meanings, and phrases – not corrections to O.E.D. proper,' he wrote. When completed, 'it would be fused together into one alphabet with the existing O.E.D. Supplement'. The Press would have to reckon on a first reprinting of *OED* without this new addition, in say 10–15 years' time; meanwhile, 'discreet preparations', not 'urgent or easy to accomplish', should begin straight away. Given that the most important function of a new Supplement was that it would feed efficiently and profitably into all the Oxford English dictionaries (it was evident, by now, that the former Quarto dictionary was not performing this role as Chapman had hoped in 1933), the material for the new Supplement, '<u>as it came in</u>, would be used for revision of the lesser dictionaries, so that they would have sucked it dry before it appeared in print as a quarry for competitors'. This implied the need for 'one supervisory editor . . . at a fairly early stage' who was to be in charge of all the Oxford dictionaries. The Press should fix a scale for the project – i.e., limits on the size and length of the Supplement, which 'the editor will tend to exceed'. 'Assuming 1965 as a possible finishing date', Sisam guessed that there should be '400 pages of new matter – certainly not more in the plan; and the proportion of each letter should be roughly calculable (not, of course, by reference to existing Supplement, which is wedge-shaped.)'[23]

'In mitigation of a big task', Sisam pointed out, all major editorial and compilatory issues had already been settled. The *OED*'s present style and form had proved its worth and need not be changed, and there would be no new articles like those for *of* and *set* (*set*, notoriously, was the longest entry in the Dictionary), and no old words of uncertain meaning.[24] Instead, there would be a high proportion of hard words (easier to define and illustrate than common, more indeterminate words) and 'the relaxed standards applicable to any short supplement which can be corrected if another supplement follows it'. Judicious control of both input (sources for new words and senses) and output (the eventual dictionary) was essential: 'Everything depends on good collections and a practical editor who will keep limits in a province which has few natural limits, and not be perfectionist in anything except performance in time.'

Outlining the main sources for the new Supplement, he divides them into scientific and technical words on the one hand, and on the other, 'general words and usages that are new developments'. Where the former were concerned, the Press should identify them with the help of other, specialist, dictionaries, but make sure that they had good examples of actual usage to illustrate their function and currency. Sisam suggested employing outside consultants (at £50 to £100 for a trial year in the first instance) to monitor areas such as maths, physics and medicine, while 'The Economist might be inspired to watch over Economics, Sociology, Politics, the R.H.S. over Horticulture, the B.B.C. over Wireless and Television; the Meteorological Office over its popular province'. He thought 'The Economist staff (which would be invaluable if willing to help) would probably not be greedy, if slips and such like out-of-pocket expenses were supplied.'

As for non-English English, Sisam reluctantly concedes that US words 'of a certain status and permanence must go in', even if they are not found in English authors, 'because so many American books are printed or current in England, and one must please the Americans'. The 'English speaking Dominions . . . must also be pleased by our dictionaries', he adds, cynically or realistically. He thinks 'the ideal would be that a discreet professor in each should put a good student on to a thesis on local new words, phrases and senses of good status conforming with the Supplement's leaflet of hints to readers. That would be enough . . .' and he warns, 'They are likely to want too many native names of plants and animals.'

It would be much more difficult to identify, select and get good quotations for quotidian vocabulary sources. 'The general words, senses or phrases, such as one might find in a Times leader, or good literary work are much less easy to distinguish define and illustrate: they may turn up anywhere and there is no obvious place in which to look for them. Here, if the job is to be done well, one must start with voluntary collectors, as was done for the original O.E.D. One could make a list of good or very well-known books from 1930–, hope to add to it as the work progressed, and try to find intelligent volunteers to read specified books and select anything they thought interesting. This would cover the ground best.'

But how should one come across and identify such volunteers, who would have to be sufficiently knowledgeable about OED not to repeat the material already covered there or in the first Supplement, and sufficiently dedicated to the Press and its purposes to commit time and energy without payment? Sisam looked to those already associated with the Press, in one capacity or another. 'I think first of people like Chapman, Costello . . . Butt, Horseman [*sic*], (not to speak of industrious women) who are conscientious and unlikely to be wild at first,' he said, listing names of academics who had recently published books with the Press, along with the still intellectually active Chapman, and R. C. Goffin, a long-term Press employee (soon to play a significant ancillary role in the creation of the new Supplement).[25] 'But the list would grow if you could kindle any enthusiasm for this great national and international work, and encourage those who showed aptitude as collectors. At a late stage one might ask for volunteers in T.L.S., R.E.S. [*Review of English Studies*], N.&Q. [*Notes & Queries*; both academic journals published by the Press]. The reward would be naming in the Preface.'

What as to method? 'Collectors or enquirers would need a leaflet of hints, including a specimen slip in facsimile (this was done for O.E.D. Supplement) . . . . they must be warned to avoid nonce-words, rare technical words . . . pure slang, dialect, transparent and unlimited kinds as negative in <u>un-</u>, or proper noun adjectives in <u>-ian, -an</u>.' This should be done as soon as possible, 'and Craigie and Onions, who know all the faults of voluntary readers, could advise on the draft'.

Sisam thought this ruthlessly restricted project could be started without an editor, with the Press making an initial outlay of a few hundred pounds a year. Once an editor (assumed to be male) was found – and the search should begin straight away – he would 'take over the collections and collectors, and begin the work of filling gaps, writing articles, and stirring the enthusiasm of readers to do at least a fraction of the work which the volunteer readers for O.E.D. did without any sure hope of a result'. The new editor would probably need no more than 'a clerk-typist at first', and then, later on, 'a young man who could be trained to succeed'. The important thing, once such an editor was appointed, was 'to settle a programme <u>in time</u> for the Supplement'. Then the Press could commit itself to an annual outlay of '£2000–£3000 a year for a defined period of editing and general supervision of dictionaries at the present value of money'.

The great virtue of this plan was that it would not commit the Press 'too heavily too soon', and that 'anything it produces will be useful'. Its weakness was that it would call for a good deal of personal supervision by the publishers themselves in the early stages. But 'there is much to be said for doing something while you still have the early experience of Craigie and Onions to fall back on . . . . A good editor with no collections would waste a lot of time. Craigie, the most productive dictionary editor, always had the smallest staff, seldom more than two under him; and Wyllie was the same in his most productive period. On O.E.D. Supplement we found that multiplying subordinate staff – then easily obtainable with good University training – had no effect whatever on production: they all became absorbed in timeless researches'.

Over the next few months the Press considered and debated this advice. They accepted Norrington's view, outlined in October 1952, that there was no point in 'trying to damp down sales of <u>O.E.D.</u>' Although the Dictionary would be expensive to reprint, delay would not reduce cost, and was 'repugnant to business common sense. Provided that we keep adjusting our selling price to current replacement costs,' Norrington thought, 'we need not be afraid of doing our duty.' The existing Supplement would have to be reprinted along with the main Dictionary when stocks ran out, around 1962, and at this point 'we shall have to show our hand; tell the world that we are engaged in a big new project, the addition of a volume to OED that will cover the 40 years since it was published (1928–?1970)'. His conclusion was that they could not therefore 'wait longer than 1962 (or whatever earlier date) before appointing and proclaiming an Editor'. He guessed, with admirable prescience, that the new Supplement might appear in 1972.[26]

But was a wholesale revision of the *OED* really out of the question? When the publishers brought their plans for the Supplement to the Delegates' meeting of July 1953, not everyone was convinced of this. Davin and Norrington were sent away to reconsider this issue, as well as to begin (or in fact, to continue) the search for a new editor for the Supplement, which it was agreed should be the priority: at this stage, the Delegates still 'hoped that Mr Wyllie will eventually take charge as editor of the revised Supplement' – while agreeing 'that this must not interfere with the completion by him of the Oxford Latin Dictionary'. Wyllie had by then spent some months in the Warneford and it still seemed possible he might recover. Meanwhile, they fastened on an interim caretaker, R. C. Goffin, who would begin the vast work of sorting through all the files constituting the 'O. E. D. collections' and putting their contents in order – 'in consultation with Mr Wyllie'. Once Goffin had made a preliminary assessment of their nature and quality, it would be possible to form a view on the question of whether the new Supplement should contain 'corrections of existing material in the main work, in addition to new words and senses'. All this was discussed in relation to the overarching priority, namely 'the general question of the maintenance of the Delegates' English dictionaries'. The heart of the whole enterprise must be set beating again. Consequently, the Delegates' minute records, 'the Secretary was instructed to consider plans for the establishment of a permanent staff and the training of a young lexicographer, and to report further'.[27]

Where supplementation, as opposed to revision, was concerned, the arguments Davin and Norrington were to return to the Delegates seemed unanswerable. They spent a further year discussing the question exhaustively with Craigie and Onions, with Sisam again, and between themselves. Although Onions later said that the decision to abandon plans for a revision was a 'grief' to him, all the others were firm, and he too had seen it at the time as the only way forward. In October 1953, Davin reported that Onions had 'expressed himself very strongly to the effect that it would be impossible to produce a supplement which gave an adequate treatment of all the errors in the main work. He thought that unless we strictly confined it to new words, senses and phrases we should get nothing done at all. He thought we would have in any case great difficulty in finding an editor competent to deal with it, failing Friedrichsen [on whom see p. 147 below] and Wyllie'. Craigie – still, despite his extreme age (87), regarded as a valuable counsellor – agreed in April the next year. 'To seek out and correct all the errors in the main text would be a huge task even if we had a fully-trained team of lexicographers immediately available.' Nevertheless, they should 'continue to collect revision material for the main work against the time when we might be in a position to issue another and different kind of supplement of corrections or even revise the main work'. Craigie confirmed the wisdom of getting Goffin to work straight away, knew of 'no young philologists we could rake in . . . and clearly did not feel any confidence that Wyllie would ever recover enough to take over'.[28]

A consensus gradually emerged, which more or less repeated the conclusions of Sisam's memorandum. It was impossible, at this stage, to revise the main Dictionary. The original *OED* had 'pre-eminent authority as an accurate picture of the language at the time of publication. Only revision comparable in quality to the original work is worth contemplating or would be judged adequate. And nothing less could justify the immense expense of resetting the longest lexicographical work in the world.' Such a project, they thought, would cost the Press something in the order of £1 million (taking into account the costs of setting up a new staff, the necessary years of editorial preparation, and the complete resetting required of the twelve volumes of the 1933 reissue). Another option, incorporating a selection of corrections into the existing *OED*, was impracticable. Given that 'our existing collection of corrections, though considerable, are merely those which various people have sent in at various times, and are unsystematic and fortuitous', such a policy would lead to inconsistencies and unevennesses.

Instead, what was needed was the addition to the Oxford record of new words and senses since the first Supplement had appeared. Collecting could start immediately, without prejudice to the question of who ultimately was to edit, so as to amass 'enough material for a supplement of new words, senses and phrases to be ready as an editorial basis in about 3–5 years'. And they could expect to spend, not £1 million, but perhaps £30,000 in the process. This meant, of course, that they would 'not be able in any foreseeable time to correct the main body of the dictionary'.[29]

The Delegates finally agreed to this proposal in 1954, though not without misgivings. In the words of their new Secretary, C. H. Roberts, the papyrologist (and former Delegate) who had that year left his academic studies to throw his lot single-mindedly into publishing, 'even a Supplement is a formidable enough undertaking; if I ever had any tendency to be light-hearted about dictionaries, reading the introduction to the last volume of O.E.D. has sobered me'.[30] But it was also agreed, as Craigie had advised in April 1954, that the Press would continue to collect and store information about words and usages relating to the period covered by the original OED, in the hope that, at some point in the future, this could feed into a full-scale revision.

The caretaker editor R. C. Goffin, determined on in July 1953, had already begun work (part-time) collecting words and quotations and sorting the OED revision material previously accumulated, following the lines set down by Sisam in his memo of September 1952. Employed for many years in the Press's India office, Goffin had also found time to publish several books (encompassing a wide range – the life and poems of the seventeenth-century poet William Cartwright, abridged versions of Chaucer's *Troilus and Criseyde*, Sabatin's *Scaramouche* and Wren's *Beau Geste*, notes on Indian words, and a couple of anthologies of radio broadcasts for English language learners). His signal virtue, apart from being a hard-working, methodical and reliable person, was that he would certainly have retired by the time the projected Supplement was completed. Consequently the Press would not then be faced with finding him further employment. Davin planned to find 'a room for him in Oxford' – at 40 Walton Crescent, as it turned out – and 'set up the machinery for collecting and organizing material, on lines followed with the original OED and with SOED'. 'Though not a lexicographer, he has had some experience in philology [the notes on Indian words, presumably, which had been published as an SPE tract] and some familiarity with our methods of work.' And crucially, he would have ready access to Craigie and Onions.[31]

In October 1955 the Delegates formally offered an interim post to Goffin. Davin had done his best to provide him with wisdom and advice and had set up a number of meetings for him with the experts: Onions and Craigie first and foremost, but a number of others too, including Professor Norman Davis of Glasgow University, the New Zealander whom Sisam was accustomed to consult on medieval and philological matters, and the editors of the languishing Quarto, now named Oxford Dictionary of Modern English, E. McIntosh of Exmouth (who was principally giving his time to successive editions of COD and POD), and C. T. Carr of St Andrews. Davin had also attempted to locate the papers that seemed to be missing from the past, spurred on in part by a 'tiresome request' from the general dictionary editor at Merriam-Webster in the US, who asked whether his company might acquire the OED slips. Davin thought this was a bad idea, since 'they would use the fact that they had the slips in order to boost themselves in competition with us'. However, 'this has raised the question of where the slips are. Onions says that there was a considerable collection of slips in the dictionary papers stored in the Bodleian and he thinks that most of these, if not all, would be contributions towards a full revision of the O.E.D. or Supplement. Do you happen to know anything of these or of the whereabouts of any other slips? I am reluctant to plunge into the vast back files.' No reply to this letter is preserved, although it indicates that the whereabouts and status of Wyllie's 'O.E.D. Collections' were now in question.[32]

By November 1955 it was possible to put some facts and figures together on the proposed new enterprise. As Sisam had suggested, the new Supplement, complete by perhaps 1965, was to be 400 pages of new matter, which, estimating 10 items a column, would give 12,000 new 'articles' (or entries).[33] 'Fused' with the 1933 Supplement (the latter corrected 'wherever possible'), it would come to about 1,278 pages; the editors were 'to work out a rough scale per letter as the work advances'. Its style and form were to be exactly the same as for the parent Dictionary, except that the 'lemmas' – the head words for each entry – were no longer to begin with a capital letter. The Press was also considering whether two former members of staff, Mrs Alden (who as Miss Savage had worked on the first edition of the Shorter with Onions in the late 1920s) and J. W. Birt (who had joined Onions's staff aged 16 in 1906), might be persuaded to help.[34]

The strategic role that this new dictionary was to play in the lives of the other Oxford dictionaries was carefully noted: 'a subsidiary function of the editor will be to see that new materials will be passed on, where useful, to the editors of the subordinate dictionary [the Shorter]'. At present, apparently, this task was regularly discharged by Davin, 'but a new method will probably have to be worked out in the light of experience as new sources of material begin to give results'. Reciprocally, the editors of both the Shorter and the other Oxford dictionaries were to send their words and quotations to Goffin in the central second Supplement office.[35] Davin thought that 'special attention should be paid to the prospect of a new edition' of the *Shorter* and that at some future stage they might decide to work on the two concurrently, perhaps with the same editor in charge. (This long-sighted proposition was to be fulfilled in 1993, when Leslie Burnett, a senior editor on Burchfield's staff, produced a fourth and entirely rewritten edition, the *New Shorter Oxford English Dictionary.*)

Where readers were concerned, the publishers decided at this stage to limit requests for help to their own personal contacts, and to defer public appeals till they could see 'what success can be got on a narrower front'. And it was judged best to postpone 'drawing up a list of important books since 1930 and assigning these to readers', since their 'experience with ODME [the Quarto] did not show this to be very successful'.[36] Instead, Davin thought, 'it would be better to go on looking out for suitable readers and let them read what they fancy'. A 'useful basis' for such reading, nevertheless, would be 'the new edition of *Annals of English Literature* which should be ready in a year or two'. The second edition of this compendious bibliography of literary works, revised by Chapman, duly appeared in 1961. Its identification as a foundation source of quotations for the new Supplement was a good indication of the importance that literature – in *OED*'s second sense of the word – was to continue to play in the Dictionary in the second half of the twentieth century.[37]

Search for a permanent editor

Meanwhile, the hunt for an editor proper had already begun. 'I do not expect Sisam to agree,' Norrington wrote to Davin on 7 October 1952, 'but I am convinced that Wyllie is the best choice for Editor. He is much the best definer – and indeed all-round lexicographer – that we know of, apart from the over-age Craigie and Onions. As it turned out, it was lamentable that he was ever involved in <u>Latin</u> lexicography, and the sooner he gets back to English the better.' Norrington conceded that the priority was completing the Latin dictionary but believed 'that the prospect of O.E.D. Supplement work and a start on printing O.L.D. will heave Wyllie along'. He thought it certain that 'the knowledge that someone else will edit O.E.D. Supplement, or an avoidance of a decision on this point, will ruin Wyllie, and probably ruin O.L.D., on which we have now spent, I guess, £50,000', an investment he had no intention of jeopardizing. Hoping that the Latin dictionary might be completed in five years, he suggested that they should seek out someone to 'organize operations' over that period 'in preparation for Wyllie's editorship'.[38]

The favoured candidate for this task was the etymologist G. W. S. Friedrichsen, whose experience stretched back to the time of Murray (on whose staff he had been employed from 1909 to 1914), and whom they had recently contacted in an unsuccessful attempt to persuade him to take over the ailing ODME (they had turned to C. T. Carr instead).[39] He was now working with the British Joint Services Mission in Washington, DC, but had collaborated with Onions on his *Dictionary of English Etymology* and had proofs for this at his elbow as he wrote back to Davin, as early as 26 May 1952, exploring whether they could provide a salary of around £2,740 to match what he was getting at the moment. He was evidently puzzled by the proposition being put to him, which at this stage involved the possible collaboration of the Press's former employee O'Loughlin (lately editor of the Odham's dictionary reviewed by Chapman in 1946, and also lecturer in English at Oxford and librarian of the faculty's English library), and on 2 June wrote again to say, 'I have no idea how a partnership with O'Loughlin would work, with me here in Washington. I do not even know what the new edition of two volumes, presumably, would mean. I am still waiting for some illumination from you.' Would the Supplement deal with corrections, he asked, or just additions? As an example of the need for the former he pointed out that 'if you look at the word HOWITZER [defined by Murray in an *OED* fascicle published 1899], you will see that this gun was "designed for horizontal fire with small charges": would that be dealt with in the Suppl.?' (In fact, this word – accurately defined in the *Concise Oxford Dictionary* in its first edition of 1911 – had been picked up by one of Murray's correspondents as early as 1913: 'I don't know who can have given you the definition,' Major John H. Leslie had written. 'Horizontal is the exact contrary. It is essentially a high-angle firing weapon, and would never, under any circumstances, be fired horizontally.' It escaped Burchfield's notice in the second Supplement, as it did Craigie and Onions's in the first, and remains as Murray left it both in the second edition of the *OED* in 1989 and in *OED Online* today).[40]

Once it was clear that Wyllie's mental health ruled him out altogether, the publishers for a long time hoped they might 'lure' Friedrichsen back on terms 'as attractive as possible'. But they also recognized that a man in his sixties was not the best choice for a project encompassing a decade and more, and while they were prepared to face a salary of the order of £2,000, they would not be in a position to compensate his American wife who might have to sacrifice her pension.

Casting around for younger men, they thought of O'Loughlin on his own – 'less able than Friedrichsen', Davin judged, and not highly rated by either Onions (who had trained him) or Sisam – and a number of university philologists.[41] They knew, however, that it was unlikely that candidates such as these could be tempted from their academic posts and that 'our chances of finding a young philologist are very slim'.[42] A despairing memo reads: 'It is clear that suitable young men will be difficult to find. Those of the right qualifications – always few – tend to be taken by the universities and they prefer the more leisurely work of a university teacher with its good vacations to the regular hours, and short vacations of the lexicographer.'

It was Sisam to whom Davin repeatedly returned for advice, although this was seldom cheering. 'Don't hope,' Sisam wrote on 10 July 1954, 'that by an apparatus of super-editors, committees, special staff, etc etc you will be relieved of the main worry, which is to see that the Supplement is published before it is obsolete.' And he stressed the crucial role that the publishers played in managing the lexicographers, thus ensuring timely and efficient production: 'only the office can oppose single-handedly the natural dilatoriness of lexicographers . . . . It is the exception for any huge dictionary to be finished', at the same time insisting that efficiency, diligence and dispatch were the cardinal virtues required for the task: 'it is a matter of hard work, common sense, some learning, and the best use of time, rather than of high lexicographical technique'.[43]

For a time it seemed that salvation might come in the form of Norman Davis (1913–89). Like Sisam before him, and also Davin (a fellow student at Otago University, with whom he shared his year of birth), Davis was a New Zealand Rhodes scholar. He arrived at Merton College, Oxford, in 1934, and developed into an organized and productive scholar of formidable intellectual power. He had spent the war acting as a spy for the British Government in eastern Europe (for which he was awarded an MBE in 1945), and then returned to the UK to take up a chair of English Language in Glasgow. Testimonials from a range of sources confirmed his scholarly aptitude, and he was moreover 'very sane', 'level-headed' and 'not easily rattled' (Onions's and Sisam's verdicts; delivered, presumably, with Wyllie's more volatile characteristics in mind).[44] In July 1954 Davis was reported to be considering proposals to 'come to Oxford and act as Editor of this project and other dictionaries subject to satisfactory financial proposals being made'. On 29 October 1954 the Delegates' minutes record that he is to be paid £2,500 per annum, but on 12 November 1954 they state that he had declined. A letter explains why:

The temptation is considerable, but in the end I conclude that I ought to resist it. Though I am very much interested in dictionary work I am not quite certain that I should find the daily grind at it an acceptable change from the greater freedom and variety of my present job . . . . I don't know whether I am right or not, and I may live to regret it; but 'No' it is, thank you very much.[45]

Davis was later to take up the Merton chair in Old and Middle English at Oxford and to act as adviser to the various subsequent stages of the Supplement.

So once again, the Secretary was 'instructed to see if a young scholar could be found who could be trained as a lexicographer at the Delegates' expense'. A year passed. Then in November 1955 they were relieved to be able to offer the job to another New Zealander, Alan (E. A.) Horsman (b. 1918), one of the academics Sisam had early identified as a possible volunteer contributor.[46] Horsman got straight to work, visiting the old lexicographers as had Goffin a year before him, and braving the elderly Onions's 'characteristic querulousness' in agreeing to undertake what Davin felt to be unfathomably obscure 'prep': looking up and comparing old pages of Supplement copy with the eventual printed product.[47] But another blow fell when Horsman was offered, and accepted, a chair of English in New Zealand, only months after taking up his post in Oxford.

When informed of this in an urgent appeal from Davin, Norman Davis suggested falling back on an earlier candidate. 'All things considered, I should vote for Burchfield,' he wrote on 3 November 1956. 'He is clearly not ideal, for he hasn't had much experience yet and still has his way to make in the academic world. But, as I have told you before, I have a high opinion of his practical good sense and punctual execution of whatever he takes on'.

R. W. Burchfield (1923–2004) was, by his own admission, yet another member of 'the New Zealand mafia'.[48] After serving in the New Zealand Artillery in Italy during the war, he took an MA with first-class honours at Victoria University College, Wellington. In 1949 he followed Sisam, Davin and Davis to Oxford with a Rhodes Scholarship, in his case held at Magdalen College, Oxford, where he read for a second BA in English and gained a second-class degree in 1951. He then embarked on a postgraduate degree and taught undergraduates in a variety of language subjects while holding lecturing jobs at Christ Church (to which he was appointed in 1953) and at St Peter's College.

At Magdalen he had become acquainted with Onions, and in 1955 had taken over from him as honorary secretary of the Early English Society (EETS) – the body set up by Furnivall in 1864 to publish scholarly editions of Old and Middle English works, partly to feed earlier examples of English usage into the OED. Davis said he was 'delighted' with the way in which Burchfield did his EETS job. 'There is no doubt that he is quite adequately equipped philologically, and I am sure he would soon pick up the specialist techniques – especially since he gets on well with CTO and could get some tips from him. Of course you know better than I do whether he wants it – I should suppose he would be glad of it, since I gather his House [Christ Church] post is likely to end soon.' Davis went on to apologize for being 'so barren of suggestions ... but after all we have been through the same process before and it isn't likely that anything new will emerge'. And the only other person he could now think of was 'one Macdonald at Newcastle ... but though he is knowledgeable and sensible he is also extremely dilatory and could not, I think, be trusted to press on as the job requires'.[49]

Dilatory was not an adjective that could be applied to Burchfield, and this was in Sisam's eyes the significant virtue. He wrote on 8 November 1956 to reassure Davin that Burchfield was 'well trained in philology, conscientious in his work, & as business-like as you could expect'. Sisam's experience of him was limited to the EETS (for whose press Sisam and his daughter Celia were then preparing an edition of the Salisbury Psalter, to appear in 1959). 'That he is promising as a lexicographer I cannot say: that is mostly a matter of natural aptitude (and all your candidates are equally unproved) and of training which, since Wyllie's aberration, you have nobody to give: he could learn a lot by studying definitions in the best part of O.E.D. itself.'

Sisam suggested that Burchfield be put to learn with Craigie, who has 'exactly the qualities and practical methods needed in a Supplement, as he proved when O.E.D. Suppl got bogged with a large & apparently well trained staff: nothing will get the work done without practical method .... Anyway I commend him as a possible success – no obvious reason why he shouldn't succeed.' Davin replied on 13 November to say, 'I think we shall have to take the chance on his becoming a lexicographer. It is unlikely we shall find anyone better.' Onions too approved, and thought Burchfield's lack of lexicographical experience no disadvantage, since he would share this characteristic with 'all the recruits to the staffs of the Oxford Dictionary whom I can remember being engaged during the last sixty years .... It is a craft by itself, and solvitur ambulando ['it is solved by walking', i.e. experience on the job].'[50] It seems clear that the decision had already been made, since by then they had asked Burchfield for a curriculum vitae ('a sheet of paper which will record your virtues rather than your vices'), and had settled on a salary. Burchfield had declared himself 'well satisfied' with £1,500 p.a. (significantly less than the sum of around £2,500 for which the Press had been bracing itself); the Dean of Christ Church was 'glad a suitable post had offered itself', and all that was left was for the Delegates to agree, which they did on 16 November 1956.[51]

Back in New Zealand, Burchfield's father was interviewed by his local newspaper: 'With a family of three children and work on the supplement ahead of him, there seemed little chance of his being able to return to New Zealand for a long time, said his father, Mr. F. Burchfield, Pitt Street, Wanganui, today.'[52]

The expected completion date for the new dictionary was put at 1967, when the Press hoped to publish both the first and second Supplements together, merged in a single volume. In fact, the second Supplement was to take twenty-nine years, and four volumes, to publish in full. But Burchfield's tenacity and steely-minded resolve were to make the task far less agonizing for his publishers than the first time round.

The vital importance of such qualities to the successful completion of a major dictionary was impressed upon the publishers only a few months later. On 1 August 1957, C. T. Carr finally pulled out of the ODME (Quarto) project in which Sisam and Chapman had earlier invested such hope, writing to Davin to say, 'I find I am so jaded by the work and nauseated by the thought of the messy part which still awaits revision that after much anxious thought and hesitation I have decided to tell you that I cannot continue. I know this will cause you embarrassment and trouble, but I fear there is no alternative. Lexicography gets one down after years of labour and I don't want to get myself in the same state as Wyllie. I am very conscious that I am letting you down.'[53] In 1958, Davin still hoped that when 'work on the new supplement to O.E.D. is well advanced', one of its editorial team, 'familiar with the new sources that become available in the course of preparing the new supplement', would turn their hand to the job. But by 1970 it was acknowledged that the end of the road had been reached for this dictionary. Boxes containing thousands of carefully filed papers and slips for the ODME, said by Davin to be four-fifths completed in 1957, were stored away in the *OED* archives (where they still survive), a solemn warning to the tiro editor of the new *OED* Supplement.[54]

VI

Burchfield's Supplement (1): Producing a Dictionary

First days at the office

Years later, Burchfield recorded his memories of starting his unusual new job. 'My recollection of the time', he wrote, 'is that I felt like a pioneer arriving in a new colony and finding a log cabin to house me but no other resource except a rather superior Man Friday to assist me.' These terms, consciously or unconsciously, recall Murray's description of himself at a similarly early moment in the creation of his new dictionary: 'I feel that in many respects I and my assistants are simply pioneers, pushing our way experimentally through an untrodden forest, where no white man's axe has been before us.'[1] Burchfield, dealing with a much smaller compass of years, did not have so substantial a forest to hack his way through, but seems keenly to have felt himself in a scholarly and methodological wilderness so far as lexicography was concerned. After the enforced departure of Wyllie – about whom he seems to have known little – there was no *OED* lexicographer in post to induct him into the mysteries of either the institution or its most formidable dictionary.

He took up his appointment on 1 July 1957, exactly one hundred years after his predecessors Coleridge, Furnivall and Trench had been established as a committee of three by the Philological Society 'to collect unregistered words in English' (a 'cherished coincidence', so Burchfield felt).[2] On his first day, he reported to the Oxford University Press and was shown to 40 Walton Crescent, 'a small back house in a back street' nearby, with the disadvantages that it functioned partly as a private house and partly as a catch-all office for a number of other OUP projects.[3] One of his first visitors was the caretaker's dog, followed soon afterwards by the caretaker's baby grandson, dressed in his pyjamas, along with other members of the same family who lived in the building. Other occupants turned out to include the secretary to the panels of the translators of the New English Bible, and one of the editors of another of the Press's English-language reference books, the *Oxford Illustrated Dictionary* (the successor to the Encyclopaedic Dictionary Sisam had planned many years earlier, on which Jessie Coulson had worked).[4] In his new room, Burchfield found 'a telephone on the bare kitchen-table, a chair, and a small book-case with a set of O.E.D. and a few oddly assorted books in it'. He expected, he says, 'the telephone to ring, and that someone – presumably Dan Davin – would summon me and tell me how to go about compiling a large-scale dictionary on historical principles. It quickly dawned on me that I would simply need to organize the whole project myself from scratch. There were no courses, no conferences, no seminars, no handbooks or manuals of lexicography.' So Burchfield started his first day's work instead by reading through his copy of *The Times* (a newspaper routinely scanned by Wyllie, as we saw in Chapter III, and also regularly excerpted by Eleanor Bradley in the 1930s), working methodically through the issue in its entirety from the advertisements, then printed on the front page, to the weather forecast on the back. He copied out all words and meanings which he could not find treated in the parent Dictionary or its Supplement. 'The results,' he found, 'were a revelation':

The *OED* was shown at once to be a product of the Victorian and Edwardian period, and not up-to-date at all. The reigns of George V and George VI had witnessed wars, scientific discoveries, and social changes of immense importance, but these were very poorly reflected in the *OED* and its 1933 *Supplement*, *body-line bowling*, *Bolshevism*, *questionnaire*, and such unmissable terms apart. The early centuries of English vocabulary had been scrutinised and analysed with meticulous care. But the language that had come into being in the period since 1879 (when J. A. H. Murray undertook the *OED*) had been collected and dealt with only in the manner of a Sunday painter [which term Burchfield was to define as 'an amateur painter, one who paints purely for pleasure']. Subject for subject, word class for word class, the first *OED* Supplement of 1933 was a riffraff assemblage of casual items, in no way worthy of the magnificent monument to which it formed an extension.[5]

To understand the full force of this cruel judgement, it is useful to remember *OED*'s own definition of *riff-raff* (s.v. *riff-raff*[1] sense 3b): 'Of things: Worthless, trashy'. As we shall see, the main way in which Burchfield's project was to differ from that of Craigie and Onions was that, unlike them, he had the luxury of many years of preparation, and in particular the opportunity to plan and carry out extensive reading programmes, systematically sweeping recent publications for new words and usages. By contrast, the first Supplement was based largely on the accumulated notes and corrections that both readers and lexicographers had amassed in the course of their undirected and incidental exposure to contemporary language. Burchfield's results, unsurprisingly, were superior.[6]

Burchfield's previous existence had been that of a typical temporary Oxford tutor in the humanities. In the 1950s, the Oxford colleges had a small number of fellows, and then as now relied on a badly paid penumbra of college lecturers to deliver a portion of the mainstream tutorials to their undergraduates.[7] Burchfield, employed by Christ Church on a short-term contract expiring in 1957, fell into this unstable category: a young man of promise and ability, but as yet untried and unproven in his academic career, with no secure future in prospect. He had 'for some years' assisted Onions 'in an informal way', from whom he 'learned the meaning of astringency and its relevance to scholarship'. He had taught many tutorials in English-language topics, specifically on the language of great writers like Shakespeare, Spenser, Milton and Dickens, while his research was 'a vast piece of work on the *Ormulum*', a long collection of versified sermons written around the year 1200 by an Augustinian canon called Orm, for which he was carefully producing a transcription and an index of words (under the supervision of J. R. R. Tolkien).[8] These activities he now put aside in order to pursue his new career.

With his family responsibilities, he was no doubt delighted to land a properly paid job. But he was leaving a life which, although precarious and exigent for the untenured college tutor, was in many ways more comfortable and less exacting than the one he was to enter. Colleges were social institutions, where small numbers of men lived and worked together (only five, out of around thirty, Oxford colleges admitted women as fellows or undergraduates). The assumption was that work was life and life was work, with no clear line between one and the other, and certainly very little time-keeping. In the humanities, many clever and erudite scholars did not publish, or published very little, devoting themselves to reading, thinking and teaching. Productivity, of the sort weighed in vulgarly quantitative terms, was not then an academic value. The wide range of philological teaching, and the substantial research project on which Burchfield had been engaged since 1951, necessitated, in his own words, 'a knowledge of the linguistic monuments of Old English, Old Norse, Gothic, and other Germanic languages, also of Old French, and a professional knowledge of all the elements of comparative Indo-European philology that had a bearing on the vocabulary and grammar of medieval English'. Acquiring and extending knowledge of this sort was not a finite or measurable activity, but an indeterminate process with no fixed end in view.

Burchfield was now stepping into a different world. As he himself observed, 'My qualifications at the time, in 1957, entitled me only to express gratitude for the opportunity that had been put before me . . . as a young Oxford don, I had never had to manage a department or look after editorial staff. I was thirty-four years of age, with a family to bring up . . . . I was only partially equipped to deal with the problems ahead.'[9] Gentlemanly and relaxed though the Press may have seemed as a working environment, Burchfield had been engaged for a specific task and for a specific period. Common-table discussions over college dessert were not part of office life: he was on his own, without the distractions of teaching but without the stimulus and diversion of academic fellowship either. It seems clear that the publishers – particularly Sisam, who far away in the Scillies still exercised strong influence on his successors – were, in the early years, keen to impress upon him the importance of delivery and dispatch. Institutional memories of lexicographical delay and digression haunted them, and Sisam tried to make sure, in his letters to Davin, that these memories did not dim.

Burchfield's main colleague at Christ Church had been the literary critic J. I. M. Stewart (who found the time to publish many successful detective novels under the pseudonym Michael Innes). Before he left, Stewart had warned Burchfield that 'the afternoons will seem long', and advised him to establish a new pattern of work.[10] This advice Burchfield most notably acted on. There seems to be no evidence in the *OED* files and papers (those which are at this date available to outsiders) that their new editor ever gave the publishers cause for anxiety or even, after the initial stages of appointment, doubt. This in itself was a distinctive achievement for an *OED* lexicographer. Having got through his first day and read and noted his copy of *The Times*, all the indications are that Burchfield drew up a clear plan of attack, and acted on it with promptness, efficiency and authority.

Burchfield's 'Man Friday', installed in the room opposite his, was the loyal interim editor R. C. Goffin, 'a loquacious and extraordinarily genial companion' who explained that he had 'spent the preceding months [more accurately, years] preparing the way for the new Editor to arrive', Burchfield's immediate predecessor having 'disappeared like greased lightning' when offered his New Zealand chair. Goffin made Burchfield welcome and impressed him, he says, with his use of Anglo-Indian words like *Hobson-Jobson* and *bandobast* (neither of these words was included in the *OED* or its first Supplement, but both were later to find a home in Burchfield's own dictionary, the first with quotations from 1829 and the second from 1776).[11]

Goffin's 'main contribution' during the period before his arrival, Burchfield says in faint praise, ' for which I have been everlastingly grateful, was to cause two cabinets of wooden boxes to be built, 72 in all, of a size able to contain 6 inch times 4 inch slips placed in orderly sequence'. As in the past, this was the form in which quotations were supposed to be stored, although many of them actually arrived in the office on 'used envelopes and other scraps of paper'. Goffin had done a little more as well, 'painstakingly start[ing] to cut up copies of M. Reifer's *Dictionary of New Words* (1955) and Hinsie and Shatzky's *Psychiatric Dictionary* (1940 [the second edition of which Wyllie had received on behalf of the Dictionary in 1953]), filing slips for the entries as he went along', and also attempting to locate and check through the letters sent to the *OED* since 1933 pointing out errors and omissions – a difficult task in which, as we saw in Chapters III and IV, neither he nor, later, Burchfield's staff, were wholly successful, perhaps because Davin (p. 145 above) had not been able to find them all.[12]

From his days at Magdalen, and his work on EETS, Burchfield knew Onions well enough to have gathered at least some information and advice from him already, both on how to set about collecting material and on how to process and represent it – although Onions seems to have been tantalizingly discreet about 'the main lines of disagreement' on this between, say, Murray and Craigie.[13] As one might expect, Onions's counsel was 'deeply cautionary'. Many years later, when lecturing to an audience at the University of Kent at Canterbury, Burchfield described some of his lugubrious warnings. 'From a note I made of a conversation we had on 1 August 1957 [days after he had taken up office], I see that he told me, for example, that professional scholars should be consulted only when all other sources have failed. "They are admirable if asked to criticise a provisional entry, hopeless if asked to do all the work."' Burchfield was urged to be similarly cautious with his subordinates: 'You will need one or two itinerant lexical assistants. They must not be men with degrees, or anyone seeking advancement or higher pay.'[14] As ever, the fear was that time would be wasted and money drained away.

Davin thought it was too much to burden Craigie (who died later that year, aged 90) with the task of training up the new recruit, as Sisam had suggested. Instead, he prevailed upon Sisam to do this job instead, and packed Burchfield off to the Scilly Isles for four days (12–15 August 1957), arranging for him to stay in a hotel so as not to inconvenience Mrs Sisam. Burchfield reports this advice, which largely reprised that already sent to the Press, as quite as admonitory but more detailed than that of Onions.

Burchfield was to set himself a time limit (seven years), stick to one volume of about 1,275 pages, base his dictionary on 'the English of educated people in English' (no colonialisms), and keep specialized scientific jargon and the like to a minimum. Burchfield found this vision a deeply unattractive one. Sisam's 'broad view about the exclusion of overseas English', he wrote later, 'had all the classical hallmarks of Dr. Johnson's *Dictionary of the English Language*'. He believed, wrongly in Burchfield's opinion, that 'an insular policy was desirable because it brought with it the certainty of verification of meaning. People who could verify the meanings of English English words were at hand in Oxford. Abroad was not, as Nancy Mitford had said, *bloody*, but, in terms of its vocabulary, likely to be difficult or meretricious in one way or another.' Technological and scientific words 'should be included only in so far as the words could be explained to an intelligent layman'. Sisam, moreover, 'expressed contempt for the poetical vocabulary of poets like Blunden and de la Mare' (who seem to have been instanced not on account of their singular characteristics but only in so far as they represented contemporary poetry generally): contemporary literary sources had not been a strong feature of the 1933 Supplement, and there was no reason to depart from this policy.

One way or another, Burchfield was to flout all these directives, regarding them as cramped and small-minded. But the main burden of Sisam's advice was compelling, and unanswerable. Compiling a large dictionary such as this, he said, was like swimming the English Channel. Burchfield must 'make the crossing before the tide turns or you will never get across'. Delay, for good reasons or bad, would mean that the enterprise would founder under the waves of new words dashing against its frame.[15]

Initial stages

Burchfield returned to Oxford with a good deal to mull over, and busied himself in the next few months establishing a proper office. Over the next few years, he persuaded the Press to convert his 'shabby Victorian villa' into a more businesslike establishment, capable of providing a decent working environment for the expanding editorial staff together with their accompanying equipment and materials. He dug out the former office's old reference books, damaged and filthy from storage, and had them rebound, and unearthed the slips only partially used by the first Supplement editors – 140,000 of them – that Sisam had had packed up and stored away. Months were spent sorting through and filing this material, integrating it into the collection already established by Goffin of the more recently acquired bundles of slips amassed by Rope, Troubridge, Chapman and others, and distinguishing between the quotations to be saved for revision of the main *OED* and those immediately usable for the Supplement. (In 1961, Burchfield reported in a summary of the post-1933 history of *OED*-related activities that the inter-Supplement years had seen 'no systematic reading or collecting of slips' other than by these few independent readers, indicating that he was still unaware of the precise nature of the role Wyllie had played between 1933 and 1954.)[16] He was joined by an assistant, Jennifer Dawson, in October 1957, and by a secretary early in 1958.

What must have been most gratifying to the publishers in the early years was Burchfield's regular production of annual reports. These indicate organized progress through a clearly articulated programme of reading and research. Taking very seriously his ten-year time-limit, Burchfield began by planning to complete his programme of reading and accumulation of quotation evidence by the summer of 1961. The new Supplement was to 'carry the record down to the end of the 1950s as a convenient terminal date', recording all the new words and senses that Burchfield and his staff could lay their hands on. Improvements to existing entries already printed in the first Supplement were to take the form of ante-datings (if earlier quotations for an entry could be found) and of 'revised definitions where these are needed (for example, the definition of *shop-steward* as "the foreman of a workshop" can no longer be considered adequate)'.[17] Burchfield then expected to devote three years to processing the results for the earlier letters of the alphabet, with the aim of getting the first tranches of copy in front of the Printer by early 1964. While this was in production, he would continue preparing the material for the letters that came behind.

Five years into the project, this plan was successfully under way.[18] Half a million quotations had been stored in the office's boxes, which Burchfield estimated would yield about 30,000 new words, senses and phrases. In his first five-year report, July 1962, he proudly declared that 'the collecting of material for the revised Supplement is now complete (except in so far as a skeleton team of readers has been retained for the perusal of current newspapers and for the filling of gaps in the reading as they are discovered)'. This meant, he predicted – with an optimism now somewhat painful to read, except that the Dictionary was to be the better for his failure to fulfil his prediction – that 'these figures will not alter substantially' before publication. In the event, his Supplement, whose first volume (published in 1972) took a further ten years to appear, contained in total not 30,000 but 69,300 entries.[19]

The backbone of the project in these early years was the reading programme, divided between internal and external readers. In 1957, Davin had passed on to him a list of 'illustrious names': distinguished academics, and men and women of letters, who Davin hoped would flood the Dictionary offices with sound examples of valuable new words and uses. Not a bit of it, Burchfield found. It was impossible to rely on outside readers who were already occupied in full-time jobs. 'One by one they declined an invitation to read, or undertook the reading assigned to them in such a leisurely fashion that it would have been A.D. 2000 before the Supplement could appear.' He was forced to rely instead on 'free-lance readers', 'retired school-masters', and 'the wives of university teachers'. The problem was that 'many of the people best fitted to do the readings could not be persuaded to accept any task by a definite date because of more lucrative work easily obtainable elsewhere'. Nor, in fulfilment of Onions's grim prophecy, had academics been a good source: 'with one or two exceptions university teachers of English have not come forward to help at the reading stage'; though Burchfield hoped that he would 'be able to call on their advice and criticism on particular points as entries are being assembled'. The exceptions, however, were distinguished and their production of slips more numerous than this testy account indicates: among others, Roland Hall, Emrys Jones, Douglas Gray, Derek Brewer, Elsie Duncan-Jones, E.G. Stanley and M. B. Parkes, all contributed copiously to Burchfield's quotation files and are named in the various prefaces to the volumes as they appeared, as well as in Burchfield's later T. S. Eliot lectures on his early years as Supplement editor.[20]

The outside readers were volunteers, and their support had been drummed up through a variety of means. As with the original Dictionary and the first Supplement, appeal lists – thirteen of them by 1962, listing 10,000 new words, senses and phrases – were published in *The Periodical* and *Notes & Queries,* and several more specialised sources were tried too. These yielded variable results; Burchfield reported that the aeronauts reading the *Journal of the Royal Aeronautical Society,* for example, 'were not very clever at this game' and sent in disappointingly few examples of the large number of new words which had appeared in their field. A better way of drawing in keen amateur word enthusiasts seemed to be the pages of the *Sunday Times* – at least for a few issues. The journalist Godfrey Smith, with whom Burchfield struck up a useful personal relationship, published a glowing article on the new lexicographical venture in the issue of 1 February 1959, appending an appeal list of ten words for which earlier quotations were sought: *A-bomb* used as a verb – in fact Burchfield eventually included neither verb nor noun as a separate lemma, despite printing several quotations in which the word *A-bomb* occurs, which means that the word still lacks a proper entry in *OED*;[21] *academic,* 'as in "of academic interest only"'; *accommodation address*; *put on an act* 'in the figurative use'; *actor-proof*; *aficionado* (1926 – later ante-dated to 1892); *afters* 'of sweets, pudding entremets or dessert'; *be your age* 'act in a fashion becoming to your age'; *in aid of* 'colloquially' (1956 – later ante-dated to 1837). Four further lists were published over the next six months, though at gradually lengthening intervals. About twenty letters were received in response to each list, most of them with printed evidence earlier than that they already had: a significant haul. But 'the interval between lists lengthened . . . presumably because the editor of the Sunday Times felt they had less news-value than we had hoped'. Nevertheless, the publicity was valuable, leading to a seven-minute film on the Oxford Dictionaries on BBC television, in which both Burchfield and Onions (now 85) participated – and Godfrey Smith himself was cited as first user of the word *logophile*, which appeared in the first of these articles: 'We are pretty sure that since all *Sunday Times* readers are natural and inveterate logophiles . . . he [i.e. Mr. Burchfield] will get some invaluable assistance.'

Further readers responded to articles published in the daily press, for example *The Times*, especially when this newspaper reported the *Periodical* appeals in attractively energizing terms: 'there is no close season for the lexi-cographers; they pursue their quarry, all the year round, in every covert of print. Now the greatest of them all – the master of the shire pack that has run so many elusive words to a kill – has uttered a loud "Halloo" and may count on a large field of enthusiastic . . . followers.' Other articles followed in the same paper, advertising the Supplement's search for ante-datings of words such as *bus-conductress, business as usual, bubble-gum, cocktail party, cat's whiskers, Chinaman* (cricket), *Churchillian, chain-smoking, Chelsea-bun* – the last of which, like several of the others, successfully sparked a correspondence.[22]

External readers, acquired one way or another, were vital to the success of the project, since they provided as many as half the total number of quotations over the course of these first five years: 30,000 slips came in from volunteers in 1958, Burchfield reckoned, going up to between 60,000 and 67,000 a year between 1958 and 1961 and making an impressive total of around 223,000. Burchfield's own staff matched this figure, which brought the total stored in the specially carpentered boxes up to about half a million by 1962. Of the outside readers, 'substantial' contributors numbered about 100 in all, so this averages out at perhaps 2,000 slips a head – a notable achievement for individuals not formally connected with the enterprise they were supporting. A few of these were collectors who had a professional reason for amassing their quotations – Clarence Barnhart, the American lexicographer, who in 1958 sent them from his files in New York 'a set of some 4,500 slips drawn from 1955 issues of *The [New York] Times, Science News Letter*, and other sources', or H. W. Orsman, who 'presented to us his unique collection of some 12,000 quotations from New Zealand works' from the time of James Cook to about 1950.[23] But most were neither linguists nor academics, simply individuals who felt impelled, for one reason or another, to devote their time and effort selflessly to a magnificent scholarly undertaking.[24]

In 1962, Burchfield reported the names, occupations and totals of the principal contributors:

Miss M. Laski	31,000	(author & journalist)
Mr R A Auty	26,000	(retired schoolmaster)
Mrs A S C Ross	12,000	(wife of university teacher)
Mr W Kings	8,000	(retired schoolmaster)
Mr R Hall	7,000	(university teacher)

These were the 'few Heaven-sent enthusiasts' that Chapman had hoped for in 1935 (p. 82 above); although their contributions were dwarfed by those for the first edition of *OED* (detailed in the prefaces to its succeeding fascicles), they had been accumulated over a much shorter time-scale, and under very different conditions. As Burchfield told an audience of lexicographers in New York in 1973, 'Notwithstanding the change of social climate since the Victorian period, and the virtual disappearance of a leisured or semi-leisured class, some excellent readers came forward. The instruction we gave them was quite simple: copy out a quotation for any word, sense, or phrase occurring in the source that is not already adequately dealt with in the O.E.D. or its Supplement (1933).'[25]

Of those appearing in the list above, only Roland Hall (b. 1930), a dedi-cated servant of the *OED* who continues to identify numerous *OED* ante-datings, is alive today.[26] Auty (who died in 1967) was a retired schoolmaster from Faversham in Kent, who undertook to read the entire works of James Joyce, with the exception only of *Finnegans Wake*. 'Like a medieval scribe,' Burchfield said later, 'he copied in his own handwriting many thousands of 6 × 4 inch slips on which he entered illustrative examples for any word or meaning that occurred in Joyce and was not already entered in the Dictionary.'[27] Mrs Ross was Stefanyja Olszewska (1907–73), wife of the linguist who had complained of the first Supplement's faint-hearted omis-sion of four-letter words in 1933 (p. 122 above); she had studied under Tolkien in Leeds, published several articles on Old and Middle English philology, and read for and worked on the first Supplement in the early 1930s.

Laski (1915–88) differed from the others in being a public figure. In Burchfield's words, she was a 'writer, broadcaster, journalist, and lexico-graphical irregular supreme', moreover 'renowned' both at Oxford and throughout her life 'for her beauty, her forceful personality, and her obses-sion with religious and secular beliefs'. After writing a series of novels in the 1940s and 1950s (including *Little Boy Lost*, later made into a musical starring Bing Crosby – at which Laski was apparently furious, having earlier sold the rights to John Mills without realizing how they might be used), she turned to 'more thoughtful and literary works' in the 1960s and became well known as a broadcaster on programmes such as *Any Questions*, *The Brains Trust* and *The Critics*. One of her obituarists remarked on 'her clear, immediately recognisable voice with a slight touch of petulance or arrogance always there'.[28] In 1958, while 'momentarily starved of reading matter' (she thought it might have been when she was 'holding on to the telephone so as to be put through to Passenger Inquiries'), she idly picked up 'an eight-page pamphlet containing double-columned lists of some 450 words in alphabetical order and running from *alabamine* to *astrophil*', the second appeal that had been enclosed with a copy of *The Periodical*, 'the O.U.P.'s classy publicity handout'. So began her irresistibly compulsive habit of noting down, in a succession of small black notebooks (some now preserved in the *OED* archives), any words from her wide range of omnivorous reading that she thought might be useful for the Supplement, or for 'the Great Jubilee' (a hoped-for day when a revision of the whole Dictionary might be set in hand), and 'carding' the results. She continued to dispatch a steady stream of cards to Burchfield right up to the publication of the final volume of his Supplement in 1986, by which time her 'extraordinary contribution' had come to a total of around 250,000 quotations, all copied out in her distinctive spidery script.

In order to flood the *OED* offices with such abundant accumulations of linguistic booty, 'she dredged numerous bulky Edwardian sales catalogues for the names of domestic articles, she read much of the crime fiction published in the twentieth century [and reviewed it for the *TLS*], and she scoured the whole rich literary world of twentieth-century (and some older) books and magazines for their unregistered vocabulary'. Laski herself mentions G. B. Shaw, Beerbohm, Hemingway, MacNeice, Elizabeth Bowen, Graham Greene, Ogden Nash, John Osborne, Dorothy Wordsworth's journals and G. M. Hopkins's prose as sources read for the Dictionary. One of her enthusiasms was the writing of Charlotte Yonge; as a result this novelist's representation in the *OED* seems to have risen sharply between the first and second editions (on whose relationship see further below).[29] In 1968 she published a series of articles in the *TLS* on reading for the *OED*, in which she recounted the delights of 'treasure hunting with the near certainty that treasure will always be found'.[30] She described her daily trawl through the *Guardian*, speculated on whether the *kimono shirt* she remembered the theatre critic Kenneth Tynan wearing at a student party in Oxford would make the grade along with *bush shirt* and *Hawaiian shirt*, reported what was then standard *OED* Supplement wisdom, that five examples of a new word's use in printed sources were required for it to get into the Dictionary, listed the words unrecorded in the *OED* that she had discovered by reading the first edition of *The Times* in 1788 ('thanks to the postal strike I had some spare working hours'), and noted how 'the non-historian can seldom know whether [the *OED*] is delinquent or accurate' when consulting it to check the names for historical events, persons and phenomena.

The drawbacks of relying on volunteer readers, even those as comparatively skilled and erudite as Laski, were well known to Burchfield. As he pointed out, 'it means that the dictionary is to some extent in danger of omitting words or senses that individual readers overlook or deliberately refrain from copying through inexperience or any other factor'. He tried various methods of offsetting these likely disadvantages, for example double reading of 'important sources', or what he describes as 'an instruction [to the reader] to follow what was virtually a concordancing procedure' for other sources. Burchfield's determination to press on as swiftly as possible with the reading programme, as a prior and separate stage to processing the results of the reading, meant that, as we have seen, an initial central corpus of quotations was established between 1958 and 1961. As he later told his New York audience, 'this was before computer-aided processes and electrostatic copiers became available. The accumulation of quotations therefore proceeded along the same lines as those adopted by the editors of the main dictionary almost a century ago': manual copying and manual sorting – though by 1971 they had begun to use office duplicators, manual guillotines and in-house photocopiers.[31]

To begin with – in great contrast to later on – Burchfield restricted himself to a small staff. From the end of 1958 he 'usually' had 'four full-time assistants in Oxford, a secretary, a part-time assistant for filing slips, and a full-time assistant in London'. Alert to the pitfalls of his predecessors, he kept a watchful eye on his employees and allotted them carefully specified remits. Half were put to compiling entries from the quotations and reference books already amassed in Walton Crescent, and half to verifying quotations, filling in gaps in the collections, and 'establishing the first or earliest use of a word so far as this can be done'. It was crucial to differentiate sharply between these two activities. 'The assistants drafting entries make rapid progress because they are freed from the time-consuming task of verifying material themselves.' Confined to the office, they were willy-nilly restrained from the 'drift to Bodley', there to pursue 'the "endless research" that Charles Cannan complained of during the preparation of OED itself'. The research assistants in London, on the other hand, could 'make use of the considerable resources of the various libraries in London (which collectively are superior to those in Oxford [Burchfield is referring to nineteenth- and twentieth-century material in particular, and perhaps thinking of the Colindale (newspaper) Library]), and can plan their work so that it complements that of the drafters without themselves being involved in the compilation of entries'. This task was by no means insubstantial. 'It must be remembered,' Burchfield pointed out in 1959, 'that a large percentage of the material sent to us is in the form of clues to possible quotations, quotations taken from secondary sources, and so on, and that almost every entry calls for examination of appropriate sources in a large library.'

Needless to say, staff management was essential, as without a firm hand on the reins the second Supplement could waver and drift in its progress, tending towards some of the disastrously time-consuming practices of the two previous lexicographical enterprises. Equally important was a clear sense of the likely length of the Supplement and of the nature of the material it would treat. Most important of all was the programme for assembling and processing the raw material, writing and editing the entries, and eventual publication.

Burchfield estimated that his new material would be about three-quarters the length of the existing Supplement. This would make a total of 1,500 pages for the merged work (as agreed, the new Supplement was to subsume material from the old), which Burchfield was confident he would not exceed. His 1962 lengthy report also discussed sources in considerable detail: his readers had undertaken vast swathes of literary reading (novels, drama, poetry), and perused periodicals and specialist publications from a wide range of disciplines, including linguistics, art history, ornithology, psychology, politics, history, philosophy, and many branches of science and technology. (External readers had been good at working through 'the main prose works of the period' along with newspapers and periodicals, he had found, while poetry and more technical material had been best entrusted to his own staff.) About 50 per cent of the new material would be technical or scientific, and Burchfield went into some detail about the issues and prob-lems in selecting and defining this vocabulary, anxious to avoid 'filling the Supplement in Webster-like fashion with neologisms of doubtful perma-nence and rapidly changing sense'.

In this analysis and treatment of sources, Burchfield was consciously reviewing, and intending to improve on, the work of Craigie and Onions. In one respect – the inclusion of literary sources – he was reaching back to the aims and methods of the original *OED*; in another – the inclusion of scien-tific and technical ones – he was developing and surpassing them. Early on in his editorship, he had discovered that 'the existing Supplement, though technically sound in the presentation of the material it contained, suffered from the defect, in a literary instrument, of not being based on a proper reading of the literary works of the period 1884–1930'. Burchfield was disturbed by what he saw as a dereliction of one of the main duties of the *OED,* that of acting as a treasure-house of the vocabulary of great writers. 'It is clear,' he continued, 'that no systematic reading of the works of any author was attempted after about 1890 when the main period of organized reading for the Dictionary ended. Thus, Kipling, Conrad, Henry James, Shaw, Arnold Bennett, and other writers who flourished after 1890 are hardly represented at all in the [first] Supplement, and the poets are ignored. There are in fact a few quotations from Hopkins and from Hardy's *The Dynasts* (published 1903–8) in the 1933 Supplement but these look very odd against the rest of the material. It therefore seemed advisable to add some 1884–1930 sources to others being read'. Burchfield listed the principal sources that were being tackled by the readers for the new Supplement, which by contrast put literary sources first:

1. The main literary works of the period 1930–1960
2. A selection of important scientific and technical works, 1930–60
3. Runs of literary, scientific and technical periodicals, 1930–60
4. Current newspapers, esp. *The Times, Listener, TLS* and *Economist*
5. The main Commonwealth sources, mostly 1930–1960
6. As many literary works of the period 1884–1930 as could be managed in the time available.

The enormously expanded range of sources from which the second Supplement was to draw its quotations was a significant break with *OED* tradition, as Burchfield later acknowledged, correctly describing it as 'wider than that attempted for any post-medieval century in the main Dictionary'.[32]

Finally, the 1962 report contained a reassuringly specific and apparently realistic report on the time-scale for production. As we have seen, Burchfield had now accumulated half a million quotations, and he believed that this material contained all the major new words and senses he needed to put in the Supplement. The next stage was scrutinizing this vast and various archive to choose items for inclusion, deciding which quotations were to be printed to illustrate the words, and writing the definitions and etymologies. He still believed that he would be able to start putting copy before the Printer by the end of 1963 or beginning of 1964, and keep up a steady supply thereafter. 'Whether publication can be achieved in 1967, the year originally proposed, must remain an open question until it is seen how rapidly my staff can prepare and cope with all the research and verification involved, and also on other not readily assessable factors. But I trust enough has been said to show that the preparations are well advanced, and that my staff and I are proceeding with all possible speed while endeavouring to maintain the high standard set by the OED itself.'[33]

All this seems measured, rational and highly systematized. Burchfield had grasped the way to accumulate material for a dictionary and was running a well-organized programme. His 1962 report gives the impression of total control of the project and of the staff, so far as such a thing is possible given human frailty on the one hand and the vagaries of chance on the other. But was writing a dictionary really to be so straightforward?

No doubt there were bumps and false starts even by 1962. And despite these carefully planned and meticulously described advances, and the hoped-for publication date of 1967, the second Supplement's completion was still twenty-four years away. The first volume, covering A–G, appeared in 1972, the second (H–N) in 1976, volume three (O–Scz) in 1982 and volume 4 (Se–Z) in 1986. Such procrastination might seem to justify Sisam's observation that there was little reason why any sane man, comfortably provided for, should ever finish such an enterprise. But to take this view would be unfair to Burchfield, who was strongly conscious of the burden of responsibility resting on his shoulders. 'Lexicographers are generally long-lived – they need to be – but many fail to complete their course,' he wrote in 1989. 'This was a threat that haunted me for twenty-nine years.'[34]

Expansions, distractions and delays

Why did the second Supplement take so long? This is not a straightforward question to answer. As in the past, vast quantities of correspondence survive in the OED archives from interested language-users (academics – including William Empson again, probing the sexual connotations of the verb *possess* which had been missed by OED,[35] teachers, commercial firms seeking to discuss the Dictionary's use of trade names, 'amateur' word-fanciers, and many others) who wrote to the OED with queries, corrections and specula- tions.[36] By contrast, the documents relating to editorial activities thin out from the 1960s onwards, virtually disappearing after the early 1970s. One explanation may be that face-to-face meetings superseded the exchange of memos between offices, so that fewer physical records survive from this period. Another is that, as one would expect, documents on editorial appointments are kept in personal files not yet available to the public, since many staff members are both alive (indeed in flourishing health) and still employed by the Press. Numerous other papers in the archives, some possibly relating to the second Supplement, have yet to be sorted and filed by recently appointed staff who have infused new order into these massively extensive records.[37] Thus it is probable that fresh information will come to light in the future, both within and without the offices of the Oxford University Press, and this will be accommodated in Peter Gilliver's history of the *OED* currently in preparation (Burchfield indicated the character of some of this information in 1989 when he hinted that salaries had been a contentious issue for Supplement staff).[38]

Fortunately, however, the increasingly exiguous archival evidence can be glossed and put into its larger context by Burchfield's own accounts of editing the Supplement, published in numerous sources over the next few decades. Much of this writing is entertainingly anecdotal – Burchfield had a good eye for a telling or punchy quotation – and also helpfully informative, some of it a little self-congratulatory or complacent, some fiercely defensive in response to the (remarkably few) criticisms that came his way. Naturally, appearing as they did over a stretch of years, these narratives overlap or to some extent contradict each other. Piecing all this material together, however, it seems two chief factors played determining roles in the delay.

The first of these was Burchfield's determination to deal better with new vocabulary than had Craigie and Onions, and the consequent vast expansion in quotations and quotation sources. As we saw earlier, on his first day at work he had been horrified by the deficiencies of the first Supplement in recording new words and uses. Further acquaintance with the *OED* editors' ability to treat current and incoming vocabulary did not improve his judgement of it. At a conference of European lexicographers in Leiden in 1977 he spoke of his surprise at the evidence of their ineptitude in *OED* proper as well as the Supplement. 'The only thing that can be said about the principles of choice,' he thought, 'was that they were *ad hoc*'; and he instanced *vagarity*, *vagrant* (v.), *vague* (v.), *variolitization*, *variolization* and *vaudouism*, as words which should have been omitted from Craigie's editing of *OED1*.[39] But it was not just that Burchfield wanted to avoid including words that would in a decade or two, or even less, look absurd (*atocha*, *olivescent* and *promovable* are examples of several such words from the first Supplement which slipped through his fine mesh, as it happens): he also wanted to make sure that he did include words his dictionary would subsequently look absurd to have omitted.[40]

In this respect, the publication of Philip Gove's *Webster's Third New International Dictionary* in 1961, marketed as 'the greatest vocabulary explosion in history', was a bombshell. This excellent work was the first twentieth-century dictionary to attempt a policy of honest descriptivism in relation to language, in that it included vast numbers of words used on a daily basis in (American) English that had never before made it into the pages of an accepted lexicographical authority on the language as a whole. Examples 'ranged all the way from *breezeway* and *split-level* to *fringe benefit* and *sit-in*, from *airlift* and *no-show* to *deceleration* and *astronaut*, from *beatnik* and *den mother* to *wage dividend* and *zen*', as one review had it. (All these words, except *wage dividend*, subsequently found their way into the second *OED* Supplement.) Serious lexicographical treatment of uses such as *ain't* ('used orally in most parts of the U.S. by many cultivated speakers') and *of* (for *have*, in phrases such as 'I should of') were greeted with horror and execration by newspapers and journals across the United States – a book of the reviews was later published as an academic textbook written by linguists – and changed twentieth-century lexicography by hugely increasing its remit.[41]

As Burchfield himself wrote, 'the sheer quantity of words included in [*Webster's Third*] made it apparent at once that I had seriously underestimated the task of collecting modern English vocabulary wherever it occurred. The whole editorial process had to be delayed – in the event by several years – until my editorial assistants and outside readers had assembled evidence on this majestic scale. Lists of words and senses are one thing; supporting illustrative quotations are quite another.'[42] The impact on his plans of this publication alone is a sufficient explanation for Burchfield's protracted delay in assembling, producing and printing his own dictionary. In 1968 he visited some of the main dictionary establishments in the States – G. and C. Merriam Co. (publishers of *Webster* dictionaries), Random House, American Heritage and the *Dictionary of American Regional English* – to discuss lexicographical method and content, and in the same year he made an arrangement with Philip Gove to pool resources in the accumulation of quotations. Merriam cancelled this arrangement in 1977, something Burchfield described as 'a grievous blow'.[43]

By the 1970s, Burchfield was drawing his illustrations of expanding vocabulary from a number of different fields – not just American and slang uses and words from science and technology but also many other sources of World English: the English of Australia, New Zealand, the West Indies, India and elsewhere. Increased hospitality to these new sources grew with the dictionary itself, and put further strain on his staff's time and capacity. To explain his Supplement's gradual expansion, Burchfield (in the Preface to his second volume) quoted, with apparent insouciance, Dryden's *Preface to the Fables*: ''Tis with a Poet, as with a Man who designs to build . . . generally speaking, he is mistaken in his Account, and reckons short of the

Expence he first intended. He alters his Mind as the Work Proceeds, and will have of this or that Convenience more, of which he had not thought when he began. So has it hapned to me . . .'[44] (It is irresistible to imagine Sisam turning in his grave.)

Burchfield's determination to include the vocabulary of significant literary authors can hardly have speeded him up, given that this policy too augmented demands on both readers and editors. Where and how was he to draw a line?[45] And related to this extension of sources were two other innovations, equally prolonging of time and labour, that Burchfield introduced into existing *OED* policy: an increase in the number of quotations printed to illustrate words and senses, and an increase in the recording of combinatorial forms (Craigie's 'compounds, collocations and phrases'; p. 132 above) – on both of which, more later.

More reading, in order to turn up more quotations, in turn required more editorial time. And as he grew into the job, Burchfield's notions of appropriate treatments and techniques changed and developed. He describes how, in 1984, he reviewed material prepared in the early 1960s for the alphabet ranges *radio–radium* and *tec* to *terrazzo* (for publication in the fourth volume of 1986): 'the paper clips had all gone rusty, the old definitions for the most part had to be rewritten, and a much wider range of illustrative quotations needed to be absorbed. The vintage entries of the early 1960s represented not more than twenty-five per cent of what we sent to press. A policy of "think small" had turned into one of "think big".'[46] (The truth of this statement is strikingly attested by the difference between the sample Burchfield produced in January 1963, copies of which are still in the archives, spanning the words from *lo* to *lock-up*, and the version published in 1976. Burchfield ended up producing twice as many columns, many more words, and many more quotations. The word *lobotomy*, for example, appears in the 1963 specimen with three quotations: one (1938) from a medical dictionary, one (1952) from a literary source ('I can tell you a thing or two about lobotomising rapists down to good little pacifists'), one (1955) from the *Scientific American*. In the published dictionary this has stretched to fifteen quotations in all, and the entry bears signs of considerable additional research and redrafting.)[47]

This first factor, resulting in a gigantic increase in vocabulary deemed eligible for the Supplement and a corresponding proliferation of illustrative quotations, was bound up with Burchfield's own conception of the new dictionary's content. The second factor responsible for delay, almost certainly as important, cannot be laid at his door. This was the publishers' conception of Burchfield's brief, viewed as a whole and not simply in relation to the *OED*. The creation of a renewed lexicographic centre in Oxford was to breathe fresh life and vigour into the smaller dictionaries at its circumference, so that, in accordance with Sisam's prescription, these 'lesser dictionaries' might suck dry the new material prepared for the *Supplement*, maintaining Oxford's competitive advantage. The *Concise* and *Pocket Oxford Dictionaries* were being edited away from Oxford in Exmouth (by McIntosh), and a new edition of the *Little* was in preparation (by Jessie Coulson) in Twickenham. The editors, so Burchfield felt, were bringing 'suburban values to bear on the astringent scholarship of the original works' ('astringent' being the term characteristically used of Oxford lexicographers and especially Onions, suggesting a quality at once precise and acerbic).[48] Onions was still responsible for the *Shorter*, but his own 'astringency' was by then that 'of a caged bird'. Long retired, he worked single-handedly, and had 'no means of ascertaining the nature of lexicographical growth in the years since 1933 except by observing what came to his attention from his reading and from the casual observations of colleagues and friends'. (Burchfield tells us that the word that troubled Onions shortly before he died was *beatnik*. '"Where can it possibly have come from?" he asked me several times in or around 1965.') These years were, so his successor felt, 'a period of great peril for the smaller Oxford dictionaries'.

But under Burchfield's invigorating leadership, as he himself states, the outlying enterprises were withdrawn from the provinces and brought back to the centre in Oxford. Quotation files and information about new words and new meanings were shared between the dictionaries, which by 1984 had swelled to twenty, 'all flying the Oxford flag from their base at 37a St Giles, Oxford' (to which the dictionary establishment had moved in 1977), though from 1985 onwards Burchfield's governance of the subsidiary lexicons ceased. Staff trained on and for the Supplement were seconded to work on these other, more immediately profitable, dictionaries, providing 'funds for the survival of OUP and its scholarly publishing programme'. Nevertheless, in siphoning off time and energies from the main project for so many years, this was 'a distraction and encumbrance of indescribable proportions'.[49]

These two main causes of delay forced Burchfield to relax his deadlines for completion in common with many lexicographers before and since. An academic by training, he naturally preferred accuracy and comprehensiveness to precipitate publication: the same preference that all his predecessors would have exercised had the publishers permitted. But Sisam's severe requirements for rigorous economies of copy, and his warnings against burgeoning teams of assistants – both strictures inherited from his own predecessors – were in a few years forgotten or ignored. Estimates of the length of copy were continually revised upwards, and the dates at which it was said to be ready for printing continually deferred. It was not at first realized that, while gathering quotations was time-consuming, processing them into copy (as Onions had described in 1928) was even more so; Burchfield reported in 1973 that 'experience seems to show' that the latter activity took three times as long as the former.[50] His tantalizingly brief description of the 'editorial process' by which his Supplement was assembled, accompanied by a pyramid-shaped diagram and printed in volume 1, makes it clear that he alone was responsible for 'the bringing together and revision of all material'. This would have created a 'bottle-neck' similar to that which delayed the production of both *OED1* and the first Supplement.[51]

Even nine years into the project, Burchfield seems not to have understood (or, perhaps, made clear to the publishers) that basing his scale on that of the first Supplement was a mistake. His 1966 report states that 'drafting of words in G should be completed in 1967 and this will bring the drafting to the half-way point', since 'in the 1933 Supplement G ends at p. 440 of an 867-page work'. But the first Supplement had been, in Sisam's words, 'wedge-shaped' (it had fewer years to catch up on, relative to the date of publication of the main dictionary, as it went through the alphabet). These proportions could not apply to the second Supplement.[52] Accordingly, once Burchfield had (in 1969) persuaded the Press to publish the Supplement in two volumes rather than one, and fixed the alphabet range for the first as *A–J*, the estimate had to be revised soon afterwards – in 1971 – to three volumes.[53] At some later stage it was accepted that four volumes would be necessary.[54] Once again, no adverse comment from the publishers has survived in the records available to outsiders today: though Burchfield reported in an essay published in 1987 that 'it is no secret that the financial guardians of publishing houses [unspecified] still keep a stern eye on the waywardness and procrastination of their resident lexicographers. The estimated losses of revenue resulting from the publication of each volume of the new *Supplement* are very considerable – another subject for a future historian to reexplore.'[55]

After 1962 the Supplement staff had expanded rapidly: to fifteen (including the young Julian Barnes) by 1969, by which time the house at 40 Walton Crescent boasted a Dictionary Common Room, a Quotations Room and a Photocopying Room, in addition to office quarters; and to eighteen members by 1972, when the first volume appeared. It continued at this strength till 1983. In 1977, as we have seen, the whole operation moved to 37a St Giles, 'a splendid spacious Georgian mansion in central Oxford'. The disruption occasioned by such a move delayed them still further.[56]

The papers that do survive indicate that Burchfield operated with much more freedom than the *OED* editors before him. Perhaps this was due partly to his businesslike competence and efficiency, and partly to a different understanding of the professional relationship between publishers and lexicographers: that the partnership was a decorous and comparatively distant affair between equals, rather than an intimate one of demand and supply, of blood and tears. There were moreover differences in both character and fortune between Chapman and Sisam on the one hand, and Davin and the two succeeding Secretaries to the Delegates, C. H. Roberts (from 1954 to 1974) and G. B. Richardson (1974 to 1988), on the other. To Roberts and Richardson fell the task of steering the Press in the 1970s and 1980s through unprecedented times of turmoil and change, which easily distracted attention from an enterprise that was clearly, if slowly, making progress, from 1972 onwards receiving almost uniformly rapturous reviews, and (however expensive on its own account) generating revenue from the sales of the lesser dictionaries that it also nourished.[57]

Davin, Sisam's protégé and Assistant Secretary after Sisam's departure in 1948 until his own retirement thirty years later, was a literary man (a poet and writer called 'last of the scholar-publishers' by his *ODNB* biographer Jon Stallworthy) and must have felt a close sympathy for the task on which Burchfield was engaged. But he seems to have chosen to manage with a light hand. The one piece of criticism of Burchfield's editing to be seen in the archives, a biting critique by Sisam of some sample pages of the Supplement he read in 1965, Davin passed on to Burchfield, having tactfully scrawled a note at the top to say 'haven't time to read at the moment'. (Burchfield annotated Sisam's letter with acidly dismissive comments in carefully printed red pen, writing back to Davin: 'Contrasts markedly in tone with the other reports though the actual substance is not great. I wonder if it isn't possible for K.S. to be on the wrong side of infallibility in matters of doctrine at the O.E.D. level.')[58] There is no evidence (so far available) that either Davin or Roberts exercised close supervision and control over Burchfield's activities, nor that they relentlessly scrutinized his procedures and method, nor that they discussed, with erudition, fascination and (usually) good judgement, words to be included or excluded, nor that they insisted on a continuous supply of copy to the printers, and hauled Burchfield over the carpet, as we have seen Chapman and Sisam haul his predecessors, over increases in scale. 'Revolver-practice' through the windows of 40 Walton Crescent seems not even to have been thought of, let alone attempted. The difference, in this respect, between the conditions of production of the first and of the second Supplements could hardly be more marked. It is unsurprising that Burchfield, under far lighter supervision, took more rather than less time over a job capable of expanding into infinity.

It was problems with the printers, rather than with the lexicographers, that seized the attention of the publishers. Signs of this begin in 1970, when Burchfield complains of the slow rate at which they are processing his copy (they had been giving precedence to the reissue of the *Shorter*).[59] Insufficient swiftness of response and return soon became the norm. These troubles were not confined to the production of dictionaries: developing technologies in a range of trades were killing off many traditional processes, and hot-metal printing was one of the industries by then in terminal decline. In the Preface to volume 3 of his Supplement, published in 1982, Burchfield dourly reports that they lost their printers 'after they had set the letters O and P for this volume. The closing down of their hot-metal department in 1980 delayed the printing of Volume III by six months before new printers were found.'

These changes and others like them caused upheavals in the labour market and the resulting strikes affected the whole country. As Burchfield wrote, 'the Oxford University Press found itself locked in internal debates and wrangles about surviving in difficult trading conditions. Trading profits turned into trading losses and unpleasantnesses occurred as those responsible for the management of affairs found themselves in inevitable disputes with the union.' This meant that 'the [Dictionary] Department could not stand aside and pretend that it existed in an ivory tower of its own choice. The words *picket* and *picketer* are dealt with in this volume,' he continued: 'all of us encountered the fact of picketing at intervals while this volume was in preparation'.[60]

What Burchfield (quite appropriately) leaves unmentioned is that he himself had strongly resisted the unionization of dictionary staff and that some of the unrest came from within his own ranks. His laudable aims to manage his increased staff were implemented, so former employees report, by strict efforts to control them; it seems he resisted any attempts to assume editorial roles which might challenge his own control of the project, insisting instead on precise fulfilment of explicitly described tasks, punctually observed lunch-breaks of designated length, and severe office discipline. Although the division Burchfield had initially established, between the dictionary assistants who drafted entries and those who researched in Bodley, eventually broke down, the apparent benefit was short-lived, as those who escaped – or 'drifted' – from the repressive atmosphere of the office, away to lexicographical exploration (deemed 'frolic' by Burchfield) in Bodley, might have that privilege summarily withdrawn.

No doubt Burchfield was motivated by his fear of succumbing to the lexicographical loss of focus and dissipation of energy that Sisam had warned him were the inevitable consequence of large numbers of staff, and was determined to flog his team himself rather than suffer the indignity of being flogged by the publishers (he himself worked ceaselessly, often seven days a week, for many years).[61] But employment relationships had changed radically since the early decades of the century, and his staff were men and women of the same (or better) intellectual attainments and qualities as himself, far less likely than the 'Little People' of *OED*'s former days to feel comfortable with strict management practices, and much more likely to complain about their low salaries. One former employee compares working for OUP to working for the BBC: one was supposed to feel grateful to the institution for employing one, regardless of the poor pay and *de haut en bas* attitude of the management to its staff. Another, who wanted to leave, was refused a reference unless he sought a new job within OUP itself, Burchfield's view being that the Press trained staff for its own benefit, not for those of rival organizations. Under these conditions, it is not surprising that many left altogether – in the case of Julian Barnes, the employee who was denied a reference, for a glittering career as a novelist, one of whose short stories features a meticulous lexicographer bleakly working on the second Supplement proofs.[62] 'You either left, or were ground down,' Barnes reports. 'Joining the [union] ASTMS was really just two fingers up to Burchfield rather than any great feeling of banding together against an oppressive employer. The OUP wasn't oppressive, merely condescending and undervaluing.'[63] On the other hand, some of the best aspects of paternalism remained, as when the Press paid for private health treatment in an emergency. What additionally compensated those who stayed was the knowledge that they were engaged on a project of national and scholarly significance, which would in time receive due recognition and acclaim. And a small core of Supplement members turned their initial experiences under Burchfield's regime to spectacular account, when they embarked on the third revision of the Dictionary in the 1990s.

VII

Burchfield's Supplement (2): Editorial Policies and Practice

General

What were Burchfield's editorial policies and what sort of dictionary did they produce? Archival material may offer sparse help here, but further information can be found not only in Burchfield's published articles but also in the immensely rich pages of the second Supplement itself. Up to the 1980s, one could analyse and evaluate dictionaries only by sampling a judiciously chosen range of items, for example words in the same lexical field, and hoping that the results were representative of the work as a whole. The alternative was to read the dictionary through, entry by entry, a virtually unimaginable job where *OED* is concerned, though a number of aficionados did this with the original fascicles as they were published – for example Murray's friend, the classicist Robinson Ellis, who kept hoping Murray would up his rate of quotation from his own translation of Catullus, and jealously totted up mentions of his rivals. 'I am pleased to find two quotations from Catullus in the new part of the Dict . . . . If I were inclined to magnify this success, I might triumph in the thought that I had twice the whole number of quotations in this part which I had in the former,' Ellis wrote to Murray in 1906. '. . . Swinburne is extraordinarily successful; Jowett too much; and I think there are too many quots from J. H. Newman. I am glad to see [James] Bryce [the radical politician, jurist and historian, also a correspondent of Murray's] and R[obert] Bridges, occasionally, but not frequently.'[1] At least a couple of modern critics have meted out the same treatment, in part, to Burchfield: the academic Gabriele Stein, who analysed usage labels in the third volume of the Supplement, and the writer Clive James, who explained that the reason he had been so late turning in the copy for his review of the second volume in 1977 was that, unlike other reviewers, he had read the book in full.[2]

Since the 1990s, however, another aid has come to hand. As described in its proper chronological sequence below, Burchfield's Supplement, merged with the first edition of the *OED*, was after 1986 turned into electronic form in order to produce the second edition of the Dictionary in 1989. *OED2* was subsequently released first on CD-Rom, and then, from March 2000, on the internet. Electronic analysis allows us to penetrate the *OED* in ways previously impossible, exposing the treasures stored within and transforming our understanding of its compilation, content and inner workings. It is an invaluable tool in illuminating the nature of Burchfield's work – except that, as the separate components of *OED2* (*OED1* on the one hand, and the second Supplement on the other) cannot now be systematically distinguished from each other, one must be careful to manipulate the searches so as persuade them to yield reliable information about Burchfield's portion of *OED* rather than that of his predecessors (or vice versa).[3]

As we saw in the last chapter, Burchfield set out, either initially or eventually, to update and extend the *OED* in various specific ways. He helpfully identified these in his discussion of editorial policy in the Introduction to the first volume of the Supplement, in which he tells us, 'our aim has been first and foremost to ensure that all "common words" (and senses) in British written English of the period 1884 to the present day (of those not already treated in the Dictionary) are included'. He went on to specify the three areas of vocabulary earlier picked out by Sisam: literary language, World English, and scientific and technical English, along with a fourth, 'colloquial and coarse expressions referring to sexual and excretory functions'. Elsewhere, he mentions two other important respects in which he developed or departed from *OED* practice of the past: first, his decision to include many more illustrative quotations than the first edition, moving towards 'at least one quotation a decade' (naturally this was an impossible goal to achieve, and would have produced an unmanageably large dictionary had Burchfield been successful); and secondly, his determination that illustration of 'obvious' attributive uses of words (such as *railway director*, whose inclusion by Craigie in 1902 had excited such execration from Murray) 'should be extended and expanded to show that the twentieth century is at least as productive as those that immediately preceded it'.[4]

Both these latter innovations were shrewdly picked up by Clive James in his 1977 review, where he tells us his particular interest in the dictionary (like that of Ellis) was the quotations and their provenance: which writers were in and which were out. (He was piqued to find that Germaine Greer was in while he himself was out.) About D. H. Lawrence, he thought, the editor had no reservations:

If Lawrence said it, in it goes. God, what that man knew about life. He is in for 'life-body', 'life-demand', 'life-divine', 'life-flow', 'life-meaning', 'life-idea', 'life-quick' ('Nowadays society is evil. It finds subtle ways to torture, to destroy the life-quick, to get at the life-quick in a man'), 'life-responsibility', 'life-stupid', 'life-urge', life-this and life-that. 'Life' was a word he worked to death – here is the proof.

To these ten instances of combinatorial forms in *life-*, James could have added the further eight that Burchfield also quotes from Lawrence in the same entry (easier to pick up, amidst an abundance of other such examples, with the computer than with the naked eye): *life-anger, life-course, life-drama, life-mystery, life-clouded, life-blissful, life-force, life-empty*. Only six out of the total of eighteen quotations are not, apparently, *hapax legomena*: that is, in twelve instances, the quotation from Lawrence is the only one to be printed. Does this mean that Burchfield and his team searched for and could not find other examples (for as we have seen, he sought to provide one quotation a decade)? Or that, as James thinks, 'none of the Lawrentian life-compounds caught on, for the good reason that they were sheerly rhetorical'; in which case did Burchfield include them as examples of interesting, if unproductive, literary usage, and regard them as *en masse* illustrative of the combinatorial possibilities of *life* – even if those possibilities were not, seemingly, exploited by writers other than Lawrence? It is impossible to be sure. Burchfield's fondness for literary sources, and the puzzlement his selective duplicating of quotations can elicit from the dictionary reader who seeks to draw inferences from this evidence, are recurring features of his Supplement; while the interpretative possibilities that such quotations offer (satirized as they are by James) are recurring features of the *OED* as a whole.

Literary sources will be further discussed in the next two sections, which take one by one Burchfield's four named areas of vocabulary (literary, World English, scientific and technical, and contentious uses relating to sex and other areas, including correctness), looking at examples of his characteristic treatment in order to construct a broad-brush picture of this enormous work. Meanwhile, is it possible to evaluate how well 'all "common words" (and senses) in British written English of the period 1884 to the present day' are represented in the Supplement? The simple answer is no: Burchfield's quotation marks point to the difficulty of definition and consequently of assessment. Electronic searches cannot help here. Nevertheless, as anyone may see by turning over the pages of the four volumes, entry after entry of the vast bulk of the dictionary prepared under Burchfield's hand evidences painstaking research through a huge range of sources, with banks of quotations skilfully analysed to yield lucid, polished and apt definitions, and meticulous updatings of *OED1* material where appropriate.

It is also comparatively easy to find items that should have been updated and were not. Here one must remember that Burchfield himself set the standards from which he occasionally slipped, that these slips are tiny in relation to the Supplement considered in its entirety, and that the question of whether or not to revise or update *OED* material was not straightforward. (This last is acknowledged in one of the few surviving archival documents, a set of instructions to assistants on the choice of quotations. 'OED revision', they were directed, is in general to be avoided, but 'it is difficult to lay down rules about this, since certain national and racial terms call for urgent revision and often editorial annotation. When in doubt, ask for advice'.)[5] Aberrations when they occur are notable, nevertheless. Burchfield's intention was to incorporate the previous Supplement into his own, 'with all possible corrections and improvements', but two important items on the very first page of the earlier work were inexplicably left out.[6] For the phrase '*From A to Z*', meaning 'from beginning to end, all through, in every particular', Craigie and Onions had provided two *OED* ante-datings: one early seventeenth-century (from a translation of *Don Quixote*), the other 1815–16 (from Jane Austen's *Persuasion*, perhaps supplied by Chapman, Austen's editor). But neither was included in Burchfield's Supplement, and nor, consequently, in the 1989 second edition of *OED* and the various electronic versions, all of which follow *OED1* in dating the first occurrence of this phrase to 1819, in Keats's 'Otho'.

This omission might be understood as the consequence of Burchfield's determination not to clog up his Supplement with *OED* revisions, which once embarked upon would be endless: as he wrote in the introduction to his first volume, 'It was . . . decided to exclude, in the main, pre-1820 antedatings of *O.E.D.* words or senses from general English sources, since the systematic collection of such antedatings could not be undertaken at the present time.'[7] As it happens, though, Burchfield did include quite a number of such antedatings, dotted about the dictionary, of varying sorts of words – for example, an earlier instance, dated 1786, of *introsusception*, of *intuition* (1796), of *novel* (*sb.* 3b, 1639), *tollent* (1770), *valedictory* (1779), and many others. It is not clear why these were accepted when the majority had to be excluded. (There is some surviving archival evidence that the date before which new quotations might be inserted varied: one (post-1972) set of instructions to staff specifies 1850, but altered this to 1830; another specifies '*c* 1820 or so', but the '2' is scribbled over and '4' written over the top).[8]

Worries about revision do not explain the other omission from Craigie and Onions's first page, the definition of *A.B.C.* to mean a teashop run by the Aerated Bread Company. Burchfield includes the first of Craigie and Onions's quotations (from *Punch* of 1894: 'I pass an A.B.C., Where I purchase two or three Cakes and scones'), drops the next two – including, sadly, a characteristic one from former *OED* editor Furnivall: 'Dear Sir, come to tea with me tomorrow, Thursday, at the A.B.C.' – and substitutes one from Edmund Blunden of 1941: 'Afterwards we went to a Lyons tea-shop, at which he [Thomas Hardy] was a little alarmed, being used only to an A.B.C.'[9] But though Burchfield defines *A.B.C.* as 'Aerated Bread Company', he does so without explaining, as Craigie and Onions do, that in these circumstances it means one of their teashops. As before, *OED2* (and *OED Online*) reproduces the second Supplement's omission.[10]

Other omissions are more striking. As Burchfield rightly pointed out, he could not add 'later examples to words and senses whose illustration ends in the Dictionary with nineteenth-century examples. In the earlier letters of the alphabet such a policy would have entailed the addition of late-nineteenth-century or of twentieth-century examples for virtually every word and sense listed in the Dictionary.'[11] Nevertheless it was a mistake to leave untouched, in volume 1 of the second Supplement (published in 1972), the *OED*'s reference to the Conservative Party as 'one of the two great English political parties', the other, evidently, being the Liberal Party (similarly unaltered four years later in volume 2). Burchfield's neglect of these key political terms continues into *OED2* and today's *OED Online*, which to this day provide these definitions unaltered. This is an extraordinary lapse. *Labour Party* fares little better. Understandably omitted from the *L–leisurely* fascicle (1902) of *OED*, the term was picked up by Craigie and Onions for the first Supplement and placed in the ragbag category of attributive uses of *labour*, illustrated by six quotations dated between 1886 and 1922. Burchfield reproduced their definition almost verbatim ('a political party specially supporting the interests of labour; in the United Kingdom [Craigie and Onions had said 'England', not United Kingdom'], the organized party formed in 1906 by a federation of trade unions and advanced political bodies to secure the representation of labour in Parliament'), added four more quotations, and kept the term in the same minor position – sandwiched between *labour-pains* and *labour-relations*. (Clearly Burchfield had not the same relationship with the political leaders of the day as Murray, who wrote to Asquith in 1913 to check with him his recently written entry for *Tory*.)[12]

Such flaws, tiny dots on the Supplement's huge canvas, were not obvious to most reviewers, and from the first volume on, the new dictionary was received with almost undiluted praise. 'The dangerous silent period [1933–71] was over and *OED* was back in business,' as Burchfield put it himself, looking back in 1988. He quoted a choice selection of comments on the *A–G* volume which reflected the interests of the various reviewers. 'Those **** words make the Oxford' was how the *Daily Express* announced his embrace of lexical descriptivism, while the *Guardian* judged that he was 'Gazumping Old Onions'. Kingsley Amis observed that he had 'never come across any kind of lexical work with so many references to drinks as this one contains. Quite uplifting', and Tom Stoppard thought that 'if he had been the Oxford University Press he "would have put the first copy on a decorated float and driven it around the town, or, if modesty forbade, merely announced it in *The Times* under births and left it at that." In short,' Burchfield concluded, 'the volume received the kind of welcome usually accorded to a Grand Wedding, or to the winners of the Grand National or the boat race.'[13]

One of the most important developments Burchfield made to existing *OED* policy, one likely to have significantly improved his treatment of 'common' words, was to increase the proportion of quotations from newspapers and periodicals. In this he suffered much less embarrassment or criticism than Murray. It was reading *The Times* on his first day at work in 1957 that had revealed to Burchfield the quantities of recent vocabulary unrecorded by the first Supplement, and a glance through any of his own pages indicates the wealth of material he was able to find both there and in many other such sources (the importance of which had also been recognized by Chapman and Wyllie).[14] His example has proved productive for his third-edition successors, who now routinely trawl vast electronic databases of newspapers in successful searches for ante-datings to *OED*'s original quotation evidence, vindicating Murray's view that 'newspaper quotations are the <u>most valuable</u> of current instances' (p. 118 above).

What of Burchfield's deliberately increased hospitality towards illustrative quotations and combinatorial forms? In 1965, Sisam had commented adversely on a sample of Supplement copy sent out to him in the Scilly Isles: 'Generally I should criticise the specimen for many kinds of profuseness. In the main O.E.D. and the first Supplement there were general rules for scale to standards of inclusion which are not obvious to me in [Burchfield's] specimen, though they may be clear when the principles are explained . . . . The quotations are long, and sometimes unnecessarily multiplied.' Burchfield strongly resisted some of Sisam's specific criticisms – against his disapproval of the length and layout of his treatment of compound forms in *astro-* he jotted angrily 'This kind of remark is no help at all'[15] – but any Supplement reader might concede that the 'profuseness' of quotations, uneven as it is, raises questions rather than answering them.[16] In his updating of the first edition's entry for the noun *alibi* (originally published in 1884), for example,

Burchfield supplied two extra quotations, one an ante-dating and one a post-dating, so that the new quotation range reads 1743, 1774, 1855, 1862, 1939 (this last from Eliot's *Old Possum's Book of Practical Cats*). Useful, but a curious contrast to his treatment of the newly identified transitive verb *alibi* ('to clear by an excuse, to provide an alibi for'), whose first appearance he dated 1909. Here, he printed not one or two, but instead seven quotations, dated 1909 (two from the same source), 1917, 1926 (again, two from same source), 1930 and 1958. Whatever one should infer from this, the most obvious inference, that the verb *alibi* is either more frequently used or in some way more important than the noun, is (surely) erroneous.[17] Instead, this must be an example of the *OED*'s habit of favouring eccentric diction at the expense of the core lexicon, something deplored by Murray from the early days of his editorship but still, evidently, hard to avoid. (Murray famously complained that 'of *Abusion*, we found in the slips about fifty instances: of *Abuse* not five'; but Murray had not replicated that imbalance in the Dictionary itself.)[18]

Even more striking are the thirteen twentieth-century quotations Burchfield supplied for *mantra*, nine of which come from the years 1962–73, although according to Burchfield's normal rule the word did not need updating since it was already furnished with a quotation of 1883.[19] Contrast that with the three quotations for *manufacturer* (1752, 1832 and 1901), three quotations for *Labour Government* (1926, 1945, 1971), two quotations (both eighteenth-century), for *labour-pains*, and three twentieth-century quotations for the noun *rape* meaning sexual assault – all of which, incidentally, refer to male homosexual rape.

Where the verb *rape* is concerned, Burchfield's practice – reproduced unchanged in *OED2*, and hence the current (autumn 2006) version of *OED Online* – is so startling that it is worth examining in more detail. *OED* had supplied four quotations for sense 3, which it defines as 'To ravish, commit rape on (a woman)', dated 1577, 1641, 1861 and 1885 (all with women as the object of the verb). Burchfield added a further gloss to this sense, 'Also, with a man as the sexual object and a man or woman as the subject', and provided five quotations as follows (four from one decade clumped together):[20]

1928 *D. H. LAWRENCE Let.* ? 28 Oct. (1962) II. 1096 Why do men only thrill to a woman who'll rape them? **1971** *Southerly* XXXI. 6 The first of the series of sexually voracious women who seek virtually to rape him. **1972** *Times* 31 Oct. 2/4 The girls had taken their clothes off and intended to rape him. **1977** *New Society* 1 Sept. 449/2 These women have been confined for a variety of offences, chief among which are soliciting and manslaughter. When a man finds his way into their midst, he is promptly raped. **1977** *New Yorker* 24 Oct. 64/3 A man . . . claimed he had been assaulted and raped by four other prisoners.

As it stands, the quotation evidence gives rise to the inference that after the turn of the twentieth century, when female–male rape began (if it existed before, the word *rape* was not used for it), there was no longer any male–female rape. While it is understandable that Burchfield wanted to print sufficient evidence to demonstrate that the new sense he had identified was established in the language, the result flies in the face of one of the most significant of the functions of *OED*, namely that it reflects the culture whose language it records (or as *OED* puts it itself, the Dictionary 'not only provides an important record of the evolution of our language, but also documents the continuing development of our society').[21] As the 'essence of the work' (in Murray's words, p. 128 above), quotations play a crucial role in it. Burchfield might easily have printed quotations illustrating the use of the verb as applied to male–female rape, thus providing twentieth-century evidence for the continued use of this sense, as he did for many others.[22]

Further examples of this sort of variation between the numbers of quotations provided for different entries, and the consequent puzzle as to how it should be interpreted or what it is intended to imply, can be found simply by leafing through Burchfield's pages: 18 quotations for *pizzazz* and 5 for *pizzeria*, 16 for *plonk* (= cheap wine) and 6 for *press-up*, and so on.

Sisam's other main objection, to the proliferation of combinatorial forms, raises another set of questions. Murray's close friend W. W. Skeat had written to him about this in 1878, right at the start of his editorship: 'The mere piling up of additional words, especially of words of wh. the meaning is self-obvious, gives no value to a Dict^y, but rather decreases it' (though he thought exceptions might be made 'in cases where the works of famous men have made such words famous').[23] Murray had taken the same view: as we saw in Chapter I, Craigie got into terrible hot water with him for putting *railway director* in the Dictionary as a derivative form under *railway*. It was totally unnecessary to include such phrases, Murray felt, as their meaning was transparent. Yoking two words together in this way was how the English language expressed 'the genitive relation' (that is, ownership or belonging), and was, in Murray's words, 'a grammatical, not a lexicographic matter. *Railway director* is simply our ordinary way of saying *director of a railway*, and the one phrase has no more business in the Dictionary than the other, or than such a phrase as *man's life*, *manufacturer's employees*, or *officer's valet*.'

Murray's furious condemnation of Craigie's practice here is quoted by Burchfield, as is Murray's view that including such combinatorial forms was 'not in accordance with the principles and method of the Dictionary . . . much valuable space appears in consequence to be consumed on what is of no practical value'.[24] In fact, when the original portion of this section of OED appeared in 1904, the first fascicle for which Craigie was responsible, it turned out that he did after all include *railway director*, along with *railway porter*, *railway cat*, *railway sandwich*, and a host of other similar phrases. There is certainly a good argument that Murray was right and that there was little point in their inclusion; indeed Craigie puts in a comment that almost suggests as much: 'The great development of railways in the 19th c., leading to an extensive use of the word in various connexions, has given rise to many attributive collocations of a more or less permanent character, while the number of those which may be formed at will is infinite. The examples given here have been selected mainly as being instances of some of the more usual combinations . . . .' It seems that Craigie recognized the force of Murray's objections but held out all the same for putting all these quotations in (twenty-seven of them). He has another (shorter) section altogether, sense 4, for 'special' combinations where one cannot infer the meaning from the two separate words – e.g. *railway-creeper*, 'a plant conspicuous at railway stations in India', and *railway spine*, 'an affection of the spine produced by concussion in a railway accident'.

Such collocations uncontroversially deserve inclusion and definition: the problem is to decide when, or if, a transparent combination has become a 'special' one (compare, for example, *shop door* with *shop window* and *shop floor*: *shop door* generally means just that and no more; *shop window* can mean a place inside a shop's window for showing off goods as well as the window of a shop; *shop floor* now usually has a figurative meaning). Murray was well aware of the difficulty: in 1879 he told the Philological Society that, 'like other Dictionary-makers, I have found the question of questionable compounds a very difficult one to settle'; and his own portion of the OED also contained a good number of 'obvious' combinations, as can be seen from the statistics published in the prefatory material to most of the fascicles.[25]

But Burchfield felt that Craigie was right to put in an abundance of phrases of the transparent type. He comments, perhaps in allusion to Sisam's 1965 objections, 'It would be foolish if I were to say that I have sailed through OEDS without similar problems to those [of Craigie]. Some of these have arisen because of my insistence that this very class of words, "obvious" attributive uses, should be extended and expanded', in order to show that this form of word-formation was in as fine fettle now as in previous centuries. And despite the fact that this use of *railway* was perfectly adequately illustrated in OED1, with quotations as late as 1880, Burchfield chose to add nearly a hundred more (occupying almost two columns) when he came to Craigie's entry for this word, in the third volume of his Supplement published in 1983, although according to his own rule – no new material if nineteenth-century quotations were already in the *OED* – such updating was quite unnecessary and the new insertions added nothing material to the information and evidence already present in the Dictionary (the space might have been better used for a few twentieth-century quotations for male–female *rape*).

If Burchfield had consistently added further evidence of this sort, he would have doubled or even tripled the size of the Supplement and greatly extended the length taken to produce it. As it is, the most casual glance through any of the four Supplement volumes indicates that combinatorial forms of this sort do take up a remarkable amount of space in Burchfield's additions (as under *bed, bank, plain, stone, word,* and hundreds of other entries).

One way of assessing Burchfield's policy on combinations is to compare it with that of the parent Dictionary. Both Murray and Burchfield give figures for the number of words they define, and for the number of combinations (both defined and undefined) they also include. The original *OED* treated 307,270 words, and 107,555 combinations (414,825 words in all), a ratio of 3:1. Burchfield, on the other hand, treated 62,750 words, and 64,000 combinations (126,750 words in all), a ratio exceeding 1:1.[26] This means that, proportionally, Burchfield included vastly more combinations than Murray and his fellow editors. Certainly Burchfield's record can persuade us that such combinations are as easy to make now as in previous centuries. But what it chiefly tells us is that he had a particular zeal for collecting examples of such forms, not that the twentieth century was either more, or less, 'productive' than 'those that immediately preceded it'.

'A literary instrument'?

'The great majority' of the combinatorial forms in the second Supplement, so Burchfield claimed in 1973, are 'from literary sources'.[27] This interesting statistic is impossible to verify, but it is a characteristic indication of the importance he attached to such sources. Consciously adopting the mantle of his predecessors, Burchfield began with a strong sense of the centrality of literature both to language and to the *OED*: as we have seen, reporting to the Delegates in 1962, he put 'the main literary works of the period 1930–1960' at the head of his list of sources tackled by readers for the new dictionary, and even hoped to remedy, so far as might then be possible, the failings of the first Supplement in this respect. He preserved to the last his determination to quote from 'great writers', on occasion expressing a strong sense of embattlement against the destructive practices of modern linguists, whom he characterized as 'great marauding bands', 'scholars with shovels intent on burying the linguistic past and most of the literary past and present'. To ignore 'our greatest living writers' left one, he felt, 'looking at a language with one's eyes partly blindfolded': and if the *OED* had had room for the vocabulary of the canon Orm (whose work had been the subject of Burchfield's own projected graduate thesis), then he too 'could, and must, admit the vocabulary of Edith Sitwell and Wystan Auden'. [28]

According to Burchfield's own report, his love for literary sources played a determining role in prolonging the production of the second Supplement. This was owing to a strategy he devised in order to deal with adverse comment on the sample of Supplement pages which he produced in 1963. The reports on this sample surviving in the archives are wholly positive ('quite first rate', 'excellent', etc.), but apparently there had originally been some objections to 'poetical items': Burchfield reports that his inclusion of T. S. Eliot's *loam feet*, quoted from *Four Quartets* – 'Lifting heavy feet in clumsy shoes, Earth feet, loam feet, lifted in country mirth' – was disapproved of both by some of the consulted scholars (unnamed) and by his 'publishing overlords within OUP'. (Sisam's contempt for 'poetical vocabulary' had perhaps been passed down to his successors.)[29] Nevertheless, Burchfield decided to retain this quotation, together with one he had also included from a poem by Donald Davie ('Come with me by the self-consuming north (The North is spirit), to the loam-foot west And opulent departures of the south'), which he thought might have been influenced by Eliot's use. He explains why: if he increased 'the coverage of every realm of English vocabulary throughout the English-speaking world', then 'poetical combinations of the *loam-foot* kind would be mere golden specks in the whole work'. Despite alleged resistance from his staff – 'my staff (I don't know about anyone else's) have a genuine horror of poets. I love poetry and poetical use has been poured into the Supplement, because it is my own preference compared with that of my colleagues' – this new policy met with the publishers' assent: 'to their eternal credit the senior officers at the Press did not intervene, and the editing continued on the basis of the specimen together with my newly formed principle of swamping somewhat unpopular items, or rendering them semi-visible, by enlarging the whole structure. It was the moment, I now [1988] realise, when the one-volume Supplement that had been planned inevitably turned into a four-volume work.'[30]

The view that the distinctive uses of literary writers are on the one hand the backbone of the language and must be faithfully recorded by the *OED* if it is to explain the history and development of English, but are on the other hand 'golden specks' which must be swamped by a welter of other entries so that they are not too visible, is not entirely coherent. As his predecessor Henry Bradley recognized in 1904, some writers – he instanced Lydgate, Malory, Caxton, Spenser, Shakespeare, Pope, Johnson and Walter Scott, among others – have had a marked influence on language, 'either because of their boldness in the introduction of new words and new senses of words, and the extent to which their innovations have found acceptance, or because their writings have afforded abundant material for literary allusion'. Others, by contrast, have not – or at least, not in clearly demonstrable ways – for example (Bradley suggests, contentiously) Chaucer, Milton and Carlyle.[31] All these writers are generously quoted by the *OED*, to the delight and satisfaction of generations of readers who value the Dictionary as a treasure-house of the writings of major contributors to the literary canon. But *OED*'s quotations from such sources tell us as much about the values of the lexicographers and their readers as about the language itself: as we saw in Chapter IV, some writers – late sixteenth-century, or male, for example – were favoured over others – eighteenth-century, or female – for cultural, not linguistic, reasons.

Burchfield emphasizes many times his fondness for inclusion of the *hapax legomena* and eccentric usages of literary writers (Beckett's *athambia*, Joyce's *impotentising*, Woolf's *scrolloping*, Edith Sitwell's *Martha-coloured* – 'the result of a personal memory . . . . As a child, I had a nursery maid called Martha, who always wore a . . . gown . . . exactly the colour of a scabious', Hopkins's *unleaving*, etc.).[32] But he never tackles the paradox at the heart of the relationship between literary language and the language of the tribe: that (as countless scholars, and writers themselves, have investigated), literary writers often choose to express themselves by deviating from 'ordinary language' rather than merely exemplifying it. (Famously, Thomas Gray said that 'the language of the age is never the language of poetry . . . poetry . . . has a language peculiar to itself'; though T. S. Eliot warned that poetry 'must not stray too far from the ordinary everyday language which we use and hear', nor 'lose its contact with the changing language of common intercourse', and G. M. Hopkins thought that poetic language 'should be the current language heightened, to any degree heightened and unlike itself, but not . . . an obsolete one'.)[33]

Sometimes such deviation is linguistically productive and the resulting locutions and coinages have caught on in the language – whether the supposed usage of Shakespeare (*scotch the snake*), or of Spenser (*chevisance* – for which he was chided by the *OED* lexicographers), Carlyle (*gigman*), Tolkien (*hobbit*), or of Sinclair Lewis (*Babbitt*) – and sometimes not: as the term 'specks' suggests, many literary usages (the 'literary fungi' we saw

Herbert Coleridge complain of in 1860) seem to have been peripheral to general usage rather than to have influenced it in any substantial way (e.g. *Martha-coloured*).[34]

In the event, several critics complained that the coverage and treatment of some literary sources was insufficient, thus illustrating how difficult it was to please everyone. Geoffrey Hill, for example, resented Burchfield's inclusion of words like *tofu* at the expense of adequate treatment of Hopkins's language, in particular the exclusion of *unchancelling*, asking, 'is the name of an easily analysable substance which has appeared on a million menus more real than a word, peculiarly resistant to analysis, which has lodged itself in a few thousands of minds?'[35] Such a question indicates the impossible burden of expectation that the *OED* has to bear: how can it conceivably record all the vocabulary, or even the significant vocabulary, of all the writers that might be judged, by whatever criteria, to deserve a place within its pages? And how can a dictionary do full justice to the way that poets use language, which is often context-dependent on the one hand, and polysemous (in that the reader is expected to summon to mind a wide range of possible connotations) on the other?

Who these writers should be, and how their work should be handled, were nettles only partially grasped by Burchfield. In 1989, looking back on early days at the Supplement, he wrote, 'the entire works of writers like Eliot, Auden, Joyce, Lawrence, and many others, needed to be indexed in the manner that the readers of sources drawn on for the *OED* had indexed the works of Chaucer, Malory, Marlowe, Shakespeare, Milton, Johnson, and all the other famous writers of the past'. (Elsewhere he picks out Edward Thomas, Dylan Thomas and Roy Fuller as, what he calls, 'significant authors'.) Setting aside the question of how such writers should be identified, indexing of this sort was specifically disclaimed by Murray: 'forming complete verbal indexes to all books ... is not only impossible, but the results would be unmanageable' as he told the Philological Society in 1884 although his assistants had made a start on some books in 1879.[36] Clearly, despite the regrets of Hill and others, indexing would have been equally impracticable for the second Supplement. There is no indication that it occurred; indeed, in the Introduction to volume 1, Burchfield apologizes for his policy of 'liberally representing the vocabulary of such writers as Kipling, James Joyce, and Dylan Thomas', as against the *OED*'s 'policy of total literary inclusiveness for the earlier centuries ... [of] all the vocabulary, including *hapax legomena*, of such authors as Chaucer, Gower and Shakespeare'. This last remark is baffling. Any regular user of the parent Dictionary can attest that *OED* did not, and could not, achieve 'total literary inclusiveness'.

Inconsistency was unavoidable in a policy such as this, and Burchfield freely acknowledged that he changed his mind as he went along, for example deciding in 1973 – after the publication in 1972 of his first volume, treating the letters *A–G* – to include all rather than just some Jabberwocky coinages, with the consequence that, of this group of words, only *borogove, callay, callooh, frumious,* and *gimble* are omitted from the *Supplement*.[37] He also acknowledged that 'the pattern of admission' of such words

> was governed as much by the choice made by the readers as by any abstract principles adopted by the editors. If a reader made a slip for such an item it was likely to be included, with small regard for consistency in comparable words, or in words drawn from other writers, in other parts of the Dictionary. Conversely a word that was not copied by a reader had little chance of inclusion since the editorial staff would almost certainly be unaware of its existence.[38]

The results can be seen in any Supplement author whose works are checked in detail against the dictionary itself. A typical case is that of Auden, named several times by Burchfield as an indexed source, with around 750 quotations altogether – many for unusual words (*ingressant, lanterloo*), but others for more ordinary ones (*clambake, cocktail*).[39] Some of his poems are not cited at all, despite the fact that they appear in volumes listed in the Supplement bibliography (published at the end of volume 4 in 1986), and contain many words and usages just as eligible as ones which the Supplement does record. Different editions and dates are cited for the same work: 'Under Sirius', for example, first appeared in the journal *Horizon* in 1949, and subsequently in the collection *Nones*, published in New York in 1951 and in London in 1952. All three dates are in different places assigned by the Supplement to vocabulary recorded from the poem. In any one poem, some of the unusual words will get into the dictionary and some will not (*rundle* is not recorded, but *semble* is; they occur six lines apart in 'Thanksgiving for a Habitat' (1965); *flosculent* and *maltalent* (n.) are not recorded, but *ubity* and *videnda* are; they occur a few pages apart in the same work). When such words are cited by the Supplement, they are variously, and apparently inconsistently, labelled as *arch[aic], isolated later example, nonce-word, Obs. exc. poet., poet[ic], rare* (or *rare⁻¹*, meaning that Auden's is the only example found), with no indication how these labels were assigned or what the distinction between them is.[40]

Reading through his copy of the second volume of Burchfield's Supplement in 1976–77, Clive James saw that its citation of authorities delivered judgements on a cultural as well as a linguistic world:

Some critics have noticed, with barely concealed anger, that Martin Amis is in with 'ludic' [Anthony Burgess had pointed out that his own use (1966) antedated that of Amis (1973)].[41] There has been something like a boycott of his father, Kingsley, who is among those authors cited for 'Lefty' but who so far as the editors are concerned might never have written *Lucky Jim*. If 'James Bond' is in the language then 'Lucky Jim' (or at least 'Lucky Jimmery', which is in frequent use) ought to be in as well. So should 'Jimmy Porter', but there is no mention of him, either: John Osborne only gets in for 'legit' (Archie Rice said it in *The Entertainer*) . . . . Of the younger ladies, Margaret Drabble is in but once, for 'lit. crit.'. *The Female Eunuch*, however, is quoted so often that the whole volume might as well have been called *Beauties from Germaine Greer*. With due allowance for envy on my part, I'm bound to say that Ms Greer seems to have made a big hit with the editors, who must have read her book to pieces. She is a fountain of examples not just on her own subject but on every other subject as well. She is in for 'Hollywoodise.' She is back a few entries later for 'hoodlumise'. She is in for 'inauthentic' . . . She is in for 'largactil', 'lovenest', 'Marcusian' . . . but enough. Face it lads: old Germs is the Shakespeare of our generation.

Noting the *life-* compounds already mentioned, James fastens on D. H. Lawrence as 'Most-Mentioned Male'. On the other hand, 'there is a tendency to down-grade Dr Leavis. He is not in for "life-enhancing" – an unhistorical omission', while (and here James points out the importance of what the quotations say, not just where they are from) 'the entry for "magazine" quotes the *Listener* to make Leavis sound cranky ("Leavis didn't apologise that his terms of reference should be the Robbins Report and Harold Wilson and the magazine sections of the English Sundays")', and that for *literarism* makes him sound paranoid ('the term "literarism" was in fact coined by the late Aldous Huxley for use against me').[42]

Irresistibly, the reader constructs a world view from these citational choices. The lexicographers articulate no cultural manifesto, but time after time, in entry after entry, they choose – whether conscious or not of the cumulative effect – to quote one source (and one type of content) rather than another, and therefore to reinforce a particular set of cultural values. The enormous array of scholarly information assembled in the Supplement, as in the parent Dictionary, gives the impression (justly) of utterly punctilious and impartial erudition. But the readers and the lexicographers made prior decisions, not necessarily on linguistic grounds alone, about which sources were worth reading and recording. These decisions affected the dictionary they produced.

Preferences and biases, of whatever sort, become clearer when we contemplate the larger picture: and it is here that the electronic searching enabled by *OED Online* comes to the fore, since it allows us to distinguish the relative intensity with which sources are quoted in the Dictionary. We can now see, as neither James, nor even Burchfield himself, could have seen at the time, that Greer was cited 131 times in all (58 times in volume 2, the one James was reading). Where male-authored literary sources were concerned, James was right to pick out Lawrence as a favourite. Burchfield seems to have applied a literary canon of sorts: Joyce, Wodehouse, Lawrence, Aldous Huxley and Auden are the twentieth-century authors most frequently cited in the Supplement, in that order, from around 2,000 quotations down to 750 – far more than 'Shakespeare' Greer.[43] But female authors were a different kettle of fish, in the Supplement as in the *OED* itself. Top of the list in Burchfield's dictionary – but with far fewer quotations than male authors – were Ngaio Marsh (the New Zealand crime writer), Dorothy Sayers and Agatha Christie, at around 450 quotations each, followed at some distance by more literary writers such as Elizabeth Bowen and Woolf (around 340 and 230 respectively).[44]

As already demonstrated (Chapter IV), the *OED* is constructed from its quotations. Do these figures and ratios, whether of male or female authors or both, tell us about the relative contribution such writers made to the English language? Or instead about the reading preferences of Burchfield, his staff and his volunteers (with the indefatigable Marghanita Laski, an enthusiastic reader of crime novels, perhaps playing a significant role)? Almost certainly the latter.

Excursus on writers and dictionaries: the example of Auden

In including words like *asile* (used by Hardy), *baltering, soodling* (Auden), *stelled* (Edmund Blunden), and many others, Burchfield may have been remembering the epigraph from Horace's *Epistles* that Dr Johnson printed on the title-page of his dictionary:

> [The good poet] will do well to unearth words that have been long hidden from the people's view, bringing to light some splendid terms employed in earlier days by Cato, Cethegus and others which now lie buried by grimy dust and the years' neglect.[45]

As we saw earlier, Johnson selected his quotations from a body of major literary and philosophical writers from up to two hundred years before his own time. One of his intentions was to record the language used by these writers and thus to influence the usage of modern writers: he hoped, he said, to 'contribute to the preservation of antient, and the improvement of modern writers'.[46] Burchfield no doubt felt the same. His term 'literary instrument', used of the *OED* in his 1962 report to the Press, suggests not only the Dictionary's role as a key to great writers of the past, but also its function as quarry for great writers of the future. Horace's words remind us that writers as well as lexicographers may wish to preserve language, and by re-using a word keep it alive or even resurrect it from the past.

The regenerative and formative role of a writer in the development of language is several times meditated on by T. S. Eliot, for example in a BBC radio discussion broadcast at a time of national crisis in November 1940. Here he drew a Trenchian parallel between the greatness of a nation and the greatness of its language: 'If a nation to be great must have a great language, it is the business of the writer as artist to help to preserve and extend the resources of that language.' Such a person must prevent 'the language from deteriorating or from getting ossified', helping 'to choose, from among the new words and idioms in current speech and in current journalism, those which justify themselves, which deserve to be fully licensed and preserved'. But writers do not do this on their own: there is 'a continuous collaboration between the few who can write it and everybody who speaks it', a collaboration which is recorded (Eliot's interlocutor Desmond Hawkins suggests) in the pages of the dictionary, a book in part written by the 'non-literary dead', 'the ancestral Man-in-the-Street', 'the ones who weren't writers'. The dictionary, consequently, is 'a book to which every professional writer is infinitely indebted'.

'Quite so,' Eliot replies, and proceeds to develop the idea: 'The dictionary is the most important, the most inexhaustible book to a writer. Incidentally, I find it the best reading in the world when I am recovering from influenza, or any other temporary illness, except that one needs a bookrest for it across the bed. You want a big dictionary, because definitions are not enough by themselves: you want the quotations showing how a word has been used ever since it was first used.' (This tempts one to think that Eliot was thinking of the *OED*, but Valerie Eliot confirmed to Burchfield in 1988 that 'her husband possessed a copy of the *Shorter Oxford* but not of the *OED* itself'.)[47]

The unmatchable qualities of a dictionary as reading material, and its suggestive powers for poets and authors, have been observed by many other writers. Emerson believed that 'neither is a dictionary a bad book to read. There is no cant in it, no excess of explanation, and it is full of suggestion. The raw material of possible poems and histories', a sentiment chosen by Murray in 1895 as one of the illustrative quotations for the *OED* entry for *dictionary*. Years later, OUP marketing staff found an echo of Emerson (perhaps deliberate) by the novelist E. Annie Proulx and printed it as one of the puffs on *OED* publicity material in 2003: 'Here is the greatest treasure of words waiting to be assembled . . . All the raw material a writer needs for a lifetime of work'.

Oliver Wendell Holmes had explained one of the reasons why in 1831: 'When I feel inclined to read poetry I take down my Dictionary. The poetry of words is quite as beautiful as that of sentences. The author may arrange the gems effectively, but their shape and lustre have been given by the attrition of ages. Bring me the finest simile and I will show you a single word which conveys a more profound, a more accurate, and a more eloquent analogy', thus anticipating Trench's later musings on Emerson's term 'fossil poetry': 'Many a single word also is itself a concentrated poem, having stores of poetical thought and imagery laid up in it' (the *OED* also liked the formulation 'fossil poetry' and found two occasions to quote it in the Dictionary).[48] Auden said much the same in his inaugural lecture as Professor of Poetry in Oxford in 1956 (perhaps attended by Burchfield, who was lecturer at Christ Church, Auden's college, at the time), when he remarked that 'the most poetical of all scholastic disciplines is, surely, Philology, the study of language in abstraction from its uses, so that words become, as it were, little lyrics about themselves'.[49]

One way in which words can be thought of as 'little lyrics about themselves' is in etymological terms: how a word's philological components tell a story about its development through time. This brings us straight back to the dictionary, and more specifically to *OED*, whose individual entries on words might, however fancifully, be thought of as 'poems', often containing miniature essays on etymology as well as the mosaic of quotations illustrating a word's use in (canonical) literary sources. Auden was a famous, even notorious dictionary reader, and once declared that if marooned on a desert island, he would choose to have with him 'a good dictionary' in preference to 'the greatest literary masterpiece imaginable, for, in relation to its readers, a dictionary is absolutely passive and may legitimately be read in an infinite number of ways'.[50] His poems (particularly the later ones) are peppered with abstruse vocabulary, and the only way a reader can understand what he is saying is to turn to a dictionary for elucidation, sometimes a dialect dictionary but often *OED*. Auden's obsession with this work originated in his early years, and may have been related to his other early passion for geology; in both cases (as Trench and others had seen) meaning could be discovered by exploring the layered strata of the past.[51] Humphrey Carpenter's biography describes how, while an undergraduate at Christ Church, Auden impressed many of his contemporaries with his voracious appetite for words:

In his conversation as in his poetry, he used a vocabulary drawn from scientific, psychological and philosophical terminology, and from his discoveries among the pages of the *Oxford English Dictionary*. Words like 'glabrous', 'sordes', 'callipygous', 'peptonised' (which all appeared in his poetry during this period) delighted him but disconcerted his listeners. 'I did not understand much of what Wystan said,' recorded one undergraduate contemporary, who nevertheless 'felt it was important because of the portentous manner in which he said it.'[52]

And Carpenter gives a memorable account of the pride of place enjoyed by *OED* in Auden's study in his house at Kirchstetten, Austria:

Auden's workroom – the upper room, reached by an outside staircase, and always shown proudly to visitors, was . . . bare, with piles of books (no bookcases), a desk on a raised platform by the window, and a portable typewriter on which Auden composed his book-reviews and articles and made fair copies of his poems. The most prominent object in the workroom was a set of the *Oxford English Dictionary*, missing one volume, which was downstairs, Auden invariably using it as a cushion to sit on when at table – as if (a friend observed) he was a child not quite big enough for the nursery furniture.[53]

By 1972, when he returned to Oxford (to live in grace and favour lodgings at Christ Church), Auden's copy of *OED* was so worn out he was considering buying a new one.[54]

The effect on his poetry is one on which critics have remarked with some asperity. As Frank Kermode points out in a review of *Epistle to a Godson*, a collection of Auden's poems published in 1972, 'sometimes you find two learned freaks together, in such a way that it looks as if the poet has only that morning been browsing [through the dictionary]: eutrophied, eucatastrophe; obtemper, obumbrate'.[55] Denis Donoghue reacted with similar tartness to the same collection, in a review entitled 'Good Grief': '. . . Mr Auden, it is well known and in part approved, has been making merry with the dictionary in recent years. I suppose he thinks of them as pure poetry, containing thousands of words virtually untouched by human hands; marvelous words now archaic, obsolete, and for that very reason waiting to be resuscitated by a poet addicted to that pleasure . . . .'[56] A particularly preposterous poem is entitled 'A Bad Night' and subtitled 'A Lexical Exercise'. It is crammed with words lifted from *OED* which, out of context, are virtually unintelligible: *hirple, blouts, pirries, stolchy, glunch, sloomy, snudge, snoachy, scaddle*, etc. In context, however, they are much more communicative: 'Buffeted often/By blouts of hail/Or pirries of rain/On stolchy paths . . .' [57] The syntax, together with the sound qualities of these unfamiliar words, roughs out for us a perfectly adequate impression of their meaning, and *OED* functions as a useful reference point, giving us the definitions of the words and instances of their use that Auden himself presumably read and pondered upon as part of the 'exercise' of composing the poem.

OED is helpful not only in explaining to us what Auden apparently meant, but also in providing clues as to why he chose as he did. Auden's use of *hirple* at line 8 ('Far he must hirple,/Clumsied by cold') may have been prompted by one of *OED*'s citations for *hoast*, a word which crops up further down in the poem ('Fetched into conscience/By a hoasting fit'), from Ritson's *Scotish Songs* (1794): 'He hosts and he hirples the weary day long'. *OED* citations may also explain Auden's choice of the word *curmur* in 'Thanksgiving for a Habitat X' ('two doters who wish/to tiddle and curmurr between the soup and fish/belong in restaurants'), where the reference is to the undesirability of cooing lovers as guests at a dinner party. *OED* defines *curmur* merely as 'to make a low murmuring or purring sound'; the single illustrative quotation (from *Blackwood's Magazine* in 1831) more precisely connotes the behaviour of two lovers over a meal: 'They two [cats] sit curmurring, forgetful of mice and milk, of all but love.' The verbal noun *curmurring* gets a separate entry in *OED*, and is defined as 'a low rumbling, growling, or murmuring sound'; the two illustrative quotations (one from Burns, one from Scott) both use the word to refer to the noise made in digesting food – suggesting prandial connotations closer to Auden's use than to the *OED* definition. It seems possible, perhaps likely, either that the various quotations suggested the context of the word in Auden's poem, or that his context reminded Auden of the quotations, and hence recalled the word *curmur* to him for use in this instance. Earlier in the same poem, Auden's apparently archaic use of the word *port* as a verb ('only cops port arms') may similarly have been triggered by reading the last quotation for this sense in *OED1*, dated 1711: 'They had ported arms without license.'

One can go on playing this game indefinitely, returning to the Dictionary with the words Auden seems to have lifted from it in the first place, and trying to retrace his readings through the pages of *OED* in an attempt to shed some light on the way his mind connected disparate contexts. According to Burchfield himself, Auden several times urged him to insert particular words into the Supplement. On one occasion, he 'pressed me to include the word *disinterested* in the "now established sense" of "uninterested"' (Burchfield did so, but called it 'a loose use').[58] On another, Burchfield was sitting working quietly in his room at Christ Church when the door burst open and in rushed an excited Auden, waving a sheet of paper in his hand freshly torn out of his typewriter, to insist Burchfield should put back into the *OED* an obscure word in a poem he had just that minute written. In telling this tale – to an audience of historical linguists at a conference in Oxford in 1988 – Burchfield gave it as his opinion that 'Auden was not a scholar and often didn't know what words meant', echoing, if unconsciously, Murray's complaint about Robert Browning, who 'constantly used words without regard to their proper meaning', and 'added greatly to the difficulties of the Dictionary' (Browning had earlier told Murray 'that he found the Dictionary "most delightful" and intended to read every word of it'.)[59]

A number of Murray's surviving letters are to writers, inquiring what precisely they had meant when they used a particular word. The replies were not always helpful: answering a query about the meaning of *thwarteous*, a word he had used in his drama 'The Christian Captives' in 1886, Robert Bridges told Murray, 'As I remember nothing about this word I think it best to say nothing . . . . As soon as I had finished [the play] I began something else, and have scarcely thought of it again. Whether I coined the word or found it I cannot say.'[60]

It is not surprising if Murray was sometimes sceptical of the value of such testimony. Responding to an inquiry about the meaning of the word *voidee cup* in a work of Dante Gabriel Rossetti's ('Then he called for the Voidee-cup:/And as we heard the twelfth hour strike,/There by true lips and false lips alike/Was the draught of trust drained up'), he told a correspondent, 'I see no trace of Rossetti's phrase in English of any age, and I suppose he invented it himself.' After some guesses at how Rossetti might have arrived at the phrase, deriving it perhaps from Old French, Murray continued,

One must not take the language of poets too seriously. One cannot now ask Rossetti where he got it or how he coined it; but if I may infer from the results of appealing to other poets for explanation of their cruces, he would probably say 'I have really forgotten; I was under the impression that I had seen or heard it somewhere; can I have been under a misapprehension? what terrible people you dictionary fellows are, hunting us up about every word; you make life a burden.' That is the general sort of answer one gets, which means 'we write for amusement, & not to be studied as texts; if you will make school-texts of us, yours be the responsibility!' I believe Browning once answered a request for explanation of a passage, with 'I really do not know; ask the Browning Society!' I know he once confessed ignorance to me of the meaning of one of Mrs B's lines.[61]

(In fact he was wrong to impugn Rossetti in this way. Craigie included *voidee* in the *Visor–Vywer* fascicle, published five years after Murray's death in 1920, and defined it as 'a collation consisting of wine accompanied by spices, comfits, or the like, partaken of before retiring to rest or the departure of guests . . .', illustrating the word with quotations from Chaucer up to the mid-seventeenth century, along with this very instance from Rossetti (1881) as an example of an 'attributive' use.)[62] Murray enjoyed a far more productive relationship with Thomas Hardy, illuminatingly explored by Dennis Taylor, who describes how 'Hardy snatched up the volumes of the dictionary as they appeared, [while] Murray's readers snatched up the volumes of Hardy as they appeared, in order to incorporate their distinctive words' into the *OED*.[63] His granddaughter records, however, that Murray 'held all his life to the opinion that novel reading was a waste of time'.[64]

Several of Auden's words, quoted in the Supplement, are labelled '*isolated later example*', or '*Obs. exc. poetic*'. One member of the Supplement staff, Julian Barnes, later described how – given Auden's predilection for treating *OED* 'not as a Supreme Court but as a flea-market where cast-offs can be acquired at little expense' – the *OEDS* team had often to decide, as they sat and pondered their collection of quotations, 'how far Auden's re-use of [a] word constituted a genuine revival of it, or whether it was merely a nonce-archaism'.[65] But the only time that Burchfield acknowledges the phenomenon of which these instances may be examples – the *OED* putting back into its pages a word that a writer found there in the first place – is in a comment on his inclusion of James Joyce's use of *peccaminous* (for which *OED1* had recorded only two quotations, 1656 and 1668): 'It is the kind of word that Joyce may have picked up from the *O.E.D.*' – though it has been questioned, by Vincent Deane, whether Joyce did actually use *OED* as a source. This word has recently been revisited by the lexicographers at work on the third edition of the *OED*, who have found a further modern use of the word since Joyce. It seems that the lexicographical loop between writers and dictionaries continues.[66]

Other sorts of echoes and re-uses, whether inside or outside the *OED*, Burchfield enjoyed recording. He added the word *cessile* (= 'yielding') to *OED* in his first volume in 1972, quoting first a poem by the Scottish poet Alexander Hume of 1599 ('The massiue earth reposis still, Suspended in the cessil eire'), then a quotation from it ('cessile air') by Quiller-Couch (1911), and then a further echo of it ('Scintillant circumambient cessile air') in Joyce's *Ulysses* (1922) – Quiller-Couch had included the poem in his *Oxford Book of English Verse* of 1900 (many times reprinted) and Joyce may have read it there. In defining the word Burchfield explains that it is 'applied only to the air, in imitation of the first quot.' And in the rag-bag collection of combinatorial forms under the adjective and adverb *plain* he prints a chain of quotations on the term 'plain-sewing', a word used by Auden to refer to mutual masturbation (along with 'Princeton-First-Year' which Burchfield also adds to *OED*). They include a snippet from the *Observer* (1971) reporting that 'one of my [W. H. Auden's] great ambitions is to get into the OED, as the first person to have used in print a new word. I have two candidates at the moment', which Burchfield sandwiches between two other references to Auden's use of the term.

OED3 revised this entry in December 2005, excising the 1971 quotation and with it Burchfield's revelation of Auden's *OED* ambition, and choosing instead a later example, a letter from Derek Attridge to the *TLS* (part of a correspondence discussing the term): 'Auden . . . once boasted to me . . . of his having been the first to use "Plain-Sewing" in print, and explained it as a sailor's term for mutual masturbation' (18 April 1980, p. 441). This new choice of quotations perhaps better explains the usage of the term (it is arguable), but does so, regrettably, at the cost of drawing our attention to the *OED*'s own incestuous relationship with dictionary-reading writers.

World English

In Chapters V and VI it was mentioned that Burchfield received a couple of substantial donations of non-UK material from the New Zealander lexicographer H. W. Orsman and the US lexicographer Clarence Barnhart. But he initially accepted Sisam's view that uses peculiar to North America and to the 'Dominions' should be kept to some sort of decent minimum. His report of 1962 had been clear on this: 'No systematic treatment of Commonwealth sources is being attempted but Australian, New Zealand, and South African words already in *OED* will be joined by a relatively small number of additional words and senses which now seem to deserve a place in O.E.D. pending the preparation of regional dictionaries of various kinds of English.'[67] Australian English, he thought, was 'more productive of new words and senses than the other main regional branches of English (except American English) and there may be as many as 500 items in the new Supplement'. But from 'New Zealand, South Africa, and Canada', on the other hand, 'there will be perhaps about 300 items each'. Other Commonwealth sources would be represented simply by 'a few' words – '*bhoodan* and *gramdan* from India, *calypso* from the West Indies, and so on'. Where US words were concerned, Burchfield gave no figures, but planned that 'vocabulary that has become established in this country will be included (e.g. *accident-prone*, *acronym*, *automation*, *deadpan*, *disc jockey*, *egghead*, *rat race*, *soap opera* and *supermarket*) together with a relatively small number (of which any selection must be rather arbitrary) of words and senses more or less restricted to the United States but encountered in American fiction, at the cinema, and elsewhere, as *comfort station, motorcade,* etc.'[68]

But by the time the first volume appeared, in 1972, this policy had radically changed. Burchfield described how he was now making 'bold forays into the written English of regions outside the British Isles, particularly into that of North America, Australia, New Zealand, South Africa, India, and Pakistan'. In 1975 he explained why: 'it is now [as opposed to in Murray's time] a legitimate function of a historical dictionary, even one prepared in Britain, to record and treat overseas words that are virtually unknown in this country' (e.g. the Australian phrase *to lob in,* 'to arrive in', New Zealand *marae,* 'a space in a Maori settlement set aside for social functions', South African *lappie,* 'a dish cloth, a small rag').[69] In 1984 Burchfield declared, 'English is English wherever it is spoken and written as a first language, and the natural repository for all of it, subject only to the physical difficulty of collecting it, was the *Supplement to the OED'*.[70]

Why did he change his mind? One clue may lie in a memo of 15 November 1967, one of the comparatively small number of editorial papers in the archives from this period, recording a talk Burchfield had heard delivered by the young linguist David Crystal, in which he outlined his plans for a new 'Dictionary of the English-Speaking Peoples' to be published by Cassell. Burchfield – along with his companions Norman Davis and C. L. Wrenn, who had succeeded Tolkien as the Oxford Professor of Anglo-Saxon in 1945 – had been disturbed by the boldness of Crystal's proposal to include material from 'all the English-speaking areas including the United States, the Antipodes, the West Indies, India and Pakistan, the Philippines, and so on'. He was moreover 'scandalised by the blandness with which Crystal admitted that he was pillaging standard dictionaries to obtain his material' rather than doing primary research (though as Burchfield must have known, many, if not all dictionaries, including the *OED,* have from the earliest days borrowed from their predecessors, and no shame need attach to such pillaging).[71]

Crystal's dictionary seems not to have come off, but the idea may have planted (or nurtured) a seed in Burchfield's mind that grew and prospered. Today, it seems right, and inevitable, that Burchfield should have jettisoned the 'unblushingly "Britocentric"' views of Murray, and later Sisam, understandable though both had been in their time.[72] Full coverage of World Englishes, nevertheless, would have been both impossible and (in view of the proliferation during the 1960s, 1970s and 1980s of dictionaries of regional English from Oxford and elsewhere) unnecessary. How did

Burchfield decide what to put in and what to discard? Unfortunately, he leaves no record of how he considered the difficult issues involved in spreading his net as widely as he describes he eventually thought he should. But to talk of 'the written English of regions outside the British Isles', as he had in his Introduction to the first volume of the Supplement, skirts round the problem of determining whether words recorded in some of these areas – for example Maori *marae* – should be considered as English in the first place; and Burchfield evinces no recognition that the standards of spoken and written English, in countries such as India, that approximate most closely to British norms are achieved by people for whom English is a second language.[73] At least one Supplement reviewer pointed out that Burchfield's inclusion of American English was remarkably inconsistent, and demonstrated this by listing terms found in a number of recent dictionaries of new US words (some of which were listed in Burchfield's bibliography, and also included quotations illustrating usage) that had not found their way into the Supplement – e.g. *service break*, *sexy* in the sense 'generally attractive or interesting, appealing', *vinify* 'to make wine' (*service break* was one of the 5,000 new words and senses added in OED2, *vinify* was added in an interim 'Additions' volume of 1993, while this sense of *sexy* is still unrecorded in the OED).[74]

Burchfield himself drew attention to one of the results of his change in policy over the years, namely unevenness between the volumes, so that (for example) words from 'countries such as the West Indies and even Scotland . . . have better coverage in the range H–P [vol. 1] than . . . in A–G [vol. 2]'.[75] Investigating the degree to which such unevenness occurs is not straightforward. Sometimes the provenance of a word is mentioned in the section of the entry describing its etymology, and sometimes in the section with the definition; abbreviations used in the *OED* are not always consistently distinguishable (e.g. electronic searches for *Sc.* turn up the label 'Scottish' but also the abbreviation '*sc.*', = 'obviously'). Consequently it is difficult to devise systematic tests of *OED*'s relative coverage of regional vocabulary which are not also prohibitively time-consuming. One imbalance is notable, however: the threefold increase in words of Chinese origin added to the Supplement after Burchfield's own visit to China in 1979 (e.g. *pipa*, *pyotonghua*, *Little Red Book*, *running dog*, *scorched earth*).[76]

Burchfield's handling of the many hundreds of foreign terms and loan words he introduced is additionally difficult to investigate since [||] it is not possible to search electronically for the vertical parallel lines [||], or 'tramlines' (the lexicographers' own term), that are used to indicate 'alien' or not yet naturalized words, with which he often – but not always – marked these terms. In the original *OED*, Murray had acknowledged that the treatment of such words was determined by somewhat subjective calls of judgement. 'Words may be classed as *naturals, denizens, aliens,* and *casuals,*' as he described in his 'General Explanations', and he went on to draw careful distinctions between these four classes, attempting to demarcate with some precision the successive degrees of strangeness. But in the end, Murray said, 'opinions will differ as to the claims of some that are included and some that are excluded, and also as to the line dividing *denizens* from *naturals,* and the position assigned to some words on either side of it. If we are to distinguish these classes at all, a line must be drawn somewhere.'[77]

Craigie and Onions did not use tram-lines at all, perhaps because they did not want to make this distinction.[78] Burchfield reintroduces the symbol with apparent enthusiasm but on principles hard to discern. Of his examples quoted above, the two Hindi words *bhoodan* and *gramdan* are thus marked, but *calypso, marae* and *lappie* are not. Other Hindi words, however, are unmarked, for example *dhoon, dhoona, dhrupad, dhyana.* On the same page, *diable* and *diable au corps* are 'tram-lined', but *diabolo* is not. A theory that words that seem to require (for native English speakers) difficult pronunciation is scotched when one sees that *déjeuner* and *déjà vu* have no tram-lines either. There is no clear policy here, nor do the quotations offer any further help, as there seems to be no consciousness of foreignness in the quotations themselves (rendering a word in italics, for example) that correlates with the presence of tram-lines.

Reviewers greatly appreciated the wealth of such terms in the Supplement and praised the extension in *OED* policy to which it was due. Burchfield quotes the judgement in 1977 of the Anglo-Saxonist Fred Robinson, who reported that the new *OED* Supplement was 'making it possible for Americans to read Australian, South African, and other novels and newspapers' with far less bewilderment:

> If an Australian novel baffles American readers with words like *hoon, middy,* and *nork,* the *Supplement H–N* will tell him [*sic*] they refer, respectively, to a lout, a measure of beer, and a woman's breast. If an Afro-American novel perplexes Australians with *honky, jive-ass,* and *kelch,* the Supplement is there with the answers. South African *lekker,* Nottinghamshire *lerky,* West Indian *limer,* and many words like them are precisely explicated.[79]

Scientific and technical vocabulary

This vocabulary had caused Murray a good deal of trouble. In 1883, the Delegates had urged upon him the principle that 'slang terms and scientific words should both be limited to such as were found in literature'. His granddaughter sympathetically reports his dilemma:

> 'What,' asked the exasperated Editor, 'is classed as literature?' He confessed to inability to give an answer: 'I could at most omit those as to which I have a strong subjective feeling that they are not likely to be used at present in literature . . . running the risk that any day they may burst on the world as famous poisons, disinfectants, anaesthesians, or cholera prophylacts, & so be in every body's mouths.

Precisely this fate afflicted Murray with the word *appendicitis*, an example of 'crack-jaw' medical jargon that one of his specialist advisers had warned him against in 1891, but from which Edward VII was to suffer in 1902.[80] Another notorious omission was the word *radium*. In August 1902, Murray found this word in Craigie's *OED* proofs for the fascicle *R–Reactive*, and counselled him to omit it. Conceding that Craigie had 'probably got the opinion of a responsible chemist', he said that he himself had meanwhile consulted 'a chemical student who has just taken his degree', who thought that the identification of this new chemical element 'is quite premature and may turn out to be a regrettable blunder'. The word was excised. Murray's misjudgement here may well have been a source of mirth among the staff: as Peter Gilliver describes, H. J. Bayliss produced a sample entry for the word which admirably satirized the forms and conventions their chief editor had so expertly established as the *OED* norm (illustration 4).[81]

In his 'General Explanations', published with the first fascicle in 1884, Murray explained that a lexicographer should include 'such of the scientific, technical, slang, dialectal, and foreign words as are passing into common use, and approach the position or standing of "common words," well knowing that that the line he draws will not satisfy all his critics'. But in practice, as can be seen by the most superficial glance at his pages, he included a substantial number of words that fell some way beyond any line credibly drawn by a layperson.[82] For their part, Craigie and Onions had expressed reservations about their treatment of 'the more esoteric scientific terms' – 'it cannot be hoped or pretended that this problem has been solved in every instance with infallible discretion', they said – given the vast increase in these terms since *OED* had begun.[83] Burchfield's task, after even vaster expansion in scientific activities and terminology since 1933, was correspondingly greater. To help him with this formidable undertaking, and in defiance of Onions's and Sisam's advice, he broke new ground by employing science consultants on the *OED* staff, whose job it was to take 'general responsibility for the drafting of entries in these disciplines'.[84] This 'radical departure from the policy adopted by the editors of the main Dictionary' was, he explained, in part influenced by his visit to North American dictionary departments in 1968.[85] The proportion of space in his dictionary occupied by the mass of scientific terms that resulted is very substantial (again, there is no systematic way of searching for them), and in 1973 he estimated that 'about a third of the words and senses in Volume I . . . are scientific or technical'. Many are instanced only in specialist periodicals and other abstruse sources, and are defined in ways not accessible to the general public (e.g. *axopodium*, 'a pseudopodium, stiffened by an axial filament, found in some Heliozoa and Radiolaria', or *diphosphopyridine nucleotide*, 'one of the names of the co-enzyme nicotinamide-adenine dinucleotide'). As with World English, the lexicographical problem appears intractable: where and how should the line be drawn between inclusion and exclusion?[86]

Some sorts of technical vocabulary, however, Burchfield initially did try to limit according to criteria which would have been approved of by the Delegates of 1883. Justifying his inclusion of various sorts of specialized entries, including trade names, in the Supplement, he explained in 1975 that 'Many rose- and pear-names – *Gloire de Dijon*, *Maréchale Niel*, *Marie Louise*, and the rest – will owe their presence in the dictionary as much to their appearance in the works of Charlotte Yonge or Oscar Wilde or John Galsworthy as to their place in the hierarchy of trees and fruits.'[87] The implication is that it is use in literature that guarantees a place in the Dictionary.[88]

But by 1977, as he reported in a discussion at a lexicography conference, Burchfield had categorically dropped the 'literature criterion' so far as the sciences and social sciences were concerned. 'We have decided . . . that it is unworthy to treat scientific and technical vocabulary only in respect of those words which make their way into the common language and into fiction . . . . We are attempting to treat with consistency the central vocabulary of psychology, sociology, physics, chemistry, and so forth.' One of the other lexicographers attending the same session pointed out, 'I must say there is some difficulty in deciding what is meant by the central vocabulary.' It is also difficult for anyone who is not an expert in a particular field to determine exactly how well Burchfield fulfilled this formidable aim.

One feature of Burchfield's coverage of individual areas of specialized vocabulary is pointed to by David Crystal (the young linguist who had so agitated the older guard of scholars with his scheme for a wide-ranging dictionary in 1967). In 2000, Crystal noticed that one of his own books, *Systems of Prosodic and Paralinguistic Features in English*, which he had written with Randolph Quirk in 1964, had been quoted only for its use of ordinary words rather than for the technical vocabulary for which it might have been thought an especially apt source. Surveying the vocabulary he used in the book and the items selected for inclusion, Crystal asks, 'Is there a principle underlying the words that the lexicographers chose?' and answers, 'I can discern no principle here. The selection process may well have been at random'; and he shows that 'the lexicographers virtually ignored [his book's] emergent academic vocabulary'. Crystal also found that quotation from individual sources was not evenly distributed over the alphabet. Another of his books, the introductory paperback *Linguistics*, 'was evidently brought in at the point where the lexicographic team had reached letter I . . . and it seems to have stopped being used at the end of letter P (apart from an isolated example from letter S). There are thirty-seven citations from it. Most are indeed directly concerned with linguistic topics, but the book was, once again, used as a general source for items that had nothing to do with linguistics.'[89]

Even summary and specific analysis such as this has rarely been conducted. Most reviewers warmly praised the scientific and technical content of Burchfield's dictionary, and noted that the abundance of new senses recorded in his pages indicated the quality of scientific advice his staff supplied. In the journal *Notes & Queries* alone was he significantly criticized, for patchy treatment of technical vocabulary relating to non-scientific subjects – horse-riding, cookery, pottery, sports (with the exception of cricket, whose terminology was fully covered), and for some curious examples of favouritism – comprehensive treatment of terms from surfing, for example, as against marked omissions from philately.[90]

Contentious words and uses

In his account of his editorial policy in the introduction to volume 1 of the Supplement, Burchfield singled out words related to sex and excretory functions as one of the areas he had specifically extended the *OED*'s remit to include. Since he also developed *OED* policy on other fields of contentious vocabulary – racist terms, and usages considered contentious for reasons relating to correctness and politeness – it is convenient to treat them here all under the one heading. As we saw in Chapter IV, the 1933 Supplement had been taken to task by A. S. C. Ross for its omission of four-letter words and various other slang items, in accordance with 'Victorian' values which Ross thought should be discarded. Here Burchfield confidently and boldly introduced change. In an article in the *TLS* entitled 'Four-letter Words and the *OED*', published to coincide with the appearance of his Supplement's first volume in 1972, he treated his readers to an entertaining account of the changes in public mores and lexicographical practices following the publication by Penguin Books of *Lady Chatterley's Lover* in 1960, quoting carefully phrased correspondence between the editors of the underground magazine *Oz* and the Delegates' Assistant Secretary Davin, in which the latter had sought in 1969 to defend the *Shorter Oxford*'s omission of *fuck*.[91] Now, however, Burchfield explained, '*nous avons changé tout cela*' (the slip into French perhaps indicating the enjoyably *risqué* character of this new policy, whatever the claims of dispassionate philology). In common with other English-language dictionaries, the *OED* was opening its doors to items of vocabulary previously shunned on grounds of taste or obscenity. The words *come* (verb), *condom, cunnilingus, fellatio, French letter, frig, frigging,* among 'numerous others', were all included in Burchfield's first volume, fully supported by etymologies and quotations (which in many instances had long been on file in the *OED* offices).[92]

Burchfield valuably extended the range and remit of *OED* in including such terms, though his treatment is at times uneven. The word *come* is said to be 'slang', *bugger* 'coarse slang', whereas *frig* and *frigging* are unmarked (consistency and transparency of labelling in the Supplement seem to have raised insuperable problems). And as he worked through the items in the parent Dictionary, some of them, in various ways, escaped his net. An example is *twat*, one of the instances Murray had perhaps been thinking of when he complained that Browning had 'constantly used words without regard to their proper meaning'. The term had been defined only obliquely in *OED*: Murray simply referred the reader to a quotation of 1727, an entry from one of Bailey's dictionaries which read 'Twat, *pudendum muliebre*' – no help to readers without Latin – and added a note to say 'Erroneously used (after quot. 1660) by Browning', who in his poem *Pippa Passes* had been 'under the impression that it denoted some part of a nun's attire'. The 1660 quotation, from *Vanity of Vanities*, reads 'They talk't of his having a Cardinalls Hat. They'd send him as soon an Old Nuns Twat.' Browning had written (though Murray partially saved his blushes by omitting to quote him):

Then owls and bats
Cowls and twats,
Monks and nuns, in a cloister's moods,
Adjourn to the oak-stump pantry![93]

Burchfield kept all of Murray's entry, added five more quotations ranging from 1919 to 1973, but did not trouble to elucidate the Latin definition. His entry was reproduced without change in *OED2* and therefore continues to this day.

Two other definitions similarly untouched by Burchfield, whether or not for reasons of 'Victorian prudishness', were those for *Sapphism* and *tribade*. *Sapphism* had been included by Bradley in the *S–Sauce* (1909) fascicle in *OED1*, where he defined it as 'unnatural sexual relations between women', referred to a medical dictionary of 1890, and proffered a single illustrative quotation, dated 1901, from the *Lancet*: 'As yet in this country the novelist . . . has not arrived at the treatment in romance of excessive morphiomania, or Sapphism, or vaginismus, all of which diseases will be found in French novels'.[94] Further research is needed to discover whether this remark justly represents usage, by whatever group of people, at the time. By 1982, however, when Burchfield published his *O–Scz* volume, Bradley's definition (whatever may be thought of his quotation) was plainly unacceptable and should have been updated; Burchfield's addition of three fairly neutral quotations for the newly evidenced derivatives *sapphist* and *sapphistically* indicates that he reviewed the entry. Murray had been even more condemnatory than Bradley in his treatment of *tribade*, which he defined as 'a woman who practises unnatural vice with other women', but again the Supplement passed it over. (Both terms were among the tiny number of existing items to be changed in the second edition of the Dictionary in 1989, which dropped the references to 'unnatural' and 'vice' in the definitions, found recent quotations for *tribadism*, but retained the *Lancet* quotation as the single illustration for *Sapphism*.)

Burchfield did take action on the word *lesbian*, however. *OED1* had defined this word simply as 'of or pertaining to the island of Lesbos'; as we have seen, the additional sense referring to sexual relations between women had been discussed, and on Craigie's insistence rejected, in 1930. Burchfield adds unproblematic definitions for both adjective and noun to indicate their sexual applications, but his choice of quotations is another matter, particularly for the noun. They include Aldous Huxley: 'After a third-rate provincial town, colonized by English sodomites and middle-aged Lesbians, which is, after all, what Florence is, a genuine metropolis will be lively', and C. Day Lewis: 'I shall never write real poetry. Women never do, unless they're invalids or Lesbians or something.' Were such examples the only ones available to him? Or do they illustrate a personal, or perhaps more general, societal, view? Here it is instructive to compare the quotations for *homosexual*, another term new to the Supplement (first recorded 1892), which are almost all neutral (e.g. Stella Gibbons: 'There were many homosexuals to be seen in Hyde Park', or the *Daily Telegraph*: 'Homosexuals and lesbians make up a sizeable minority of the population').

Where racist language was concerned, Burchfield took justifiable pride in establishing the claims of descriptive lexicography, quoting Chapman's view that 'it is no part of the duty of a lexicographer to pass judgement on the justice or propriety of current usage'.[95] In a riveting account of the perils of defining ethnic terms, he describes how the editor of the 1951 *Concise* – E. McIntosh, who had also reported De Valera and his party *Fianna Fáil* 'taking the oath' in 1927 – 'unwisely entered the word *Pakistan* in his dictionary . . . unwisely, because names of countries as such do not normally qualify for an entry in Oxford dictionaries – and defined it as "A separate Moslem State in India, Moslem autonomy; (from 1947) the independent Moslem Dominion in India"'. The definition lay unnoticed by all save (unknown to Burchfield) J. M. Wyllie, who wrote to Davin about it in 1951 and was apparently ignored.[96] But in 1959, 'somebody [else] must have pointed it out':

> The Pakistanis, understandably, were outraged, and called for a ban on the *COD* in Pakistan and for all unsold copies in Pakistan to be confiscated. The OUP admitted that the definition was 'tactless' and 'locally irritating', but pointed out that the intention had been to show that Pakistan was in the familiar, triangular section of territory which had always been called India on maps and in geography books . . . . The Karachi police raided bookstalls in the city and seized 215 copies of the fourth edition of the *COD*. They also raided the Karachi office of the OUP, and seized the only copy of the dictionary on the premises, which was, in fact, the typist's copy. Copies in government offices were commandeered by the police, and apparently hundreds of copies were collected from public offices, schools and colleges.[97]

'High-level' diplomatic manoeuvres produced a temporary solution, that OUP should insert a correction slip for all copies of the dictionary sold in Pakistan. The Press subsequently decided to remove the word *Pakistan* 'from the main-line Oxford dictionaries altogether'.

Similar problems arose with the definition of *Palestinian* (in the sixth edition of the *COD*) in a way first of all offensive to the Arab League ('(Native or inhabitant of) Palestine; (person) seeking to displace Israelis from Palestine'), and then, after it had been changed, to Jewish organizations. On this occasion the Press stuck with the revised definition, which remains in Oxford dictionaries today ('*n*. Native or inhabitant of Palestine. *a*. of, pertaining to, or connected with Palestine').

Both these fracas were due to lexicographical error or misjudgement. Many others were not: Burchfield describes protracted battering from various pressure groups to get the Press to banish from their dictionaries definitions of words sometimes used with derogatory connotations (like *Jew* and its derivatives), or always used in this way (*wog, wop, dago*). Burchfield staunchly resisted, despite a death threat. 'In the end,' he concluded, 'in their function as "marshallers of words", lexicographers must set them all down as objectively as possible to form a permanent record of our time, the useful and the neutral, those that are decorous and well-formed, beside those that are tasteless, controversial, or worse.'[98]

Burchfield repeats this statement in his Preface to volume 2 (p. xviii) of the Supplement, in which such terms seem first to have been encountered. Not only did he insist on including all offensive terms, suitably labelled, if they were to be found in common use, but he also determined, 'in order to avoid misunderstanding and consequent hostility, that the historical record of words like *Jesuit, Jew, Negro, nigger* and others already entered in the *OED*, should be brought up to date in volumes II and III'. As ever, this admirable policy was difficult to sustain with consistency. By the time Burchfield had reached this view, his first volume (covering the alphabet range *A–G*) had already appeared, which meant that words such as *bogtrotter, bohunk, blackie, darkie*, and no doubt others, unidentified as racist or derogatory in *OED1*, continued similarly unidentified in his Supplement.[99] In addition, a number of other racist definitions, labels and usages in *OED1* from *H* onwards, presumably unexceptionable(?) at the time they were written, escaped the process of updating: for example Murray's reference to 'superior blood or race' s.v. *half-blooded*, to 'wild or savage races' s.v. *hubbub*, or Onions's definition of *white man*, first published in 1924, as 'a man of honourable character such as one associates with a European (as distinguished from a negro)'. (*OED2* rewrote the definition for *white man* but retained those for *half-blooded* and *hubbub*, which thus survive into today's *OED Online*.)

Burchfield actually introduced a racist formulation under *interlocutor*, one of whose new senses he defined as 'the compère in a group of nigger minstrels'; while in adding two new uses of the word *Chinaman* to his first volume, he had furnished neither these nor the existing sense ('a native of China') with any warning labels – although across the Atlantic the editor of *Webster's Third International*, Philip Gove, had been forced to make a correction in later printings after his original entry for *chinaman* had been published without a usage label or note.[100] (The two new senses were *Chinaman's chance*, a US term meaning 'a very poor or negligible prospect (of gain, survival, etc.)', and *Chinaman*, 'a left-handed bowler's offbreak to a right-handed batsman'; once again, both – along with the mention of the 'nigger minstrels' – are reproduced without change in *OED2* and today's *OED Online*.)

Owing to the difficulties of producing so substantial a piece of work over so long a period of time, Burchfield seems never to have settled on a standard procedure for treating contentious items.[101] Sometimes he uses definition alone (*nig-nog* is unlabelled but defined as 'A coarsely abusive term for a Negro'); sometimes label alone (*coon* is labelled '*slang.* (Derog.)' but defined simply as 'a Negro'). In rather more cases, he labels the word simply 'slang', but indicates the term's offensiveness in the definition (as with *kike*, defined as 'A vulgarly offensive name for a Jew'; *wog*, defined as 'A vulgarly offensive name for a foreigner, esp. one of Arab extraction'). Sometimes the warning or comment appears as a note separate from both label and definition (as, for *honky*, 'Disparaging in all applications'; *wop*, 'Now considered *offensive*').

He later pointed out that he had had little to guide him in this respect. 'Notes on ethnically sensitive vocabulary and usage notes such as mine on **miniscule* [the asterisk indicates the word's questionable status] and on *hopefully* are now routine in all major English dictionaries,' he wrote in 1988. 'They were very rare in the heady days of the 1960s and early 1970s.'[102] This is certainly true of UK dictionaries, although in the US usage notes had become common from the mid-sixties, after the heated controversy which greeted the publication in 1961 of *Webster's Third New International Dictionary* and its alleged failure to provide sufficient warning against a large range of controversial vocabulary. The *Random House Dictionary* (1966) and the *Houghton Mifflin American Heritage Dictionary* (1969) were among the first to provide generous quantities of information, of various sorts, on the register and acceptability of the words they defined.

Burchfield had a special interest in matters or usage relating to correctness, the final topic we glance at in this section. In 1996, ten years after he had completed the Supplement, he published a third edition of Fowler's *Modern English Usage*. One might expect there to have been tension between the broadly descriptivist attitudes that we have seen him adopt towards (most) racist and sexual vocabulary, and the expectations of readers hoping for an updated copy of the beacon of prescriptivist usage that Fowler's dictionary represented. This seems to have been so. In some respects he outraged Fowler lovers by his permissiveness in this new edition – one reader suggested that 'Burchfield's wildly descriptionist perversions of the classic prescriptionist masterpiece have assured him a definite place in Hell' – but in others he enthusiastically embraced the role of *arbiter elegantiae*, authoritatively prescribing on a range of usage matters, notably pronunciation and spelling.[103]

The same unevenness marks his work in the Supplement. Burchfield had from the beginning retained *OED1*'s use of the paragraph sign (¶) to indicate 'catachrestic and erroneous' usages. But his use of this discriminating mark was often at odds with the quotations he printed as evidence. Thus under one such stigmatized use, *data* (the plural form used with a singular construction), he includes a quotation of 1965 that states '. . . by general usage *data* is now accepted as a singular collective noun'. Such discrepancy between quoted evidence and editorial judgement is redolent of the prescriptivist position of Derwent Coleridge, Marsden, Brodribb and others (Chapter IV above) that a lexicographer should act as an arbiter of usage rather than a disinterested recorder of it. But *OED*'s claim to authority is based on its unique method of constructing definitions from its quotational evidence. Where does Burchfield's judgement come from if not from his quotations?[104]

Burchfield's addition of usage notes was a newly enunciated policy, again introduced part-way through the Supplement, this time in volume 3. Here he noted the recent prescriptivist backlash against the 'markedly [*sic*] linguistic descriptivism of the post-war years', and commented, 'One small legacy of these great debates is that here and there in the present volume I have found myself adding my own opinions about the acceptability of certain words or meanings in educated use', whether or not 'users of the dictionary . . . find these editorial comments diverting'. Such a departure from the stated principles of the parent Dictionary comes as a shock, but in fact Burchfield had already entered comments of various kinds in the earlier volumes – for example that use of the plural form *agenda* with a singular verb was 'now increasingly found but avoided by careful writers', or that *nite* was 'A widespread vulgarism'. Assertions of personal taste, like the latter, were again often curiously out of step with the quotation evidence Burchfield also printed, seeming to indicate that the editor was turning his back on the duty, identified by Trench, to be historian rather than critic.

The debates Burchfield referred to had taken place in various forums in the UK in the late 1970s and early 1980s, including the House of Lords, where 'eloquent voices', he tells us, had been 'raised against the use of modish words like *ongoing*, *relevant* and *viable*'. But no warning of any sort, not even a neutral comment, appears in Burchfield's treatment of these three words in the Supplement itself. Nor do the plentiful quotations with which he illustrates their use indicate the basis for judging these words to be in any way problematic. And it is easy to find a significant number of similarly unlabelled words or usages in his Supplement which are by contrast proscribed or disapproved of by contemporary sources (e.g. *parameter*, *envision*, *prior to*, *decimate* and many others).[105]

In the same preface, Burchfield robustly advocated liberalism in language matters. 'The English language is alive and well, in the right hands,' he declared.

Expressions like *right on* and *hopefully* bring out the worst and the best in men and women. They stand as emblems of social and political divisions within our society. These and other elements lying strewn in the disputed territory of our language are at any given time not numerous but are charged with a significance that goes beyond the mere linguistic. [Despite these remarks, Burchfield does not indicate the 'emblematic' status of either term in the body of his dictionary: *right on* is labelled 'US slang . . . Freq. in Black English in the U.S.'; *hopefully* is said to be 'avoided by many writers'.] If you are tempted to fulminate against them, or to feel uneasy about them, bear in mind that the English language has been in the hands of linguistic conservatives and linguistic radicals for more than a thousand years and that, far from bleeding to death from past crudities and past wounds, it can be used with majesty and power, free from all fault, by our greatest writers.[106]

On the one hand he puts up the barriers with his *ipse dixits*, just as Marsden et al. advised; on the other he defends varied usage by pointing out that such variation has contributed to the language's present richness. However, his appeal to the standard set by 'our greatest writers' poses more questions than it answers. Do they, whoever they are, by definition use language 'free from fault'? Or does language when used by our greatest writers somehow undergo transmutation, so that in their usage 'faults' become acceptable?

Coda

At a lexicographical 'round table' conference held in Leiden in 1977, attended by dictionary-makers from Europe and North America, Burchfield was challenged, possibly with some exasperation, by A. J. Aitken (Craigie's *DOST* successor): 'I would like to ask Mr. Burchfield this question: what are your principles?' Burchfield demurred, explaining that he did not want to keep his audience from their lunch, that he stuck pretty much to Murray's techniques, and that 'in the end the judgments are subjective'. 'The central core' of vocabulary, he felt, 'no one is in any doubt about at all and need not be demonstrated'. Where the rest was concerned, 'if you can include the items and edit them and illustrate them sufficiently and still get your dictionary out in a reasonable time you go ahead'. He described one of the problems:

there is a factor which I call staff resistance and that is that the assistants who work with one on a dictionary frequently hold very different opinions about inclusion from those which one holds oneself. I am afraid that

I become at that moment terribly autocratic and simply say that it is going to be such and such and proceed. And then I don't lie awake at nights wondering about the conclusions but simply press on . . . . The personal element, I think, in dictionaries is still extremely important. The generations to come will have to blame the wrong choices on the personality or the preferences, the place of birth and the personal experiences of the general editor, but I see no option but to proceed in that manner.[107]

Such frank acknowledgement of subjectivity is both courageous and disconcerting. Perhaps the most striking thing about Burchfield's tendency towards individualistic comment and editorial choice (of whatever sort) in the Supplement is that it is as slight as it is, given the enormous amount of material he dealt with to produce his work. It is also remarkable that the second edition of the *OED*, compiled with the advantage of electronic aids, was quite as inconsistent as Burchfield himself when dealing with the manifestations of his individualism, and could make no more than sporadic attempts to curb or discipline it – though no doubt this was in part due to the speed with which this edition was compiled.

Burchfield himself seems to have been motivated by intense feelings about language, the *OED*, and the role he played in relation to both. He reports with pride that his colleague at St Peter's College, Oxford (Francis Warner), would introduce him to guests dining in college as 'custodian of the English language'.[108] He wrote, in an essay on 'The *Oxford English Dictionary* and its Historical Principles', that 'apparently Edward Elgar once said, "the people yearn for things that can stir them". I believe this to be profoundly true, and I believe too that, in the right hands, the *Oxford English Dictionary* is a work that can satisfy this yearning.' He bitterly resented attacks on his dictionary, few as these were, and piled contumely on the professor of linguistics who had dared to challenge the historical authority of the enterprise: 'I suspect that the professor has withdrawn into his quotationless, Saussurean author-free shelter, or somewhere like that, as I have heard no more from him'. (The offender was Roy Harris, singularly prolific in publication since sparring with Burchfield in 1982.)[109]

The reception of the Supplement was in most cases warmly gratifying. Burchfield quoted, slightly out of context, his former employee Julian Barnes's judgement of his work as 'an overflowing treasure-chest, rich argosy, super-stuffed silo . . . Well, it *is* magnificent, scholarly, and impressive', and thus forgave Barnes both the rapier thrusts dealt to some sample definitions and his deft unveiling of insufficiently imaginative searches for illustrative quotations.[110] Other reviewers responded with the same feelings of passion that Burchfield displayed himself: Anthony Burgess told how he had 'taken this book like a mistress to bed (a weighty one but handleable)'.[111] The *TLS* observed that its publication was 'no doubt the most important event in English lexicography since the completion of the *OED* itself in 1928', supplying 'what for many will be easily the most entertaining and readable of all dictionaries of English'; *The Times* that it was 'a work which will last longer and prove more influential than anything else published . . . this half-century'.[112]

Burchfield cast himself as heroic adventurer, beginning as Robinson Crusoe (p. 152 above), and finishing as victorious general. At the end of the Preface to his fourth volume, he signed off from lexicography by quoting George Washington's words in December 1783: 'Having now finished the work assigned to me, I retire from the great theatre of action.' Washington went on to become first President of the United States, Burchfield to re-edit Fowler's *Modern English Usage*; the parallel did not seem to strike him as absurd. He was confident that his dictionary work, now complete, would 'stand as a lasting testament to the fruitfulness and inventiveness of the language of our age'.[113]

In this he was surely right. For despite the unevenness detectable when any specific category of Supplement vocabulary is examined, the huge mass of material in his pages – amounting to some 69,300 entries and 527,000 illustrative quotations – is simply far greater than that found in any other late twentieth-century dictionary of the English language.[114] Any attempt to evaluate a dictionary systematically will tend to identify inconsistencies and imperfections, letting the vast bulk of entries slide by unnoticed. But the wealth of lexical data Burchfield accumulated during his twenty-nine years writing the Supplement dwarfs the discrepancies and irregularities occasioned by his rethinking various aspects of the project as he went along. Such defects can be easily turned up by reviewers of his work today, enabled – as Burchfield was not – by electronic searches, but they should not detract from the strengths his pages also amply display. His dictionary valuably extended the range of its great predecessor, and its abundance of information about the vocabulary of the twentieth century – however unevenly selected and illustrated – created a broad springboard for the next major stage in the history of the *OED*.

VIII

The 'New *Oxford English Dictionary* Project'

Start of the project and the production of *OED2*

Well before Burchfield's last volume was published in May 1986, and the lexicographers, publishers and assorted guests had celebrated with a drinks party at Rhodes House in Oxford, other plans were afoot. OUP's publicity material had claimed the completed second Supplement as 'the final piece in a great jigsaw which gives the fullest possible treatment of the English language from the middle of the twelfth century until the 1980s'. But it had already become a cornerstone of an entirely new enterprise.

As the Supplement approached its final stages, the Press had to contemplate, as in 1928 and 1933, the implications of bringing a substantial lexicographical project to a close. Against the desirability of reducing expenditure had to be set the importance of maintaining the value of the initial investment – both that of *OED1* and of the recent Supplement – and of supporting the numerous English-language dictionaries into which, up to now, the latter had most satisfactorily fed. *OED1*'s fifty-year period of copyright had come to an end in 1983, leaving it vulnerable to exploitation by others. Piracy was already suspected. In the gracious Georgian mansion at 37a St Giles, meanwhile, there was now assembled a uniquely skilled team of historical lexicographers, whose abilities had been demonstrated not only in work on the Supplement, under Burchfield's control, but also in more independent projects such as the *New Shorter*. Since 1957, the Supplement had acquired great quantities of quotations of literarily incomparable value, a substantial library, and an established administrative system. Was this all to be disbanded as in 1933? At what future cost to the Press?[1]

The answer to this question was both simple and bold. The Press decided to throw itself into the vanguard of the technological revolution, then in its infancy, by converting its most illustrious reference book to an electronic medium. This ambitious project would create the Dictionary afresh, transforming its structure and radically altering the ways in which readers would be able to access its content. It would safeguard *OED* from outside depredation by renewing copyright in this different form. It would preserve its team of lexicographers, already at work on new words, thus maintaining the Press's world position in lexicography. And it would harness, in ways as yet not fully foreseen, the opportunities offered by this extraordinary new technology.

The beginnings of change in traditional methods of book-making had been signalled both in Burchfield's third preface, in his warnings of rumblings in the printing industry, and in his fourth, in his elegiac notice that the volume in which it appeared might be 'the last major book to be set up in type by the hot-metal process'.[2] Also in this preface, Burchfield explained that his work in its final stages had overlapped with 'the merging in electronic form of the twelve volumes of the *OED* and the four volumes of the Supplement'. This 'imaginative project', Burchfield said, without specifying further the implications for the Dictionary or for its readers, 'should ensure that the Oxford tradition – indeed its pre-eminence – in historical lexicography will be maintained into the twenty-first century and beyond'.

Looking back on these years with the advantage of elapsed time and experience, it is curious to see (or remember) how difficult it was to understand the implications of digitalizing the *OED* – or any other work – and with what suspicion such technological wizardry was often received. In the *TLS*, Eric Korn thought 'the [New *OED*] project provokes speculations about how far technology leads research, and how far it is the other way round', while a subsequent correspondent darkly observed that 'computer ironmongery is no substitute for solid scholarship'.[3]

By contrast, the Press itself was swift to grasp the potential of the new technology, and its particular aptness for *OED*. Preliminary explorations had begun in March 1982 under Burchfield, who had supervised a study of the various ways in which the Dictionary might be electronically exploited.[4] Its results determined 'the senior Officers of the Press. . . at once to pursue the idea'. Calculating that 'the *OED* could be regarded as a kind of national monument', they decided it was 'quite proper to solicit assistance, whether financial or technical, from Government departments, research institutions, or industrial companies'. Richard Charkin, then head of Reference Publishing at OUP – and the person chiefly responsible for the brainwave of safeguarding *OED*'s past and future by turning it into electronic form – initiated approaches to various possible partners. In March 1983 a small team was set up to write an 'appeal booklet', to be put before institutions wishing to contribute in one way or another, and over the next few months the project's likely constituents and phases gradually emerged. In particular, it became clear that full revision of the *OED* would have to be deferred to a later, rather than early stage, as otherwise 'it would be far too long before any new edition of the Dictionary could be published'.[5]

The 'New *Oxford English Dictionary* Project' was first officially announced on 15 May 1984. As *The Times* reported the following day, all the main details were by then in place. 'It will take 120 keyboard operators 18 months to transcribe the 500 million characters in the 21,000 pages of the printed edition,' the article explained, while by contrast it would take 'the most advanced computer . . . 10 minutes to read it'. The Press hoped to produce the 'New Oxford Dictionary' in four years – in fact, under the project's director Timothy Benbow, it took five years, a notable piece of timeliness in comparison with the three predecessors – and it was to cost them a total of £7 million. Of this sum, £300,000 had already been promised by the Department of Trade and Industry, in 'recognition of the national importance of the project'. A further £1 million had been invested by the British subsidiary of IBM, and two other partners were on board: a special unit at the University of Waterloo in Canada, and the United States computing subsidiary of Reed International.

But what benefits, exactly, would the electronic medium bring, and what was involved in this vast expense? Two of the senior editors on Burchfield's Supplement had been identified to take charge of the editorial side: John Simpson and Edmund Weiner, both of whom had joined the staff in the mid-1970s and risen through the ranks to emerge as architects of the new project. In 1985, Weiner published a fuller description of the project in the *Journal of English Linguistics*. He could not resist drawing parallels, he said, between the enterprise the Press had embarked upon in 1879 when they signed the contract to publish the original Dictionary, and that which they had now begun nearly one hundred years later. 'Like its predecessor, the New OED Project is designed to break completely new ground in more than one discipline, is conceived primarily as a service to scholarship and only secondarily as a source of revenue, and is on a very large scale, requiring considerable investment of money, time, equipment and staff.' But he thought there was an important difference. Where the first *OED* was concerned, the Press had either failed to see 'or only dimly perceived' the magnitude of its new commitment, 'whereas all parties to the *New OED* have entered in with their eyes wide open both to the potential and to the problems of the task'.[6] (Whether the Press would now agree that this was so may be debatable: over twenty years on, it is not easy to predict an end to the rather more extensive project to which, as it turned out, they were then committing themselves.)

Weiner set down a clear and analytic account of the new enterprise's proposed aims and constituents, which he called 'a Skeleton Guide'. First, they would acquire 'the knowledge, staff, equipment and procedures' necessary in order to turn the two existing dictionaries – Murray's and Burchfield's – into a machine-readable form. This would include analysing the various components of the texts, no simple task given the inevitable variations in editing over so many years (broadly speaking they needed to work out the basic 'kit' with which each entry was supplied: headword, etymology, label, definition, quotation, and so on). Next would come the creation of the machine-readable Dictionary itself, which would involve keying all the suitably tagged constituents into an electronic medium, followed by meticulous proof-reading; the result would then be published in print form (to create *OED2*). Thirdly, they planned to create the *New OED* database, which would entail devising software to allow the contents of the new Dictionary to be accessed and its hidden treasures brought to light. Fourthly, they envisaged a range of prospective means by which this database might be developed and exploited – adding new entries to keep it up to date, enhancing it with the addition of new elements (maps? Thesaurus-type information? Entries from other specialized dictionaries?), and a number of other possibilities, including its analysis 'by researchers in Artificial Intelligence'. 'Moving into even bluer skies than those that smile on the projects suggested above,' Weiner added, 'one can tentatively predict a time when not only textual and graphic data is added to the database, but audio and visual material as well. It looks as if the optical data will be able to take such mixed media into its stride.'[7]

This is a prescient account of the marvellous possibilities of the new medium – whose delighted optimism has in some respects been exceeded by events (for example, in the transfer to online publication). One thing is striking, nevertheless: 'revision' is mentioned at only a single point in the article. 'It is no secret that several aspects of the *OED* require revision', Weiner writes. 'When conventional methods were the only ones envisaged' – and here we may remember what Chapman had thought in 1933, or 1946, or what his successors had decided in the late 1950s – 'the likelihood that revision would ever be done was remote.' Now, however, the electronic medium would allow researchers to identify, for each entry, the constituent requiring revision – pronunciation, say – then deal with it globally and consistently. Once this was done, 'the revision process would be carried out and the changes in the data applied to the database'.

Much of the meat of the lexicographical task is only gestured at here – including the months and years of necessary reading through the texts of both past and present missed by previous editions of *OED*, together with those still to come that the new edition would wish to take in its stride. Fleet-footed such reading was about to become, owing to electronic aids, but at every stage human judgement would be as vital and as time-consuming as it had ever been. The dull plodding endured by Johnson, by Murray and his colleagues, and by Burchfield and his staff, is still an inextricable part of the lexicographical process. In the 1950s, when the Press debated the question of whether to revise or supplement, the financial and scholarly costs of such plodding were constantly in their minds. In the whirl of this technological moment, plodding disappears from view, although the internal document submitted to companies tendering for the technological transformation of the Dictionary clearly indicates the enormous scale of changes that would, eventually, have to be made to the pre-Burchfield material.[8]

In all this calculation, the second edition of the *OED* (*OED2*) – the publication in hard copy of the initial merging of *OED1* with Burchfield's Supplement – figured as a sort of by-product of the main aim, the 'New *OED* Project' itself. But to the outside world these other schemes were scarcely apparent. The second edition hit the Anglophone literary world with enormous impact in 1989, quite dwarfing the visionary project to which it was a mere stepping-stone. According to the Press's biographer Sutcliffe, when the publication of the last volumes of the first edition of *OED1* were rumoured to be imminent in the late 1920s, the American man of letters H. L. Mencken described how 'his spies in Oxford had told him that plans were underway for celebrating its completion with "military exercises, boxing matches between the dons, orations in Latin, Greek and the Oxford dialect, yelling contests between the different Colleges and a series of medieval drinking bouts"'.[9] In the event, the 1928 celebrations were dignified and continent. Mencken's account would have been more fairly applied to the publicity jamboree which accompanied the delivery to the world of *OED2*.

The main celebrations were held at Claridge's on 29 March 1989, with a series of speeches from 10.30 to 11.55, followed by questions, drinks and luncheon, and finally a speech from Lord Jenkins, then Chancellor of Oxford University. Guest speakers were Christopher Ricks, Malcolm Bradbury and Daniel Boorstin, former Librarian of US Congress. 'For me,' Boorstin declared, 'this is like being present at the revelation of the second edition of the Bible.' The mother country had given the US 'two great gifts', he continued,

the Magna Carta and the English language . . . . For a democratic people the *OED* provides the living scriptures. Our vernacular language is the most democratic of all our products . . . . The *OED*, using the oldest and

11. 'framulous' by Don Addis.

least appreciated of our technologies, not only conquers time. It makes the whole past a common treasure. It makes every word become not merely a carrier of messages but a historical phenomenon, a kaleidoscope of meanings.[10]

Along with the speeches, Geoff Robinson of IBM UK Ltd, the company that had generously donated its technological expertise, presented a commemorative plaque to the Secretary to the Delegates, George Richardson. Lunch, though a more moderate spread than that prepared for the Goldsmiths' banquet, was of a sufficient munificence (quenelles of pike, roast rack of lamb, savarin of rum, accompanied by 'Bourgoyne Blanc and Claridge's Claret').

The Press's own account of the affair (in *OED2 News*, a series of in-house pamphlets) gave slightly more detail.

From 9 o'clock onwards the hotel was swarming with television and cameras – up to four different crews at one point – and with [them] were several journalists rushing around, either interviewing John Simpson or Edmund Weiner [the two editors in chief] or waiting to do so, or rushing to file their stories. There was a lot of news coverage both on

Wednesday (BBC1's lunchtime news, for example), and in the papers the next day . . . . The speeches in the morning were widely judged to have been very successful and to have hit exactly the right note.[11]

The publicity department had secured exhaustive coverage: national and regional papers, periodicals, magazines and a good range of overseas media all carried the story, many with a photograph of the two editors propping their elbows against a tower of the twenty volumes and looking cheerful. The success of this marketing operation was phenomenal: by 13 March 1989, 680 sets (costing £1,500 each) of the twenty volumes had been sold, rising to 3,200 sets round the world by the publication date itself a fortnight later. The *OED2* publicity campaign was chosen as the best promotion of the month in a competition sponsored and judged by *Publishing News*.[12]

OED2 News itself quoted a choice selection of the many plaudits so far received, for example that of Philip Howard in *The Times*: 'An epic of the English language, which will . . . record and influence the way we speak and write until the end of time'; of Christopher Bigsby in the *Listener*: 'The *OED* is all things to all men'; of Trevor-Roper in the *Sunday Telegraph*: 'This immortal work'; of the *Daily Express*: 'The greatest dictionary ever compiled'.[13]

But next month, the trade publication the *Bookseller* carried an entertainingly carping article in its 'Critics Crowner' column.[14] It poked fun not at the Dictionary itself but at reviewers' attempts to get to grips with its twenty volumes. Unlike the scholar or casual reader, David Holloway (of the *Daily Telegraph*) had complained, 'the reviewer, against a deadline, must seek his shortcuts. One way is the sampling method: he can take a letter and read it. The extremely lazy one will choose "X" (12 pages) . . . . The real glutton for punishment might choose "S", a letter that requires just about 2,500 pages . . . The best method, surely, is serendipity', or the game of 'Who's in and who's out' – which could apply both to words and to cited authorities.

This recognition of the difficulty of understanding and evaluating the dictionary – any dictionary, but especially *OED* – was long overdue. How could one begin to grapple with the content and quality of so gargantuan a publication, whether up against a deadline or not, so as to produce a reasonable evaluation? The remarkable thing about the reception of the second edition is how few of its admirers can have read its pages with enough attention to notice that entry after entry of 'the most authoritative and comprehensive dictionary of English in the world', with its 'comprehensive selection of chronologically arranged quotations', was supported with quotation evidence that mysteriously petered out in the 1880s or earlier, with nothing to represent the last hundred years.[15] Evidently this could not be otherwise, especially for the earlier part of the alphabet, since Burchfield's brief had been only to update those entries lacking nineteenth-century quotations (see p. 179 above). Nor did they observe the archaic quality of some of the definitions, nor the unevenness with which the twentieth-century portion of the Dictionary – prepared, as we saw in the last chapter, on principles increasingly different from those of *OED1*, especially where science and world English were concerned – sat against that of the centuries before. (Admittedly this last is not easy to distinguish: one of the unfortunate characteristics of the second edition of the *OED* is that there is no typographic, or electronic, distinction between the first edition and second Supplement: one cannot see where Murray et al. stopped and Burchfield started.) And almost nobody seems to have asked themselves whether the much-vaunted new content of this second edition – a mere 5,000 additional words, less than 1 per cent of the total – justified the £1,500 selling price, given that many of the purchasers, whether libraries or individuals, would already possess the Dictionary in its original form of twelve (or thirteen) volumes of first edition plus four volumes of Supplement.[16]

Growls emerged from some quarters nevertheless. They seem to have begun with G. F. C. Plowden, an expert on Pope, who wrote to the *TLS* expressing his sense of injury that the 'handful of corrections and amplifications' he had sent in to the *OED* over the years – supplying ante-dating quotations, pointing out omissions, and offering rectifying evidence – had all been 'politely acknowledged and suppressed', although the acknowledgement for one had been 'in the Editor's own hand and regretted that it had come too late for the first volume of the Supplement'. 'Naturally,' Plowden said, 'I expected to find them in the second edition, but to my disappointment none of those I can remember is included.' He asked, 'If the Dictionary cannot absorb scraps that are fed straight in by the post, what chance is there that they will have taken account of the far more voluminous and significant work of scholars who contribute antedatings etc to journals such as *Notes & Queries*? Have they also been neglected?' And had other *TLS* readers been able to divine from the publicity for the second edition that the dictionary took no account of information that had long been available?[17]

Two weeks later, another correspondent hammered in some nails. 'The four volumes of the Supplement,' he pointed out, 'in no sense constitute a revision of the main body of the dictionary. Whereas the latter has stood still for over fifty years, English studies have not.' And he gave some examples, to conclude, 'no amount of sales promotion by the Oxford University Press can conceal the fact that the "new" *OED* is still no more than a magnificent antique'.[18] In the same issue, an injured subscriber to the Dictionary claimed that he had, in effect, been cheated by the Press. He had originally bought the *OED* in its 'compact' form – the two-volume photographically reduced version of the first edition published in 1971, with four original pages to each of its own and a magnifying glass thrown in free – and he had then bought each of the Supplement volumes as they appeared, though the price of these had risen steeply from £15 to £90. 'Now, however, we are told that the second edition includes everything in the first edition and in the Supplement, but with the addition of an extra 5,000 words and meanings which have entered the language since the Supplement was completed.' But how was a subscriber to get at this material without buying the new edition in its entirety, at a cost of £1,500, thus duplicating a mass of material he or she already possessed? 'Isn't this a breach of faith?' he asked.[19] No answer to this (presumably tongue-in-cheek) challenge was forthcoming but, six weeks after the first complaint, the *TLS* printed a carefully written and emollient reply from John Simpson, co-compiler of *OED2*.[20] Courteously thanking Plowden for his contributions over the years, he pointed out that in producing the new edition, 'Oxford University Press has had to consider the relative priority of a number of different aims, and has in fact achieved an ambitious target in a short space of time'. He went on to specify the main elements of that target: amalgamation of *OED1* with the four-volume Supplement, addition of the 5,000 new words and senses, conversion of Murray's pronunciation scheme to IPA (International Phonetic Alphabet), and 'the rewording of many definitions to reflect historical and modern usage'.

He then explained, in some detail, how the Press could not possibly have undertaken the task they were now being criticized for neglecting, namely wholesale revision of the main Dictionary. He noted that the 'scraps . . . fed straight in by the post' by helpful correspondents 'represent only the tip of the iceberg'. 'Many thousands of additional antedatings' could be extracted from the dictionaries prepared since *OED1* had been completed, from scholarly publications, and indeed (one might add) from original texts. Digesting them appropriately would necessitate redrafting entries on a significant scale.

This was an unanswerable case. *OED*'s claim to pre-eminence rests firmly on its quotation base. New quotation evidence would require editors to redraw their semantic maps, rethinking the relationships between different senses of words that Murray and his colleagues had sketched out so many years ago on the basis of what was now appearing insufficient and incomplete material. This, Simpson explained, would be the task of the third edition, already in progress. He finished by urging *TLS* readers to continue to send *OED* their corrections and amplifications. 'Such contributions,' he said, 'have always been a great strength of the *OED*, and will continue to make it an endeavour in which all word-lovers can share.'

Helpful and informative as this letter is, it sidestepped the issue. It conceded the complainants' point without addressing their injury, encouraging them to keep faith with the Dictionary they loved by continuing to heap their treasures – the voluntary contributions on which the *OED* had always relied – at its feet. It is tempting for an outsider to speculate that *OED* had been put in an impossible position by the financial imperatives driving its masters. The strategy appears clear. At long last the Press had determined on revision rather than further supplementation. But it had also recognized that this project was an undertaking of many years, necessitating punitively heavy expenditure. How could it keep its flagship Dictionary in the public eye during this period, while at the same time generating an immediate financial return to offset future costs (and protecting the copyright of the original work)?[21] The answer was a marketing triumph, exploiting the ambiguity in the *OED*'s own definition of 'edition': a 'differing form' from that of the original work, certainly, but essentially the same content. Libraries and institutions everywhere bought this handsome new publication, beautifully presented and magnificently advertised, and displayed it on their shelves as the standard work. They consigned their earlier volumes to storage or the second-hand market without seeming to realize that the expensive replacement contained little that was truly different.

OUP was repeating a different form of the trade-off it had determined on in the 1950s. Then, however, the long-term project of full revision was indefinitely postponed. The significant compensating factor this time round, allowing one to forgive if not excuse the second edition, was the Press's eventually wholehearted embrace of this formidable undertaking. After sixty years and more, the original *OED* was to be completely overhauled, in a revision that would amount to entire rewriting.

Content and character of *OED2*

Meanwhile, the public were left with the second edition, dedicated like its predecessor to the reigning monarch (Elizabeth II). What precisely did these twenty volumes contain? Volume 1, covering the alphabet range *A-Bazouki*, began with sixty-eight pages of introductory matter. The Preface explains clearly, in its first sentence, that this second edition 'amalgamates the text of the first edition, published in twelve volumes in 1933, the *Supplement*, published in four volumes between 1972 and 1986, and approximately five thousand new words, or new senses of existing words, which have gained currency since the relevant volume of the *Supplement* was published'. Two paragraphs down, the waters are muddied. 'The aim of this Dictionary is to present in alphabetical series the words that have formed the English vocabulary from the time of the earliest records *down to the present day* [my italics], with all the relevant facts concerning their form, sense-history, pronunciation, and etymology.' This was largely true of the first edition, published in 1928 and 1933, but could not be true of the second, published in 1989, given that most of the material in the second edition was carried over without change from the first.

Merging the dictionaries in this way produced some strange results. One of the significant changes the second edition made was to introduce IPA into the *OED*, rightly asserting that 'IPA has the advantage that it is very widely accepted and understood, and can be used to represent the sounds of regional and dialect English and foreign languages as well as of standard English'.[22] For *OED2*, all the pronunciation indicators in the first edition were painstakingly updated to this modern system. But *OED1*'s system had been based on Murray's own pronunciation, around a hundred years out of date in 1989, as the lexicographers themselves acknowledged: they described it as 'extremely "precise" [the implication of their inverted commas is not clear], conservative, and (in present-day terms) old-fashioned' (p. xx).[23] This makes nonsense of Murray's own remarks, reprinted (though without identification of any sort) a few pages on in *OED2*'s Introduction, which, conversely, insist on the importance of recording *current* pronunciation:

> The pronunciation is the actual living form or forms of a word, that is, *the word itself* [Murray's italics], of which the current spelling is only a symbolization – generally, indeed, only the traditionally-preserved symbolization of an earlier form, sometimes imperfect to begin with, still oftener corrupted in its passage to our time. This living form is the *latest fact* [Murray's italics] in the form-history of the word, the starting-point of all investigations into its previous history, the only fact in its form-history to which the lexicographer can personally witness. For all his statements as to its previous history are only reproductions of the evidence of former witnesses, or deductions drawn from earlier modes of symbolizing the forms of the word then current, checked and regulated by the ascertained laws and principles of phonology. *To register the current pronunciation is therefore essential* [my italics], in a dictionary which deals with the language on historical principles.[24]

One of Murray's scholarly idiosyncrasies was pronouncing the initial *p* in words beginning *ps*, such as *psoriasis*, *psychic*, *psychical*, *psychiatrist*, etc., many of which words in *OED2* are thus most peculiarly given this as the first of two possible pronunciations (e.g. ps-, sɒˈraɪəsɪs). *All* 'ps' words (other than *psalm* and *psalter*) would be thus marked were they not interspersed with additions introduced only in Burchfield's Supplement, and now merged in alphabetical sequence in *OED2*. Thus it appears that you can say '*p*sychiatrist' (pronouncing the *p*) but not '*p*sychedelic', since Burchfield, who was responsible for adding the latter word, unsurprisingly did not choose to reproduce Murray's eccentric pronunciation. Nothing could have been further from Murray's intentions regarding 'current pronunciation', as the extract quoted above makes clear. Murray's tic, preserved in this curious form of aspic, is most unlikely to have been a 'living fact' in 1989 (though those who knew Onions (d. 1965) attest that he too pronounced the initial *p*, perhaps influenced by Murray's example).[25]

Similar observations, *mutatis mutandis*, applied to various other sporadic changes introduced by the *OED2* lexicographers. Sometimes *OED1*'s editorial comments on etymology and pronunciation occurring at the beginning of an entry were reproduced without change in the new dictionary, so that a late nineteenth-century view was represented in *OED2* as being that of 1989, despite the fact that it had since been overturned by intervening scholarship or was otherwise unacceptable (a case in point is the phrase 'irretrievably mutilated by popular use', which is how Murray characterized, in 1909, the pronunciation of those who dropped the initial *p* in *ps*- words. No post-1960 linguist would use such an expression). Elsewhere, *OED1* comments were partially rewritten, so that a mixed view, part nineteenth-century and part modern, was represented as being that of 1989.[26] Consequently, all temporal adverbs appearing in *OED2*'s explanatory comments – 'still', 'now', 'recently', 'formerly', etc. – have to be treated with great caution, and the user must look up the corresponding entry in both *OED1* and the 1972–86 Supplement to discover which of three possible time-frames is being referred to (that of *OED1* – itself stretching over forty-four years, from 1884 to 1928 – or of the 1972–86 Supplement, or of 1989). To say the least, this is a grave inconvenience.

As the Introduction acknowledged, 'the short time available' in preparing this edition 'meant that there had to be rather strict limitations on the extent of the changes made'. Other inconsistencies abound. One oddity, striking the curious reader of the new edition, is the attribution of a series of quotations, without date, to '*Mod.*' (e.g. s.v. A *adj.*[2]1c, and three other places on p. 4 of volume 1). As the introductions to both *OED1* and *OED2* (p. xxxi) explain, this is the way that unattributed quotations 'embodying typical recent usage of a word or sense' are indicated.[27] In fact, as his granddaughter tells us, they were made up *ad hoc* by Murray when he had been unable to find any bona fide contemporary examples. So 'As fine a child as you will see', to illustrate an adjectival sense of *a*, and 'the new arrival is a little daughter', to illustrate *arrival* (sense 6), were Murray's own purpose-made quotations, on both occasions devised as he was correcting proofs while sitting at the bedside of his wife Ada, who had just given birth to a daughter (Elsie) in 1882.[28] The *OED2* user will readily guess what *Mod.* stands for, but will not necessarily be aware that these quotations are modern in terms of the 1880s, not the 1980s. Usage has not changed for the two examples just given, but others look stranger – e.g. '*Mod.* At present, when small-pox is about' (s.v. *about* sense 9), or '*Mod.* The pawnbroker declined to advance more than 3 shillings on the article. I will advance him £50 on your note-of-hand' (s.v. sense 8a of the verb *advance*)'.

As well as adding 5,000 new words and senses, *OED2* also undertook 'the rewording of many definitions to reflect historical and modern usage' (as explained in Simpson's *TLS* letter of 1989). Since there is no means of systematically distinguishing these additions and changes, other than comparing the edition entry by entry with its predecessors, searches must proceed by guess and luck. (The publicity brochure given to attenders of the Claridge's lunch included a sheet of paper entitled 'Some Facts about *OED2*', telling its readers that of the new words, 1,200 were from the sciences; and of those from the arts and social sciences, 175 were from politics, 95 from economics, 57 from linguistics, 74 from the law; no further information seems to have been supplied.)[29]

A swift survey would indicate that special attention was given to sexual words (though it may be that the present writer, like Dr Johnson's two ladies in the anecdote, was looking for them). Julian Barnes told readers of *Harpers & Queen* that his special remit under Burchfield had been 'sports and dirty words', and that he had 'once tried to get *blow-job* into the *OED* Supplement and presented my admittedly thin evidence to the editor. He considered my application but declined it. "I'm afraid there isn't as much of this about as you imagine," he commented sympathetically, and so in 1972 the term was deemed not to exist.'[30] It got in in 1989, with quotations from 1961, as did the verb *blow* (= 'fellate'), with quotations from 1933. (The first was labelled 'slang', the second 'coarse slang'; it is difficult to divine the reason for the distinction.)

As we saw in the last chapter, the definitions for *Sapphism* and *tribade*, left unchanged by Burchfield, were carefully rewritten in *OED2* to remove the mention of 'unnatural' sexual relations and of 'vice'. A strange amalgam appears s.v. sense 20 of *cock*. The first edition, with commendable frankness, defined this as 'Penis', adding a note to say 'The current name among the people, but, *pudoris causa* ['for reasons of modesty'], not admissible in polite speech or literature; in scientific language the Latin is used.' Three citations were identified by date and name of authority, but the quotations were not themselves reproduced, presumably because their content was thought inappropriate. Burchfield in his 1972 volume added earlier and later examples, this time printing them in full (e.g., from a text of 1618, 'Oh man what art thou? When thy cock is up?'). OED2 runs all this material together, bafflingly mingling quoted with unquoted authorities, and reproduces OED1's note unchanged, with its anachronistic reference to 'the people', its untranslated Latin, and its strange implication that scientists *c.* 1989 are unable to bring themselves to refer to the penis in their own language.

Political correctness, of various sorts, seems to have driven a number of the (proportionally tiny) changes introduced elsewhere. The entry *bohunk* in the Supplement had not been identified as a derogatory term, but this information was added to the definition in OED2, perhaps as a result of A. J. Aitken's remarks in his 1973 review of the first volume of the Supplement.[31] OED1 had defined *darky* (sense 3) as 'a negro, a blacky', and had labelled it *colloq.*, with quotations from 1840, 1883 and 1884. Burchfield had let this stand, but the OED2 compilers adjusted the definition and added a usage note: 'A Black, esp. a Southern U.S. Black (usu. considered patronizing or mildly offensive).' By contrast, *bogtrotter*, untreated by Burchfield, is left unidentified as a racist term by OED2, as was *Paki*, a term Burchfield had introduced into OED2, without a label to indicate that it could be derogatory (as of March 2005, it is now, in the revision of OED3, labelled 'usu. *derogatory* and *offensive*').[32] Other material from the first edition, overlooked in error by Burchfield, survived untreated into OED2 in the same way, for example the racist definitions or remarks in the entries for *Chinaman, half-blooded, hubbub* and *interlocutor*, all identified in the previous chapter. As of October 2006, none of these terms (except *Paki*) had been revised by the third edition of the OED, so they have been reproduced without change in today's OED Online.

Sometimes feminist considerations seem to lie behind the decision to select a particular item for rewriting. OED2 picked out *jury* and redefined it as 'a company of persons (orig. men) sworn to render a verdict. . .' (unfortunately we are not told precisely when women were first allowed to serve as jurors). A spot check of other definitions which might be held to be sensitive on grounds of sexism turns up a new (OED2) addition to sense 9 of *chair* (sb.): '. . . Now also used as alternative for "chairman" or "chairwoman", esp. deliberately so as not to imply a particular sex', and a note on *spokesperson* deriving from Burchfield's Supplement: 'A manufactured substitute for "spokesman" or "spokeswoman". One of numerous words used to avoid alleged sexual discrimination in terminology.' On the other hand, *housekeeper*, in the most common (I would imagine) current sense (*OED2* sense 4), is unembarrassedly gender-specific, and carried over without change from *OED1*: 'A woman engaged in housekeeping or domestic occupations; a woman who manages or superintends the affairs of a household; *esp.* the woman in control of the female servants of a house-hold' (quotations range from 1607 to 1859). And while there was an entry for *camera-man* (deriving from Burchfield's Supplement), defined as 'a man who uses or operates a camera professionally' (sense 3d), there was none for *camera-woman* or *camera-person* (both of which terms had by 1989 been current for some years among television and cinema photographers).[33] Notes on or definitions of *man, men, mankind,* all to denote women as well as men, or *girls* instead of *women* used in collocation with *men* in certain contexts, seem to yield no further examples where feminist objections, then considered in many quarters standard, were acknowledged.

If changes like that made to *jury* were part and parcel of a general policy of revision in *OED2* to eradicate the intrinsic sexism of *OED1*, such a policy was doomed to failure. The speed with which the second edition was produced meant that consistency in its execution was unattainable; while the attitudes of the original editors, or of their culture, were preserved not only in their definitions and comments on words, but also in their choice of quotations – whether in those for *woman* in *OED1* (which famously included such items as Congreve's 'Nor Hell a Fury, like a Woman scorn'd' and Pope's 'every Woman is at heart a Rake'), or in Burchfield's subsequent inclusion of unpleasant remarks on lesbians, or, say, his choice of 'The Dry Martini . . . is a drink which certainly sorts out the men from the boys and the girls from their principles', as one of the illustrations for *man* sb.[1] 4c (perhaps one of the references to drink which Kingsley Amis found so uplifting). It would be impossible to make any real changes to the sexist balance of the *OED* without, in many instances, starting again from scratch. And it could certainly be argued against such a policy that *OED1*'s (and the Supplement's) choice of quotations, in common with its defini-tions, bears valuable historical witness to the sociolinguistic attitudes of a particular period.

Another area to which the *OED2* lexicographers gave attention was that of the usage labels of their own predecessor, the editorial *ipse dixits* Burchfield introduced, 'oil to preserve the mucilage from inspissation', when he was half-way through the alphabet. But these had been inconsis-tently presented in their original form in the Supplement. Some had been attributed (to 'Ed' – although this is not a term appearing in Burchfield's list of abbreviations), but some had not; some condemnatory comments had been accompanied with the paragraph mark (¶) used by Murray to indicate 'catachrestic or erroneous' usage, but some had not; some had been enclosed within brackets, and some printed in a different, smaller typeface, but again some had not. And despite Burchfield's indication that editorial comments of this nature were a new departure in volume 3, a few were also to be found, as we saw in the last chapter, in the two earlier volumes of his Supplement. It is therefore unsurprising that Burchfield's status labels and comments were variably treated by the *OED2* compilers, notwithstanding the (in general) formidable accuracy of their digitalization of the Dictionary. Some were tagged 'R.W.B.', for R. W. Burchfield (though 'R.W.B.' was not included in the list of abbreviations), some were reproduced without being identified as due to Burchfield, and some were dropped altogether. One of those omitted was the note Burchfield had inserted, in possibly disingenuous response to Auden's prodding, on *disinterested* – 'often regarded as a loose use'. But on what grounds should this have been excised in 1989, given that other contemporary dictionaries continued to warn against it, and that it recorded a historical fact of judgement by a major *OED* editor of the past (whether deemed idiosyncratic or not)?[34]

One could go on. But such criticisms seem in the end unfair, for how could the second edition of the *OED* be otherwise? As the lexicographers themselves acknowledged, 'it may be said without exaggeration that the apparently straightforward task of amalgamating the two texts [*OED1* and Supplement] turned out to have ramifications and implications so multifarious, protean and unpredictable that the project team occasionally despaired of detecting them all'.[35] Heroic though their endeavours were, they had had no time to sift minutely through the 321,500 entries (and many more words)[36] they were combining into a single dictionary, or to achieve consistency or evenness in their treatment of definitions, labels and other material written over a period of a hundred years, during which enormous social as well as linguistic changes had taken place. Just as importantly, they could not possibly have undertaken the updating of the thousands of entries whose last quotations were a hundred years or more out of date and whose definitions were written in nineteenth-century locutions no longer current.[37]

Many observations of this kind were made in a punishing review of the second edition by E. G. Stanley, a stalwart friend and prolific contributor to the Dictionary for decades.[38] His remarks were hotly contested by a poorly briefed senior officer of the Press and an exchange of letters was printed in the pages of the journal in which Stanley's piece had appeared, *Review of English Studies* (then edited by R. E. Alton, a fellow of St Edmund Hall, Oxford), which was itself published by OUP. Stanley, who was on the editorial board of the 'New *OED* Project', was driven to conclude that 'some of the editorial aims outlined in the Managing Director's letter and in the introduction to the 1989 edition have led, in the opinion of a reviewer who is a constant user of *OED*, to a version of *OED* published before it was fit for publication as a second edition'.[39]

The pain caused to some users, and no doubt the *OED* and the Press itself, by some of the circumstances of the creation and reception of the second edition was considerable. And it was indisputably the case that for many non-scholarly purposes, the combined edition of *OED1* and Supplement was more convenient than their previous incarnations, whether used separately or in conjunction. Those twenty superbly produced volumes did present (and still do present, since this edition continues to be the only printed one available), in a single publication, all the work so far carried out by *OED* lexicographers and put into book form, even if the date of its respective stages of completion was not always evident. Most importantly of all, it was a significant interim juncture in the creation of the third edition. While it was not 'the state of the art' dictionary that the *Daily Telegraph* claimed, it was 'an extraordinary co-operation of literature and electronics, of history and technology ... monumental, indispensable', as Sebastian Faulks said in the *Independent* magazine. Another warm tribute, by William Golding in the *London Evening Standard*, recounted how 'in the high days of Queen Victoria a dictionary was conceived, not to say dared, which matched her iron bridges, her vast ships and engines'. In ways not yet expected by most of those heaping praise on *OED2*, the Press and its lexicographers were soon to be engaged on a magnificent counterpart to their predecessors' 'stupendous achievement'.[40]

Intervening stages: the *Additions* and the CD-Roms

In 1989, the Press still took the view that 'the most important way in which the *OED* can be updated is by the addition of new words and senses'.[41] Work on this had begun well before Burchfield's Supplement was completed, and was a vital element in the Press's lexicographical strategy conceived as a whole. In their Introduction to *OED2*, the new editors John Simpson and Edmund Weiner explained why. 'Fifty years before, the remainder of the team responsible for the *OED*, having completed the original Supplement' – that of Craigie and Onions in 1933 – 'dispersed, and there followed an interval of a whole generation during which no original historical lexicography was carried on at OUP.' (As we saw in Chapters III and V, Wyllie and others had in fact preserved collections and made searches at least to some degree in those intervening years, though the circumstances of Wyllie's departure wiped this from institutional records.) 'Because of this,' Simpson and Weiner continued, 'the new *Supplement* had to be started virtually from scratch, and needed many years to make up lost ground [again, as we saw in Chapters VI and VII, this was partly because the project was reconceived during those years, and not just because it 'started from scratch']. It was imperative to avoid the repetition of such a hiatus at the completion of the *Supplement*'. So in order not to make the same mistake this time round, the Press set up, towards the end of 1983, a 'small editorial group', drawn from those who had drafted Supplement entries for its fourth and final volume.

Simpson and Weiner take up the story again in the first of the three volumes of *Additions* subsequently printed (the first two in 1993 and the third in 1997), a series of new entries for *OED* on words and senses spread across the alphabet, designed to be a stopgap between the publication of the second edition in 1989 and what they then envisaged as the publication of the third in a further ten years or so. Their initial plan had been to 'add these entries to the OED database during the course of revising the Dictionary for its Third Edition'. But given the quantity of words in hand, their intrinsic interest, and the increasing uncertainty about when, exactly, a third edition might appear, it seemed desirable to go ahead and publish them straight away. An additional factor was now as previously playing an important part in the Press's general plan. All the Oxford dictionaries benefited from the existence of a central lexicographical unit, whose job was to gather together and analyse new information on words and language: 'It is an integral part of the *OED*'s role today to provide fully researched and edited new material for the range of dictionaries produced by the Oxford University Press,' Simpson and Weiner wrote, specifying the then-forthcoming *New Shorter Oxford English Dictionary*, the eighth edition of the *Concise* – both edited by former Supplement senior editors, respectively Leslie Brown and R. E. Allen – and the *New Oxford Dictionary of English* of 1998 (an Oxford dictionary of an entirely different cast, compiled from re-analysis of much of the core vocabulary using the British National Corpus, i.e. spoken as well as written contemporary sources).[42] Nevertheless, the entries in the *Additions* volumes were not just recent neologisms; they also 'represented a heterogeneous collection of accessions to the language over the past few centuries'. Some were surprising omissions from *OED1* or its Supplements (e.g. *mundane* in the sense 'everyday, ordinary . . . banal, prosaic', etc.), some were examples of the technical, or non-UK English, vocabulary to which the *OED* was becoming increasingly hospitable (e.g. *Multics*, a computing acronym, or *mulloway*, a type of fish found in Australian coastal waters), and some refined and expanded *OED* definitions as well as its quotation record for certain items (e.g. *mumbo-jumbo*).

These volumes, valuable as they were, seized public attention far less than the CD-Roms that were released over the same period, first of the original edition (in 1987), and then of the second edition (1992, subsequently reissued in upgraded versions in 1999 and 2002). The rapidity of technological change robbed the user of these new gifts almost as swiftly as it issued them (so it sometimes seemed): existing copies of the first CD-Rom can no longer be played on today's computers, which have far outstripped their predecessors' capabilities in all respects except this single most important one. This means, alas, that it is impossible to search *OED1* electronically, and thus distinguish the contribution of Burchfield from that of his predecessors. But the uses to which these CDs could be put enchanted a new lexicographical audience of literary computing enthusiasts, and many rapturous reviews are still available online.[43]

It was 'digitalization', also, that truly excited the 'project team' behind the second edition, as can be seen from the intensity and detail with which their pages on electronic transformation are written (towards the end of *OED2*'s Introduction). They talk of their use of 'technically sophisticated methods, more redolent of engineering than lexicography', which were 'unprecedented in the history of the Oxford Dictionaries', but 'necessitated by the scope and scale of the project'. And they strive to give some idea to the layperson of the magnitude of their task:

> Data capture, the keying of about 350,000,000 characters over 18 months, took 120 person-years; computer development took 14 person-years; automatic processing of the text took 10 months; interactive integration took 7 person-years; the two rounds of proof-reading, undertaken by over 50 people, each took 60 person-years; and final composition of the integrated text involved the setting of approximately 20,000,000 characters per week.

Naturally, they were themselves well aware of the significance of this switch from print to electronic technology, describing it as 'without doubt, their chief contribution to the future of the *OED*' – rather, it is implied, than any editorial contribution.[44] In this they were surely correct. For tagging the various elements of a word in this way enabled their retrieval according to a variety of different criteria, or taxonomical principles, so as to enable both lexicographers and users to access the Dictionary in radically new ways. In a word, *OED* was now poised to escape the tyranny of alphabetization.[45]

In 1915, *The Times* had portrayed the historical treasure buried in the *OED* as though it were easily accessible. 'If indeed we wish to trace the

history of different periods and study their innovations and ideas,' a journalist wrote, 'we can find these dated with curious accuracy by the appearance of the new words in which they are embodied. For just as the
archæologist, when he excavates the site of some ancient city, finds the
various forms of its civilization arranged in chronological strata, so we find
evidences of each past generation and its activities in the superimposed
strata of our vocabulary.'[46] This description (which uses the imagery of
geological discovery that had pervaded scientific and other sorts of
discourse during the nineteenth century, p. 109 above) assumes, and implies,
that it is a simple matter to trawl the Dictionary for data on new usages,
quotation provenance and dating, etymologies, etc.

The first-edition lexicographers themselves may well have understood how
the OED represented an archaeological treasure-house, with thousands of
different items comprehensively described and docketed. But to the casual
readers this information was available only at the level of the individual entry,
and even the intensively habitual user could not hope to construct, from an
overwhelming multiplicity of individual items, the complete picture, 'the
various forms of . . . civilization arranged in chronological strata' that The
Times describes. In a work of this size, organized by alphabetical order of the
words defined (and not by meaning, date, content or any other intrinsically
motivated taxonomy), such information can only be garnered piecemeal.[47]

Digitalization has changed all this. Now it is possible to think of the taxo-
nomic principle on which one wishes to arrange this vast store of lexicographical information, tap search terms into boxes, and receive a slew of
results – often partial, unwieldy and at first indigestible, but susceptible to
further processing and investigation. Various sorts of archaeological strata,
sometimes of compelling interest and value, then loom into view, the gaps
and absences in evidence often as suggestive and significant as the evidence
itself.

However, access to the OED in its electronic form has not of itself
redeemed the second edition. On the contrary, it has provided the diagnostic
tools to reveal, to both users and (more especially) today's OED lexicographers, just how badly needed was the thoroughgoing revision of the
Dictionary on which the latter were now about to embark in earnest,
seventy years and more after the first edition had been completed. It is no
exaggeration to say that this new stage in the history of the OED has revolutionized the ways in which the Dictionary can be both used and compiled.
Its consequences can be considered under two separate (although linked)
heads: first, the characteristics of the electronic version of the OED, and
secondly, in the remaining sections of this chapter, the nature of the major
revision of the Dictionary now taking place.

The electronic *OED*

The most obvious, and least interesting, advantage of the electronic *OED* is the speed with which one can look up a word – an advantage significantly multiplied if one is investigating several items together: one touches a few keys, instead of grappling with numerous heavy and cumbersome volumes. The disadvantage of viewing the Dictionary on-screen is that it is impossible to compare two or more entries meticulously side by side to try to discover how and why the lexicographers have made changes to *OED2* during the course of preparing *OED3*. Even (to use Chapman's and Burchfield's term) the most chalcenterous dictionary user will blanch at the task of comparing the new version of the verb *make*[1] with the old, whose many dozens of subdivided senses have been substantially recast.[48]

The really valuable gain in accessing the Dictionary electronically is of a different order altogether. The trouble with the printed form is that its massed ranks of alphabetically ordered items presented an intimidatingly unanalysable front, behind whose battle lines it was logistically impossible to penetrate. How could one identify and make use of linguistic data scattered across thousands of entries, in a work treating nearly half a million words? How could one divine the editorial policy behind the immensely varied range of quotations? But there are now many ways in which one can cut interrogative swathes through *OED*'s fabulously rich content. Searching for specific prefixes, suffixes, spelling forms, etymologies and other word characteristics gives linguists access to priceless information about the history and development of the English language. This can in turn be used to illuminate the language of specific authors or periods. Most important of all, however, is the information that can now be elicited about the nature of the *OED* itself, in the light of which all such subsidiary evidence must be interpreted. As we saw in Chapter IV, it is now possible to identify *OED1*'s most-quoted sources – after Shakespeare comes Sir Walter Scott (with far fewer quotations than Shakespeare, 15,800-odd), then Milton (*c.* 12,000), Chaucer (*c.*11,000), Dryden (*c.* 8,800) and Dickens (*c.* 8,200); whereas the Bible (in various translations) is quoted around 25,000 times and the medieval work *Cursor Mundi* (a 30,000-line composition in verse expatiating on the history of the world, based on scriptural and other sources) around 11,000.[49] It is the language of these texts and others like them whose history the first edition of *OED* charts, at the expense of hosts of others that may have significant contributions to make to the historical record. These in turn can be identified in the same way – one such example being Anna L. Barbauld (1743–1825), cited eighteen times in *OED2*, a distinguished, productive and contemporarily acclaimed poet and essayist, whose

Poems went through five editions between 1773 and 1777 and were described by the *Monthly Review* as having 'a justness of thought, and vigour of imagination, inferior only to the works of Milton and Shakespeare', and whose other works were also often reprinted. Her writing is full of lexical material which would augment and enhance the *OED*'s record. Many other such examples can be adduced.[50]

Another type of analysis is examination of the number of quotations recorded in *OED* over its chronological range (illustration 9 presents the result for the years 1500–1899). It is tempting to think that this graph's peaks and troughs represent the varying rate of word coinage over the centuries – but they don't, of course: or at any rate, they needn't. Instead, as with the representation of individual authors, this data primarily registers what the lexicographers chose from the material available to them to put into their dictionary. Not surprisingly, there is often a correlation between peaks in word recording, and the intensive excerpting of an individual source or sources. So the steep rise in quotations between the first and second decades of the sixteenth century is almost half accounted for by a single text, Palsgrave's *Lesclarcissement de la langue francoyse* of 1530, a bilingual English–French dictionary from which the *OED1* lexicographers took over 4,600 quotations. What the *OED* does not tell one, however, is the relationship between Palsgrave's lexicon and general usage of the day, on which any interpretation of the Dictionary's evidence in this respect must rest.[51]

The eighteenth century is a particularly interesting example of how the lexicographers' methods, in combination with prevailing literary views of the time (and also with chance), determined the eventual content of the *OED*.[52] Soon after the first set of reading lists for *OED* volunteers was drawn up by the Philological Society members concerned, it was decided to assign the eighteenth-century period to American readers. The Society's *Proposal for the Publication of a New English Dictionary* (p. 6) reported in 1859 that 'the whole of the 18th-century literature has been handed over to our American collaborators', to be organized by a subcommittee of which G. P. Marsh was to act as Secretary, and in May 1860 Herbert Coleridge explained to Trench that this period 'would have a less chance of finding as many readers in England'.[53]

Why did Coleridge feel that British readers would be uninterested in the eighteenth century? Many Victorians took a low view of the literature of this period, as instanced in remarks like those of Swinburne, whose book on William Blake reminded his readers that his author lived in a time 'when the very notion of poetry, as we now understand it, had totally died and decayed out of the minds of men; when we not only had no poetry, a thing which was bearable, but had verse in plenty; a thing which was not in the least bearable'. Such disregard was not universal (Pope was much admired), but was apparently sufficient for Coleridge to judge that the eighteenth century was better off in the hands of the Americans.[54]

But this turned out to be a misjudgement. Twenty years later, when Murray became editor of the *OED* in 1879, he found that there was a serious deficiency in eighteenth-century quotation slips. In the *Appeal* he issued that year, he reported

it is in the eighteenth century above all that help is urgently needed. The American scholars promised to get the eighteenth-century literature taken up in the United States, a promise which they appear not to have to any extent fulfilled, and we must now appeal to English readers to share the task, for nearly the whole of that century's books, with the exception of Burke's works, have still to be gone through.[55]

Murray's *Appeal* was accompanied by a 'List of books for which readers are wanted', on which a note on the section for the eighteenth century begins: 'the literature of this century has hardly been touched. Readers are safe with almost any eighteenth century book they can lay their hands on'. Forty-six works or authors, many literary, are named as 'books that ought to be read'.

It is clear that Murray toiled heroically to fill the 'serious gaps' he found in the quotation material he inherited from Furnivall in 1879. In 1884, he described how 'for more than five-sixths of the words we have had to search out and find additional quotations in order to complete their history, and illustrate the senses; for every word we have had to make a general search to discover whether any earlier or later quotations, or quotations in other senses, exist'.[56] But the evidence we can now turn up from electronic searching of the *OED* suggests that, where the eighteenth century was concerned, Murray was less successful than he had hoped. Illustration 9 plainly indicates disproportionately low documentation in the *OED* of this period of the language. Further searches reveal that around 18,000 words, in currency in both the seventeenth and the nineteenth centuries, altogether lack eighteenth-century documentation in the *OED*.[57] Is it really plausible that these words simply ceased to be used in the eighteenth century, only to revive a hundred years later? The answer must (at least in many cases) be no.

Whether the comparative paucity of quotations in the *OED* from the eighteenth century is due to under-reading of this period and hence a comparatively low stock of quotations to draw on, or instead to the lexicographers' preferences for certain sorts of quotation sources over others – or, perhaps most likely, to a combination of these two factors – we cannot now discover. But its effect on the Dictionary is significant, given that the quotations in the *OED* are not so much illustrative as constitutive of meaning – for that is the implication of the definition methods described by Murray and Onions, quoted in Chapter IV. This is fully recognized by the present-day *OED* lexicographers as well as by their predecessors. Thus Penny Silva, Director of *OED3*, writes, 'the discovery of meaning in the quotations was acknowledged by Murray when he noted that "the explanations for the meanings have been framed anew upon a study of all the quotations for each word collected for this work", and explained that it was from the quotations "and the researches for which they provide a starting point", that "the history of each word is deduced and exhibited"'.[58]

Fewer quotations from the eighteenth century meant less evidence of usage for this period, and less opportunity for eighteenth-century lexical productivity and innovation of one sort or another to impress itself on the lexicographers in the manner graphically reported by Murray in 1887: 'You sort your quotations into bundles on your big table, and think you are getting the word's pedigree right, when a new sense, or three or four new senses, start up, which upset all your scheme, and you are obliged to begin afresh, often three or four times.'[59] What aspects of eighteenth-century language might have started up in front of the eyes of the lexicographers had their eighteenth-century evidence been fuller? What examples of characteristic or uncharacteristic language usage in this period may they consequently have failed to document in the *OED*?

This example reinforces the points made above. The *OED* reflects the sources chosen by its lexicographers and readers. Both nineteenth- and twentieth-century lexicographers were limited by constraints of time and resources, and had to be dependent on material not always accurately or thoroughly assembled. The electronic *OED* allows readers to discover, investigate and attempt to understand all these things for the first time, while it enables the lexicographers themselves to measure and analyse their own practices in revising the original *OED* and bringing its record up to date. The striking inequalities in the way that different sources were represented in the *OED* reveal previous editors' prior assumptions about the importance of certain periods over others, certain genres over others, certain texts over others, and male authors over female ones. Such inequalities invite the present-day lexicographers to formulate and explain their own policies: can they defend and should they maintain their predecessors' preferences? Or should they revise the *OED*'s policies and practices? If so, how and why?

When the second edition of the *OED* was published, it sometimes seemed that the editors themselves had underestimated the monumental task of revision necessary. 'It is a matter of common knowledge that many elements of the original *OED* require revision,' the editors commented at the start of their Introduction (p. xi), providing an 'outline agenda' for this process (pp. lv–lvi). But they felt that 'this new edition represents the first, and almost certainly the most arduous, step towards [the] goal' of full revision and updating. As it has turned out, digitalization has pointed the way to many more, and more arduous, steps than those taken in the creation of *OED2*. The extraordinary variability of quoted authors, sources and periods now brought to light reveals that the job of full revision and updating the original Dictionary, conducted on whatever principles, is an enormous one.

The third edition: general

The origins of the third edition of the *OED* were established well before the second edition was published. By 1993, initial plans had coalesced into a more definite form. John Simpson was appointed editor and Edmund Weiner deputy editor, and in 1994 the new project was formally announced in a widely distributed leaflet. Here, the scale of the new endeavour was fully acknowledged, Simpson explaining that 'the greater part of the text is still substantially that which was published in the late nineteenth and early twentieth centuries by Sir James Murray and his successors'. Resorting to the same means as previous *OED* lexicographers, the new editor made a detailed and eloquent appeal for help from the public, especially any scholar 'working on a literary, social, or other historical text who has found a discrepancy between the material with which they are working and an entry in the *OED*'.[60] Completion, originally planned for 2010, has since been deferred; Simpson suggested in 2003 that 'we expect to complete the main cycle of revision in twenty years or so, depending on a number of factors (budget, growing experience of staff, new computer routines, etc.)', but this projection too is now out of date and has not been publicly replaced.[61]

Meanwhile, the project has been reconfigured. *OED Online* was launched in March 2000 as an internet site, giving access both to the electronic version of *OED2* and to the revised portions of the Dictionary as they are successively completed. In its accompanying publicity pamphlet the Press announced that it was now committing £34 million to bringing the *OED* up to date, making the revision programme 'the world's largest humanities research project'. For the first time, OUP is repeating the level of institutional support it had given to the original *OED* – indeed in many respects, not least managerial, it is substantially increasing it. A large team of lexicographers works in the OUP offices at Walton Street under the leadership of John Simpson and Edmund Weiner (with an outpost in New York under

12. Editors of *OED*: (from right to left), John Simpson, Edmund Weiner, R. W. Burchfield, W. A. Craigie, C. T. Onions, Henry Bradley, and (top) J. A. H. Murray. From Oxford University Press publicity pamphlet for *OED Online* (2000).

Jesse Sheidlower), and the operation is directed by administrative officers in the Press and supported by technological staff.[62] The third-edition lexicographers began with the letter *M*, reaching *O* by March 2004 and *P* by March 2005 (at the time of writing, autumn 2006, they are in the second half of *P* with entries up to *Pomak* completed).[63] Production is steady, with chunks of revised entries released every quarter.

To begin with, *OED Online* could be accessed through subscription only, with individuals being charged in the region of £350 for a year. The cost has now come down to £195 for a year ($295 in North and South America). More importantly, as the result of an admirable recent initiative, a 'landmark agreement' between Oxford University Press and the Museums, Libraries and Archives Council in the UK, *OED Online* is now available free at many public institutions (such as local UK libraries). Perhaps connected with this recognition of *OED* as an essential resource for educational purposes is its recent identification as one of the fifty-odd 'icons' of Britain.[64]

The third edition of *OED* – which may never be published in print form – returns to the ambitious standards of the first. It is not a 'scratch Supplement' like that of Craigie and Onions, and it has not, like Burchfield's dictionary, been undertaken (by the lexicographers at any rate) with insufficient initial awareness of its eventual likely scope. To the extent that the new Dictionary changes as it grows, alterations can be (and have already been) made retrospectively to the material already published, bringing it in line with contemporary policy, so that this version of the Dictionary, unlike all previous ones, can maintain consistency throughout the alphabet. The procrustean constraints of print have been shuffled off in other ways, too: electronic publication means that entries can expand according to intrinsically motivated needs, rather than the space available on the printed page. This is a decisive break with the past. In two important respects, nevertheless, the new edition adheres to the methodology of its predecessors: it is based on the analysis of quotations from many textual sources, and it interprets the meanings of words in relation to historical evidence of their past usage. Unlike the two twentieth-century Supplements, it is not conceived as an appendage to the original edition, with all the limitations to lexicographical scope that that implies. Instead, it is a new work in its own right. It is a major step forward in lexicographical practice and representation, unparalleled in the *OED*'s history to date.

The website has mutated through various forms since its initial release. It offers a substantial range of information and resources, from extensive archival material on the history of the *OED* to sophisticated search options. The former (free to non-subscribers) includes a lucidly written and informative Preface. The main elements of Murray's page and entry layout, designed in 1884 to be 'eloquent to the eye', are by and large preserved, in traditional lexicographical form, but one can choose to turn these features on or off – pronunciation, spellings, etymology and quotations – so as to clear the screen if one wishes. An additional optional feature, very useful, is a date-chart which represents the distribution of quotations in diagram form, revealing the chronological spread of the evidence on which historical and semantic analysis of a word is based. Switching between one screen and the next is swift, owing to the limited graphic content (though the same is not true, unfortunately, of sifting the results of searches). The site designers have thought carefully about how to exploit the new possibilities provided by the electronic medium for viewing, accessing and cross-referencing information, and there are many imaginative and helpful options such as the ability to view contiguous lemmas listed by date or by entry, or an 'entry map' (a schematic diagram of the word's identified senses, hierarchically organized).

A particularly valuable feature of this new edition and its ongoing revisions is its historical transparency: most changes to the site are recorded as they are made. So it is easy to see, from the front page, the list of quarterly updates, charting the successive releases of batches of revised and new vocabulary (e.g. *pi-mesic* to *pleating* was released on 15 June 2006, *philanthropal* to *pimento* on 16 March 2006, *perfect* to *philandering* on 15 December 2005, and so on), while a summary account of the site's history records and dates such events as the fresh design in December 2005 and the addition of advanced search tools in January 2002. It is also possible to access lists of the entirely new words that have been added to the online version, together with the date of their inclusion (e.g. *mixability, moaner's bench, mobile vulgus, modem, body-swerve, clunky, dysfunctional, dyspraxic, lurve, toe-curling*), both those across the whole alphabet range and those within the specified ranges under systematic revision, as well as the entries to which new meanings have been added (e.g. *abductee, black water, centaur, cringe, exfoliate, spacer*).

Such transparency allows the dictionary user to identify which changes and additions have taken place at which stage in the process of compiling the recent revisions to the Dictionary (subsequent to *OED2*). If one takes the view that the *OED* is not an impartial record of language and its users, but instead a selection governed by all sorts of individual factors relating to the lexicographers concerned and the conditions under which they worked – including their own views on and assumptions about language and what their job of dictionary-compiling entailed – then one wants to have as much information as possible about who did what to the Dictionary, and when.

This is something *OED Online* implicitly recognizes by documenting its own actions in this way, and also by clarifying the bewilderingly various stages through which it has passed since its initial digitalization in 1989: six different forms since 1986, representing the progression from print to the third edition in its online medium, via *OED2* and the three volumes of *Additions*.[65]

OED Online also contains a bibliography, to which many of the quotation authors cited under entries are electronically linked (not always correctly). This must be used with caution. It is a conflation of Sweatman and Bayliss's bibliography (formerly 'Register') of 1933 (p. 65 above) with that of Burchfield (printed at the end of *OEDS4* in 1986). But the first made no claims to completeness, and neither work has been revised. Works cited for the first time in *OED3* are not as yet included. So there is no entry for the work Rose Macaulay was reading in the 1930s, for example, *A Brief Summe of Geographie* by Roger Barlow (d. 1554), from which both she and the *OED3* editors were able to ante-date various geographical and natural history terms (p. 100–01 above) – nor for any other of the numerous new texts that *OED* is now citing in significant quantities.

How do *OED3*'s new entries compare with the old? In marked contrast to previous revising editors, who had to content themselves with supplementary, and inevitably inconsistent, patching, the lexicographers working on *OED3* are delivering a root and branch reworking of the first edition. The semantic structure of each entry has been reconsidered and in many cases recast, so that identification of the various senses of a word may be partially or completely different. In all necessary cases, which in practice means almost all cases, surviving definitions have been rewritten in contemporary English, replacing the late nineteenth- or early twentieth-century locutions that now look quaint, outdated and/or, for one reason or another, unsuitable.[66]

The recasting of entries has been driven by the accumulation of additional quotations, to which a vast amount of well-directed energy has been devoted. Many students of pre-contemporary texts will have come across examples of words which ante-date *OED1*'s quotation evidence, and many users have provided the lexicographers with evidence and lists from the publication of the first fascicles onwards. For the first time, this evidence has been drawn on and incorporated into a new version of the Dictionary, and also, evidently, backed up with much independent research. The body of quotations has been reconfigured, with some alterations (both additions and, very occasionally, subtractions), many of which even out the chronological spread of attestation. Many existing quotations have been checked and re-dated.[67] As one would expect, in a dictionary whose claim to revolutionize English lexicography was based, as Craigie and Onions recognized in 1933, on its bank of empirical data, this new information is transforming the *OED*. The truth of Murray's contention that taking into account additional quotations, when inferring meaning, obliges one to rethink and adjust one's original hypothesis, could not be more powerfully demonstrated.

Other categories of treatment – for example, spelling forms, phonology, word labelling (see further below) and explanatory headnotes – have been overhauled and in many cases expanded, changed or rewritten. Etymologies, or what Murray called 'Morphology or Form-History', have been wholly revised (under the supervision of Philip Durkin).[68] The result of such various and substantial labour is that this version of the Dictionary has left clear water behind it. Readers wanting to get a representative idea of the scope and detail of the sweeping changes that have been introduced may wish to examine old and new versions of, for example, *magic*, *Martian*, *martyr* – or indeed *make*, possibly the most substantially rewritten and reworked item to date.[69]

Perhaps most pressingly of all, *OED3* is engaged in bringing the record up to date. The absence of twentieth-century quotations for huge numbers of entries in *OED2* is now being rectified. This anomaly had been one of the most disfiguring aspects of the second edition, belying its claims to be 'authoritative', 'up to date' and 'comprehensive', since for its twentieth-century component it had relied almost exclusively on Burchfield's four Supplement volumes of 1972 to 1986. But the principal aim of these volumes had been to identify and record new words or senses since 1928, not to update the quotation record for words already treated in *OED1*. Consequently, *OED2's* attestation and treatment of pre-existing words – the bulk of the English lexicon – during the course of the twentieth century was extremely thin, and its reprinting of out-of-date definitions disconcerting or even absurd.

Entry after entry in the portion of the alphabet range so far revised in *OED3* displays new quotations from twentieth- and indeed twenty-first-century sources, repairing the gaps left in documentation for the last hundred-odd years. Taking the range M–*monnisher* as a sample, and using *OED Online*'s search mechanism, it is possible to calculate that, whereas Burchfield supplied 18,203 quotations for this section of the alphabet, the new revisers have to date supplied 37,873. In other words, *OED3* has doubled the number of quotations from recent sources.[70] It is difficult to overstate the value of this material (or the extent to which it was overdue).

The new edition has also re-evaluated the currency of many items in nineteenth- and twentieth-century vocabulary. Burchfield had said of his

Supplement, 'Our policy depends upon the realization by users of the Dictionary that any word or sense not marked "obs." or "arch." is still part of the current language.' But one has only to turn over a few pages of *OED2* to find example after example of words quite unfamiliar to a mid- to late twentieth-century user, not marked 'obs.' or 'arch.' but quite evidently not 'part of the current language'. Most of these (so it appears) are now being caught by the third revision. The lexicographers have presumably looked for and failed to find subsequent quotations for numerous such words documented in *OED1* with nineteenth-century quotations but left untouched by Burchfield in the 1970s and 1980s, and consequently also by *OED2* in 1989 (e.g. *magiric, magirist, magism, magnase, magnetiferous, maidenism, manificative* and countless others), and at long last applied the label 'obsolete' (in some instances, especially where Murray or his co-editors marked a word 'rare', it may well have been obsolete for a hundred years or more). The same has been done for those words (far fewer in number) documented in *OED1* with only pre-nineteenth-century quotations (sometimes only one), not then identified as obsolete, and also left unmarked by Burchfield (e.g. *miskenning* adj., last quotation in *OED1* (& 2 & 3) 1608, *melonist*, two quotations in *OED1* (& 2 & 3) dated 1629 and 1727).[71]

Conversely, some words labelled archaic in the first edition, and again left untouched by Burchfield, have had the label removed – thus *misdoubt* (the noun, not the verb) is supplied with three twentieth-century quotations, and *misenter* now has its single *OED1* quotation, dated 1675, sandwiched between one of 1598, and one of 1999 (though this leaves an odd gap).[72] And some words which, one might have thought, should have been labelled obsolete or rare in the second edition have now been shown to have had a new lease of life. Thus *magnanerie*, a silkworm house, had two quotations (1887 and 1885) in *OED1*, was passed over without comment by Burchfield, and now in the third edition is demonstrated as having been both earlier and later used, with additional quotations from 1835, 1966 and 1969. This last word is unlabelled; that it is quoted from a volume of poetry by Kenneth White and from Nabokov's *Ada* may give one pause for thought. Are these isolated examples of literary resuscitation, possibly from the pages of the *OED* itself, like Auden's revival of *baltering*, or Joyce's of *peccaminous* and *cessile*? It would be helpful to have some editorial comment on this possibility, as with many other unlabelled words whose use is sparsely illustrated, from unusual or eccentric sources, over the last hundred years or so (though this is supplied in the case of (so far) eight words, *maltalent, melpomenish, menalty, muskin, nan, nannicock, nippitatum* and most recently *peccaminous* itself, all identified as (revived) 'from dictionary record' – two of them used by Auden and three by Joyce).

The wealth and variety of differences and revisions between *OED3* and its predecessors make it difficult to form a clear idea of the character of the new Dictionary as it unfolds before us. One way of tackling this problem is to examine a particular area of revision, however limited, to see what hints it can give us about the Dictionary as a whole. The next two sections discuss editorial labels and notes, then quotation sources, to try to form a view of the aims and qualities of the *OED* lexicographers' gigantic new undertaking.[73]

Editorial labels and usage notes

In his 'General Explanations', published in the first fascicle of *OED* in 1884, Murray described how he used a range of terms and symbols to characterize a word, and this account was amplified and refined by the *OED2* editors in 1989 to explain the practice of the original Dictionary more clearly. They identify three main categories of label: by *subject* (e.g. *Mus.* for 'music', *Bot.* for 'botany'), by *variety* of English (e.g. *U.S.*, *Austral.*), or by *status*, that is, 'where there is any peculiarity, as *Obs.* (obsolete), *arch.* (archaic or obsolescent), *colloq.* (colloquial), *dial.* (now dialectal)'.[74] This last category is particularly interesting. Such labels were often used to indicate a word's social and other connotations, so that they now reveal cultural assumptions that have since changed but may be difficult to identify from other sources. As observed by Richard W. Bailey, one of the participants at the Leiden conference in 1977 at which Burchfield acknowledged the personal element in his own dictionary (p. 210 above), 'labelling is the least scientific and most artistic part of the lexicographer's task. We cannot form a judgement of usage on the basis of the character of the speaker (whether real or fictional) or the speech setting or, for most dictionaries, the frequency of a sense or form in the corpus. Status labels arise from a judgment about usage rather than a judgment about meaning, and hence emerge from the lexicographer's sense of the language.'[75]

Inevitably, over so long a period of compilation, labelling practices changed and developed. Consistency, however desirable, was never a practicable possibility (so *clavicembalo*, a name for a harpsichord, is labelled '*Mus.*' in *OED2*, but *clavichord* and *clavicithern*, immediately following, are not).[76] In his Introduction to the Supplement, Burchfield tells us that the 'system of labelling is unchanged' between *OED1* and his Supplement, and that 'it would have been inappropriate to have a different system in the Supplement from that used in the Dictionary itself'.[77] This statement glides over the inconsistencies of labelling in both *OED1* and Supplement, and also obscures the fact that Burchfield did treat labelling, of various kinds, differently from his predecessors – most strikingly in his introduction of

Johnsonian *ipse dixits* from volume 3 onwards (p. 209 above). The third edition revisers have thus had their work cut out to regularize and systematize editorial labels, an especially important element in an electronic dictionary where users can be expected to employ label tags, and status descriptions of one sort or another ('vulgar', 'regrettable', 'loose', 'poetic'), as one of the ways in which to organize searches for various different sorts of material. For example, how many of the quotations from Auden are of words judged to be 'historical' or 'archaic'? What words occurring in a particular play of Shakespeare's are still in use in the twentieth century, but have shifted in register in some way or other? Editorial labelling tells us not only about the connotations of words but also about the attitude, sometimes unconsciously expressed, of the lexicographers towards their material.

The third edition revisers' policy is evolving gradually, as the present writer has found to her cost. Investigating *OED3*'s treatment of a number of labels ('historical', 'archaic', 'obsolete', 'rare' and others) over a sample stretch of text, shortly after it went online, I found a number of puzzling inconsistencies: some words were labelled 'archaic', some 'historical', some 'rare', when the same sorts of quotation evidence were adduced in each case. Passing my notes to the editor, John Simpson, for comment, I was taken aback to learn that many of the inconsistencies had already been noted and corrected. He wrote back to me to explain that

> soon after we started publishing online in March 2000 we recognized that there was a problem of consistency with our obsolete/rare labelling. This arose because the system we were using (developed from that in use on the Supplement) had too many unnecessary complications – and so the system was being applied slightly differently by different editors. As a result, in late 2000 we reviewed our policy and decided on a simpler approach. We are using this new policy now, and have applied the changes to much of the online text (as part of an ongoing procedure). I suspect you conducted your research on these labels before we had started to implement the new policy.

This helpfully illuminates *OED3*'s recognition of the importance of labels (if also the disconcerting volatility of the Dictionary's new form). The benefits of such renewed scrutiny are apparent in many of the changes now being made to *OED2*. For example, historical words supported with one quotation alone are now routinely described as 'rare' as well as 'obsolete', whereas before they were labelled 'obsolete' but not necessarily 'rare' (as in the case of *magnatical*, supported with a single seventeenth-century quotation; *magnicaudate*, which had a single nineteenth-century quotation; *magnisonant*, two quotations dated 1843; and many others). Some of the apparent lapses from consistency turn out to be explicable according to rational principle. Thus, the answer to my query why *misincline* is labelled obsolete, but *misimprision* labelled both obsolete and rare, when both are illustrated by a single seventeenth-century quotation, was as follows: 'It would have been easy to label both as obsolete and rare, but in fact *misincline* is supported by other early evidence (see *misinclined* and *misinclination*), whereas *misimprision* appears to be isolated. On the basis of this wider evidence it seems reasonable to withhold the "rare" label from *misincline*.' This is a defensible if not transparent policy.

Inconsistencies remain, nevertheless. The last quotation for *nealing* (n) is dated 1839, and that for *neckclothed* dated 1864, but neither is labelled obsolete, whereas other words last quoted in the 1870s *are* labelled obsolete (as *necking* (n^1), *neckbreak* (adv), and many other examples); *neckland* is labelled obsolete but not rare, despite having only two quotations (1598 and 1627), whereas other pre-1870 words with two (or more) quotations are described as obsolete *and* rare (*orbate, orbation*), etc., etc. Individually, these examples and others are trivial; cumulatively, however, they may be important, given that labels are one of the discriminating features by which the *OED*'s wealth of material can be electronically searched. But it is impossible to test the current revisers' consistency in labelling by any method which is itself consistent: sophisticated as the improved search features introduced into the *OED Online* site in January 2002 are, they do not enable searches which reveal how third edition labels compare with those of the previous editions in relation to quotation dating and quotation frequency, nor do they allow one to search for labels as a separate category – i.e. separately from all the other material that appears in the 'definitions' text. It seems therefore impossible to do more than comb through entry by entry, serendipitously happening on this or that.

The search facilities do, however, open up some promising avenues of investigation into the comparative use in one edition or another of labels and labelling, and consequently into what this suggests about the various sorts of criteria applied by the lexicographers. Thus one can get a list of the occasions on which 'Now *rare*' appears in the 'definitions' text of *OED2* entries, and count those instances occurring within (for example) the stretch of revised material over the letter *M* – the answer is 170. The same query applied to *OED3* yields 928 results, an enormous increase. It may be that the new application of this label identifies words in regular use in the late nineteenth century, but now on their way to obsolescence, and that searching for this label in *OED3* is a potentially valuable tool for various sorts of lexical research. But to investigate *OED3*'s use of the term in any more detail one would need to go through every one of those 170 and 928 entries, check that 'now rare' was indeed being used as a label, and compare *OED2* with *OED3*, looking in each case at the date and range of quotations, together with any other editorial comment.

Another promising label to explore (since it may tell us something valuable about any changes either in the revisers' choice of sources, or their judgements about particular usages) is 'literary'. The word *literary* occurs 140 times in the 'definitions' text of *OED3* over the range of entries beginning with *m*, but only 58 times in the corresponding *OED2* text – quite a big difference, and worth looking at further. (Have the revisers chosen to label as 'literary' usages previously unlabelled? Or have they simply identified additional 'literary' senses of words, or added more 'literary' terms or quotations?) In one instance (so far), the *OED3* editors use a more refined version of this term, i.e. 'consciously literary' – a useful label, one might think, if tricky to apply, given the Dictionary's predilection for unusual, writerly diction of one sort another: the revisers say of *make* in the sense 'compose, write' (verb 1, s.v. 4a), that 'The principal modern use is of poems or verses, though even this is somewhat *arch.* or consciously literary.'

Distinguishing between 'archaic' (not 'arch') and 'consciously literary' as they do here seems helpful, but may be specious. We need to know how these terms are understood by the lexicographers (and other terms like them, e.g. (not consciously) 'literary', 'poetic', both of which may shade into 'obsolete', and/or 'historical', and perhaps also deserve the addition of '(now) rare'). What are the new criteria for assigning editorial labels, and what are the labels already in use in the Dictionary? *OED3* will eventually give us a comprehensive list, it appears, but we will have to wait a little longer for it. In an article published in 1999, one of the lexicographers refers to 'a terminological glossary' in preparation for *OED3*. 'The editorial policy of the third edition is still under development,' he tells us, 'and given the immense diversity of types of lexical information which the *OED* may choose to record, it will be some time before the list can be made generally available.'[78] Meanwhile, some labels (as yet undefined and undifferentiated) appear in the list of abbreviations inherited from *OED1*, available both in print and online – e.g. *colloq., derog., vulg., arch., hist., obs., poet.* – but others, not being abbreviations, do not – e.g. *affected, coarse, coarse slang, emotional feminine, humorously pedantic, illiterate, improper, low, ludicrous, now rare, rare, shoppy, well known*, and a number of other terms.[79]

Some of these labels, unsurprisingly, have been dropped in the current revision, reflecting as they do attitudes or social judgements now out of date (though they still have value as indicating the connotations, of whatever sort, which words may have had in the past, in the eyes of the lexicographers). Perhaps the most striking instance of label change in *OED3* is the revisers' complete eschewal of the terms 'erron.' (i.e. 'erroneous'), and 'catachr. (i.e. 'catachrestic'), as applied to usage, both of which occur many times in previous editions of the *OED* to indicate 'incorrect' or contentious uses of one sort or another. Similarly, they no longer use the paragraph sign to proscribe such uses. Their avoidance of these terms of condemnation points to a significant change in lexicographical position. All the *OED* lexicographers, from Trench onwards, have paid lip service to the ideal (variously stated) of descriptivism, but the *OED3* editors are the first to prefer description to prescription in what seems to be uniform practice as well as theory. They have turned their back on Burchfield's *ipse dixits*, as on *OED1*'s more covert proscriptions of one form or another.

These few examples give some idea of the way in which editorial labels can tell us about the lexicographers as well as the words they describe. In addition – if the search engines can be persuaded to divulge this information – labels can reveal a significant picture of the types of source the lexicographers are choosing to document, and hence the quality and function of the *OED* as a whole. Transparency, comprehensiveness and consistency in both label explanation and label application are therefore vital.

The third edition's decisive change in attitude in matters of 'correctness' is additionally illustrated by the usage notes that have been rewritten or inserted for the first time in *OED3*. These admirably present what Bailey called the lexicographer's 'sense of the language' – something apparently intuitive, and therefore individual and personal – while at the same time preserving objective authority. On the words in the portion of the alphabet treated to date the revisers have produced a number of notes which depart from Burchfield's arbitrative approach, while providing the sort of information on issues of correctness that dictionary users often crave. Their practice is no doubt influenced by current practice in contemporary dictionaries (not least OUP's own *New Oxford Dictionary of English*), but the *OED* has the peculiar additional advantage of its range of quotations throughout the history of a word's use, which uniquely inform and substantiate the editors' views. These place any remarks on usage in a historical perspective, illuminating comments such as the editors make on *masterful* sense 2 (in the sense 'masterly'): 'Use in this sense, which seems to have declined somewhat during the 19th cent., has been criticized in usage guides, app. starting with H. W. Fowler Dict. Mod. Eng. Usage (1926) 344' (quotations from 1425 to 1988).

The newly inserted note on *media* as a singular noun is another good example of how to treat matters of correctness and usage. Burchfield had reported this use in the second volume of the Supplement (1976) but in the same breath described it as 'erroneous', notwithstanding his inclusion of a quotation by Kingsley Amis dated 1966, which seemed to point to its increasing acceptability (however regretted) ten years before: 'The treatment of *media* as a singular noun . . . is spreading into the upper cultural strata'. The *OED3* revisers, by contrast, write that 'the use of *media* with singular concord and as a singular form with a plural in -*s* have both been regarded by some as non-standard and objectionable' – and they quote Amis again – but they define the word, with dispassionate descriptivism, as 'the main means of mass communication, *esp.* newspapers, radio, and television, regarded collectively; the reporters, journalists, etc., working for organizations engaged in such communication. Also, as a count noun: a particular means of mass communication.' The treatment of *nigger* appears equally exemplary: additional quotations both ante- and post-date previous *OED* evidence, enabling a semantic re-analysis of the word accompanied by usage comments which are clearly congruous with the quotations rather than at odds with them. These changes and others like them are significant and valuable developments of *OED*'s existing policy. They reflect the far greater importance that the editors of *OED3* attach to methodological self-consciousness and consistency.

Quotation sources

The overwhelming breadth and range of material in *OED*, in all its versions, is exhibited in its apparently comprehensive list of words and in its rich banks of quotations. One of the most fruitful ways to explore the Dictionary, therefore, is to investigate its criteria for choosing the sources from which those words and quotations originate. Notwithstanding its overflowing abundance, *OED*'s content has been selected and shaped according to constraints (whether chosen by the lexicographers or imposed upon them) which have varied from time to time in its history. Its picture of the English language varies correspondingly.

These constraints have sometimes been overlooked by its admirers. As we saw in Chapter IV, it is easy to be tempted into the view that this huge word-book reflects the world of things, and certainly of thought, as well as the world of words. Readers of the *OED* have described this 'vast storehouse of the words and phrases that constitute the vocabulary of the English-speaking people', as 'a history of English speech and thought from its infancy to the present day', or 'a history of thought and civilization'.[80] Simpson has on occasion taken a similar view, remarking in the Preface to the third edition that 'the *Oxford English Dictionary* is an irreplaceable part of English culture. It not only provides an important record of the evolution of our language, but also documents the continuing development of our society. It is certain to continue in this role as we enter the new century.'[81]

This statement goes to the heart of *OED*'s role and function as the supreme authority on the English language. But the concepts to which it refers – '*English* culture' '*our* language', '*our* society' – are dangerously labile, and certainly hard to pin down and define in ways equally acceptable to all users of the language. As we know, the first and second editions of *OED* represented various aspects of 'English culture' unevenly. What changes are the *OED3* lexicographers making as they revisit and revise the quotation sources for their new dictionary?

The importance of quotation sources, and the variability of their treatment in the past, is fully addressed by the lexicographers themselves. In his Preface, Simpson recognizes that *OED* has in the past been criticized for its apparent literary bias. He comments, 'A closer examination of earlier editions shows that this view has been overstated, though it is not entirely without foundation.' By contrast,

> The revised text makes use of many non-literary texts which were not available to the original Victorian readers and their immediate successors, particularly social documents such as wills, inventories, account books, diaries, journals, and letters such as the York Civic Records, Gilbert White's Journals, and the Diaries of Robert Hooke. The inclusion of material from sources such as these allows the editors to provide a fuller picture of the vocabulary of (especially) the Early Modern period. Further reading of similar sources will doubtless result in additional significant discoveries, as will the re-examination of texts already 'read' for the Dictionary.[82]

Elsewhere, discussing 'The Reading Programme' for the new *OED*, Simpson writes,

> The original Dictionary relied heavily on a small number of authors (notably, of course, Shakespeare) for its coverage of Early Modern English (1500–1700). Today, readers systematically survey a much broader spectrum of texts from this and other periods. A separate Historical Reading Programme has been created to serve this function . . . . In addition to the 'traditional' canon of literary works, today's Reading Programme covers women's writing and non-literary texts which have been published in recent times, such as wills, probate inventories, account books, diaries, and letters. The programme also covers the eighteenth century, since studies have shown that the original *Oxford English*

Dictionary reading in this period was less extensive than it was for the previous two centuries. Also carefully perused are the books and articles by other scholars who have studied the language of individual authors of the Early Modern English period . . . . Taken as a whole, these Reading Programmes represent one of the most extensive surveys of the English language ever undertaken. Since the first publication of the *Oxford English Dictionary*, the breadth of materials available and the means of retrieving and analyzing those materials have expanded incalculably. Despite the changes, the original aim of the programme remains unaltered since the days of James A. H. Murray: to collect examples of the changing vocabulary of English from a highly diverse range of published sources spanning the entire English-speaking world, and to provide the *Oxford English Dictionary*'s editors with a constantly updated and ever more detailed record of English past and present.[83]

Since *OED3* has yet to update its bibliography or detail the rates of quotation from these new sources, the only way to investigate the new material is to look through the new entries and to guess what comes from new sources or from old sources revisited. Then one can experiment by typing different terms into the search boxes with the hope of getting interesting results – though even if one does, one cannot know what relation they will have to the third edition as a whole (that is, when the lexicographers have extended this wave of revision through the whole of the alphabet).

It is possible to get a good sense of some early trends, nevertheless. Quotations from wills and inventories, examples of the 'social documents' identified by Simpson in his discussion of new sources, had more than doubled by July 2006 (from around 400 to over 850).[84] As *OED3*'s deputy editor Edmund Weiner observes, 'There is no guarantee that literary authors in any age before the nineteenth century would conveniently mention all the items and occupations of everyday life. Many of the concerns of the kitchen, the workshop, and the farmyard need never feature in literature at all. If we are to find attestations of this kind of vocabulary, account books, wills, and similar documents are much more likely sources. As one would expect, if the records exist, a word is likely to be attested in what one might call "ordinary" everyday use before it appears in the "artificial" environment of literary writing'.[85]

Such sources were not of course neglected in *OED1* (Weiner points out that the *Durham account rolls* were cited more than 700 times in the first edition of the Dictionary, and the *Testamenta Eboracensia* and *Ripon Chapter Accounts* more than 500 times each.) Nevertheless, the lexical wealth of non-literary writings, insufficiently tapped by *OED* in the past, is indicated by the large number of new quotations from inventories and other non-literary sources which is now flooding into the revised Dictionary, for words such as *mullen*, 'A headstall or bridle for a horse', *ox-harrow*, 'A large and powerful harrow used on clay lands, originally drawn by oxen', *pinsons*, 'pincers, forceps', and the like. This new material will help correct the bias towards vocabulary from literary sources.

OED3 is also making extensive use of online sources. These are a mixed bunch (the lexicographers need to be wary lest their easy access to such gateways, created for one reason or another, to vast quantities of text skews their representation of the lexicon in the same way as did their predecessors' preferences for literary sources). One of the earliest used by the lexicographers was Chadwyck-Healey's *Literature Online*, 'a fully searchable library of more than 350,000 works of English and American poetry, drama and prose, 180 full-text literature journals, and other key criticism and reference resources'.[86] This is therefore made up almost entirely of literary texts: not very different from previous *OED* sources. But another electronic database, *Eighteenth Century Collections Online*, gives access to a much broader range of texts – literary but also legal, historical, horticultural, architectural, technical, scientific and so on. Searching databases such as this, which have been created by digitizing page images of the original works, brings its own problems – sometimes the facsimiles are illegible or yield misleading results – but the wealth of new material is remarkable. Many of the other electronic databases regularly used by *OED3* open windows on to other areas or periods of writing hitherto neglected in the first edition of *OED* or Burchfield's Supplement: women's writing, newspapers, US language, business and technical English, etc.[87]

So what is happening to the *OED* in consequence? Comparing the representation of individual authors in *OED2* and *OED3* is fiddly but interesting. Taking female writers as an example, we can pick a handful of authors and look at the results. Starting with the medieval period, we might expect the two best-known women writers of the fourteenth century, Margery Kempe and Julian of Norwich, to be more often quoted in *OED3* than in *OED2*, and indeed this is true. Neither is quoted in *OED2* (Margery's autobiography was not discovered and published until after the 1933 Supplement had appeared; while Julian's work – although in print in the 1870s – was perhaps judged ineligible because the manuscripts in which it survives were post-medieval).[88] Over the alphabet range *M–Pomak* in *OED3*, however, this has changed: Margery is quoted 55 times and Julian 14. Neither has an enormous *oeuvre* (though Margery's is not four times the size of Julian's, as these figures might suggest); the numbers are nevertheless tiny beside those of fourteenth-century male authors (e.g. the lexically rich *Gawain* poet, quoted *c.* 3,700 times in *OED2* throughout the whole alphabet).[89] But comparisons are very difficult here. The quotations from these two authors are mostly for ordinary words (*madwoman, manacle, mayor, meddle, nought*); does that make them more or less likely sources for the Dictionary? Should the *OED* quote these female authors (both of whose texts survive in MSS written by male scribes) in some sort of ratio to their perceived significance on account of gender? Would that mean quoting them very extensively indeed (since half the English-language-speaking community at that time were, presumably, women)? Or quoting them hardly at all (since almost none of these women produced written texts)? If the criteria for selecting quotations are instead claimed to be wholly linguistic, what characteristics of these two writers make them more, or less, suitable as quotation sources?

In fact, the *OED3* lexicographers may have taken no conscious decisions here. Although these figures look staggeringly low in comparison to those for Chaucer – who jumps from 1,465 quotations in *OED2* over *M–Pomak* to 2,348 over the same range in *OED3* – the difference between *OED2* and *OED3* may be due to the latter's use of material from the *Middle English Dictionary*, one of the projects first mooted by Craigie in 1919 (see p. 29 above), and finally completed in 2001. The quotation evidence in this specialist dictionary, which engaged in primary research in the medieval period far in excess of anything possible for *OED1*, has been extensively adopted in the revised *OED* and has resulted in a significant increase in quotations, apparently concentrated in the fourteenth century.[90] Whether the methodology of the *MED* where gender (or anything else) is concerned should dictate that of *OED3* is another question, to which *OED3* may wish to return in due course.

Moving swiftly forward several hundred years, to the example of Virginia Woolf, we find a different state of affairs. Woolf was quoted 237 times in *OED2*, a low number in comparison with the male authors with whom we naturally group her (e.g. Lawrence and Joyce; see p. 190 above). In 1966, the reader allotted to Woolf, Marghanita Laski, instructed to 'treat her work as poetry', commented that it was peculiarly unyielding of useful quotations ('still she supplies remarkably few words,' Laski wrote to Burchfield. 'I should have guessed her to be immensely rich in formations, wouldn't you?').[91] Woolf citations have nevertheless jumped sharply, from 40 over *M–Pomak* in *OED2* to 266 in *OED3*: it is tempting to think that this may be because she is now being cited for bread and butter uses as well as distinctive locutions. Further experimentation reveals that this is an unusual increase for a female author. Some – e.g. Frances Burney, George Eliot, Jane Austen – have significantly higher rates of quotation in *OED3* compared with *OED2* (though overall totals remain low in comparison with 'equivalent' – in terms of literary stature – male sources); others seem to have received less attention – e.g. Emily Dickinson, up from 8 to 15 quotations.[92]

Substantial as some of these increases are, they scarcely compare with those of canonical male authors already heavily quoted in *OED*. Thus Lawrence, Woolf's contemporary and one of Burchfield's favourite authors, was quoted *c.* 270 times in *OED3* over *M–Pomak*, and has now been bumped up to *c.* 580 quotations in *OED3*; while Dickens, quoted *c.* 1,010 times in *OED2* over *M–Pomak*, is now up to *c.* 1,460 quotations in *OED3*. Contrast the increase in quotation from George Eliot, *OED*'s most-quoted female author, from *c.* 430 to 675 quotations. This is slightly more in percentage terms than Dickens – 57 per cent as against 45 per cent, but much less in absolute numbers – 240-odd quotations as against 450. (It is additionally surprising to find that such literary authors, of either gender, are being quoted more often in *OED3* rather than less.)

Analyses of this sort are crudely inadequate in the absence of any study of the quotations concerned and the words or senses for which they are cited. At first sight they point to (continued) gender differentiation, but it is impossible, at this early stage, to be sure of their significance. Nevertheless gender is an important, if difficult, issue that *OED3* needs to confront (it has been boldly grasped by its sister reference work, the *Oxford Dictionary of National Biography* published in 2004, which has greatly increased, in its new edition, the previous ratio of women treated relative to men).[93] How are the lexicographers to determine the appropriate proportion in which female authors (or any other category of source, whether chronological, generic or authorial) should be quoted? Should the proportion reflect the number of female authors in print as compared to male? Or the number of female speakers compared to male? How do the lexicographers determine whether one quotation is preferable to another? To what extent should gender play a role in that judgement? If it is really the case, as stated in *OED3*'s Preface, that this dictionary 'documents the continuing development of our society', what aspects of society should it aim to document? Given that the *OED* is based on its quotation sources, these questions cannot be avoided.

Where quotation from periods, rather than authors or works, is concerned, it is possible to make more systematic searches. Counting up the numbers of quotations in *OED2* and *OED3* over 1500–1899, and comparing them in successive stretches of revised alphabet range, it seems that the third revision began by replicating the proportions of period coverage of *OED2* – generous quantities from the late sixteenth century, fewer from the eighteenth, copious amounts from the nineteenth – but has more recently 'corrected' these proportions. Between December 2004 and December 2005, *OED3* increased its *relative* collection of eighteenth-century quotations (at the expense, apparently, of sixteenth-century quotation collection) so as to bring the rate of quotation over the years 1700–99 more into line with that from the centuries on either side. If this recent trend continues, then the proportions of quotations per century in the *OED* may look very different in the next few years. In turn, this may lead us to change our minds about the lexical productivity of different periods in the history of the English language.[94]

But it remains a major undertaking to examine the *OED*'s sources, notwithstanding the electronic aids we are now able to use. Random searches like many of those described above may mean almost nothing when conducted in a piecemeal way. Setting them in a framework, and understanding how they fit into the *OED*'s representation of the lexicon overall, are undertakings that require substantial labour, conceptual on the one hand and factually detailed on the other. The third-edition revisers are doubtless themselves engaged in such reflection on their work and will in due course tell us how the sources for the *OED* have been selected to produce this major new revision of what has been called 'the internet's biggest, most prestige-laden reference book'.[95] In doing so they will greatly aid our understanding of the true nature of this magnificent accumulation of knowledge and information.

Coda

The number of words in the *OED* has substantially increased since 1928. So has the range and ambition of the lexicographers, as they have gradually shrugged off the remnants of Victorian assumptions that some words and usages are better than others, or that England is central to the English tongue. The flood of dictionaries now appearing of non-UK varieties of English – South African, Australian, Caribbean and many others – is greatly facilitating *OED3*'s geographical expansion, if at the price of complicating decisions as to which words, of any variety of English, should be included and which excluded in the most authoritative dictionary of the language as a whole.[96]

By contrast, much in *OED* method and methodology has remained unchanged since the first edition was completed. In 1986, Burchfield recorded his sense of 'marvel' at 'the permanent value of so much of [Murray's] editorial policy, and even of his clerical procedures'; just like their predecessors, Burchfield and his staff perused books, papers, journals, noted down usages that appeared to them novel or otherwise interesting on slips of paper, listing the author, title of work, date of edition, and a brief quotation of the word and its context, and filed them away.[97] A visitor to the Dictionary in 1933 specially commended the 'simplicity of methods of the staff working in the Old Ashmolean' – 'twenty people without the click of a machine'.[98] Today, the offices of the *OED* staff, far more numerous, resonate with the quiet whirr of computers accessing electronic texts in databases all over the world, but paper (whether quotation slips, 'found on every desk in the *OED*'s current offices', or the pages of printed books) has not yet been banished from Oxford lexicography.[99]

Is it appropriate that so little should have changed? Over the 150-odd years since the Dictionary was first thought of, the academic discipline of linguistics has wholly reshaped the study of language. In 1982, Roy Harris attacked the *OED* for its implicit assumption that words can be understood only through an analysis of their historical use over time (diachronically), rather than – or as well as – in relation to other words in the current language (synchronically). 'It is rather like insisting that the modern container lorry is just an updated version of the horse and cart.'[100] For the last twenty years, other dictionaries have been availing themselves of the matchless range of information to be found in corpuses of various kinds, and have explored new ways of representing language to illuminate contemporary usage, whether syntactic or semantic.[101] Enabled by the electronic transformation its publishers so farsightedly put into place in the 1980s, the *OED* is now poised to take advantage of this new information; its deputy chief editor recently suggested 'linking the *OED* to other online dictionaries' and incorporating 'a thesaurus element to enable searching by semantic fields and synonyms'.[102] (The etymology of the word *thesaurus* – which means 'treasure-house' in Greek – points to the richness inherent in such different methods of organizing language.) These changes would start to address some of Harris's concerns, and would help users access evidence on, say, the relative frequency with which a word has been used in a specified body of texts (so that one could better understand its connotations and potential meanings): small beginnings which would help the *OED* move forward to tackle, or at any rate acknowledge, more theoretical issues, such as the question of how words mean, and what role the dictionary plays in recording and constructing that process.

Many of its readers, however, use and love the *OED* precisely for the reasons criticized by Harris: the wealth of accurate historical information it so lavishly provides, and the sources from which its quotations are drawn. The level of public interest in this great monument of scholarship was demonstrated by the success of the recent *Wordhunt*, a joint venture by *OED* and the BBC in a twenty-first-century incarnation of the appeals issued by the early lexicographers from the late 1850s onwards. This invitation to the general public in the UK to come up with quotations for recent words was received with enthusiastic delight. The results helped the *OED* enhance its quotation store for *back to square one, Beeb, bonk, chattering classes, full monty, management speak, minger* and many other terms, and the BBC TV series, *Balderdash and Piffle,* which reported the appeal and its response, enlisted further devoted readers for the Dictionary: word-lovers across the country enrolled themselves as valuable unpaid contributors, a notable example of wholly beneficent continuity with the past.[103]

The revision of the Dictionary now under way at Oxford University Press gloriously rescues the *OED* from the condition of a 'magnificent fossil' – something Marghanita Laski, one of its staunchest supporters, feared in 1972 might be its fate.[104] It does so at significant cost to its publishers, a private institution whose unsubsidized support of the national dictionary, to the tune of several million pounds a year, is unparalleled in the world. Since its inception in 1857 this dictionary has consumed the lives of successive editors. It has at all times been the source of tension, sometimes benign and sometimes terribly conflictual, between the uncompromising search of its lexicographers for accuracy and completeness, and the necessarily commercial aims of its Press – for whom financial survival, and a marketable and timely product, have been paramount. Vision, doggedness, selflessness and heroism have all, in various ways, characterized the *OED*'s past and present editors. In marvelling at and praising their great achievements, one should also pay tribute to the Dictionary's successive publishers, who first shouldered, and now continue to bear, a burden which may not roll from their backs for many years to come.

APPENDIX 1

Examining the *OED*

(Note on author's *OED* website and on electronic searching of *OED*)

The charts reproduced on pp. 125 and 128 are taken from *Examining the OED* (*EOED*, published at http://oed.hertford.ox.ac.uk/main/), a research project which sets out to investigate the principles and practice behind the *Oxford English Dictionary*. They are based on analysis of the electronic form of the Dictionary, *OED Online* (published by Oxford University Press at www.oed.com, a subscription site freely available at public libraries and many other institutions in the UK), and thus represent the evidence to be found in *OED2*. However – as explained in Chapter VIII above – most of the pre-twentieth-century material in *OED2* derives from the first edition (completed 1928), and the charts can therefore be taken as more or less accurate reflections of the quotations gathered for this first version of the Dictionary. (For a full description of the methods of collecting and analysing the electronic data see pages at http://oed.hertford.ox.ac.uk/main/content/category/11/43/161.)

EOED is wholly independent of the *OED* itself, and seeks to provide scholarly commentary on and analysis of this great dictionary's history, methodology and practice. Its main focus is on exploring and analysing *OED*'s quotations and quotation sources, so as to illuminate the foundations of the Dictionary's representation of the English language. Much background material and further information on issues related to this book can be found on *EOED*'s various pages, e.g. Johnson's influence on the *OED*, the compilation of *OED* and the gathering of its sources, the coverage by *OED* of different historical periods and authors in the English language, photographs of original historical documents and of the editors themselves, and a library of downloadable articles on *OED* originally published in academic journals and books.

APPENDIX 2

Glossary

The list of the specialist terms relating to *OED* used in this book is partially excerpted from http://oed.hertford.ox.ac.uk/main/content/view/73/183/, where more items can be found.

- ¶ (paragraph mark): symbol printed at beginning of entries in *OED1*, *OEDS* and *OED2* (but not the 1933 Supplement or *OED3*) to indicate 'catachrestic and erroneous' uses.
- ‖: symbol (referred to by the lexicographers as 'tram-lines') printed at beginning of entries in *OED1*, *OEDS* and *OED2* (but not the 1933 Supplement or *OED3*) to indicate words which are 'not naturalized, alien'.
- †: symbol printed at beginning of entries in all editions of the *OED* (except 1933 Supplement) to indicate obsolete words.
- **Addenda** = '[list of] those things which need to be added' (Latin): standard term in dictionary-making, referring to list of new items added to successive printings, or editions, of an existing dictionary. Sometimes includes and sometimes distinguished from **Corrigenda**.
- **Additions** (also **Additions Series**): three volumes supplementing the second edition of the *OED*, containing new entries prepared for the third edition, edited by John [J. A.] Simpson and Edmund [E. S. C.] Weiner (vols 1 and 2) and Michael Proffitt (vol. 3) (Oxford: Clarendon Press, 1993–97). These entries are incorporated into the online version of *OED2*; see pp. 229–30 above.
- **Corrigenda** = '[list of] those things which need to be corrected' (Latin): see **Addenda**.
- **Delegates of OUP** (**Delegates of the Press**): a group of senior members of Oxford University (including the Vice-Chancellor, Proctors and – more recently – the Assessor) who, according to the University's statutes, 'have charge of the affairs of [Oxford University] Press'. As

explained on the OUP website, 'the chief executive of the Press, currently Henry Reece, is also known by the traditional title of Secretary to the Delegates. He chairs the Group Strategy Committee (GSC) which is in charge of the day-to-day management of the business' (http://www.oup.com/about).

- **Dictionary**: this book uses the term 'Dictionary' (with upper-case 'D') to refer to the *OED* as opposed to other dictionaries.

- **fascicle** (also *fasciculus*, pl. *fasciculi*, Latin): *OED1* defines the relevant sense of this word as 'A part, number, "livraison" (of a work published by instalments)'; it is the term used of the successive instalments in which the first edition of the Dictionary was published between 1884 and 1928.

- **General Explanations**: account of the English language and of *OED*'s editorial practices and printing conventions, written by J. A. H. Murray and first published as part of the introductory material to the first fascicle of *OED1* published in 1884. Subsequently reproduced unchanged in the first volume of the Dictionary (containing the first four fascicles, covering letters *A–B*, published in 1888) and in the 1933 edition of *OED1*. Also printed, with some slight changes, in *OED2* and reproduced from there on *OED Online*. Pagination varies according to which printing is cited.

- **hapax legomenon** (pl. *hapax legomena*) = 'said once' (Greek): 'A word or form of which only one instance is recorded in a literature or an author' (*OED2*). This term was not recorded in *OED1* and was added to the Dictionary by Craigie and Onions in their 1933 **Supplement**, illustrated with two quotations dated 1801 and 1882. Burchfield included it in the second volume of his **Supplement** (1976) and added a further four quotations. Evidently the status of a *hapax legomenon* is always volatile: the word may exist or have existed in wider oral use, but not been written down; or if written down, the place of record may not have been noted by *OED* readers or lexicographers.

- **Historical Introduction**: account of inception, development and completion of *OED1* written by W. A. Craigie and C. T. Onions and published in the 1933 reissue of *OED1*. Subsequently reproduced with minor modifications in *OED2* and *OED Online* (at http://www.oed.com/archive/oed2-preface/history.html).

- **lemma**: 'A lexical item as it is presented, usu. in a standardized form, in a dictionary entry; a definiendum' (*OED*). This sense of the word is not recorded in *OED* before the 1997 volume of *OED* **Additions** (from which this definition is quoted). It was not included by Burchfield when he updated *OED1* for the 1972–86 **Supplement**, indicating that the term had yet to achieve general currency; although the **Additions** prints a quotation from him (dated 1974) as an example of *lemma* used in this way.

- **New English Dictionary (NED):** the name given to *OED1* in its early years and also subsequently, in tandem with '*OED*'; see also **Philological Society's Dictionary**. It derives from the Philological Society's *Proposal for the Publication of a New English Dictionary* (1859), itself thus titled to draw attention to the view propounded in this document that, instead of supplementing existing dictionaries as previously suggested, the Philological Society should oversee the preparation of an entirely new work (see **Historical Introduction** for more information). In 1928, Onions recorded that 'A New English Dictionary' was the official title in use at Oxford University Press, adding 'not that there is any quarrel with those who prefer O.E.D., the symbol for the *Oxford English Dictionary*, a style adopted now for many years on the covers and wrappers of our sections and parts, and on the binding cases of the quarter-persian edition, but not incorporated in the title page' (Onions (1928b: 1)). (The first cover of a fascicle to bear the designation 'Oxford English Dictionary' alongside that of 'New English Dictionary' had been that for *Deceit to Deject*, published 1 Jan. 1895, and every fascicle issued after 1 July of that year included both titles.) Many users were perplexed as to which was the more correct title to adopt. In 1927, R. W. Chapman (Secretary, i.e. chief executive, of OUP) published a letter in *The Times* (18 May, p. 17) pointing out that '"New English Dictionary" is not adequately descriptive without the rest of the formula ("on Historical Principles")', and that the OUP Delegates had therefore for some years 'permitted the hope that the shorter "Oxford Dictionary" might ultimately gain acceptance'. In 1930, his deputy Kenneth Sisam wrote to a still puzzled correspondent as follows: 'On the whole we think the short form O.E.D. = Oxford English Dictionary is more distinctive than N.E.D. = New English Dictionary, as the latter has an element of anachronism and vagueness, but we have no particular wish that N.E.D. should fall into desuetude. Internally we use O.E.D. In strictly philological publications N.E.D. is better established. I am sorry I cannot be more precise' (OED/B/3/2/19, 11 Mar. 1930). From 1933, 'Oxford English Dictionary' appeared on the title-pages of the Dictionary, but many scholars continued to refer to *OED1* as *NED* long after this (e.g. George Kane and E. T. Donaldson, in *Piers Plowman: The B-Text*, London: Athlone Press, 1975).

- **nonce-word:** as J. A. H. Murray wrote s.v. *nonce* (sense 4) in *OED1*, this is 'the term used in this Dictionary to describe a word which is apparently used only for the nonce', i.e. (as *OED3* now explains) 'on one specific occasion or in one specific text or writer's works'. *OED3* tells us that 'nonce-word' was 'one of a number of terms coined by James Murray especially for use in the N.E.D.' (another such term was *echoic*; see *OED2*).

- *OED*: the *Oxford English Dictionary*. See **NED**.
- *OED1*: the first edition of the **OED**, published 1884–1928 and reissued in 1933 with a Supplement. Edited by J. A. H. Murray, Henry Bradley, W. A. Craigie and C. T. Onions.
- *OED2*: the second edition of the **OED**, published 1989, a merging of *OED1* with the four-volume **Supplement** of 1972–86, with the addition of about 5,000 new words and senses (identified for inclusion since the respective volume of the second **Supplement** was published). Compiled by J. A. Simpson and E. S. C. Weiner.
- *OED3*: the third and ongoing revised edition of the **OED** edited by John (i.e. J. A.) Simpson, published online from March 2000 onwards and updated every quarter.
- *OED Online*: available to subscribers at www.oed.com. Contains two versions of **OED**: (1) *OED2*, and (2) *OED2* merged with the portion of *OED* which has been revised to date for the third edition of the Dictionary (e.g. *M–Pomak* by October 2006).
- *OEDS*: Burchfield's second **Supplement**, published in four vols 1972–86.
- *OUP*: Oxford University Press, which took over responsibility for publishing the Dictionary and paying its staff in 1879.
- *The Periodical*: OUP's own in-house journal (published 1896–1979), appearing quarterly, reporting news and carrying articles about books published by and matters relevant to the Press. Several issues were devoted to **OED** matters (e.g. in 1915 to Murray's death, in 1928 to the completion of *OED*, in 1933 to the reissue of *OED1*).
- **Philological Society's Dictionary**: the London Philological Society (founded 1842) originally proposed the dictionary that was to become *OED1*, and it was by this title that the Dictionary was often referred to. Long after most other users had dropped the attribution, the Philological Society continued to refer to 'the Society's Dictionary', and up to 1982 printed a paragraph on the back cover of each volume of its *Transactions* stating that 'The Society's New English Dictionary on Historical Principles, edited by the late Sir James A. H. Murray, Dr. Henry Bradley, Professor Sir W. A. Craigie, and Dr. C. T. Onions, and published by the Clarendon Press, was completed in 1928'. See also **New English Dictionary**.
- **The Press**: = Oxford University Press.

- **reader**: term used to denote one of the host of volunteers who have offered their services to the Dictionary, from its early days onwards, to read through sources and copy out quotations for individual words and senses. As indicated by the acknowledgements in every fascicle and volume of *OED* published from 1884 to 1989, the Dictionary has always been crucially reliant on this voluntary labour (which continues today: see the current Appeal for more readers, and http://www.oed.com/readers/research.html for information about how to contribute).
- **s.v.**: = *sub voce* or *sub verbo* (Latin), meaning 'under the word'. An abbreviation used by lexicographers, philologists, etc. to refer the reader to material recorded under (s.v.) a particular **lemma**. Thus Murray's definition of *nonce-word* can be found in *OED1* s.v. nonce (sense 4).
- **Second Edition**: see *OED2*.
- **Secretary to the Delegates**: see **Delegates of OUP**.
- **slip**: the term used for the pieces of paper, about 4 × 6 inches, on which quotations for the *OED* were copied by readers according to certain set conventions (it was important to specify the date, edition, title, author, etc. of the work from which they were taken). Once submitted to the Dictionary, they were sorted into alphabetical order and additional material, on 'topslips', supplied by the *OED* staff and editors (etymology, pronunciation, definition, etc.). Bundles of slips for each entry were then sent to the printers. See Chapter IV (pp. 127–9).
- **Supplement**: The first Supplement, edited by W. A. Craigie and C. T. Onions, was printed as a separate volume in the 1933 reissue of *OED1* and given away free to all existing *OED* subscribers (see Chapter II). The second Supplement, edited by R. W. Burchfield, was published in four volumes in 1972 (*A–G*), 1976 (*H–N*), 1982 (*O–Scz*), and 1986 (*Se–Z*). Not to be confused with the **Additions**.

Notes

Introduction

1. See the Glossary, pp. 259–63 above, for an explanation of the terms 'New English Dictionary', 'Oxford English Dictionary', 'fascicle' and other specialized expressions used in this book. A bibliographical account and list of fascicles and parts can be found in McMorris (2000); facsimiles of the title-pages (specifying the editor responsible), plus individual prefaces, are reproduced in Raymond (1987).

2. Vice-Chancellor to RWC, OED/B/3/2/17, 28 Apr. 1928; *The Periodical*, 15 March 1934, p. 5. The Dictionary had earlier (in the fascicle for January 1898) been dedicated to Queen Victoria. Papers in OED/B/3/2/16 (e.g. a letter of 5 June 1927 from the Vice-Chancellor to RWC) record anxious discussion among the publishers and the University of the propriety of 'depriving Queen Victoria of the Dedication of the N.E.D., and re-dedicating it to the King'; it was decided that 'presenting' it to the King was the better option.

3. E.g. *The Periodical*, 15 Mar. 1928 (reproduced at http://oed.hertford.ox.ac.uk/main/content/category/15/85/288/). The two classic accounts of the inception and progress of the first edition of *OED* are the lexicographers' own 'Historical Introduction' first published with the reissue of the first edition of the Dictionary in 1933 (partially reproduced in *OED2* Preface and online at http://www.oed.com/archive/oed2-preface/history.html), and the biography of the chief editor, J. A. H. Murray, by his granddaughter (Murray (1977)). More recent accounts include the highly readable Winchester (2003) and the scholarly Mugglestone (2005).

4. CTO to DMD, SOED/1951/14/3, 22 Mar. 1951.

5. KS to HM, OED/3/2/16(1), 6 Apr. 1927; see Trench (1860 (1857)).

6. Murray (1977: 136) tells us that when Coleridge learned he would not recover 'he is reported to have exclaimed, "I must begin Sanskrit tomorrow", and he died working on the Dictionary to the last, with quotation slips and word-lists spread on the quilt of his bed'. See also 'Historical Introduction', p. x; in fact Coleridge's consumption appears to have been an established condition in 1858 (*DNB*). For more on Furnivall, an attractive, infuriating and quixotic figure, see Munro (1911), Benzie (1983), Pearsall (1998).

7. From its first fascicle on, the *OED* was published by the Clarendon Press, an imprint of OUP publishing its more scholarly books, though 'Oxford University Press' was the imprint used for publications distributed in the UK but published by others (university presses, for example, or foreign publishers). The official biographer of the Press, Sutcliffe (1978: 167), reports that 'Cannan [Secretary to the Delegates 1898–1921] was the only person to know the difference between the Oxford University Press and the Clarendon Press, and nobody dared ask him what it was'; the

two became increasingly indistinguishable when OUP gave up its London base, latterly (from 1966) in Ely House, Dover Street, in 1976.

8. *Saturday Review*, quoted in *The Periodical*, 15 Feb. 1928, p. 26; *Athenaeum*, 2 Feb. 1884, pp. 177–8 (reviewer identified as C. A. M. Fennell in Bailey (2000a: 213); *The Times*, 26 Jan. 1884, p. 6. A full list of reviews appears in Bailey (2000b).

9. *Academy*, 12 Nov. 1898, p. 251.

10. Quoted in *The Periodical*, 15 Feb. 1928, p. 29.

11. This figure is quoted in *The Periodical*, 15 Feb. 1928, p. 25. Sutcliffe (1978: 223) states that in 1928 'the debit balance appeared to be in the region of £375,000, but nobody knew quite what that meant. Overheads were not included, and the value of money had changed since the first outlay' (no source given). Many papers in the OUP archives attest to the poverty and low wages of the *OED* staff. See further pp. 33–6 below.

12. As early as 1878, the Sanskrit scholar Professor Max Müller, advising the Press in a privately printed report on the Dictionary, declared that he had 'no misgivings as to the merely commercial aspect of the undertaking' ('Observations . . . on the Lists of Readers and Books Read for the Proposed English Dictionary', OED/B/3/1/2; available at http://oed.hertford.ox.ac.uk/main/content/view/199/331/).

13. *The Oxford Dictionary: A Brief Account* (1916: 16).

14. Quoted in *The Periodical*, 15 Feb. 1928, p. 25.

15. *The Times* of 15 June 1899, for example, offered a 'new subscription price for the whole work' of £17, while reissued parts at that date cost 3s. 6d. For a price index, see Webb (2006).

16. Bailey (2000a 213); Skeat quoted in *The Periodical*, 15 Mar. 1934, p. 14.

17. *The Periodical*, 15 Feb. 1928, p. 25.

18. Quoted in *The Oxford Dictionary: A Brief Account* (1916: 8). Curzon was picking up on a phrase originally used by Charles Cannan in a letter to J. A. H. Murray (OED/B/3/2/3, 23 Jan. 1905). The term was repeated in the note prefixed to the *Standard–Stead* section of the ninth volume of the Dictionary, which marked Murray's death and was published on 1 Oct. 1915, and was worried at by Bradley in a letter to Cannan the previous month: 'To call the Dictionary an "engine of research" seems at first sight to mean that it is a tool which persons engaged in research can use. This is the only sense in which the designation can be applied to the Dictionary as a book. In the sentence as it stands, "the Dictionary" seems to be put as a sort of hypostasis of the body of people engaged in producing the book, and their collective activities. That, if you like, is an "engine of research", that is still going on working, though perhaps not always tirelessly so far as its individual wheels or cranks are concerned' (OED/B/3/2/7, 9 Sept. 1915).

19. Baldwin (1928:5). The Worshipful Company of Goldsmiths had become involved with the project when they contributed £5,000 towards the cost of producing volume 6, treating the letters *L*, *M* and *N*, in 1908. See Murray (1977: 291–2).

20. HM to RWC, OED/B/3/2/17(1), 14 Jan. 1928. The culprit was the American publisher George H. Doran, who was added to the invitation list in March. The seating plan for the banquet (at which he was placed on Milford's left) can be seen on pages at http://oed.hertford.ox.ac.uk/main/content/view/211/334/.

21. RWC to Pember, OED/B/3/2/17(1), 12 Jan. 1928. Lord Cave died before the banquet was held, precipitating another set of anxious memos about who should take his place.

22. RWC to Craigie, OED/B/3/2/17(1), 13 Jan. 1928. A handful of women had worked as paid staff members of the project, including (from 1899 to 1920) another of Murray's daughters, Elsie (1882–1952).

23. For Eleanor Bradley's subsequent work see pp. 38, 80, 81. At least one of the female guests to whom such accommodation was offered declined. Agnes Carwell Fries, wife of the American lexicographer and linguist Charles C. Fries, recorded 'It

was explained to me that being "skied" meant that women could sit in the balcony above the hall and watch the men eat. I felt insulted and refused to go under those circumstances'; quoted Bailey (1985: 200–1, n. 3). As Bailey notes, '*Skied* in this sense does not appear in the *OED*'.

24. The menu can be seen at http://oed.hertford.ox.ac.uk/main/content/view/207/333/ (with wine list on next page).

25. RWC to HM, OED/B/3/2/17(2), 3 May 1928. Baldwin's speech is at http://oed. hertford.ox.ac.uk/main/content/view/275/351/.

26. Both letters OED/B/3/2/17(2), 7 June 1928.

27. Chapman had made a special plea to the Vice-Chancellor on Maling's behalf. 'He is a good scholar and has done a great deal for the Dictionary. He is over 70 and has been away from work for 3 or 4 months suffering from rheumatism. Recognition might give him a fresh lease of life' (OED/B/3/2/17(1), 27 Apr. 1928). In the same year, Craigie also received an honorary doctorate from the University of Cambridge and a knighthood. The Public Orator was A. B. Poynton, a distinguished classicist, curator of the Bodleian Library (1912–37), and Master of University College (1935–37).

28. RWC to A. B. Poynton, OED/B/3/2/17(2), 24 May 1928.

29. F. Madan to RWC, OED/B/3/2/17(2), 25 May 1928. Madan's contributions to *OED* are noted in Onions (1928b: 2); he also contributed to the Supplement.

30. Baldwin (1928: 5). Craigie also acknowledged his staff's essential contributions in his speech at the banquet: *Oxford English Dictionary, 1884–1928: Speeches Delivered in the Goldsmiths' Hall, 6 June 1928* (1928: 15–16).

31. The Grimms' dictionary was eventually completed in 1960 and the Dutch dictionary in 1998: see Osselton (2000) for an account of these and other European dictionaries of the period. For words in use both before and after 1150, the *OED* quoted from works before 1150 if possible.

32. See illustration 4 and p. 201 below.

33. Copies are preserved in OED/B/2/1/2.

34. Hall's comment is printed in OUP Delegates, 'New English Dictionary. Correspondence and minutes (April 24 1896)', p. 5 (OED/B/2/2/1). One enthusiast, G. G. Loane, published a list of over a thousand items for inclusion in 1920 and another in 1931 (Loane (1920, 1932)).

35. Quotation from the Preface to the Supplement in Murray et al. (1933: v).

36. KS, 'Dictionary', OED/B/3/2/17(1), 3 Mar. 1928.

37. RWC to Vice-Chancellor, OED/B/3/2/22, 31 May 1933.

38. A term used by Vice-Chancellor Pember in his speech at the 1928 banquet (*Oxford English dictionary, 1884–1928: Speeches Delivered in the Goldsmiths' Hall, 6 June 1928* (1928: 28)).

39. Grimm et al. (1854: 315), translated Ganz (1973: 21).

40. See e.g. pp. 49, 227 below.

41. The equivalent dictionary in France, covering a shorter time-span than the *OED*, is *Le Trésor de la Langue Française: dictionnaire de la langue du XIXe et du XXe siècle* (Imbs (1971)) whose title points to the same function.

I Press and Dictionary in 1928

1. R. W. Chapman and Kenneth Sisam are both listed, without institutional sobriquet, among those who had 'made noteworthy contributions or have maintained a continuous interest in the collection of evidence' for the first Supplement (Preface in Murray (1933: vi)); Sisam is also acknowledged, again as a private individual, in various of the *OED* fascicle prefaces.

2. The row with Jowett is described in Murray (1977: 221–32). The 1896 battle on size, or 'scale' (a topic discussed in more detail below), is recorded in OUP Delegates, 'New English Dictionary. Correspondence and minutes (April 24 1896)', OED/B/2/2/1; an account of Gell's dealings with the Dictionary is in Murray (1977: 250–8).

3. RWC reported that 'M' was where 'the real smash came': he had 'battered on the walls of the old Ashmolean' (where the lexicographers had their offices), though making 'hardly any breach in the fortifications' (RWC to T. B. Strong, (Bishop of Ripon) OED/B3/2/12, 5 Jan. 1923; Strong was a Delegate and had previously been Dean of Christ Church; he returned to Oxford as bishop in 1925.)

4. See Murray (1977: 289), who notes, among other references, Gladstone's quotation of OED for *put up job*, as reported in *The Times*, 6 Dec. 1893, and *Punch*'s article of 25 May 1904, pp. 367–8, on a fictitious debate, with Murray in the chair, of the topic 'Should we not strain every nerve to enlarge our language?'

5. Cf. Murray (1977: 280, 9–90).

6. Chapman's editorial work on Austen has recently been reassessed; see Sutherland (2005).

7. See the *DNB* entry written by L. F. Powell, who worked on the *OED*. Chapman's bicycling was witnessed in the 1940s by Derek Brewer, then an undergraduate at Magdalen (to which college Chapman was elected a fellow in 1931) and later a medievalist and Master of Emmanuel College, Cambridge (personal communication to the author).

8. RWC to CTO, 20 Jan. 1922, OED/B/3/3/1.

9. Information in this paragraph and below from Ker (1972), who supplies a full list of publications and reports that the anthology (Sisam and Tolkien (1921)) had sold over 60,000 copies by 1972. Sisam edited a variety of other works and produced an important body of scholarly articles; his *Studies in the History of Old English Literature* and *The Structure of Beowulf* were published by OUP in 1953 and 1965 respectively. For Tolkien's connection with *OED* lexicography see Gilliver, Marshall and Weiner (2006).

10. Sutcliffe (1978: 178, 197–8). More information about Sisam and his family can be found in Sisam (1993).

11. OUP Finance Cttee Minute Book 5, 12 Oct. 1922, no. 9 (p. 442). On 25 Mar. 1924 (no. 14, p. 469) it was agreed that Sisam's salary was to rise by annual increments of £50 up to a limit of £1,000.

12. Sutcliffe (1978: 198) whose comment must be seen as hyperbolic, as the two would have met regularly at Delegates' meetings and other events.

13. The 1933 Supplement corrected *OED*'s record for *Wiltshire* (from 'a kind of "smoked" bacon' to 'an undivided side of bacon'), but Burchfield subsequently decided not to include this correction in his later Supplement and the error therefore still stands in *OED2*. KS to CTO, OED/B/3/2/17(2), 17 and 27 July 1928.

14. Reported by Ker (1972: 410–11); Davin (1913–90), also a Rhodes Scholar, was appointed as Junior Assistant Secretary by Sisam in 1945 and became Assistant Secretary on his retirement in 1948.

15. Sutcliffe (1978: 198), who records his generous aid e.g. to indigent refugee scholars such as Paul Maas (pp. 257–62), suggests this relationship. E. G. Stanley reports Sisam's help to 'younger or coeval scholars, among them Dorothy Whitelock' (personal communication to author).

16. KS to DMD, OUP/BoxOP1713/PB/ED012869, 10 July 1954; quoted Burchfield (1984: 115).

17. *The Periodical*, 15 Sept. 1915, p. 198.

18. See *DNB*, *ODNB*, and Murray (1977), from which some of these details are taken; also Mugglestone (2005).

19. Murray (1977: 178–82, 314ff.). See pp. 127ff. below for how the Dictionary was made.
20. His collected papers include significant discussion of the authorship of the Middle English poem *Piers Plowman* and a memoir of Bradley by their editor, his friend Robert Bridges (Bradley and Bridges (1928)).
21. A distressing letter survives in the OUP archives detailing his financial position. It was 'very generally assumed as a matter of course' that his pay would have risen since Murray's death, but in fact 'I am at present receiving only the same amount as it was originally agreed that I should be paid when, after a year's work under Dr. Murray, I should become the responsible editor of a part of the Dictionary. I did not in fact receive this amount of salary for many years, because I found it impossible to fulfil the expectations of the Delegates – to which at the outset I had assented as reasonable – with regard to quantity of production. . . .[he has found it hard to bring himself to speak of the matter at all, 'in this sad year'] Only, in a month from today my age will be "threescore years and ten", and though I feel I am still able to do a fair day's work, the end of my working day cannot be far distant.' He had only recently managed to save anything [owing to heavy expenditure necessitated by illness], 'and the time remaining for making provision for those whom I shall leave behind is short. On this ground I felt bound to ask you to put the case before the Delegates.' He apologizes for his 'regrettably small output' this year, the chief reason for which was the loss of two assistants, so that he had to do much of the work from scratch. 'On the other hand, the two salaries have been saved' (HB to Cannan, OED/B/3/2/7, 3 Nov. 1915).
22. Murray (1977: 257–8, 62–4, 81–2).
23. Onions (1923: 23).
24. KS to HB's son-in-law A. S. Ferguson, 9 May 1927; RWC to HM, 6 May 1927, both OED/B3/2/16 (1).
25. James Murray was the son of a clothier, Bradley of a farmer and partner in a cloth-mill, and Onions, whose father was a designer and embosser of metal, came from a family of bellows-makers (information from Murray (1977) and from the *ODNB*).
26. *Oxford English Dictionary, 1884–1928: Speeches Delivered in the Goldsmiths' Hall, 6 June 1928* (1928: 15).
27. *DNB*. Aitken took over the *Dictionary of the Older Scottish Tongue* from Craigie after his death in 1957. The *DNB* serves the Oxford lexicographers variably: Aitken's portrait is warm and admiring (see note 30 below); Onions writes a cool account of Murray, but is himself far more generously treated by J. A. W. Bennett; Craigie is mealy-mouthed about Bradley. These biases are varied in the revised entries published in the *DNB*'s successor, *ODNB*.
28. Murray (1977: 282–3).
29. Burchfield (1989: 194–5); see pp. 182–4 below. Craigie perhaps always chafed under Murray's yoke. Two years before Murray's death, for example, he wrote sharply to complain that 'In an article on the Dictionary, which appears in to-days [*sic*] *Daily Chronicle*, I am very much annoyed to find myself referred to, in the tail-end of a paragraph, as one of your "assistant editors". Presumably the phrase (like some other inaccuracies) is the interviewer's, but as it will naturally be attributed to you, and will certainly convey to the outsider an impression not to my advantage, I trust that you will ask the writer, or Editor, to withdraw it, and replace it by something giving a fairer idea of the facts. A simple statement of the time (now 12 years) during which I have edited separate sections of the Dictionary would put the matter in its proper light' (MP Box 22/2, 1 Nov. 1913). See Mugglestone (2005: 56) for a further example of Murray's rebuking of Craigie; also Murray (1977: 288).
30. Aitken's *DNB* entry on Craigie displays the respect due from a pupil to his master; as he told his own students, he 'sat at Craigie's feet' as a young lexicographer. Nevertheless he 'was aware that the coverage of the language provided in Volumes I

and II [of *DOST*; i.e. Craigie's portion, created in his old age] was inadequate', and greatly improved the dictionary he inherited, for example by 'more than doubl[ing] the list of sources', refining sense analysis, and upgrading the importance in an entry of illustrative quotations (Dareau (2002a: 216–17); see also Dareau (2002b)). I am grateful to Marace Dareau, Caroline Mcafee and Iseabail Macleod for help with Aitken's judgement of Craigie. E. G. Stanley reports that Stefanyja Olszewska (p. 273 n. 6 below), who worked intimately with his material, judged him the weakest of the four editors, while the editor of *OED3*, John Simpson, has 'always felt he was the most unsympathetic . . . . It is difficult to track characteristics of his personal style in smaller entries, as they are likely to have been drafted by his more junior colleagues. The main point we notice is that he had a tendency to prefer splitting what Murray would have seen as complex single meanings into several sub-senses, and to structure large entries by grammar or syntax (e.g. by transitivity). This latter is not a policy Murray or *OED3* follows' (personal communication to author).

31. Wyllie (1961: 291); see Mathews (1979), Adams (1998).
32. Murray (1977: 316).
33. CTO report on J. W. Birt, OED/B/3/2/22, 22 Nov 1933.
34. Quotations from Bennett's obituary of Onions in *ODNB*.
35. Chapman used the term 'astringent' of Onions in 1946, to be echoed by Bennett in his *DNB* entry (from which the quotation here is taken) and later by Burchfield; as we have seen, Onions also used it of Murray. See Chapman (1946); Burchfield (1989: 194); also p. 170 below.
36. 'Blanket' detail is from notes towards Bennett's British Academy obituary supplied to him by Burchfield (uncatalogued Burchfield papers in *OED* archives, 8 May 1979).
37. Neither word is included in his etymological dictionary.
38. Several letters survive on this matter, e.g. KS to Wyllie, 26 Apr. 1932, CTO to KS, 28 Apr. 1932; both OED/B/3/10/4 (1).
39. CTO to KS, 31 May 1932 (see associated letters), OED/B/3/10/4(1). The contributor was the editor of publications at Brooklyn Public Library, Louis N. Feipel, who had been put out by the lack of acknowledgement; Sisam insisted Onions should write to him.
40. Murray (1977: 287).
41. *The Periodical* (15 Mar. 1934, p. 4) reported final averages for all four co-editors: Murray averaged 224 pages a year in 32 years, HB 155 pages in 29 years, Craigie 109 pages in 27 years, CTO 52 pages in 16 years.
42. Craigie to Cannan (in Craigie's hand and signed by the three co-editors); 'To the Members of the Dictionary Staff' (both OED/B/3/2/7, 8 Dec. 1915). The following year, Craigie also produced an optimistic schedule detailing completion by 1920 (Craigie to Cannan, OED/B/3/2/8, 29 Dec. 1916):
43. The beginnings of the 'scale' arrangement are described in Murray (1977: 207–9). Murray's letters to Hucks Gibbs of 12, 15 and 25 Feb. 1882 (MP Box 5) indicate that at this date it is Murray, not the Delegates, who is using Webster as a comparator, but by 1896 (see document cited in note 2) the comparison has become a standard means of measuring the progress of the Dictionary. The 1864 Webster's was the fourth edition of Noah Webster's pathbreaking *An American Dictionary of the English Language* (1828); see Micklethwait (2000).
44. Full and at times heated discussion is recorded in the OUP Delegates' document of 1896 (see note 2). In October 1903 Murray's scale (over 18⅔ pages) was 10.66, Bradley's (over 7⅔) 18.4, and Craigie's (8⅔) 4.72; but the next month Craigie's scale, over 11 pages, had shot up to 33 (Sutcliffe (1978: 154)). Wyllie (1961: 280), whose hatred of the Oxford publishers makes him an unreliable witness, claims that Craigie took a strong line on 'scale' in 1906–7, when he discovered that, unknown to

the lexicographers, their copy was being ruthlessly pruned by a specially employed member of staff whose job it was to ensure a 1:10 scale.

45. HB to RWC, OED/B/3/2/9(1), 12 May 1920; RWC to CTO, OED/B/3/2/15, 23 Sept. 1926; by this time they had decided to 'let the scale rip. Craigie is gone [back to Chicago], and we know from experience that to press for reduction would cause delay and nothing else'. Four years later, Sisam noted that the scale of *Well* was 80 times that of Webster (OED/B/3/2/13, 15 Oct. 1924); in Jan. 1926 they were still 'trying to give every ounce of energy to expediting W' (RWC to Craigie, 28 Jan. 1926), and in March remarking on its 'extraordinary difficulty' (RWC to Lt.-Col. G. T. Raikes, 2 Mar. 1926; both OED/B/3/2/15). 'Alphabet fatigue' is Noel Osselton's term: see Osselton (2007).

46. 24 March 1920, OED/B/3/2/9(1).

47. OED/B/3/2/9(1), 18 Mar. 1920. Thus *Ti–Tz* should have resulted in 561⅓ pages but was actually 565; V should have been 323 ⅔ but was actually 333, W–*Wagonette*'s 15⅔ proof pages turned into 16 corrected ones.

48. RWC to D. H. Nagel (one of the Delegates), OED/B/3/2/9(1), 26 Mar. 1920.

49. RWC to Raleigh, OED/B/3/2/9(1), 26 Mar. 1920.

50. OED/B/3/2/9(1), 13 May 1920.

51. Wyllie (1961: 280).

52. Craigie to RWC, OED/B/3/2/9(1), 27 Mar. 1920; the timetable was over-optimistic, envisaging that 'by 1 Oct. 1921 . . . at least half of W should be completed, and the preliminary work done for most of the remainder'.

53. OED/B/3/2/9(1), 22 Apr. 1920. Although Bradley had been able to write to Cannan on 9 Sept. 1915 (OED/B/3/2/7) 'I cannot allow your clerk wickedly to defraud me of my one and only splendid boast in respect of "scale". Five and a third!! But you will find it will bear examination', subsequent reports indicate this was an exception: thus *Ward* is reported to be 15, *Yoke* 10.66, *Yokeable–Yokle* 15.4, *Yoklet–Yomerly* 33.

54. Craigie to RWC, OED/B/3/2/9(1), 27 Mar. 1920.

55. OED/B/3/2/9(1), 30 Mar. 1920.

56. HB to RWC, OED/B/3/2/9(1), 2 Mar. 1920.

57. Ghosh and Withycombe (1935). This work lists the principal publications of each year together with an alphabetical index of authors with their works. In fact the *OED* staff were to work not on this but on a closely allied project which was called the 'Register', a list of works cited in the *OED*.

58. Craigie to RWC, OED/B/3/2/9(1), 30 Mar 1920.

59. Furnivall published a letter in the *Academy* of 9 Feb. 1884 (pp. 96–7), in which he exhorted readers to buy fascicles, volunteer to sub-edit, etc., and send in slips; he gives some examples of his own findings regarding which he has 'no doubt that they will enable a very valuable Appendix to the Dictionary to be made'.

60. Murray's remarks on the Supplement are quoted, from an unpublished source, on the last page of Mugglestone's account on the *OED* in Cowie (2008); for the Furnivall reference see Benzie (1983: 108). Physical evidence for the Supplement exists only from 1913 onwards: many slips are marked 'Suppl', to indicate 'this slip is for the Supplement file', in the handwriting of the assistant C. G. Balk, who left the project in that year (I am grateful to P. Gilliver for this information).

61. Craigie to RWC, OED/B3/2/15, 12 Jan. 1926. Craigie and Onions's Preface records that Mr Pallemaerts worked with Miss I. B. Hutchen. Hutchen was Craigie's sister-in-law and later became the single largest contributor to the collections for his *Dictionary of the Older Scottish Tongue* (Aitken (1987: 98) supplies further details).

62. OED/B/3/2/12, 15 Nov. 1923; *Daily Mail*, 14 Nov. 1923.

63. Craigie to RWC, 12 Aug. 1924; subsequently discussed by Craigie, e.g. in letter to D. G. Hogarth (chairman of the Press's Finance Committee 1921–27), 13 Oct. 1924 (both OED/B3/2/13).

64. For the distinguished scholar Eugene Vinaver's judgement of Sisam as 'a King among medievalists', unjustly passed over for this chair and subsequently snubbed by Oxford academics, see Sutcliffe (1978: 270), who offers no source.

65. Wyllie (1961: 281–2). Craigie mentioned in a letter to Chapman on 12 Sept. 1927 that 'the University refused to recognise [his long service to the OED] as entitling him to any benefit under its pension scheme, and this refusal was one of the reasons which made it advisable and even necessary for me to leave Oxford'; OED/B3/2/16 (2).

66. Craigie (1919); his 'first soundings' of the Press had begun ten years earlier (Aitken (1987): 112, n. 4), who cites a letter to William Grant of 28 Jan. 1916). Quotations in text are from the memorandum of 1922 preserved in OED/B3/2/14.

67. Craigie (1919: 10) (note added in 1925).

68. As Craigie told KS in 1927 (noted in KS to RWC, OED/ B/3/2/16(1), 22 Apr. 1927).

69. RWC to Delegates, OED/B/3/2/14, 15 Oct. 1925. A number of letters in the files for this period show that Craigie involved the Philological Society on his side in this debate with the Press (the Society, as originator of the OED, had an interest in the fate of the slips first gathered under its auspices).

70. CTO to RWC, OED/B/3/2/14, 12 Nov. 1925.

71. RWC to HM, OED/B/3/2/14, 13 Nov. 1925. For the term NED as opposed to OED see Glossary.

72. HM to RWC, 12 Dec. 1925; RWC to Craigie, letter drafted 7 Dec. 1925 and sent 17 Dec. 1925 (all OED/B/3/2/14). 430,000 quotation slips from OED were eventually sent to Michigan to help compile what was to become the *Middle English Dictionary* (Adams (2002: 100)), while about 1.5 million slips were sent to Charles C. Fries for the Early Modern English Dictionary project (personal communication to author from Richard W. Bailey; see also Bailey (1985: 201, n. 4)).

73. KS to RWC, OED/B/3/2/15, 20 Oct. 1926. 'Bolshevik' was of course a new term, shortly to be added by Onions to the Supplement.

74. HM to RWC, 29 Dec. 1925; KS to RWC, 31 Dec. 1925 (both OED/B/3/2/14).

75. Craigie to RWC, OED/B/3/2/15, 12 Jan. 1926.

76. RWC to Craigie, 28 Jan. 1926; RWC to HM, 28 Jan. 1926 (both OED/B/3/2/15).

77. Report on Supplement in OED/B/3/2/14, 11 Nov. 1925.

78. RWC to the Bishop of Ripon (T. B. Strong), OED/B/3/2/12, 5 Jan. 1923.

79. On the making of the Dictionary see further pp. 127ff. below.

80. KS to RWC, 20 Oct. 1926; RWC to KS, 21 Oct. 1926 (both OED/B/3/2/15).

81. KS to RWC, 22 Apr. 1927; RWC to HM, 6 May 1927 (both OED/B/3/2/16(1)). The later document is a collection of three slips, headed '<u>Supplement</u>' and signed 'J[essie] S[enior]', which are covered with a brief account noting that Supplement material was to be selected from a larger body of corrections and additions covering historical as well as current vocabulary (14 June 1927, OED/B/3/8/1; Senior had been employed to work on the Supplement in 1924: see p. 38, n. 1 below). Additional pencil jottings, perhaps in Onions's hand, indicate that Craigie was to handle 'Old Scottish' and 'Americana' while Onions was to tackle what are quaintly described as 'likely looking slips' along with the assistants Maling and Lewis.

82. It is mentioned as a one-volume project in May 1923 (RWC to Lord Braye, OED/B3/2/12, 7 May 1923). Its original author William Little had died in 1922, having 'prepared entirely without assistance the manuscript for the letters A to T and V, and . . . passed for printing about one-third of the whole dictionary' (Preface to the first edition of the SOED, p. vii).

83. Document of 7 Mar. 1900, in OUP/BoxGFGF/000131. The scheme was also applied to non-Dictionary staff.

84. A. T. Maling, F. J. Sweatman and F. A. Yockney, all members of Murray's staff, received £20, £20 and £18 respectively, and the Misses Murray, James Murray's daughters, £7 each (in common with all women workers at this time, they were paid

significantly less than men). Bradley's staff got no bonus but instead payments in consideration of long service: W. J. Lewis and H. J. Bayliss received £8 each, and W. Worrall £10 (undated document in OED/B/3/2/7; former reference PP/1915/78).

85. The OUP Finance Cttee Minute Book 5, no. 16 (pp. 392–3) records that on 24 June 1920, it was 'Agreed to fix salaries of the Dictionary staff as follows and to discontinue the payment of bonuses'; the salaries specified range from £266 10s. for Sweatman to £123 10s. for Rosfrith Murray.

86. When Powell retired from the Taylorian in 1949 the Press recognized its obligation to him and his wife (who had worked on the OED staff until 1932) and paid him £50 a year to augment his low pension (reported in documents dated May–June 1949, OUP/BoxGFGF/000131).

87. OUP Finance Cttee Minute Book 6, 28 Sept. 1928, no. 9 (p. 80).

88. OUP/BoxGFGF/000131, letters from RWC of 8 Oct. 1928; Rosfrith Murray to RWC, 9 Oct. 1928. The surviving copy of Chapman's letter to Rosfrith is impersonally formal, and it may be that she was responding to a handwritten note.

89. OUP Finance Cttee Minute Book 6, 30 Jan. 1931, no. 6 (1) (p. 136) records 'Printer submitted a provisional scheme for pensions for women, which was generally approved'.

90. OUP Finance Cttee Minute Book 6, 26 Jan. 1928, n. 10, pp. 71–2. Documents in OUP/Box/GFGF/000131 list the service periods, bonuses, and eventual pensions of Bayliss, Worrall, Maling , Lewis and Sweatman.

91. Worrall to RWC, OED/B/3/2/23, 5 Feb. 1934. In 1928, Sisam recorded that 'the average rate for sorting and the like is our own internal rate, i.e. 1/- per hour, on the assumption that two or three hour spells are worked' ([KS] to CTO, OED/B/3/2/17(2), 27 July 1928).

92. Chapman's salary is recorded in Finance Cttee Minute Book 5, 15 Jan. 1920, no. 14, p. 379 ('stipend of £1200 a year ... to rise by annual increments of £50 until ... £1500 is reached'). A full list of Dictionary staff salaries in Dec. 1924 appears on pp. 481–2 (ibid., 19 Dec. 1924, n. 14): Sweatman, Maling, Worrall: £300; Lewis and Bayliss: £275; Birt: £250; Mrs Powell: £150. Salaries appear to have stayed constant for years at a time (the 1920s was a period of currency deflation in the UK); for a price index see Webb (2006).

93. Comparator salaries quoted from Routh (1965: 68–9). Another authority, Chapman and Knight (1953: 27), estimates average annual earnings of employees in a range of occupations in 1928 as around £148, ranging from 'Agriculture and forestry' at £77 to 'Insurance, banking and finance' at £312.

94. Sisam's daughter Celia Sisam remembers that her father took pains to make himself available to staff, forgoing his right to a grand office in order to work beside his employees. He never lunched but left his door open during this period so that he could be easily visited (personal communication to author). Papers in the archives (e.g. OUP/BoxGFGF/000131) record various *ex gratia* payments made by OUP to widows and children of employees. Pitifully small as these sums of money appear, they constitute some recognition of extra-legal obligation.

II 'Beating the Track of the Alphabet': Work on the First Supplement

1. KS to Craigie, OED/B/3/2/13, 25 Aug. 1924. Her salary was £225 from 1 Jan. 1928 (OUP Finance Cttee Minute Book 6, 26 Jan. 1928, no. 10, p. 71). For other salaries see p. 272, n. 92 above.

2. Miss Savage worked with Onions on a number of subsequent projects, and (under her married name Mrs Alden) began work on the second Supplement in 1957 (p. 145 below). Miss Murray and Mrs Powell were also intermittently engaged in sorting

slips from the main *OED* that were to be sent to Michigan for the new period dictionaries under Charles Fries (C. Fries to KS, OED/B/3/2/17(2), 10 Aug. 1928; Bailey (1985: 201, n.4)).

3. See http://www.dsl.ac.uk/PRELIMS/The_History_of_DOST_Final_Version2.html.

4. E.g. in KS to RWC, OED/B/3/2/16(2), 22 Apr. 1927.

5. OED/B/3/2/17(2).

6. See p. 273, n. 6 below. Another significant female contributor was Stefanyja Olszewska, who was to supply 12,000 slips for Burchfield's second *OED* Supplement in the 1950s and 1960s (p. 161).

7. KS, 'Dictionary', OED/B/3/2/17(1), 3 Mar. 1928. (The Latin phrase (= 'Carthage must be destroyed') was familiar to schoolchildren learning the language; the sentiment was urged by Cato and heralded the beginning of the third Punic war in 149–146 BC.)

8. Sweatman to Craigie, OED/B/3/2/16(1), 22 Apr. 1927. Murray (1977: 180) reports that Murray's children especially enjoyed sorting Furnivall's slips as they were so racy; Onions (1928b: 4–5) observes that they were 'of great value' in indicating the existence or currency of particular words and meanings.

9. KS to RWC, OED/B/3/2/18, 25 June 1929.

10. See further pp. 178–9 below.

11. Preface to Supplement volume in Murray et al. (1933); Burchfield (1958).

12. See Brewer (2000: 44–50). The three editions of Murray's *Appeal* can be read on the *OED Online* site at http://www.oed.com/archive/appeal-1879–04/. Murray also published lists of 'Special wants', copies of which are preserved in the *OED* archives.

13. *The Times,* 25 May 1931. The *OED* files preserve dozens of contemporary slips for the word rather than any correspondence.

14. 'Steam Tactics', on p. 179 of the 1904 edition of *Traffics and Discoveries.*

15. In 1925 Onions had estimated the material took up 80 feet (p. 31 above); in 1933 it was stated to be 75 feet.

16. Wyllie (1961: 287).

17. Wyllie was offered the job orally at his interview and the appointment was confirmed in writing on 24 May, with a starting salary of £250 and an initial trial period of a year; 'there will be continuous employment for you and good prospects of promotion' (Wyllie to KS, 7 May 1929; KS to Wyllie, 24 May; both OED/B/3/2/18). Onions was informed on 25 June (KS to CTO, OED/B/3/2/18). From 20 Sept. 1930 to Feb. 1931 Wyllie was based in Aberdeen, where he seems to have been partly employed by the University, working 24 hours a week for the Dictionary, and undertaking to prepare copy for the Printer under Craigie's general directions at £200 a year (KS to Mr Durham, 14 Aug. 1930, OED/B/3/2/19). By April 1931 his salary had gone up to £300.

18. KS to Souter, OED/B/3/2/18, 30 Oct. 1929. Souter's life and career are described in *ODNB.*

19. OED/B/3/2/19, 7 May 1930.

20. Rosfrith Murray to RWC, 17 June 1929; CTO to RWC, 20 June 1929; both OED/B/3/2/18; Murray (1977: 136). They are still in the possession of OUP.

21. See e.g. RWC to CTO, OED/B/3/2/17(3), 13 Nov. 28; CTO to RWC, OED/B/3/2/19, 22 May 1930.

22. CTO to RWC, 22 May 1930; KS to RWC, 28 July 1930; both OED/B/3/2/19. See also e.g. KS to RWC, OED/B/3/2/20, 3 July 1931.

23. KS to RWC, OED/B/3/2/19, 10 Mar. 1930.

24. RWC to KS, 5 May 1930; KS to Craigie, 7 May 1930; both OED/B/3/2/18.

25. They are discussing Onions's treatment of the fifth sense of the noun identified in *OED* (Craigie to KS, OED/B/10/3, 6 Nov. 1931).

26. Craigie to KS, OED/B/3/10/3, 11 May 1931; CTO to RWC, OED/B/3/10/4(1).

27. Powell to RWC, 25 Dec. 1930; RWC to CTO, 31 Dec. 1930, both OED/B/3/2/19; CTO to RWC, 1 Jan. 1931, OED/B/3/2/20.
28. KS to CTO, OED/B/3/2/20, 7 Jan. 1931; the files just have an extract from the letter. Sisam wrote to Miss Marshall the same day, offering her £175 p.a., with an initial three months' trial period and a maximum of two years of work in all.
29. Letters relating to Marshall dated June–Aug. 1932 and beyond survive in OED/B/3/2/21.
30. OED/B/3/2/20.
31. He continued to be paid his full salary to the end of July that year, and was then awarded £2 a week pension 'during the Delegates' pleasure, Mr Bayliss resigning his rights in respect of bonus. It was hoped that his health might permit of his resuming Dictionary work on a basis of piece work': OUP Finance Cttee Minute Book 6, Minute no. 13 of 3 July 1931.
32. HB to RWC, OED/B/3/2/9(1), 2 Mar. 1920, speaking of both Bayliss and Lewis.
33. Bayliss's 'Press Notices' are OED/B/5/6/47; on *radium*, which with *appendicitis* was the word most frequently noted as absent from the main Dictionary, see further Gilliver (2004: 59–62) (who also discusses Bayliss) and p. 201 below.
34. *The Periodical*, 15 Feb. 1928, p. 18.
35. Sisam's term for the elderly long-term staff: KS to RWC, OED/B/3/10/3, 29 Sept. 1931.
36. CTO to RWC, OED/B/3/2/20, 21 Feb. 1931; cf. OED/B/3/2/22, 22 Nov. 1933.
37. OED/B/3/10/3, 13 Apr. 1931.
38. See e.g. Wyllie to KS, OED/B/3/2/20, 27 Mar. 1931.
39. Wyllie to KS, OED/B/3/10/3, 28 July 1931.
40. As in e.g. KS to RWC, OED/B/3/2/20, 3 July 1931.
41. See e.g. Wyllie to KS, OED/B/3/10/4(1), 1 July 1932; KS to Craigie, OED/B/3/10/4(1), 4 July 1932.
42. RWC to Vernon Rendall, OED/B/3/10/3, 28 Oct. 1931. Johnson (in his *Plan of a Dictionary*) had written 'beating the track of the alphabet with sluggish resolution'.
43. CTO to RWC/KS, 17 Feb. 1931; RWC to CTO, 24 Feb. 1931 (both B/3/10/3). When Craigie wrote to them with the same proposal to divide publication in half, Sisam responded far more respectfully (OED/B/10/3, 22 May 1931).
44. OED/B/3/2/20.
45. OED/B/3/2/20, 15 Apr. 1931.
46. KS: 'Supplement', OED/B/3/10/3, 29 July 1931. Sisam may have been miscalculating in favour of Wyllie here as the arithmetic seems out.
47. KS to RWC, OED/B/3/10/3, 29 July 1931.
48. See e.g. Craigie to KS, OED/B/3/10/3, 14 July 1931, and many other memos in OED/B/3/10/3.
49. OED/B/3/10/3, 6 and 11 Aug 1931.
50. KS to HM, OED/B/3/10/3, 24 Aug. 1931.
51. Both letters OED/B/3/10/3, 15 Sept. 1931.
52. J. Johnson to RWC, OED/B/3/10/3.
53. KS to RWC, OED/B/3/10/3, 22 Sept. 1931.
54. OED/B/3/10/3, 25 Sept. 1931; Sisam is perhaps remembering a line in *Piers Plowman*, B Pro 214 ('Thou my3test better mete the myste on Maluerne hulles'), a poem he excerpted for his anthology of medieval verse and prose.
55. KS to RWC, OED/B/3/10/3, 29 Sept. 1931.
56. See e.g. Murray (1977: 282).
57. KS, 'Supplement Programme Conference', OED/B/10/3, 14 Oct. 1931.
58. CTO to RWC, OED/B/3/2/20, 2 July 1931.
59. KS, 'Supplement Programme Conference', OED/B/10/3, 14 Oct. 1931.
60. KS to RWC, OED/B/10/4(1), 20 Jan. 1932.

61. MP Box 15, 10 May 1901, see further Mugglestone (2005).
62. RWC to CTO, 17 Feb. 1932; CTO to RWC, 18 Feb. 1932 (both OED/B/3/2/21).
63. RWC to CTO, OED/B/3/2/21, 18 Feb. 1932.
64. CTO to RWC, OED/B/3/2/21, 19 Feb. 1932.
65. OED/B/10/4(1) (see Introd., pp. 8–9 above); for Loane see p. 266, n. 34 above.
66. OED/B/10/4(1), 10 Mar. 1932.
67. KS to RWC, OED/B/10/4(1), 18 Mar. 1932.
68. 24 Mar. 1932, OED/B/3/2/21.
69. KS to Craigie, OED/B/3/2/21, 5 Apr. 1932; Heseltine worked 52 hours on the Supplement in October 1932.
70. OED/B/10/4(1), 4 April 1932. Heseltine later assisted Sir Paul Hervey on his *Oxford Companion to English Literature* and worked on various other Oxford reference books.
71. OED/B/10/4(1), 19 Sept. 1932.
72. CTO to RWC, OED/B/3/2/21, 26 Nov. 1932.
73. RWC to E. Bradley, 2 Dec. 1932; E. Bradley to RWC, 5 Dec. 1932 (both OED/B/3/2/21); p. 80 below.
74. In June 1927 it had been agreed that Craigie would take the earlier and Onions the later portion of the history ('Dictionary Supplement: further conference 15 June, 1927 – for file', OED/B/3/2/16(1)).
75. KS to RWC, OED/B/3/2/21, 30 Nov. 1932; KS to CTO, OED/B/7/5/4, 10 May 1933. The Printer was asked to reduce the print run of the large paper edition of the Supplement to 6,000 copies on 26 May 1933.
76. Baldwin (1928: 1–2).
77. OED/B/3/2/21, 28 Nov. 1932.
78. OED/B/3/2/21, 30 Nov. 1932.
79. OED/B/3/2/21, 20 Dec. 1932.; cf. Mathews (1985: 217).
80. OED/B/3/2/21, 23 and 28 Dec. 1932.
81. KS report of interview with CTO, OED/B/3/2/22, 31 Mar. 1933. Birt collapsed with lung and heart problems in November 1933 and his case was referred to the Delegates for support (CTO report, OED/B/3/2/22, 22 Nov. 1933). Lewis's pension was raised to £132 p.a. from May 1944 (KS to W. J. Lewis, 3 May 1944, OUP/BoxGFGF/000131). Lewis's book *The Language of Cricket* had been published by OUP; but this had gone out of print in 1945 with a sale of fewer than 500 copies and consequently, under the terms of the contract, no royalty had ever been due to the author (memo of 19 Dec. 1947, OUP/BoxGFGF/000131). He worked briefly for Craigie in 1946 (p. 134 below) and died aged 79 in 1947.
82. OED/B/3/2/21, 4 and 5 Dec 1932.
83. RWC to CTO, OED/B/3/2/22, 16 May 1933; see RWC, Memorandum for the Finance Committee, OED/B/3/2/22, 18 Apr. 1933. Correspondence between RWC and the President of Magdalen (Gordon) of 22–25 Feb. 1938 discusses Onions's financial situation, evidently poor, and supplies further details (OED/B/3/10/25).
84. OED/B/10/4(2).
85. 1 Aug. 1933; Craigie to [RWC], 27 May 1933 (both OED/B/10/4(2)). Mathews contributed to Craigie's American dictionary of 1936–44 and subsequently produced his own (Mathews (1951)).
86. KS to CTO 13 Apr. 1933; CTO to KS, 22 Apr. 1933 (both OED/B/10/4(2))
87. KS to CTO, 22 May 1933; CTO to KS, 25 May 1933 (both OED/B/10/4(2)); *OED Online* has since ante-dated this with a quotation from the *Wisconsin News* of 1928: 'Panning the mugg who "muscles in" on the boss each day as he goes to chow'.
88. KS to CTO, OED/B/10/4(2), 5 May 1933.
89. The bundle of slips and associated correspondence are in OED/B/10/4(2), May 1933; *The Times*, 19 Jan. 1933.

90. *The Periodical*, 15 Mar. 1934, p. 19.
91. RWC to CTO, 8 Dec. 1932, OED/B/3/2/21; Toynbee and Whibley (1935), vol. 1, p. 183 (letter to West, 21 Apr. 1741); Preface, p. vi.
92. Both Supplements were concerned to record primarily new words and senses rather than attempt to correct evidence in the main Dictionary; both nonetheless found space, on occasion, to include pre-nineteenth-century ante-datings to *OED*. See *The Periodical*, 15 Mar. 1934, p. 14 (available at http://oed.hertford.ox.ac.uk/main/content/view/317/287/) for a list of some in the first Supplement, and p. 178 below for examples in the second.
93. RWC to CTO, OED/B/3/2/22, 18 Jan. 1933.
94. Both these quotations are taken from *OEDS1* (1972), s.v. *Buchmanism*; cf. the entry s.v. *group* (n.) 3d.
95. OED/B/3/2/22, 12 Dec. 1933. On 12 May 1938, RWC wrote to Wyllie and Le Mesurier to say that he thought that the word 'was now I think naturalized and generalized', referring to a headline in 'today's *Times*': 'Abortive Putsch in Brazil'. Burchfield's quotations begin with one from *The Times,* dated 1920.
96. The menu can be seen at http://oed.hertford.ox.ac.uk/main/content/view/268/287/.
97. See RWC to Vice-Chancellor; RWC to KS and HM (both OED/B/3/2/22, 24 May 1933).
98. KS to RWC, 25 May 1933; Baldwin to RWC, 5 Aug. 1933; both OED/B/3/2/22.
99. *The Periodical*, 15 Mar. 1934, p. 26.
100. E.g. OED/B/3/2/22, 24 May 1933.
101. Chapman (1946: 492). *Chalcenterous*, meaning 'having bowels of brass', is a word almost exclusively used by twentieth-century *OED* lexicographers of themselves; see the various bibliographical references in *OED*, s.v., and Burchfield (1989: 16, n.1). The word was first recorded in Burchfield's Supplement, in a definition which does not explain the lexicographical connotations.

III After the *OED*

1. *The Periodical*, 15 Mar. 1934 (p. 8).
2. The original 128 fascicles had sold for up to 12/6 each for large sections.
3. Gordon (1881–1942) was Merton Professor of English Literature, 1920, then President of Magdalen, 1928, then in 1933 Professor of Poetry. He had been an undergraduate with RWC at Oriel in 1902; the two continued close friends and associates (RWC wrote Gordon's *DNB* entry). See *The Periodical*, 15 Mar. 1934, pp. 17–20 (available at http://oed.hertford.ox.ac.uk/main/content/view/320/287/).
4. Bradley and Bridges (1928: 153).
5. *The Times*, 22 Nov. 1933.
6. [Review of 1933 Supplement] (1934: 51).
7. For *lesbian* see further pp. 49 above and 205 below; for *putsch* see p. 63 above.
8. The difficulty of making good contemporaneous judgements is indicated by the objection of several reviewers to words they did not think 'worth their place' in the Supplement, for example *pince-nezed*, *snolly-goster*, *snookums* and *solemncholy* ([Review of 1933 Supplement] (1934: 51)). But all of these were kept by Burchfield in his revision of the relevant volume of the Supplement in 1982, and for the first two he found later quotations.
9. Burchfield (1980: 278); see p. 153 below.
10. A few reviewers made consistent searches of the Supplement in an attempt to establish, according to scholarly criteria, how it had treated specific categories of vocabulary. Thus A. S. C. Ross (1934) pointed out that it had shirked various sexual and 'coarse' words and expressions (see pp. 122 and 203 below).

11. See further *The Periodical* 15 Feb. 1928, pp. 6–8 ; also Knowles (2000).

12. Chapman (1946). The *Times* obituary of 2 Mar. 1940 was written by 'a correspondent'. For film reference see McMorris (2001: 202, 15).

13. KS to RWC, OED/QOD/1933/1, 20 Mar. 1933 (quoted Sutcliffe (1978: 221)). One of Le Mesurier's typically practical suggestions was that 'first-class dictionaries' like *OED* should be issued with a gramophone disc recording the sound of words given in the pronunciation key (as listed in *SOED*, e.g.), an idea that Sisam was 'thinking very carefully over' in May 1933. He hoped to discuss the proposition with the HMV company soon, but had reservations: 'I wonder who we should get to make the sounds? My experience is that in matters of difficulty no two persons agree, and that a great many expert phoneticians don't know the sounds they make themselves!' The idea was eventually rejected (HGLM to KS, 12 May 1933; KS to HGLM, 19 May 1933; both OED/B/3/10/4(2)).

14. HGLM to HWF, OED/B/10/4(2), 10 Jan. 1933.

15. Correspondence of 13–17 Jan. 1933, all OED/B/10/4(2).

16. The 1933 reissue of *OED* had also included a list of 'Spurious Words'.

17. OED/B/10/4(2), 17 Jan. 1933, the same source contains the later correspondence cited below.

18. Burchfield added the pronunciation of *daye/dai* preferred by Le Mesurier to the second Supplement but kept the headword spelt as in the first Supplement (i.e. *daye*), while the *Concise* spelt the word *dai* and allowed only the pronunciation 'di' (to rhyme with 'die'). Le Mesurier did not remove *lunkah* from the *Concise*, perhaps because he felt the necessity of explaining Doyle's usage was enough to merit its continued presence.

19. Correspondence in OED/B/3/10/4(2). The 1933 Supplement had included *Dáil Eireann* but defined it only as 'the Sinn Fein Parliament in Ireland', a definition emended by Burchfield in 1972 to 'The lower house of the Parliament of the Republic of Ireland (before 1922, the Sinn Fein Parliament in Ireland)'.

20. Correspondence in OED papers: ML 136–41, 27 Sept.–10 Dec. 1956; on the 'taking' of the oath see Dwyer (1999: 145–7) (many thanks to Roy Foster for his help here). There is no record of internal discussion of this matter in OUP; a briefing note (2 Oct. 1956) reports that the same definition appears in the *Shorter* (in the addenda to the revised third edition published in 1955) and states that no previous correspondence on the term exists in the files. Nevertheless a letter from HGLM to Wyllie, OED/RF, 12 Oct. 1936, thanks him for 'the great trouble you have taken to give me accurate details of *Fianna Fáil*,' indicating that HGLM had pursued the word further after his initial letter of 1933. The definition of political terms in Oxford dictionaries is a topic ripe for further study: see p. 206 below.

21. KS to CTO, 15 May 1933; CTO to KS, 18 May 1933; both OED/B/10/4(2).

22. 18 and 19 May 1933, OED/B/10/4(2). Both Wyllie and Onions corresponded with Harrod (at Christ Church, Oxford) on the various meanings of 'gold' in relation to currency in May 1933.

23. HGLM to RWC, OED/RF, 16 Aug. 1938.

24. Personal communication to author, 17 Oct. 2006; see Heilbron (1998: 126, fig. 3.3.47). Many thanks to John Heilbron, Elizabeth Baigent and Sarah Bendall for help with the correct account of a plane-table. See further Hutton (1815), 2: 191–2, which specifes a 'rectangular board'. Bennett (1987: 46–7) says the board is 'generally square', as in a clear photograph of a late nineteenth-century instrument; photographs of more recent models can be seen in Low (1952: 19).

25. Burchfield (1961: 38); OED/B/3/2/24, 3 July 1935. In 1951 Empson published *The Structure of Complex Words*, in which he found fault with *OED's* semantic analyses of a number of words (e.g. *wit* and *sense*) while acknowledging that 'such work on individual words as I have been able to do has been almost entirely

dependent on using the majestic object [i.e. the *OED*] as it stands' (Empson (1951: 391)).

26. *The Periodical*, 15 Mar. 1928, p. 30; see pp. 29–30 above.

27. Fuller discussion is to be found in Aitken (1987) and Bailey (1990). Work on the *Dictionary of Old English* did not begin until 1968–70 (in Toronto).

28. See Aitken (1987: 101–2) for helpful characterization of and distinction between these two dictionaries.

29. Adams (2002: 107, n. 20); Blake (2002: 54–9); the volume of the periodical *Dictionaries* in which these essays appear celebrates the completion of the *MED*.

30. See Bailey (1985); http://oed.hertford.ox.ac.uk/main/content/view/91/235/; http://oed.hertford.ox.ac.uk/main/content/view/92/236/; Chapter VIII.

31. *The Periodical*, 15 Mar. 1934, p. 14.

32. Sutcliffe (1978: 153–5); see McMorris (2001).

33. Quoted from H. W. Fowler's Preface to the second edition of 1929. For Sisam on 'a lexicographer's promise', see p. 51 above.

34. The third edition had some corrections in the text but was mainly improved by Le Mesurier's list of Addenda (itself largely dependent on the 1933 *OED* Supplement, as HGLM acknowledges in his Preface), which ran to 61 pages containing about 2,400 items, 'the largest addition, or indeed change of any kind, that the *COD* received before [its] revision of the '70s' (Allen (1986: 8)).

35. Sutcliffe (1978: 220).

36. Printing figure from Chapman, 'The Oxford English Dictionary and its (Oxford) Children', OED/RF, 3 Nov. 1935, p. 2; *The Times,* 17 Feb. 1933.

37. See Schäfer (1980: 53).

38. E.g. *The Times* of 1 Jan. 1935, p. 40 advertises the *OED* (1933 reissue with Supplement) at £21, the *SOED* at £3 3 s., the *Concise* (Le Mesurier's 1934, i.e. third, edn with Addenda) at 7/6, the *Pocket* (new edn 1934 with Addenda) at 3/6 (or 6s. on India paper), and the *Little* at 2s.

39. As Burchfield reports (1989:143; see further 142–4). See also the various references to this dictionary in McMorris (2001), Sutcliffe (1978: 220–2).

40. Sisam, quoted by McMorris (2001: 184); the same source also quotes Sisam as explaining that the Quarto should have 'enough obsolete material to carry a reader through the great writers back to Shakespeare' (p. 194). Craigie had proposed a similar project in 1920: '*The Oxford Dictionary of Modern English*, a work similar in character to Littré, but with the historical element reduced to a minimum, if not entirely omitted. The aim of this work would be to give a full idea of English as it now is (or as it may be about 1925), with copious illustrative material, and with the needs of the foreign student of English steadily borne in mind. The illustrative material can be readily obtained from that sent in for the *O.E.D.*' (Craigie to RWC, OED/B/3/2/9(1), 30 Mar. 1920).

41. Chapman (1946).

42. 'Telegraphese' is H. W. Fowler's term, used in the Preface to the first edition of the *Concise* (p. iv), though Fowler forgot to define it in the dictionary itself and it had to be added later, to the first set of Addenda published in the impression of 1914 (Allen (1986: 1)).

43. 'The Oxford English Dictionary and its (Oxford) Children', OED/RF, 3 Nov. 1935, pp. 3–4. Chapman added 'O.E.D. I am told often rejected quotations on the ground of familiarity. Its purpose was different.'

44. Ibid., p. 3, referring to Craigie, Hulbert et al. (1936) and Horwill (1935), a dictionary of American usage to which HGLM had contributed his specialist knowledge and advice (as described in the author's Acknowledgements). Burchfield (1989: 144) gives a list of status letters and also describes how the dictionary was to have a split page; cf. McMorris (2001: 203–5).

45. Wyllie's training is mentioned in a document (typed on pink paper) headed 'Oxford English Dictionaries', OUP/BoxOP1713/PB/ED/012869, Appendix B no. 3, 24 Nov. 1955. See CTO to DMD, OUP/ODME/11/139, 18 Mar. 1949; DMD to John Buxton, OUP/PB/ED/09256, 22 Aug. 1958. Chapman – and his wife – spent a good deal of time on this dictionary after the war, as revealed in the ODME files in OUP archives.

46. H. F. Fowler's reluctance to accept money is detailed by McMorris (2001: 239 – index entry for 'payment, attitude to (regarded as unimportant)'). Le Mesurier was similarly uninterested in money; the Press decided to pay his daughter a small but much appreciated annuity after her mother's death in 1953 (£72 a year for seven years), 'in view of her father's valuable services to the Oxford dictionaries' (A. L. P. Norrington – by now Secretary to the Delegates – to Royal Engineers' Benevolent Fund, ODME/12/73, 3 Dec. 1953).

47. Chapman, 'The Oxford English Dictionary and its (Oxford) Children', OED/RF, p. 6. Coulson continued a prolific Oxford lexicographer for many years, involved in further editions of all these dictionaries and also the *Pocket Oxford Russian Dictionary* (she also translated and wrote about Dostoevsky; I thank Della Thompson for this information). From Jan. 1967 she joined the second Supplement staff on a part-time basis (recorded in '*Oxford English Dictionary Supplement: New Edition. Report on Progress in 1966*', OUP/BoxOP1713/PB/ED/012868, 2 Jan. 1967).

48. Chapman, 'The Oxford English Dictionary and its (Oxford) Children', p. 2.

49. Ibid.

50. All quotations from ibid.

51. It is stored in various places in the archives, much of it in the as yet uncatalogued 'OED Revision Files' (OED/RF).

52. KS to HWF, OED/RF, 5 Dec. 1933; Captain of Coldstream Guards to C. H. Wilkinson of Worcester College (who passed letter on to KS), 20 Jan. 1934 and Wyllie to KS, 26 Jan. 1934 (both OED/B/3/2/22). The Director of the Public Library in Boston had written to inquire which was the right etymology on 31 Mar. 1933; see also OED/B/10/4(2), 20 Apr. 1933.

53. Letters of 26 Apr. and 6 Aug. 1938, OED/RF.

54. OED/RF, 28 Mar. 1939.

55. *OED3* revises the *OED2* entry (itself untouched since the relevant fascicle of *OED1*, published in 1904), noting that 'penal servitude' was 'a system of imprisonment with hard labour introduced in Britain in 1853 and abolished by the Criminal Justice Act of 1948' (*OED Online* s.v. *penal*, draft revision Sept. 2005).

56. Many letters back and forwards survive in OED/RF.

57. Letter to the author, 15 Nov. 2006. Wyllie was a handyman who carpentered his own pigeonholes for dictionary slips, with specially slanting slats (visible in illustration 7; information from Peter Glare). Le Mesurier asked Sisam whether he might drop the 'M'' on 9 June 1936 (OED/RF).

58. E.g. 30 Apr. 1937, 9 Sept. 1937, etc. (OED/RF).

59. A letter (on 'Latin Dictionary' notepaper) dated 20 May 1937 acknowledges receipt of a volume of the Grimms' *Wörterbuch* for what Wyllie describes as 'use on the N. E. D.'; such receipts date from 1935 and continue to at least 1939, while a document of 19 May 1952 notes an invoice for Uvarov's *Dictionary of Science*, 'which Mr Wyllie has bought for OED library'. In a letter of 20 June 1939 to a daughter of W. W. Skeat, Wyllie refers to 'a great part of the OED library' being dispersed 'five years ago', and some books being sent 'to the warehouse in Summertown' – Miss Skeat is chasing up some books of her father's that should have been returned to the King's College Skeat–Furnivall collection. (All quotations, including those in text, from OED/RF.) Information on the location of the *OLD* comes from Peter Glare, who took over the editorship from Wyllie in 1954.

60. On *Pakistan* see pp. 206 below.

61. The example given, *useage*, as in 'it has been necessary to take useage of raw materials as an indicator of output', is not convincing.
62. As Murray (1977: 305, n.12) reports, 'public interest in Minor was revived when a stone lion, all that remained of the Brewery after enemy action, was restored for the South Bank Festival of Britain exhibition' in 1949. For more on Minor see Knowles (1990) and the best-selling Winchester (1998).
63. Documentation on this dictionary is amply preserved in the OUP archives.
64. Briefing document of 24 Apr. 1972 for letter from DMD to Chadwick in response to the latter's draft obituary of Wyllie (see below; OUP/BoxOP1726/PB/ED/012933). Souter (1873–1949) instead produced *A Glossary of Later Latin to 600 AD*, published by the Press in 1949 and compiled 'from 27,470 slips composed in his own hand' (*ODNB*).
65. RWC to KS, OUP/BoxOP1726/PB/ED/012933, 30 May 1939. Bailey was a classicist now remembered principally for his massive edition of Lucretius (1947); his character and achievements are illuminatingly sketched by Jasper Griffin in the *ODNB*.
66. Information from Mrs J. E. Schuller, who grew up near Wyllie in Kincardineshire and was a friend of the family (her father had aided Wyllie in his youth and in return he helped her secure a post at OUP as secretary to Norrington).
67. KS to Bailey, OUP/BoxOP1726/PB/ED/012933, 25 Apr. 1940.
68. A copy is preserved in the National Archives and Records Administration in Maryland, USA; it has been republished at http://www.codesandciphers.org.uk/documents/cryptdict/. The editor (Tony Sale) comments, 'The Dictionary is a guide to all the specialist terms employed in Bletchley Park codebreaking. In so doing the Dictionary gives an overview of the whole range of activities as they stood in 1944. The many eccentric technical terms also reflect the special culture and humour of Bletchley Park work.' I am grateful to P. Gilliver and C. Stray for this information.
69. The linguist A. S. C. Ross, who had written a review of the first *OED* Supplement (p. 122 below) and whose wife Stefanyja Olszewska had read for both the first and the second Supplements (copiously for the latter; see p. 161 below), was also at Bletchley. See various index references in Hinsley and Stripp (1993).
70. While living in Scotland in this period, Wyllie corresponded on writing paper headed 'Oxford Latin Dictionary', with his Kincardineshire address printed on it.
71. As indicated by references to his training of staff, comments on samples, etc. in a document typed on pink paper headed 'Oxford English Dictionaries', OUP/BoxOP1713/PB/ED/012869, *c.* 1955–56 (undated).
72. Extracts from this obituary, in OUP/BoxOP1726/PB/ED/012933, are reproduced here by permission of Chadwick's estate. Chadwick's correspondence with the Press (beginning 14 Apr. 1972) is in the same location.
73. On the relationship between the Oxford and Clarendon Presses, here thought as identical by Chadwick, see Introduction, n. 7.
74. KS to DMD, OUP/BoxOP1713/PB/ED/012869, 10 July 1954; Murray (1933) 'Historical Introduction', p. xvii.
75. Document by 'BLP', OUP/BoxOP1726/PB/ED/12933, 24 Apr. 1972.
76. Quoted from Chadwick's obituary (see n. 72, above).
77. All OED/RF. Wyllie's letters are on *OED* headed notepaper.
78. All correspondence in OED/RF (the reproof to Gray is dated 26 May 1949).
79. OUP/BoxOP1713/PB/ED/012869; see further Chapter V, below.
80. OUP/ODME/11, 30 Oct. 1953.
81. The gin and Ribena are remembered by Peter Glare. Substantial documentation of the period of Wyllie's dismissal (and subsequent correspondence) is in OUP/BoxOP1726/PB/ED/012933.
82. Wyllie (1965).
83. Wyllie (1958), Book I, p. 22.

84. C. H. Roberts (then Secretary of the Press) wrote to thank him for the slips (saying that 'if at some distant date the OED is revised they would be of value') and suggested that in return he cancel Wyllie's debt to the Press in respect of his house and discharge the second mortgage (correspondence between Wyllie and CHR of May 1962, OUP/BoxOP1713/PB/ED/012870). Wyllie's family scrupulously returned all Oxford lexicographical material to the Press after his death (papers in OUP/BoxOP1726/PB/ED/012933).

IV Treasure-house of the Language: Role and Function of the *OED*

1. A discussion necessarily confined to the *OED*. See Mugglestone (2000c) for a range of essays which examine specific aspects of the making and character of *OED1*, and Béjoint (2000) and Landau (2001) for recent authoritative studies of lexicography more generally.
2. OED/B/3/2/25.
3. OED/B/3/2/24, 29 Dec. 1936.
4. OED/B/3/2/23, 13 and 15 Jan. 1934.
5. OED/RF, 23 Nov. 1937.
6. OED/RF, 6 June 1940.
7. OED/RF, 29 Nov. 1938.
8. OED/RF, 3 Dec. 34.
9. OED/RF, 13 Dec. 1937.
10. Brodribb (1928: 277)
11. OED/RF, 9 Nov. 1938.
12. OED/RF, 25 and 26 July 1937.
13. OED/RF, correspondence of May 1937 reported on document of 29 June 1937. Goffin became the first temporary editor of the second Supplement (see p. 142 below); Cumberlege succeeded Milford as Publisher in 1945; Hopkins was a staff member in Milford's office; Paul Willert worked for OUP in New York; E. G. Withycombe undertook various sorts of work for the Press: she co-edited Ghosh and Withycombe (1935), collated material for Toynbee and Whibley (1935) (see p. vii of vol. 1), and prepared *The Oxford Dictionary of English Christian Names* (1945). Burchfield later stated that the plan for the second *OED* Supplement, which he was appointed to edit in 1957, was based on 'earlier proposals written by . . . Humphrey Milford and Geoffrey Cumberlege' (Burchfield and Aarsleff (1988: 46)), but I have come across no trace of these in the *OED* archives.
14. OED/RF, 30 Nov. 1938.
15. OED/RF, 31 Jan. 1938.
16. RWC to Wyllie, OED/RF, 22 June 1937. RWC writes on the bottom of this memo that 'ODME [the Quarto] says "dialect or rare"'.
17. s.v. *higgle* 2c: 'When *A* knowing or hoping that figs will be soon inquired for, buys up all the figs in the market he higgles; but when *A* keeps a grocer's shop and asks *B* eightpence for a pound of figs and *B* offers him sixpence, then *B* haggles.'
18. OED/RF. Bunyan's vocabulary was relatively well covered in the *OED*, which quoted from his works to illustrate use of a word nearly 1,000 times.
19. OED/B/3/2/26, 3 Feb. 1940; 12 Apr. 1940.
20. OED/B/3/2/25, 18 Jan. 1939.
21. Cf. *The Periodical*, 15 Feb. 1928: 26: 'Nothing exasperated Sir James Murray more than to receive letters, as he often did, from persons alleging that this word or that was not in the Dictionary when it was there.'
22. Correspondence between RWC and W. G. Bond, OED/B/3/2/22, 27 & 28 Dec. 1933.

This sense of *spine* was added by Burchfield in *OEDS4*, with a first quotation dated 1922.

23. OED/B/3/2/26, 18 Feb. 1936; Macaulay (1935: 269).

24. Enciso and Barlow (1932).

25. OED/B/3/2/26, correspondence 8–15 June 1941. A copy of Macaulay's list is in the same file; see further Considine (1998).

26. See Fowler (2002: 54). Unlike Macaulay, Woolf seems to have been resistant to and sceptical about organizational systems like alphabeticization, in her view an arid form of male taxonomy destined to fail; in her novel *To the Lighthouse*, Mr Ramsay never reaches the meaning of 'R'. As Fowler writes, she was an admirer of Joseph Wright, and interested in the idea of collecting dialect as registering unregulated and non-authoritarian language (rather than that found in *OED*).

27. Murray (1977: 193).

28. OED/B/3/2/19, 7 Nov. 1930. According to the publishers' own account, *OED1* recorded 414,825 words (*The Periodical*, 15 Feb. 1928, p. 21); see p. 298, n. 36 below.

29. OED/B/3/2/26, 5 and 7 Feb. 1940.

30. OED/B/3/2/26, 7 and 23 Dec. 1949.

31. OED/B/3/2/23, 23 and 26 Jan. 1934.

32. OED/B/3/2/25, 3 and 4 May 1939. Burchfield added the definition, with no mark of disapproval, in his first Supplement volume of 1972, but was able to find no quotation earlier than 1955 (from *The Times*).

33. OED/RF.

34. Osborn (1933: 781).

35. D. Coleridge (1860: 155); Thackeray (1848: 7–8). Becky Sharp must have been given one of the enormously successful abridgements, since the original two-volume edition would have been too heavy to pitch out of the window in this way; see Dille (2006: 199).

36. For a history of English dictionaries, see Starnes and Noyes (1991) and Green (1997); for an account of attitudes to language at this time, see Crystal (2004: Chapters 15–16).

37. See Korshin (1974).

38. See Reddick (1990), Hitchings (2005).

39. Johnson (1958–), vol. 18, p. 89.

40. Murray (1900: 38–9).

41. Johnson (1958–), vol. 18, p. 102.

42. Schreyer (2000: 66–7). Clearly Johnson had sometimes to turn to less exalted sources: 'words must be sought where they are used; and in what pages, eminent for purity, can terms of manufacture or agriculture be found?' Johnson (1958–), vol. 18, p. 94.

43. Johnson (1958–), vol. 18, p. 29.

44. For an account of the role of quotation sources in Johnson's dictionary see DeMaria (1986); for some European antecedents see Korshin (1974); for a quantitative analysis of his sources see Schreyer (2000); for views on Johnson's policing (or not) of usage, see Barnbrook (2005) and McDermott (2005); for *OED*'s use of Johnson's definitions and quotations, see Silva (2005). Lynch and McDermott (2005) contains a useful range of recent essays on Johnson's dictionary, which is available in an electronic edition (Johnson (1996)); see also pages on Johnson at http://oed.hertford. ox.ac.uk/main/content/category/12/47/192/.

45. Reprinted Bolton and Crystal (1966: 126); see also Crystal (2004: Chapters 15–16).

46. Such transformations, which were complex and varied, are beyond the scope of this book; see further Aarsleff (1983), Dowling (1986), Morpurgo-Davies (1998). They radically affected the academic study of Old and Middle English, in which many of the *OED* lexicographers and Philological Society members – principally Furnivall,

W. W. Skeat and Henry Sweet – also played a significant role (Utz (2002)); Brewer (1996: Chapter 5).

47. Murray (1900: 49, 51). The Philological Society's *Proposal* of 1859 had described its new project, eventually to become the *OED*, as a 'new and more Scientific Dictionary than any at present existing' (p. 1).

48. Trench (1860 (1857)). The link with Passow is identified in H. Coleridge (1860: 72); see also Liddell and Scott (1843), Preface, p. vii.

49. See further Taylor (1993), e.g. pp. 281–6. Also http://oed.hertford.ox.ac.uk/main/content/view/86/195/; cf. Beer (2000).

50. Wyllie's dictum was quoted by Chadwick in his draft obituary (p. 88 above).

51. Trench (1860 (1857): 4–5).

52. Murray himself, the phonetician A. J. Ellis, and the philologist and Old and Middle English editor W. W. Skeat, all played a major role in nineteenth-century dialect study as well as in the construction of the *OED*; see further their respective *ODNB* entries and Wright (1898–1905) (a work dedicated to Skeat).

53. *Proposal* (1859: 2–3) (italics in original quotation).

54. Circular to the Philological Society members dated 9 Nov. 1862, quoted Murray (1977: 193). Furnivall was a disciple of the Christian Socialist F. D. Maurice and co-founder of the Working Men's College.

55. Concern about the size of the final product, and the consequent impracticability of the sub-editors' working methods, was expressed from very early on, for example in the detailed letter from Skeat to Furnivall, a copy of which is preserved in MP Box 1, 17 Nov. 1865.

56. Marsden (1859: 369, 386).

57. D. Coleridge (1860: 154–6).

58. Reeve (1889: 328).

59. Marsden (1859: 376). The same view is found in another critic of *OED*'s preparedness to record 'corruption' of the '"well of English undefiled"', Reeve (1889: 349). See Bailey (1996) for an account of the development of English as a world language in the nineteenth century.

60. Schlegel (1818), quoted Dowling (1986: 29). For examples of the connections Schlegel insists on between language and culture see his Lecture 1. Schlegel's ideas and their influence on English intellectual culture are discussed by Aarsleff (1983) and Dowling (1986); see also Morpurgo-Davies (1998) and Simone (1997: 197ff.).

61. First published in 1855 and 1851; my quotations are from fourth (revised) edition (1859) (Trench 1859: 5) and eighth (1858) editions respectively.

62. Moon quotes Schlegel's remarks on the first page of his preface (Moon (1865)). Again, cf. Reeve (1889: 349): 'the first duty of those who devote themselves to philological studies is . . . to defend its purity, for a corrupt and decaying language is an infallible sign of a corrupt and decaying civilisation'.

63. Trench (1858: 59–60, 5, 10). The most notable recent exponent of such a tradition was the philologist (and radical) Horne Tooke (1736–1812), whose work significantly influenced Trench. See Aarsleff (1983).

64. Richardson's dictionary of 1836–37 was another significant precursor to *OED* (along with the works of Johnson and Webster). It was particularly valued by Murray for its reliance on quotations to establish meaning: see pages at http://oed.hertford.ox.ac.uk/main/content/category/12/49/193/.

65. See Aarsleff (1983: 230–46) and Crowley (2003: Chapter 2), for an account of Trench's views on language; also Taylor (1993: 207–52) for discussion of the values attached by Trench and his contemporaries to the historical study of language.

66. D. Coleridge (1860: 157). The *OED* later defined this sense of *puddle*, relating to gold and opal mining, as 'To work (clayey or sticky wash-dirt) with water in a tub so as to separate the ore', illustrating it with quotations from 1853 onwards.

67. The term *hapax legomenon* is Greek for 'said once' and implies that the usage is eccentric as well as unique, see Glossary (p. 260).

68. H. Coleridge (1860–61). Furnivall (e.g. 1866: x) enthusiastically adopted *foolometer* and its derivatives, but it continued to be a sore spot with the Dictionary's critics and was among words identified by the OUP Delegates in 1896 as adding unnecessarily to its length ('New English Dictionary. Correspondence and minutes (April 24 1896)', p. 7, OED/B/2/2/1).

69. Trench (1860 (1857): 6).

70. Many examples of such letters are preserved in the Murray Papers.

71. Murray (1880–81a: 131–2).

72. Murray (1882–84: 523). For identification of and comment on early reviews, see Bailey (2000a and 2000b) and Bivens (1980–81).

73. Murray (1882–84: 524–5); J. Murray to B. Price ('in answer to request from the Delegates not to use newspaper quotations'), MP, Box 5, 9 June 1882; Murray (1880–81a: 129). Bradley also defended the 'better forms' of 'the much-decried "newspaper English"' in his book on language (Bradley (1904: 239)) and Onions too thought they were of 'inestimable value' (Onions (1928b: 4–5)).

74. 'newly literate' presumably refers to the Education Acts of 1870 and afterwards, which eventually established compulsory and universal primary and secondary education in Britain.

75. Brodribb (1928). Furnivall's favourite newspapers included the *Daily News* (quoted over 9,800 times in *OED*), the *Daily Chronicle* (over 4,000 times) and the *Westminster Gazette* (*c.* 7,500 times); see Benzie (1983: 107). The suspicion with which late nineteenth- and early twentieth-century intellectuals regarded both newspapers and (more complicated) education and democracy is lucidly anatomized in Carey (1992), e.g. pp. 6ff. For a cultural history of newspapers in the nineteenth century see Jones (1996).

76. Murray (1977: 196).

77. Trench (1860 (1857): 6).

78. Mugglestone (2000a, 2000b, 2005: Chapter 5).

79. *OEDS3*, pp. v–vi. Very roughly, this means something like 'oil to stop a thickish liquid from getting too clogged up'.

80. See Murray (1977: 195).

81. Ross (1934: 129); Mitford and Ross (1956). Ross's sociolinguistic study of present-day English was originally published in 1954.

82. Trench (1860 (1857): 69); Murray (1882–84: 522–3).

83. See Hoare and Salmon (2000); Gilliver (1999: 1676–77); Mugglestone (2005: Chapter 4); also Brewer (2000: 46) for some figures on comparative citation from scientific sources.

84. See Williams (1976) for an illuminating discussion of this term.

85. Reeve (1889: 328).

86. Whitney was later editor in chief of *The Century Dictionary* (Whitney 1889–91), an early rival to *OED* (see Bailey (2000a: 217–24)). References in text are to Whitney (1867: 23); Marsh (1860: 17–18). See further 'Literature and the nation' at http://oed.hertford.ox.ac.uk/main/content/view/114/271/. The phrase 'volumes paramount' is a quotation from Wordsworth's sonnet 'Great men have been among us', which celebrates the 'hands that penned/And tongues that uttered wisdom', great writers of the past (revolutionaries such as Sidney, Marvell, Harrington and others 'who called Milton friend'), 'moralists' who 'could act and comprehend' – 'They knew how genuine glory was put on;/Taught us how rightfully nation shone/In splendour'.

87. Printed in Murray (1933). This document is Bayliss and Sweatman's 'Register' (see pp. 38 above); Craigie and Onions disavow any claim that it might be regarded as a 'complete' guide.

88. *Proposal for a Publication of a New English Dictionary* (1859: 6).
89. Their names are recorded in fascicle after fascicle as the work was published. See also Knowles (2000).
90. Scott was one of the most widely read authors of the nineteenth century: see St Clair (2004), e.g. pp. 245–6, 632ff.; the concordance to his works published in 1833 would have aided their excerption for *OED* (the original work, now rare, is reprinted in *A Complete Glossary* (1974)).
91. Bradley (1904: 236).
92. Taylor (1993: 6).
93. See pp. 233ff. below and Brewer (2005–) based on intensive examination of this subject. Blake was quoted 108 times; Keats 1,483; Dickens is an exception to the bias against novelists.
94. Schäfer (1980: 13). See also Brewer (2005–) and Brewer (2000). The recognition by linguists and scholars of the limitations of *OED*'s evidence continues to be very variable. Full understanding is evinced by e.g. Algeo (1998: 64), McConchie (1996) and Nevalainen (1999: 336–9) but is by no means universal (contrast the uncritical citation of *OED* to be found in e.g. Wierzbicka (2006) and many other works).
95. *The Periodical*, 15 Feb. 1928, p. 1.
96. On Webster, see Brewer (2008).
97. On Hardy, Joyce and Woolf see respectively Taylor (1993), Deane (1998), Fowler (2002); also Chapter VII below.
98. Aitken (1971: 9).
99. Onions (1928a).
100. For an account of one such quest, see Warburton (1986).
101. See (e.g.) Becket (1787); Adams (1886); Bartlett (1894); Schmidt (1874); Cleveland (1867); Bradshaw (1894); Abbott (1875); Neve (1887); Brightwell (1869); *A Complete Glossary for Sir Walter Scott's Novels and Romances* (1974); Langley (1870). Pope and Cowper were each quoted around 5,800 times, standing out in a century in general under-quoted in the *OED*.
102. Philological Society Ordinary Meeting Book, 24 Jan. 1890 (held by OUP); quoted Murray (1977: 274) (cf. also p. 285).
103. Murray (1882–84: 509–10); cf. Murray (1977: 298)
104. A process explained in Gilliver (2004).
105. See further the pages on *OED*'s period coverage at http://oed.hertford.ox.ac.uk/main/content/category/12/52/197/.

V Supplementation or Revision?

1. An illegibly signed memorandum of 28 July 1955 records, 'Onions says that there must be masses of notes in the Bodleian in the custody of the Latin Dictionary staff'; this is preserved along with voluminous correspondence in as yet uncatalogued files containing *OED* revision material (OED/RF), some marked up by Burchfield's staff (indicating that he had access to them). On *OED3* revisers' return to these papers see p. 297, n. 8 below. Other documents on necessary revisions to *OED1* and the 1933 Supplement, some also relevant to Burchfield's Supplement but missed by him, are in publishers' papers in the *OED* archives (OED/B/3/2, etc.).
2. After 1936 Craigie continued working on the American dictionary until its completion in 1944, and on the *Dictionary of the Older Scottish Tongue* until 1955, by which time it had reached the end of letter *L*. His three-volume survey of Icelandic literature, *Specimens of Icelandic Rimur*, was published after the war, in 1952; it was described by his *DOST* successor Aitken as 'a masterly survey of a field in which [Craigie's] erudition and discernment were unrivalled' (*ODNB* entry).

3. Guðbrandur, Craigie and Cleasby (1957).

4. KS to 'File', OUP/BoxOP1713/PB/ED/012869 (the source for all references to letters and papers in this chapter except where otherwise indicated), 25 June 1941.

5. Craigie (signed), 'O.E.D. Supplement 2', 14 Oct. 1941.

6. Craigie had previously published in the series, as had Chapman and R. C. Goffin (on whom see further pp. 142ff. below); Sisam was on the SPE editorial committee.

7. See p. 21 above and pp. 182ff. below.

8. Craigie (1941); I am most grateful for P. Gilliver for identifying this tract.

9. Craigie to KS, 28 Feb. 1942. Burchfield later included one of them, though whether he found the reference in this letter or came across it independently is impossible to say. Many of Troubridge's findings were published in the journal *Notes & Queries*.

10. Craigie to KS, 19 Sept. 1942; KS to Craigie, 21 Sept. 1942.

11. The lecture was subsequently published by OUP (Craigie (1943)).

12. Craigie to KS, 17 Mar. 1943; KS to Craigie, 25 June 1943.

13. KS to J. B. Leishman (St John's College, Oxford), 4 Aug. 1943.

14. See Sutcliffe (1978), e.g. p. 248, for problems on paper rationing during the war and after.

15. KS to W. J. Lewis, 1 May 1946; Powell to KS, 7 June 1946; Lewis to KS, 28 Oct. 1946. Lewis died on 11 Dec. 1947.

16. Rope to Secretary (undated; rec'd 5 Oct. 1948); KS to Rope, 6 Oct. 1948; Burchfield (1961: 37), n. 8; Rope continued a contributor until his death in 1978.

17. DMD to W. Savage, 30 June 1949.

18. Rope to Secretary, 26 Aug. 1951; Craigie to DMD, 27 Oct. 1951; DMD to Craigie, 29 Oct. 1951. Davin later reported to Norrington (then still Secretary, but about to hand over to Roberts), on 29 Apr. 1954, that 'Craigie in fact only got as far as C', for which he thought they should pay him £50 in all rather than the £200 Sisam had negotiated for the whole alphabet.

19. Chapman (1946).

20. Sutcliffe (1978: 223).

21. These figures are recorded in an undated paper headed 'Oxford English Dictionary', perhaps written around May 1954.

22. CTO to DMD, SOED/1951/14/3, 22 Mar. 1951.

23. By which Sisam means that the first Supplement had got shorter as it went through the alphabet, since the original *OED* fascicles covering the latter half of the alphabet had been published so much more recently than had those covering the first half.

24. The 'mass of material' for *set* took something approaching forty days to digest: 'the word occupies a column more than 18 pages of the Dictionary, and extends to 154 main divisions, the last of which (*set up*) has so many sub-divisions that it exhausts the alphabet and repeats the letters down to *rr*' (*The Periodical*, 15 Feb. 1928, p. 5).

25. D. P. Costello, John Butt and E. A. Horsman were respectively a Russianist, an eighteenth-century English literature specialist, and an English literature academic of wider interests. The attraction of 'industrious women' would have been their cheapness as well as their industry, given the absence in this period of equal pay legislation.

26. Norrington to DMD, 7 Oct. 1952.

27. 'Delegates minute 8414 of 20 July, 1953'.

28. DMD to Norrington and CHR, 29 Apr. 1954.

29. Quotations in this paragraph from undated paper by Norrington, apparently after May 1954, headed *Oxford English Dictionary*.

30. CHR to DMD, 5 May 1954.

31. Undated paper by Norrington, apparently after May 1954, headed *Oxford English Dictionary*.

32. DMD to KS, OED/B/3/2/27, 30 Mar. 1954. DMD had just paid a visit to KS and reports that he is 'using up energies that I acquired in the Scillies'. Letters preserved in the publishers' files of 1952 (also OED/B/3/2/27) make it clear that the Press had earlier discussed possible ways in which the lexicographer Clarence Barnhart might use *OED* slips for the US Doubleday dictionary, and Oxford dictionary editors use the Thorndike–Barnhart quotation files.

33. Paper by Goffin, 14 Nov. 1955.

34. 'O.E.D. Supplement n/e (apparently written by Davin), dated July 1956. At this stage the Press had agreed that Horsman should become editor (see next section). Mrs Alden had also been secretary to Robert Bridges's SPE (I am grateful for this information to P. Gilliver).

35. Mentioned in Goffin's paper of 14 Nov. 1955.

36. Letters in the OED/ODME files around 1949 record repeated searches for suitable up-to-date quotations.

37. Ghosh and Withycombe (1935). For *OED*'s definition of *literature* see p. 123 above.

38. Sisam's view is quoted in part above (Chapter III). He thought 'there is nothing wrong with [Wyllie's] competence', but feared the effect of his destructive criticism on others. 'As a Lone Wolf Wyllie will be useful as long as he can work, and you should build as if he were not a necessary part of the English Dictionary organization' (KS to DMD, 10 Oct. 1952).

39. DMD to Friedrichsen, OUP/ODME/11/124, 14 Feb. 1949. Carr began work on ODME in 1949.

40. Friedrichsen had apparently been first approached by Norrington in Sept. 1951 (DMD to CTO, OED/B/3/2/27, 20 June 1951); Leslie to Murray, MP Box 22/2, 9 Nov. 1913. Wyllie had also picked up the *howitzer* error (contested by RWC); exchange of letters dated 29 and 31 Oct. 1935, OED/RF.

41. DMD to Norrington and CHR, 17 Aug. 1954.

42. DMD to CHR, 21 Jan. 1954.

43. KS to DMD 10 July 1954.

44. DMD to Norrington and CHR, 17 Aug. 1954; see Gray (1991) who describes Davis's wartime exploits in full.

45. Davis to DMD, 8 November 1954.

46. Horsmann had produced three editions of minor works; once in Otago his publications were primarily on the Victorian period.

47. DMD to Horsman, 7 Aug. 1956.

48. Burchfield (1984: 115).

49. Evidently male, so not A[gnes] M[ary] Macdonald, editor of the *Chambers Shorter English Dictionary* of 1949 and many other Chambers dictionaries subsequently.

50. CTO to DMD, 13 Nov. 1956. Davin remarks that he will pass this instance of *solvitur ambulando* on to the editor of the *Oxford Dictionary of Quotations*.

51. Discussions of likely salary are in various letters, e.g. that of DMD to KS dated 6 July 1954.

52. Burchfield (1989: 3–4).

53. OUP/BoxOP1264/PB/ED/009256.

54. DMD to John Buxton, 22 Aug. 1958; DMD to RWB, 25 Feb. 1970, memo headed *Oxford Dictionary of Modern English*; DMD to L. F. Schooling (another potential editor), 7 Nov. 1957; all OUP/BoxOP1264/PB/ED/009256.

VI Burchfield's Supplement (1): Producing a Dictionary

1. Burchfield (1984: 115–16); Murray (1882–84: 509). For *OED*'s definition of *white man*, see p. 207 below. Murray's image in turn recalls that of Johnson, who described

in his *Plan* for a new dictionary how, 'like the soldiers of Cæsar', looking on Britain as a new world, 'which it is almost madness to invade', he contemplated recording the English tongue, hoping 'that though I should not complete the conquest, I shall, at least, discover the coast, civilize part of the inhabitants, and make it easy for some other adventurer to proceed further, to reduce them wholly to subjection, and settle them under laws' (Johnson (1958–), vol 13, p. 58). Reading the *OED* in terms of such imagery – that of imperialism, conquest and subjection – is the task of a separate book; it has been partially attempted by Willinsky (1994) and by Benson (2001).

2. Burchfield (1958: 229).
3. Burchfield (1989: 190); *OEDS4*, p. xii.
4. Burchfield (1989: 190); information on dog, etc. from Burchfield (1969). (I am most grateful to A. M. Hughes, via P. Gilliver, for identifying this article.) The editor of the *Oxford Illustrated Dictionary* (see Coulson et al. (1962)) was now Lucy Hutchinson, who inherited the work from Carr (document typed on pink paper headed 'Oxford English Dictionaries', OUP/BoxOP1713/PB/ED/012869, *c.* 1955–56 (undated), p. 3); cf. p. 80 above.
5. Burchfield (1989: 190–1).
6. Craigie and Onions record in their preface that 'Mr A. J. Fowler and Mrs A. J. Jenkinson were specially engaged to read modern literature and technical works', a partial exception to this statement (though no trace of this activity appears to have survived in the *OED* papers).
7. For an account of Oxford University at this time see the near-contemporary Ziman (1963) and essays in Harrison (1994).
8. Burchfield (1989: 189). The particular interest of the *Ormulum*, not often thought literarily distinguished, is that its author-scribe used a unique phonetic spelling system to make clear to his readers how they should pronounce each word. The text is therefore an invaluable source for historical language study of various kinds. See further the bibliography at http://www.english.su.se/nlj/ormproj/bibl/biblio1.html, which records four items published (in 1953, 1956, 1961 and 1994) by RWB, one each by HB and KS, and one by the Supplement reader Stefanyja Olszewska (mentioned belowm p. 161).
9. Burchfield and Aarsleff (1988: 46, 48).
10. Burchfield (1989: 4).
11. Burchfield (1969).The earliest quotations s.v. *Hobson-Jobson* are 17c, but use the Arab form (*Hussan, Hussan*) of which *Hobson-Jobson* is a (presumably humorous, perhaps disrespectful?) corruption. Burchfield explains the word as the 'Anglicized form of the repeated wailings and cries of Muslims as they beat their breasts in the *Muharram* procession; hence this festal ceremony'; it is also the title of an Anglo-Indian glossary published in 1886. *Bandobast* (or *bundobust*) is 'an arrangement, organization; preparations'. Both words are briefly mentioned in Goffin (1934), where *bandobast* is said to be scarcely heard outside Anglo-Indian society.
12. Burchfield (1984: 116).
13. Burchfield (1989: 194).
14. Burchfield (1989: 6).
15. Burchfield (1984: 116–17).
16. Burchfield (1961: 37). As RWB wrote in an addition to his obituary, Troubridge contributed in all some 6,000 slips (*The Times*, 31 Dec. 1963).
17. Burchfield (1961: 36).
18. All the following information, unless otherwise indicated, comes from various reports compiled by Burchfield, now preserved in OUP/BoxOP1713/PB/ED/012870.
19. Figure taken from http://www.oed.com/about/facts.html.
20. Reprinted in Burchfield (1989); see p. 8.

21. It is quoted s.v. *A*, *bang*, *dirty*, *fire*, *nuclear*, *oblique*, *quantum*, *sleazoid*, *suitcase*, *tactical*, *top*.

22. *The Times*, 15 Sept. 1958; 4 Sept. 1959; 15 Aug. 1960. On *Chinaman* see further p. 207 below.

23. *OEDS1*, p. xiii. The 1962 report explains that Burchfield expected to include 300 words from New Zealand English; see further pp. 197ff. below. Barnhart's contribution was apparently the productive result of communications initially spurned by Davin in 1952. Orsman also became a lexicographer, his works including an *OED*-style *Dictionary of New Zealandisms on Historical Principles* (1997).

24. Outside readers were paid (at the rate of 7/6 an hour in 1959, 12/6 in 1966), or rewarded with books. Laski refused payment, explaining that she did so out of 'rather complicated feelings of gratitude and proper repayment' (Laski to CHR, OUP/BoxOP1713/PB/ED/012870, 9 Oct. 1959).

25. Burchfield (1973: 99).

26. Hall has written widely on subjects in philosophy and its history but is best known for his comprehensive bibliographical works on Locke and Hume.

27. Burchfield (1989: 8).

28. *Daily Telegraph*, 8 Feb. 1988, reported (like some of the information below) in Burchfield's *DNB* entry on Laski (later revised in *ODNB*). Other information is drawn from the *TLS* (note 30 below). One of her works, Laski (1961), a study of the relationship between aesthetic sensibility and moral virtue, is discussed with notable admiration by Carey (2005).

29. Laski was a founder member of the Charlotte Yonge Society and co-edited a collection of essays on Yonge in 1965 (Battiscombe and Laski (1965)).

30. Laski (1968a), (1968b), (1971).

31. Burchfield (1973: 99).

32. Burchfield (1973: 100).

33. 1962 report (last para.).

34. Burchfield (1989: 9).

35. Burchfield was 'very surprised that the dictionary [*OED*] does not record the use of possess to mean a man mastering a woman, and the use seems also to have escaped our readers since we have no quotations for it in our collections' (correspondence in OED papers: ML 74–81, July 1969). He printed the newly identified sense in his Supplement, naming Empson as his informant, and illustrated it with quotations from 1592 to 1961.

36. The legal questions raised by dictionaries recording trade names that had passed or were passing into generalized language use greatly exercised Burchfield; he discussed them in an article in *The Times* of 25 June 1981 (p. 14); see also Burchfield (1989: 96–100); and *OEDS2*, p. vi.

37. The present archivist, Beverley Hunt, builds on the meticulously detailed work of her predecessor, Jenny McMorris.

38. Burchfield (1989: 192).

39. Burchfield (1980: 278); see p. 68 and 153 above. The *V–Verificative* fascicle had been published in 1917.

40. These three words (defined respectively as 'Esparto [a type of grass]', 'Somewhat olive-coloured; of a dull greenish-yellow shade'; '= *promotable*') appear not to have survived in the language beyond their first, presumably idiosyncratic, use – in 1861, 1900 and 1920.

41. See Morton (1994) and Sledd and Ebbitt (1962), from p. 82 of which the review is quoted. Morton (p. 242) notes that Gove 'was following respectable lexicographical precedent' in recording this sense of *of*, that of Craigie and Onions's first *OED* Supplement, which had treated it as follows: 'Of, U.S. *dial.* or *colloq.* Var. of HAVE v. 24c', and supplied three illustrative quotations (1847, 1854 and 1916).

42. Burchfield (1984: 117).
43. Burchfield (1980: 277); *OEDS1*, p. xiv; *OEDS3*, p. vi.
44. *OEDS2*, p. vii.
45. On the part played in delay by Burchfield's decision to muffle quotations from literary sources in an abundance of non-literary ones, see p. 185 below.
46. Burchfield (1984: 117).
47. OUP/BoxOP1713/PB/ED/012870.
48. See p. 269, n. 21 above.
49. One such member of staff was the lexicographically acute Lesley Burnett (later Brown), who joined the Supplement in 1974 and was diverted to editing a completely revised edition of the *Shorter* published in 1993. Quotations from Burchfield (1984: 118, 1989: 14–15, 79, n. 9).
50. Burchfield (1973: 100); he is following Aitken, Craigie's successor on the *DOST* (Aitken (1971: 9)).
51. See *OEDS1* pp. xvi–xvii, and pp. 52 ff. above.
52. Nor had they been intended to. Norrington's undated document (*c.* 1954; n. 00 above) had recommended checking the new Supplement's proportions per letter with those of the other existing Oxford English dictionaries.
53. The comparison with first Supplement proportions is made in the annual report of 1966 (OUP/BoxOP1713/PB/ED/012868) and repeated in a document (proposing two-volume publication) of 29 Sept. 1969; estimates of page totals are in the annual report for 1970 (both OUP/BoxOP1713/PB/ED/012867).
54. This decision was taken by 1976, since it is referred to in *OEDS2*, p. vii.
55. Burchfield (1989: 192).
56. Burchfield (1969); *OEDS3*, p. vi; Burchfield (1984: 119).
57. The last pages of Sutcliffe's book (1978: 289ff.) gesture towards this.
58. KS to DMD, 12 Mar. 1965, OUP/BoxOP1713/PB/ED/012868. Sisam's comments are discussed at pp. 180 ff. and 182 ff. below. Burchfield's samples had attracted warm approval from other readers, e.g. Randolph Quirk, E. G. Stanley and Friedrichsen (OUP/BoxOP1713/PB/ED/012870).
59. Papers recording these problems are in OUP/BoxOP1713/PB/ED/012867.
60. *OEDS3*, p. vi. Burchfield added to this volume three new examples of the verb *picket* (from 1941, 1972 and 1977), and four for *picketer* (1930, 1972, 1970, 1978) – although as *OED1* had perfectly adequate late nineteenth-century quotations for both these words, he need not have updated them (p. 179 below). Tony Augarde, who later became the Dictionary Department's representative on the Union Committee, believes that Burchfield exaggerated the problems in his Preface to *OEDS3*. 'Picketing certainly didn't contribute to any difficulties. The Union organised occasional strikes but these were for good reason and usually only symbolic one-day events. I remember standing outside the main OUP building in Walton Street with a group of Union members, some holding placards, but nobody prevented anyone from entering' (personal communication to the author).
61. As remembered by his friend of decades, E. G. Stanley (personal communication to the author).
62. 'Evermore', in Barnes (1996).
63. Personal communication to the author. Burchfield (1989: 15–16) wrote of Barnes's departure as follows: 'The loss of Barnes and of some other very able members of staff taught me that there is an area of academic and creative territory from which it is not possible to attract and retain suitable editorial assistants. At regular intervals, and especially at the time of publication of the separate volumes, some of the more ambitious of my colleagues, seeing others in the Department as career-blockers, went off to appointments and projects elsewhere.'

VII   Burchfield's Supplement (2): Editorial Policies and Practice

1. MP Box 19/1, 7 Jan. 1906. (Swinburne was cited *c.* 1,050 times, Jowett just under 2,150 – over 2,000 from his translation of Plato alone, Newman *c.* 1,650, Bryce just over 700, Bridges *c.* 600).
2. Stein (1983); James (1977).
3. Information on how to search *OED Online* can be found on its help pages at www.oed.com and at http://oed.hertford.ox.ac.uk/main/.
4. Burchfield (1989: 195–6); in fact Burchfield here identifies his two innovations as (a) more quotations and (b) inclusion of sexual vocabulary and quotations, and sees his fondness for combinatorial forms as an extension of existing *OED* practice. For *railway director* etc. see further below (p. 182).
5. OED papers: Misc/39/3.xviii (p. 18), June 1979.
6. Burchfield (1961: 36).
7. *OEDS1*, p. xv
8. June 1979, OED papers: Misc/39/3.xviii (p. 18); Misc/39/4.iii.
9. Furnivall's fondness for the ABC teashop at 66 New Oxford Street (London), where he held open house every weekday at 4.30 p.m., was legendary (his biographer gives the teashop its own entry in the index: Benzie (1983)).
10. The Preface to the third edition of the *OED*, the major revision currently under way, states that the 'small number of brief entries found in the one-volume *Supplement to the Oxford English Dictionary* of 1933' which were omitted by Burchfield 'are being reinstated in the revised text' (http://www.oed.com/ public/guide/preface.htm#general). See p. 17 and n. 13 for another deserving candidate (*Wiltshire*).
11. *OEDS1*, p. xv.
12. Murray received a letter back from No. 10 Downing Street to say 'The Prime Minister desires me to thank you for your letter of the 4th instant, and for the proof of the article on "Tory", which he has read with interest' (MP Box 22/2, 9 Aug. 1913).
13. Burchfield and Aarsleff (1988: 51); Amis's review was in the *Observer*, 15 Oct. 1972 and Stoppard's in *Punch*, 13 Dec. 1972. For more searching reviews of *OEDS* see Barnes (1982), Strang (1974, 1977), Samuels (1988), Baker (1988).
14. Pp. 81 and 84 above.
15. KS to DMD, 12 Mar. 1965, OUP/BoxOP1713/PB/ED/012868.
16. I have also discussed these points in Brewer (2004).
17. Burchfield's choice of T. S. Eliot as his only source for twentieth-century use of the noun might well give the wrong impression that it is or was in some way an unusual, poetic or fanciful term. Detective fiction, in which as we saw Marghanita Laski was an expert, would have readily furnished other examples.
18. Murray (1879: 571–2).
19. 'Nor have we added later examples to words and senses whose illustration ends in the [first edition of the] Dictionary with nineteenth-century examples' (*OEDS1*, p. xv). *OED3* (draft entry of Sept. 2000) has culled the twentieth-century quotations for *mantra*, reducing them to six in all.
20. The document referred to in notes 5 and 8 above (OED papers: Misc/39/3.v (p. 5)) specifies that 'intervening quotations . . . should, if possible, be spaced so that the time-lag between each pair is roughly equal'.
21. http://oed.com/about/history.html#cdrom.
22. The adjectival use of the participle is illustrated by two further twentieth-century quotations, one of 'raped boys' and the other 'raped girls', which hardly redresses the balance. See also discussion of quotations for *lesbian* at p. 205, and (on *OED* and society) pp. 249–50, below.

23. Skeat to J. Murray, MP Box 24, 30 Nov. 1878.
24. Burchfield (1989: 194–5); the letter (ten pages long; B/3/8/5, 3 Dec. 1902) is also quoted in Murray (1977: 288).
25. Murray (1879: 582–5); cf. Murray (1880–81b: 267–78).
26. These figures are taken from the prefatory matter to *OED1*'s fascicles (reproduced in Raymond (1987) and analysed in unpaginated prefatory material) and from *OEDS1* p. xvii, *OEDS2* p. ix, *OEDS3* p. viii, *OEDS4* p. ix.
27. Burchfield (1973), n. 16.
28. *OEDS4*, p. x; the statement is puzzling, given that Orm, though an excellent homilist, was no literary writer and the linguistic and cultural circumstances in which the latter authors wrote were very different. These and other remarks may well have been prompted by the criticisms of Harris (1982); see pp. 211, 256 below.
29. The sample and letters reporting on it (from e.g. Friedrichsen, Randolph Quirk, Norman Davis and E. G. Stanley) are in OUP/BoxOP1713/PB/ED/012870.
30. Burchfield (1989: 12, 1980: 282). Elsewhere, as we saw in Chapter VI, he had identified other causes of delay.
31. In acknowledging that 'it might well be expected that in any notice of the literary Makers of English a large place must be given to Chaucer', but that 'it is singularly difficult to prove this by definite examples', Bradley (1904: 215–40, at p. 226) anticipates Cannon (1998). The point in both cases is that reading more widely in Middle English texts earlier than Chaucer may show that his usage was less singular than might appear; Cannon uses the evidence of *MED* to demonstrate this. Carlyle's extraordinarily eccentric vocabulary, quoted some 6,240 times, is often represented by *OED* as *hapax legomena*; but at least one of his terms, *gigman* and its derivatives, penetrated general usage (as *OED*'s definition – written by Bradley – helpfully describes: 'one whose respectability is measured by his keeping a gig; a narrow-minded person belonging to the middle class, who views "respectability" as the chief concern of life, a "Philistine"').
32. E.g. *OEDS1*, p. xiv; Burchfield (1975: 351, 1989: 173).
33. Toynbee and Whibley (1935), vol. 1, p. 192: letter from Gray to R. West, Apr. 1742 (see further Taylor (1998)); 'The Music of Poetry' in Kermode (1975: 110); Abbott (1935: 89).
34. Linguistic 'deviation' was first systematically investigated as part of the Russian formalist movement in the early twentieth century. For discussions of Shakespeare's contribution to the lexicon, see the recent useful summary by Crystal (2004: 315–29); for that of Tolkien see the book written by *OED* lexicographers, Gilliver, Marshall and Weiner (2006). Taylor (1993), e.g. Chapter 1, illuminatingly discusses related topics.
35. Hill (1989: 414). The review is of *OED2*, but the judgements Hill criticizes were made by Burchfield, who was chiefly responsible for adding Hopkins's vocabulary to the *OED*.
36. Murray (1882–84: 516; 1879: 572). It is possible the first *OED* editors established an index for Shakespeare's writings – not as difficult as it sounds, given the concordances and glossaries available – but there is no direct evidence that they did so (and no evidence now survives of indexes to any writer or work). They seem to have fallen well short of a complete record of any other writer, even those they quoted most (Chaucer, for example, is far more extensively covered in *MED* than in *OED1*, and *OED3* is now including many more quotations from his works; see p. 253 below).
37. Burchfield (1974: 13).
38. Burchfield (1989: 89); cf. similar remarks pp. 13, 84.
39. In 1959 the reading for Auden was 'well advanced' (*Sunday Times*, 1 Feb. 1959, p. 8); clearly readers went back to some authors repeatedly over the next few years in order to keep up with their published output. A document of 9 Feb. 1971 titled O.E.D.

Supplement n/e, on <u>Closing date of entries</u>, notes that 'R.W.B. favours continuous updating' and that 'this was the policy with the original Supplement. (C.T.O. was very proud of getting <u>body-line bowling</u> in, in 1933)' (OUP/BoxOP1713/PB/ED/012867).

40. For more on labels see Stein (1983), Brewer (2004); on *maltalent* see p. 243 below.

41. Burgess (1976). This is the only quotation from Martin Amis in this volume.

42. James (1977). Martin Amis was quoted a total of 134 times in Burchfield's Supplement; Kingsley Amis's total is 142 (18 times in *H–N*, the volume under discussion; 45 times in all from *Lucky Jim*). John Osborne is quoted around 50 times, though never from *Look Back in Anger* (Burchfield told Godfrey Smith in 1959, 'Yes, we read the Angry Young Men too: books like "Lucky Jim", "Room At The Top"; *Sunday Times*, 1 Feb. 1959, p. 8).

43. Burchfield also quoted Shaw, Kipling, Twain and William James in significant numbers. But these authors had been previously quoted by the *OED1* lexicographers; and since it is now impossible to distinguish electronically between *OED1* and Burchfield's Supplement, we cannot say how many of their respective quotations are to be ascribed to Burchfield. The table published by John Willinsky, who had access to Supplement data separate from that of *OED1*, indicates that these authors were quoted in as large numbers by Burchfield as Joyce, Wodehouse et al. (Willinsky (1994: 215); see further http://oed.hertford.ox.ac.uk/main/content/view/37/167/).

44. Figures from Brewer (2005–); on *OED* and gender see Baigent, Brewer and Larminie (2005).

45. Last four lines of Horace, *Epistles*, 2.2. 110–18; translation from Rudd (2005: 118). Ganz (1973: 21), quoting a letter to Karl Lachmann, tells us that Grimm also wanted 'to put before the nation the wealth and poetic force of [the German language] so that writers and poets could see and learn what was available'.

46. Johnson (1958–), vol. 13, p. 57.

47. Burchfield had suspected as much, given that the title-page of Eliot's *Notes towards the Definition of Culture* (1948) bore an epigraph 'purporting to be the entry in the *Oxford English Dictionary* for sense 1 of the word *definition*'. In fact it was from the *Shorter* (Burchfield (1989: 61; 79, n.1). See Eliot (1940), also quoted in Taylor (1993: 234); see also Taylor's Chapter 1.

48. Micklethwait (2000: 103–4); Trench (1858: 4–5); *OED* s.v. *characterization* and *fossil*.

49. Auden (1963: 35).

50. Billy Connolly specified the *OED* as his desert island luxury for the BBC radio programme in July 2002, while in 1953 Lord Birkett had said he would do the same (*The Times*, 22 June 1953, p. 3). The idea was apparently first stated by the *New Statesman* in or before 1915, as reported in *The Periodical,* 15 Sept. 1915, p. 16, and was repeated by Stanley Baldwin in his speech at the Goldsmiths' banquet to celebrate the completion of *OED* in 1928. Baldwin also commented of the *OED*, 'our histories, our novels, our poems, our plays – they are all in this one book' (Baldwin (1928: 11); I thank P. Gilliver for his help here).

51. Auden's brother became a geologist (Carpenter (1983: 108)).

52. Carpenter (1983: 66).

53. Ibid.: 390–1.

54. Ibid.: 419; apparently reliant on Rosen (1975: 219).

55. Originally published in the *Listener* in 1972; reprinted in Haffenden (1983: 470–3); *obumbrated* ('Talking to Mice') is (mis)printed *obumbated* in the original English and American editions and in the complete collection of Auden's poems published after his death, Auden (1976), but the MS in the Berg Collection in the New York Public Library reads *obumbrated*. Auden may well have found the word in *OED1*. It was not treated by Burchfield; *OED3* (draft entry Mar. 2004) updates *OED1* by defining it to mean 'overshadowed' as well as 'overclouded' and labelling it

'obsolete'; it reproduces *OED1*'s two quotations, from 1592 and 1751 (Smollett) and records no later example.

56. Originally published in the *New York Review of Books* in July 1973; reprinted in Haffenden (1983: 480–4).

57. Lines 10–21; Auden (1976: 631–2).

58. Burchfield (1969: 68). This sense of *disinterested* was already in *OED*, with a first quotation from Donne, but marked as 'obsolete'. Craigie and Onions had removed the 'obsolete' label and entered three further quotations, all of 1928, without comment. Burchfield added three more, his label 'often regarded as a loose use' apparently disapproving of Auden's endorsement. See further p. 228 below.

59. The conference was a meeting of the Henry Sweet Society, at which the present writer had just delivered a paper on Auden and the *OED*. On Browning see Murray (1977: 235) and Fowler (1998); also p. 204 below.

60. MP Box 22/1, 12 Jan. 1912. Murray put *thwarteous* in *OED* nevertheless, having found a second quotation for it in addition to that of Bridges, and defined the word as 'perverse, contrary'.

61. J. Murray to Miss Hastings, MP Box 15, 8 Mar. 1901.

62. Rossetti used the term in 'The King's Tragedy: James I of Scots' (Rossetti (1881: 129)), and it is also found in William Morris's *Child Christopher and Goldilind the Fair* (Morris (1895), vol. 2, p. 205), in both cases to refer to a ceremonial cup passed around at the end of a feast in a lord's hall.

63. Taylor (1993: 117).

64. Though she also acknowledges that this may have been 'something of a pose', and quotes him confessing that the first story in George Eliot's *Scenes from Clerical Life* 'brought tears to my eyes' (Murray (1977: 24)).

65. Barnes (1982: 21).

66. Burchfield's comment has been removed from *OED3*. See Deane (1998).

67. Quoted from pp. 12–13 of draft 1962 report in OUP/BoxOP1713/PB/ED/012870, and repeated in Burchfield (1961).

68. All of these words except for *accident-prone* were later to enter the Supplement marked as being of specifically US origin.

69. *OEDS1*, pp. xiv–xv; Burchfield (1975: 352).

70. Burchfield (1984: 117).

71. Crystal's proposal to Cassells is posted in its original typescript form on his website (http://www.crystalreference.com). It is striking not for its reliance on other dictionaries (in fact much new research is planned) but for its insistence on the importance of synchronic information about words and its suggestion of highly systematic methods to identify items for inclusion in the projected dictionary. Burchfield (1989: 147–65) explored lexicographical plagiarism further in his article on the 'Genealogy of Dictionaries', published in *Encounter* in 1984; the memo is in OUP/BoxOP1713/PB/ED12868.

72. Weiner (1990: 500).

73. For further discussion, see the essays in Quirk (1982), Burchfield (1992) – in which a much wider range of issues is treated, Moore (2001), Crystal (2003).

74. See Samuels (1988).

75. Burchfield (1975: 355).

76. *OEDS4*, p. viii. Searching *OED2* 'Entries' for '1928—' in quotation date and 'Chinese' in etymologies produces 20 results for *A–G* (vol. 1), 32 results for *H–N* (vol. 2), 32 results for *O–Scz* (vol. 3) and 100 results for *Sce–Z* (vol. 4). See also Benson (2001).

77. His remarks are reproduced in *OED2*, p. xxxiii.

78. An omission first noted by Ogilvie (2004) Tram-lines are used, nevertheless, in Onions's *SOED*, published the same year as the first Supplement (1933).

79. Burchfield and Aarsleff (1988: 53), quoting the *Yale Review* (Autumn 1977).
80. Murray (1977: 221–2).
81. Gilliver (2004: 59–62). Craigie included the word in his half of the 1933 Supplement.
82. A point made by Hoare and Salmon (2000: 164).
83. See p. 67 above.
84. *OED2*, p.xlvii. A. M. Hughes was the first of these (appointed 1968), and continues to work at OUP on *OED3*.
85. *OEDS1*, p. xiv; see Burchfield and Aarsleff (1988: 50) and Burchfield (1989: 7). *OED1* had of course regularly consulted scientists for help, as detailed in the prefaces to the original fascicles of the work.
86. Hoare and Salmon calculate, making 'a rough estimate by random sampling of all letters', that Burchfield increased more than tenfold the number of scientific head-words that '*could have*' been included in *OED1* (Hoare and Salmon (2000: 162, n. 5). This does not take into account the terms he added which came into the language after the completion of *OED1*. Burchfield included a special note in his first volume explaining that 'Lexicographers are now confronted with the problem of treating the vocabularies of subjects that are changing at a rate and on a scale not hitherto known. The complexity of many scientific subjects is such too that it is no longer possible to define all the terms in a manner that is comprehensible to the educated layman' (*OEDS1*, p. xix).
87. Burchfield (1975: 351). *Maréchale Niel* was not in the event included, though the term occurs in a Galsworthy quotation s.v. *Gloire de Dijon*.
88. As he said about a specific category of such vocabulary, 'literary currency . . . is the governing factor in the admission of proprietary terms to the *OED*' (Burchfield (1974: 16)). However, he had included in his 1965 sample a sufficient number of such terms without evidence of this sort to have drawn fire from Sisam, who told Davin that he was 'uneasy about the scale on which technical words are included without evidence in the quotations of any literary or general use'. (Burchfield had responded with red ink annotations: 'Such simple statements are of little value in practice tho' ever before us. Look e.g. at Iso- in 1933 Suppl.' – an entry under which Onions had listed an impressively large number of combinatorial forms). KS to DMD, OUP/BoxOP1713/PB/ED12868, 12 March 1965.
89. Crystal (2000: 225–6, 228, 229).
90. See Strang (1974, 1977), Samuels (1988), Baker (1988).
91. Burchfield (1972).
92. Murray (1977: 195).
93. *Pippa Passes,* Part IV, ll. 281–4, Jack et al. (1983), vol. 3, p. 90 (this edition notes a correspondence between Furnivall and Browning on the meaning of the word). I am grateful to E. G. Stanley for providing me with this reference; see also Pyles (1949).
94. The *OED* entry for *morphiomania* refers one to *morphinomania*, defined as 'addiction to morphine or opium'.
95. Burchfield (1989: 110; 109–15). Chapman was defending (in 1924) the inclusion of derogatory senses for *Jew*.
96. As Wyllie explained in a letter to *The Times* of 15 Sept. 1959 (in which he quotes two letters he wrote to Davin about the matter in Apr. 1951), the offending entry was first included in the 1944 Addenda to the third edition (1934) of the *Concise*, and for the 1951 edition was 'touched up instead of being entirely rewritten'.
97. Burchfield (1989: 111–12).
98. Ibid.: 115; Morton (1994: 204). Burchfield explains 'marshallers of words' as an adoption of Joseph Trapp's description of Dryden as 'the best Marshaller of words' (*OEDS2*, p. viii).
99. Burchfield's omission of a label from *bohunk* was an error. In 1970 he had singled out *bohunk*, along with *kike* and *wog*, as examples of words offensive to national or

racial groups which he intended to include in his Supplement (Tollenaere (1971: 126)).

100. Morton (1994: 239).

101. See further Brewer (2005), from which some of the following material is taken.

102. Burchfield and Aarsleff (1988: 52).

103. Quoted from Burchfield's obituary in the *Telegraph*, 6 July 2004.

104. As one cannot search electronically for the paragraph mark it is impossible to put together a coherent picture of Burchfield's proscriptions (or those of *OED1*). Craigie and Onions appear to have altogether eschewed use of this stigmatizing symbol in the first Supplement.

105. Similarly, one can find many examples of eccentric or unusual neologisms which Burchfield records in the Supplement without comment: e.g. the verb *romantic* (two quotations only, from 1969 and 1972).

106. *OEDS3*.

107. Burchfield (1980: 281–2).

108. Burchfield (1975: 357, n. 40).

109. Burchfield and Aarsleff (1988: 55). See Harris (1982) and the fierce correspondence in succeeding issues of the *TLS*.

110. Burchfield and Aarsleff (1988: 53); Barnes (1982).What Barnes said in full (not reproduced by Burchfield), was 'To some extent, these Supplement volumes are unreviewable; the temptation is to call the work an overflowing treasure-chest, rich argosy, super-stuffed silo, or whatever, and then waffle on about your favourite words. Well, it *is* magnificent, scholarly, and impressive; let's get that out of the way. It is also immaculately printed and proof-read, and very expensive. However, when there are blackheads on the brow of Nefertiti, we shouldn't pretend they are beauty spots. There are errors and imperfections in various fields.'

111. *Observer,* 11 May 1968.

112. Quoted in OUP publicity leaflet accompanying completion of Supplement in 1989; the *TLS* review (of *OEDS1*, 26 Jan. 1973), was by A. J. Aitken.

113. *OEDS4*, p. xii.

114. Figures from http://www.oed.com/about/facts.html. Substantial competitors, such as Gove (1961) and Stein and Urdang (1966), do not confine themselves (as Burchfield does in the main) to words and senses new to twentieth-century English, and contain far fewer quotations.

VIII The 'New *Oxford English Dictionary* Project'

1. Some of the information in this section is drawn from a pre-publication copy of Weiner (2007) (with thanks to its author), which contains a substantial bibliography of relevant publications by the *OED3* editors.

2. He adds, 'The printing house concerned, Latimer Trend of Plymouth, nobly retained its hot-metal department until the entry for *Zyrian* was safely in type' (*OEDS4*, p. viii).

3. Korn (1989); John Wilson, letter to *TLS*, 30 June–6 July 1989, p. 719.

4. Weiner (2007); the study was carried out by John Simpson, then a senior Supplement editor (later co-editor of *OED2* and chief editor of *OED3*), and Leslie Burnett, editor of the *New SOED*.

5. Quotations in this paragraph from *OED2I*, pp. l–lvi.

6. Weiner (1985: 1).

7. Ibid.: 12.

8. This is the document referred to in *OED2I* , p. li, 'A Future for the Oxford English Dictionary', 1983 (newly arrived in the *OED* archives in a collection of papers

belonging to Burchfield personally). In a more popular article, Weiner (1987) repeatedly mentions the need for revision – of definitions, pronunciation system, etymology, and also by provision of additional illustrative quotations, but at this early stage in the project was unable to report on ways and means of bringing this about. At around this time (early 1980s), *OED* staff began reading systematically through old files so as to retrieve and file revision and correction material previously submitted to and recorded by their predecessors (information from John Simpson, chief editor of *OED3*; see Chapters III and IV above).

9. Sutcliffe (1978: 223). Mencken subsequently corresponded with Sisam in 1932, hoping to publish a list of the Americanisms in the 1933 Supplement. Sisam thought him 'a great man in America whose good will we should cultivate' (OED/B/3/10/4(1), e.g. KS to Wyllie; KS to Mencken; both 19 Apr. 1932).

10. Quoted from an edited extract in the *Guardian*, 3 Apr. 1989.

11. *OED2 News,* 3 Apr. 1989, OED papers: OED2e/3/2.

12. As reported in *OED2 News* of 27 Apr. 1989.

13. OED papers: OED2e/3/2, 3 Apr. 1989.

14. 7 Apr. 1989.

15. Quotations from *OED2* publicity leaflet.

16. See p. 56 above on number of volumes of first edition.

17. Letter from G. F. C. Plowden to *TLS*, 28 Apr.–4 May 1989, p. 455.

18. Letter from John Wilson to *TLS*, 19–25 May 1989, p. 545.

19. Ibid. The Compact Edition of *OED* (1971), which photographically reduces four pages of the original to one of its own, was cheaply available ($17 in 1972, for example) for many years from US book clubs; a matching copy of *OEDS* was published to accompany it in 1987. To this day it remains the most handy printed form of the *OED* (its successor, the Compact *OED2*, with nine pages reduced to one, is virtually unreadable).

20. Letter from J. A. Simpson to *TLS*, 9–15 June, 1986, p. 637.

21. Precisely how profitable *OED2* was is not clear. According to the *Annual Report of the Delegates of the University Press 1989–1990*, p. 3, the Press invested £8 million in the computerization project; it was thought unlikely that it would recover the whole, 'and certainly not the investments made in the original work and in the *Supplements*'. The *Oxford University Gazette* of 25 Apr. 1991, on the other hand, reports that 'OUP have won a Queen's Award for Export Achievement . . . [which] also reflects the recent success of the second edition of the *Oxford English Dictionary*, published in 1989. The book has sold over 9,000 sets, more than 80 per cent of them overseas.'

22. *OED2I*, p. xviii.

23. They give three reasons for this retention: that the 'peculiar characteristics of Murray's transcription are "systematic"', that 'they constitute a useful record of one variety of English pronunciation in a particular period', and that, 'for the general user, most of them are merely small nuances for which one can make allowance'.

24. *OED2I*, p. xxxiii. As Stanley (1990) points out, pronunciation and especially accentuation are not treated historically by the *OED2* compilers even for the period 1875–1985.

25. Murray explains his preference for pronouncing the 'p' in his note on the prefix *ps-* (as words beginning *ps-* entered English from Greek, dropping the *p* was 'an unscholarly practice'; *psalm* and *psalter* were exceptions to this rule since they were borrowed from Greek during the Old English period and the *p* ceased to be pronounced at this stage in the development of the language); see further Brewer (2007b); Stanley (1990: 78–9). Onions's pronunciation of the *p* is remembered by Derek Brewer and E. G. Stanley.

26. See Stanley (1990: 78ff.). Further examples can be found by searching electronically for terms like 'recent' in the etymologies text of *OED2* entries.

27. *OED2* goes on to reproduce (without indicating its provenance) the whole of *OED1*'s remark that such quotations are 'preceded, where necessary, by a date, which is that of fascicle of the first edition in which they were first printed'. This makes little sense in *OED2*.

28. Murray (1977: 200–1). As we saw in Chapter I, Elsie Murray was to work as an assistant on the Dictionary until 1920.

29. OED papers: OED2e/11/6.

30. Barnes (1989).

31. *TLS*, 26 Jan. 1973, p. 90.

32. For discussion, see Brewer (2005: 293).

33. See Brewer (1993: 336).

34. E.g. *Collins English Dictionary* (editions of 1986 and 1998) and Oxford's own *New Shorter OED* (Brown (1993)). For Auden's request, see p. 194 above.

35. *OED2*, p. lv.

36. According to *OED Online*, *OED1* contained 252,200 entries (defining or treating '414,800' word forms); Burchfield's Supplement 69,300 entries ('Dictionary Facts', http://www.oed.com/about/facts.html).

37. The publication of a guide to the *OED* in 1991 helped users understand the special characteristics of *OED2* (Berg (1991)).

38. Stanley (1990). Another scholarly review, by John Algeo (1990), appearing in the journal of the Philological Society which had originally set out to create the dictionary that became *OED*, was called 'The Emperor's New Clothes'.

39. Asquith and Stanley (1991: 83).

40. The reviewers' remarks in this paragraph are quoted from a selection printed in a folder given to attenders of the Claridge's lunch (OED papers: OED2e/5/6).

41. *OED2I*, p. lv.

42. The British National Corpus (BNC) is 'a million word collection of samples of written and spoken language from a wide range of sources, designed to represent a wide cross-section of British English from the later part of the twentieth century, both spoken and written' (http://www.natcorp.ox.ac.uk).

43. E.g. http://www.mantex.co.uk/reviews/oxf-cdr2.htm.

44. *OED2I*, p. xii.

45. Some of the material in this section, and more especially the next two, is taken from Brewer (2004).

46. Quoted in *The Oxford Dictionary: A Brief Account* (1916: 16).

47. Alphabetical organization is nevertheless peculiarly productive in other ways; cf. Harris (1982: 935): 'the very convention of alphabetization simultaneously decontextualizes and recontextualizes words in a way which has no small element of surrealism in it. It makes the lexicographer "automatically" – in the various senses of that word – a Masson or a Magritte. He becomes the agent of a poeticization of the banal which is all the more stimulating for being the unsought consequence of a strait-laced professional practice'; see further Chapter VII, pp. 190–7 above. For the advantages of thesauruses, which do organize entries according to their semantic significance, see Hüllen (2005).

48. See note 65 below on the different stages of *make*.

49. *OED1*'s coverage of the medieval period was necessarily uneven; see http://oed.hertford.ox.ac.uk/main/content/view/81/235/.

50. See Woodfall (1773: 54), McCarthy (2004), Newlyn (2000: 134–69). In "To a little invisible being who is expected soon to become visible" (written 1795), l. 3, Barbauld provides an additional eighteenth-century quotation for *pledge* 2d ("Applied to a child, as a token or evidence of mutual love and duty between parents, or as a

hostage given to fortune"); in l. 4, an adverbial instance of *auspicious*, unrecorded in *OED2*; in l. 11, a second eighteenth-century example of *swarm* (n 2), not a contemptuous usage, by contrast with the existing quotations, to match the two sixteenth-century and nineteenth-century ones ; in "Washing Day" (1797), l. 4, an instance of *slipshod* (a, 2a) ante-dating the four nineteenth-century examples (starting with Leigh Hunt in 1815). *OED3* has added a further handful of quotations from her work over its revised alphabet range, but her total number of quotations is still tiny in comparison with many male authors.

51. On Palsgrave see Stein (1997), especially Chapters 3–5.
52. See further Brewer (2007a), from which some of the following material is taken; summary available at http://oed.hertford.ox.ac.uk/main/content/view/93/237/.
53. H. Coleridge (1860: 72); the *OED Online* archive pages contain scanned images of both Coleridge's letter to Trench and the appeal Marsh issued to his fellow countrymen (http://www.oed.com/archive/paper-deficiencies/p71.html and http://www.oed.com/archive/marsh/).
54. Swinburne (1868: 8, 11); for recent discussion of Victorian views of eighteenth-century literature and language, see the essays in O'Gorman and Turner (2004).
55. Murray (1879–80: 3). Both *Appeal* and list can be read in facsimile on the archive section of *OED Online* at http://www.oed.com/archive/appeal-1879–04/. Murray's remark seems to be the ultimate source of Schäfer's statement that 'because of a breakdown in organization', the eighteenth-century slips assigned to American readers 'never reached Murray's scriptorium' (Schäfer (1980: 53)). (American readers, particularly university academics, were subsequently enormously productive of slips, as Murray (1880–81a: 123–4) gratefully acknowledged.)
56. Murray (1880–81a: 124–5, 1882–84: 515–16). See further http:// oed.hertford.ox.ac. uk/main/content/view/90/234/.
57. On the 'Advanced search' page for *OED2*, searching for 'Entries' containing ('1800–1899' in 'quotation date') AND ('1600–1699' in 'quotation date') AND NOT ('1700–1799' in 'quotation date') gives 18,027 results. Repeating the search in *OED3* gives a total of 18,350 results (search made July 2006; 60 quotations fewer than the identical search made in January 2006, which yielded 18,410 results, indicating that *OED3* is now including more quotations from the eighteenth century). These searches do not identify the many additional entries in *OED* which have *some* quotations from the eighteenth century, but far fewer than those from the centuries on either side.
58. Silva (2000: 90), quoting Murray (1884: xxi) and Murray (1900: 118).
59. Murray (1885–7: x).
60. Simpson (1994).
61. Personal communication to author, June 2003.
62. For a list of *OED3* staff, past and present, see http://www.oed.com/about/staff.html.
63. *Pomak* is defined in the revised Dictionary as follows: 'Originally: a descendant of a group of Bulgarians who converted to Islam from Orthodox Christianity in Ottoman times. Now: a member of an ethnic group professing Islam who speak a Slavonic dialect of Bulgarian and inhabit parts of Bulgaria, Macedonia, Turkey, and western Thrace.'
64. See http://www.oup.com/online/englishpubliclibraries/ and http://www.icons.org.uk.
65. See http://www.oed.com/public/guide/citing.htm. The page does not mention the various CD editions, although it is important to distinguish between these forms: identical searches in the different electronic media often produce different results – attributable, presumably, to various sorts of technical explanations. *OED3*'s transparency is not complete. The *New Edition* entries are in avowedly draft form, and many of them have been altered since they were first released (e.g. to change or add labels, quotations, ordering and wording of definitions, etc.). The preceding

versions, which one might have cited as a stable and consultable authority, have disappeared without trace. The revised entry for (the first sense of) the verb *make*, for example, was released in June 2000 and has since been irrecoverably replaced by further revised versions (at least two), the most recent dated Mar. 2004. The online edition is a continuously evolving organism, and the editors are right to take advantage of the means to correct and revise as they go. The obliteration of its successive stages is, however, disquieting for those used to the stability and permanence of print.

66. A random example is the rewriting of the definition for *magnanimate*, a verb supported with a single seventeenth-century quotation: 'To render high-souled; to cheer, inspirit' has been replaced with 'To cheer, inspirit, give courage to (a person)'.

67. Bibliographical referencing has also been standardized, an enormous task (it was impossible for previous versions of the Dictionary to maintain consistent bibliographical standards; see http://www.oed.com/public/guide/preface_6.htm#bib).

68. See Durkin (1999).

69. See Simpson, Weiner and Durkin (2004) for an analysis of the rewriting of sample entries in *OED3*.

70. The M fascicles for *OED1* were published in 1904–8, and Burchfield's Supplement volume covering words beginning with *m* was published in 1976, so any *OED2* quotations for words over the range *M–monnisher* between 1908 and 1976 must have been inserted by Burchfield (barring a few possibly added by the *OED2* compilers; I have disregarded these as numerically insignificant). On *OED2*'s 'Advanced search' page, under 'Quotations', I searched (25 Nov. 2006) for the date range 1909–76, and counted the number of quotations for the range *M–monnisher*, to get the number of quotations inserted by Burchfield. I then repeated this search on *OED3*, to get the total number of quotations for these dates in *OED3*.

71. The Preface to the third edition (originally posted in Mar. 2000, and applying only to the range of revised material then published, i.e. *M–mahurat*) states that 'the revised sample shows 52% more words and meanings marked "obsolete" and 242% more marked "rare" than was the case in the equivalent range of the Second Edition of the Dictionary. It is just as important to monitor how and when terms fade from the language as it is to record their arrival' (http://www.oed.com/public/guide/preface_3.htm#documentation).

72. Nevertheless *misentering*, verbal noun, retains its 'obsolete' label. The latest quotation is still that of *OED1*, dated 1607, but Google hits suggest that printed sources would not be difficult to find.

73. For an illuminating account by the lexicographers themselves, see Simpson, Weiner and Durkin (2004).

74. Murray (1884), adapted Simpson and Weiner (1989: xxvii).

75. Pijnenburg and Tollenaere (1980: 310).

76. On labels in *OED* see further Stein (1983), Mugglestone (2000a), Brewer (2005).

77. *OEDS1* p. xvi.

78. Gilliver (1999: 1684).

79. On *well known* see Chardonnens (1997).

80. Quoted from *The Times* in *OED2* publicity pamphlet, cf. p. 4 above.

81. See http://oed.com/about/history.html#cdrom, and contrast Simpson (2001), which discusses the wide variety of regional (non-UK) varieties of English that constitute the English language as a whole.

82. http://www.oed.com/about/oed3-preface/documentation.html.

83. http://www.oed.com/about/reading.html.

84. For details, see http://oed.hertford.ox.ac.uk/main/content/view/156/323/.

85. Weiner (2000b: 171); see also Weiner (2000a 1997, 1994).

86. Quoted from front page at http://lion.chadwyck.co.uk/ (accessed 28 June 2006). This resource is available by subscription only.

87. For a list of some of the main electronic databases used by *OED3* see http:// oed.hertford.ox.ac.uk/main/content/view/157/324/).

88. The first edition in Middle English of *The Book of Margery Kempe* was published in 1940 (Meech and Allen (1940)); Julian's *Revelations* were first published in Cressy (1670) and were available in reprints of this work (1843 and 1902), also Collins (1877).

89. Owing to the different forms by which the *Gawain* poet's works were cited in *OED1* it is difficult to come up with a precise figure.

90. See further   http://oed.hertford.ox.ac.uk/main/content/view/155/322/; Simpson (2004) describes the reliance of *OED3* on other historical dictionaries of language.

91. Quotation from the illuminating article by R. Fowler (2002: 4). Laski explains her methods of reading in Laski (1968a), where she also comments (p. 38) on the scarcity of good *OED* material in Woolf.

92. For more information see http://oed.hertford.ox.ac.uk/main/content/view/63/150/.

93. See Baigent, Brewer and Larminie (2005: 13–23).

94. See further http://oed.hertford.ox.ac.uk/main/content/view/62/149/.

95. Quotation from the *Guardian*, for many months reproduced on the first page of *OED Online* (http://www.oed.com/public/welcome/). Cf. Durkin (2002: 76): 'A major aim of *OED3* is to make the dictionary's methodology more transparent at all levels . . . it is to be hoped that this, together with the revised data, will provide a powerful tool for future studies of the development of English lexis.'

96. See e.g. – to name only OUP dictionaries – Ramson (1988), Silva (1996), Allsopp and Allsopp (1996), Orsman (1997), Barber (2004); and cf. Moore (2001) (containing an illuminating essay by Simpson).

97. *OEDS4*, p. ix; cf. Silva (2000: 93).

98. *The Times*, 22 Nov. 1933, quoting G. S. Gordon.

99. Quotation from http://www.oed.com/newsletters/2003–06/2003.html.

100. Harris (1982).

101. Sinclair (1987) was the path-breaking dictionary in this respect.

102. Weiner (2007); cf. Simpson (2004).

103. See further http://www.oed.com/bbcwords/.

104. Letter to *TLS*, 13 Oct. 1972, p. 1226.

Works Cited

Unpublished Sources

The J. A. H. Murray Papers, Bodleian Library, Oxford.
Oxford English Dictionary archives and associated papers at Oxford University Press, Oxford.

Published Sources

Oxford English Dictionaries

OED

Murray, J. A. H., Henry Bradley, W. A. Craigie and C. T. Onions (1884–1928). *A New English Dictionary on Historical Principles* 128 fascicles. Oxford, Clarendon Press.
Murray, J. A. H. et al. (1928). *A New English Dictionary on Historical Principles*. 1st edn., 10 vols. Oxford, Clarendon Press.
—— (1933). *The Oxford English Dictionary being a Corrected Re-issue with an Introduction, Supplement, and Bibliography of A New English Dictionary on Historical Principles*. Oxford, Clarendon Press. Reissued 1st edn. 12 vols with one-volume *Supplement*. W. A. Craigie and C. T. Onions. Oxford, Clarendon Press. Reissued (1971) as *The Compact Edition of The Oxford English Dictionary*. Complete text reproduced micrographically. 2 vols.
Burchfield, R. W. (1972–86). *Oxford English Dictionary Supplement* (1972–86). 4 vols (vol. 1: *A–G*, 1972; vol. 2: *H–N*, 1976; vol. 3: *O–Scz*, 1982; vol. 4: *Se–Z*, 1986). Oxford, Clarendon Press. Reissued in 1987 in Compact Form (1 vol.).
Simpson, J. A. and E. S. C. Weiner (1989). *The Oxford English Dictionary*. 2nd edn. 20 vols. Oxford, Clarendon Press. Reissued in 1991 in Compact Form (3 vols).
—— (1993). *Oxford English Dictionary Additions Series*. Vols 1 and 2. Oxford, Clarendon Press
Proffitt, M., and J. Simpson (1997). *Oxford English Dictionary Additions Series*. Vol 3. Oxford, Clarendon Press.
Simpson, J. (2000–). *OED Online*. 3rd edn. Available to subscribers at www.oed.com.

The *Concise, Shorter, Pocket, Little Oxford English Dictionaries*

Brown, L. (1993). *The New Shorter Oxford English Dictionary on Historical Principles*. Oxford, Clarendon Press.

Fowler, H. W. and F. G. Fowler (1911) *The Concise Oxford Dictionary of Current English*. Oxford, Clarendon Press. 2nd edn 1929. 3rd edn (ed. H. G. Le Mesurier) 1934. 4th edn (ed. E. McIntosh) 1951.

—— (1924). *The Pocket Oxford Dictionary of Current English*. Oxford, Clarendon Press. 2nd edn 1934. 3rd edn (ed. H. G. Le Mesurier) 1939.

Onions, C. T., W. Little, H. W. Fowler and J. Coulson (1933). *The Shorter Oxford English Dictionary*. Oxford, Clarendon Press. 2nd edn 1936. 3rd edn 1944. 3rd edn with corrections and revised addenda 1955.

Ostler, G. and J. Coulson (1930). *The Little Oxford Dictionary of Current English*. 2nd edn 1930. 3rd edn 1941 Oxford, Clarendon Press.

Other Dictionaries

Allsopp, R. and J. Allsopp (1996). *The Dictionary of Caribbean English Usage*. Oxford, Oxford University Press.

Amos, A. Crandell, A. DiPaolo Healey, et al. (1986–). *A Dictionary of Old English*. Toronto, Pontifical Institute of Medieval Studies.

Barber, K. (2004) *The Canadian Oxford Dictionary*. Toronto, Oxford University Press. 2nd revised edn.

Coulson, J. S., H. M. Petter, D. Eagle, L. Hutchinson and C. T. Carr (1962). *Oxford Illustrated Dictionary*. Oxford, Clarendon Press.

Craigie, W. A., A. J. Aitken, et al. (1937–2002). *A Dictionary of the Older Scottish Tongue: From the Twelfth Century to the End of the Seventeenth*. Chicago, University of Chicago Press; Aberdeen, Aberdeen University Press; London, Oxford University Press.

——, J. R. Hulbert, et al. (1936). *A Dictionary of American English on Historical Principles*. Chicago, University of Chicago Press.

Glare, P. G. W. (1982). *Oxford Latin Dictionary*. Oxford, Clarendon Press.

Gove, P. B. (1961). *Webster's Third New International Dictionary of the English Language*. London, George Bell & Sons; Springfield, MA, Merriam-Webster.

Grimm, J., W. Grimm, et al. (1854). *Deutsches Wörterbuch*. Leipzig, S. Hirzel.

Guðbrandur, V., W. A. Craigie and R. Cleasby (1957). *An Icelandic–English Dictionary*. Oxford, Clarendon Press.

Imbs, P. (1971). *Le Trésor de la Langue Française: dictionnaire de la langue du XIXe et du XXe siècle*. 16 vols. Paris, Centre de recherche pour un trésor de la langue française.

Johnson, S. (1755). *A Dictionary of the English Language*. London.

—— *A Dictionary of the English Language*, ed. A. McDermott. [Electronic version of 1st and 4th edns.] Cambridge, Cambridge University Press.

Kurath, Hans, Sherman A. Kuhn, John Reidy and Robert Lewis (1952–2001). *Middle English Dictionary*. Ann Arbor–University of Michigan Press.

Liddell, H. G. and R. Scott (1843). *A Greek-English Lexicon, Based on the German Work of F. Passow*. Oxford, Clarendon Press.

Mathews, M. M. (1951). *A Dictionary of Americanisms on Historical Principles*. Chicago, University of Chicago Press.

Onions, C. T., G. W. S. Friedrichsen and R. W. Burchfield (1966). *The Oxford Dictionary of English Etymology*. Oxford, Clarendon Press.

Orsman, H. W. (1997). *The Dictionary of New Zealand English*. Auckland and Oxford, Oxford University Press.

Pearsall, J. (1998). *New Oxford Dictionary of English*. Oxford, Clarendon Press.

Ramson, W. S. (1988). *The Australian National Dictionary: a Dictionary of Australianisms on Historical Principles*. Melbourne and Oxford, Oxford University Press.

Richardson, C. (1836–37). 2 vols. *A New Dictionary of the English Language*. London, Pickering.

Silva, P. (1996). *A Dictionary of South African English on Historical Principles*. Oxford, Oxford University Press in association with the Dictionary Unit for South African English.

Sinclair, J. (1987). *Collins COBUILD English Language Dictionary*. London, HarperCollins.

Smith, A. H. and J. L. N. O'Loughlin (1946). *Odhams Dictionary of the English Language*. London, Odhams Press.

Stein, J. and L. Urdang (1966). *The Random House Dictionary of the English Language*. New York, Random House.

Webster, N. (1864). *An American Dictionary of the English Language*. Revised edn. by Chauncey A. Goodrich and Noah Porter. Springfield, MA, G. & C. Merriam; London, Bell & Sons.

Whitney, W. D. (1889–91). *The Century Dictionary: An Encyclopedic Lexicon of the English Language*. 6 vols. New York, Century.

Withycombe, E. G. (1945). *The Oxford Dictionary of English Christian Names*. Oxford, Clarendon Press.

Wright, J. (1898–1905). *The English Dialect Dictionary*. 6 vols. London: Henry Frowde.

Other Works

Aarsleff, H. (1983). *The Study of Language in England, 1780–1860*. Minneapolis, University of Minnesota Press; London, Athlone Press.

Abbott, C. C., ed. (1935). *The Letters of Gerard Manley Hopkins to Robert Bridges*. London, Oxford University Press.

Abbott, E. (1875). *A Concordance to the Works of Alexander Pope*. London, Chapman and Hall.

Adams, M. (1998). 'Credit Where It's Due: Authority and Recognition at the *Dictionary of American English*', *Dictionaries: Journal of the Dictionary Society of North America* 19: 1–20.

—— (2002). 'Phantom Dictionaries: The Middle English Dictionary before Kurath.' *Dictionaries: Journal of the Dictionary Society of North America* 23: 95–114.

Adams, W. H. D. (1886). *A Concordance to the Plays of Shakespeare*. London.

Aitken, A. J. (1971). 'Historical Dictionaries and the Computer', in *The Computer in Literary and Linguistic Research*, ed. R. A. Wisbey. Cambridge, Cambridge University Press: 3–17.

—— (1987). 'The Period Dictionaries', in *Studies in Lexicography*, ed. R. W. Burchfield. Oxford, Clarendon Press: 94–116.

Algeo, J. (1990). 'The Emperor's New Clothes: The Second Edition of the Society's Dictionary.' *Transactions of the Philological Society* 88: 131–50.

—— (1998). 'Vocabulary', in *1776–1997*, ed. S. Romaine (*The Cambridge History of the English Language*, ed. R. Hogg, vol. IV). Cambridge, Cambridge University Press: 57–91.

Allen, R. E. (1986). 'A Concise History of the Concise Oxford Dictionary', in *The History of Lexicography*, ed. R. R. K. Hartmann. Amsterdam, Benjamins: 1–11.

Asquith, I. S. and E. G. Stanley (1991). 'Correspondence.' *Review of English Studies* 42: 81–3.

Auden, W. H. (1963). *The Dyer's Hand: And Other Essays*. London, Faber and Faber.

—— (1976). *Collected Poems*. London, Faber and Faber.

Baigent, E., C. Brewer and V. Larminie (2005). 'Women and the Archive: The Representation of Gender in the *Dictionary of National Biography* and the *Oxford*

English Dictionary.' *Archives (Journal of the British Records Association)* 30: 13–35.

Bailey, R. W. (1985). 'Charles C. Fries and the Early Modern English Dictionary', in *Towards an Understanding of Language: Charles C. Fries in Perspective*, ed. P. H. Fries and N. M. Fries. Amsterdam, Benjamins: 171–204.

—— (1990). 'The Period Dictionary III: English', in *Wörterbücher: ein internationales Handbuch zur Lexikographie; or, Dictionaries: An International Encyclopedia of Lexicography*, ed. F. J. Hausmann et al. Berlin, Walter de Gruyter. 2: 1436–57.

—— (1996). *Nineteenth-Century English*. Ann Arbor, University of Michigan Press.

—— (2000a). 'The Reputation of the *OED*', in *Lexicography and the OED: Pioneers in the Untrodden Forest*, ed. L. Mugglestone. Oxford, Oxford University Press: 207–27.

—— (2000b). 'Appendix III: The *OED* and the Public', in *Lexicography and the OED: Pioneers in the Untrodden Forest*, ed. L. Mugglestone. Oxford, Oxford University Press: 253–84.

Baker, P. S. (1988). 'A Supplement to *OED*: Se–Z.' *Notes & Queries* 233: 148–53.

Baldwin, S. (1928). *The Oxford English Dictionary, 1884–1928: An Address Delivered in Goldsmiths' Hall, 6 June 1928, by the Rt. Hon. Stanley Baldwin*. Oxford, Clarendon Press. Available at http:// oed.hertford.ox.ac.uk/main/content/view/ 275/351/.

Barnbrook, G. (2005). 'Johnson the Prescriptivist?: The Case for the Prosecution', in *Anniversary Essays on Johnson's Dictionary*, ed. J. Lynch and A. McDermott. Cambridge, Cambridge University Press: 92–112.

Barnes, J. (1982). 'The Social Democratic Phase.' *New Statesman*, 16 July: 20–1.

—— (1989). '[Review of *OED2*].' *Harpers & Queen*. March 1989.

—— (1996). *Cross Channel*. London, Cape.

Bartlett, J. (1894). *A New and Complete Concordance or Verbal Index to Words, Phrases and Passages in the Dramatic Works of Shakespeare, with a Supplementary Concordance to the Poems*. London, Macmillan.

Battiscombe, G. and M. Laski (1965). *A Chaplet for Charlotte Yonge: Papers*. London, Cresset Press.

Becket, A. (1787). *A Concordance to Shakespeare*. London.

Beer, G. (2000). *Darwin's Plots: Evolutionary Narrative in Darwin, George Eliot, and Nineteenth-Century Fiction*. Cambridge, Cambridge University Press.

Béjoint, H. (2000). *Modern Lexicography: An Introduction*. Oxford, Oxford University Press.

Bennett, J. A. (1987). *The Divided Circle: A History of Instruments for Astronomy, Navigation and Surveying*. Oxford, Phaidon Christie's.

Benson, P. (2001). *Ethnocentrism and the English Dictionary*. London, Routledge.

Benzie, W. (1983). *Dr. F. J. Furnivall: Victorian Scholar Adventurer*. Norman, OK, Pilgrim Books.

Berg, D. L. (1991). *A User's Guide to the Oxford English Dictionary*. Oxford, Oxford University Press.

Bivens, L. (1980–81). 'Nineteenth-Century Reactions to the *O.E.D.*: An Annotated Bibliography.' *Dictionaries: Journal of the Dictionary Society of North America* 2–3: 146–52.

Blake, N. F. (2002). 'On the Completion of the *Middle English Dictionary*.' *Dictionaries: Journal of the Dictionary Society of North America* 23: 48–75.

Bolton, W. F. and D. Crystal (1966). *The English Language: Essays by English and American Men of Letters, 1490–1839*. Cambridge, Cambridge University Press.

Bradley, H. (1904). *The Making of English*. London, Macmillan.

Bradley, H. and R. S. Bridges (1928). *The Collected Papers of Henry Bradley*. Oxford, Clarendon Press.

Bradshaw, J. (1894). *A Concordance to the Poetical Works of John Milton*. London.

Brewer, C. (1993). 'The Second Edition of the *OED*.' *Review of English Studies* 44: 313–42.

—— (1996). *Editing Piers Plowman: The Evolution of the Text*. Cambridge, Cambridge University Press.

—— (2000). '*OED* Sources', in *Lexicography and the OED: Pioneers in the Untrodden Forest*, ed. L. Mugglestone. Oxford, Oxford University Press: 40–58.

—— (2004). 'The Electronification of the *Oxford English Dictionary*.' *Dictionaries: Journal of the Dictionary Society of North America* 25: 1–43.

—— (2005). 'Authority and Personality: Usage Labels in the *Oxford English Dictionary*.' *Transactions of the Philological Society* 103: 261–301.

—— (2005–). 'Examining the *OED*'. <http://oed.hertford.ox.ac.uk>.

—— (2007a). 'Reporting Eighteenth-Century Vocabulary in the *OED*', in *Words and Dictionaries from the British Isles in Historical Perspective*, ed. J. Considine. Cambridge, Cambridge Scholars Publishing: 109–35.

—— (2007b). 'Pronouncing the P: Prescriptivism or Descriptivism in Nineteenth- and Twentieth-Century English Dictionaries?'. *Historiographia Linguistica* 34: 2/3.

—— (2008). 'Johnson, Webster, and the *Oxford English Dictionary*', in *Blackwell Companion to the History of the English Language*, ed. H. Momma and M. Matto. Oxford, Blackwell.

Brightwell, D. B. (1869). *A Concordance to the Entire Works of Alfred Tennyson*. London, Moxon.

Brodribb, C. W. (1928). 'Our Dictionary.' *Times Literary Supplement*, 19 April: 277–8.

Burchfield, R. W. (1958). 'O.E.D.: A New Supplement.' *Periodical* 32: 231.

—— (1961). 'O.E.D.: A New Supplement.' *Essays & Studies* 14: 35–51.

—— (1969). 'O.E.D. Supplement: A Dymaxion Exercise.' *Oxford Magazine*: 68–9.

—— (1972). 'Four-Letter Words and the *OED*.' *Times Literary Supplement*, 13 October: 1233.

—— (1973). 'Data Collecting and Research.' *Annals of the New York Academy of Sciences* 211: 99–103.

—— (1974). 'The Treatment of Controversial Vocabulary in the *O.E.D.*' *Transactions of the Philological Society* 1974: 1–28.

—— (1975). 'The Art of the Lexicographer.' *Journal of the Royal Society of Arts* 123: 349–61.

—— (1980). 'Aspects of Short-Term Historical Lexicography', in *Proceedings of the Second International Round Table Conference on Historical Lexicography* [held in 1977], ed. W. Pijnenburg and F. de Tollenaere. Dordrecht, Holland, and Cinnaminson, NJ, Foris Publications: 271–9.

—— (1981). *The Spoken Word: A BBC Guide*. London, British Broadcasting Corporation.

—— (1984). 'The End of an Innings But Not the End of the Game.' *Incorporated Linguist* 23: 114–19.

—— (1989). *Unlocking the English Language*. London, Faber and Faber. [Reprints; articles originally published 1973–87.]

—— (1992). *English in Britain and Overseas*. (*The Cambridge History of the English Language*, ed. R. Hogg, vol. 5). Cambridge, Cambridge University Press.

——, ed. (1996). *The New Fowler's Modern English Usage*. Oxford, Clarendon Press.

—— and H. Aarsleff (1988). *The Oxford English Dictionary and the State of the Language*. Washington, DC, Library of Congress.

Burgess, A. (1976). 'The Long Road to Nzima.' *Times Literary Supplement*, 19 November: 1443.

Cannon, C. (1998). *The Making of Chaucer's English: A Study of Words*. Cambridge, Cambridge University Press.

Carey, J. (1992). *The Intellectuals and the Masses: Pride and Prejudice among the Literary Intelligentsia, 1880–1939.* London, Faber and Faber.

—— (2005). *What Good Are the Arts?* London, Faber and Faber.

Carpenter, H. (1983). *W. H. Auden: A Biography.* London, Unwin Paperbacks.

Chapman, A. L. and R. Knight (1953). *Wages and Salaries in the United Kingdom, 1920–1938.* Cambridge, Cambridge University Press.

Chapman, R. W. (1946). 'The World of Words.' *Times Literary Supplement,* 12 October: 492.

Chardonnens, L. S. (1997). 'Familiarity Breeds Contempt: On the Use of "Well-known" in *OED.*' *Notes & Queries* n.s. 44: 171–2.

Cleveland, C. D. (1867). *A Complete Concordance to the Poetical Works of John Milton.* London.

Coleridge, D. (1860). 'Observations on the Plan of the Society's Proposed New English Dictionary.' *Transactions of the Philological Society*: 152–68.

Coleridge, H. (1860). 'A Letter to the Very Revd the Dean of Westminster.' *Transactions of the Philological Society*: 71–8.

—— (1860–61). 'On the Exclusion of Certain Words from a Dictionary.' *Transactions of the Philological Society*: 37–43.

Collins, H. (1877). *Revelations of Divine Love, with a Preface by H. Collins.* [Based on British Library MS. Sloane 2499]. London.

A Complete Glossary for Sir W. Scott's Novels and Romances (1974). Reprinted from the original edition [Paris, 1833] in the Newberry Library. New York, Burt Franklin.

Considine, J. (1998). 'Why Do Large Historical Dictionaries Give So Much Pleasure to Their Owners and Users?', in *Actes EURALEX '98 Proceedings*, ed. T. Fontenelle et al. Liège, Université de Liège: 579–87.

Cowie, A. P. (2008). *The Oxford History of English Lexicography.* Oxford, Oxford University Press.

Craigie, W. A. (1919). 'New Dictionary Schemes Presented to the Philological Society, 4th April 1919.' *Transactions of the Philological Society*: 6–11.

—— (1941). 'Completing the Record of English'. Society for Pure English Tract 58. Oxford, Oxford University Press.

—— (1943). *The Scottish Alliterative Poems.* London, Oxford University Press.

Cressy, R. F. S., ed. (1670). Julian of Norwich. *XVI Revelations of Divine Love* [no place of publication].

——, ed. (1843). *XVI Revelations of Divine Love,* publ. by S. Cressy. Repr. [with a glossary by G. H. Parker]. London.

——, ed. (1902). *XVI Revelations of Divine Love* (based upon the edition by S. de Cressy) with a Preface by G. Tyrrell. London.

Crowley, T. (2003). *Standard English and the Politics of Language.* Basingstoke, Palgrave Macmillan.

Crystal, D. (2000). 'Investigating Nonceness', in *Manuscript, Narrative, Lexicon: Essays on Literary and Cultural Transmission in Honor of Whitney F. Bolton,* ed. R. Boenig and K. Davis. Cranbury, NJ, London and Mississauga, Associated University Presses: 218–31.

—— (2003). *English as a Global Language.* Cambridge, Cambridge University Press.

—— (2004). *The Stories of English.* London, Lane.

Dareau, M. G. (2002b). 'DOST: Its History and Completion.' *Dictionaries: Journal of the Dictionary Society of North America* 23: 208–31.

—— (2002b). 'History of DOST', in *Dictionary of the Older Scottish Tongue,* ed. W. A. Craigie, A. J. Aitken, J. A. C. Stevenson and M. G. Dareau. Oxford, Oxford University Press. 12: vol. ix–xxviii.

Deane, V. (1998). 'Looking after the Sense: Taking Stock of Joyce's English', in *A Collideorscape of Joyce: Festschrift for Fritz Senn*, ed. R. Frehner and U. Zeller. Dublin, Lilliput Press: 375–97.

DeMaria, R. (1986). *Johnson's Dictionary and the Language of Learning*. Oxford, Clarendon Press.

Dille, C. (2006). 'The *Dictionary* in Abstract: Johnson's Abridgements of the *Dictionary of the English Language* for the Common Reader', in *Anniversary Essays on Johnson's Dictionary*, ed. J. Lynch and A. McDermott. Cambridge, Cambridge University Press: 198–211.

Dowling, L. C. (1986). *Language and Decadence in the Victorian Fin de Siècle*. Princeton, NJ, and Oxford, Princeton University Press.

Durkin, P. (1999). 'Root and Branch: Revising the Etymological Component of the *OED.' Transactions of the Philological Society* 97: 1–49.

—— (2002). 'Changing Documentation in the Third Edition of the *Oxford English Dictionary*: Sixteenth-century Vocabulary as a Test Case', in *Sounds, Words, Texts and Change*, ed. T. Fanego, B. Méndez-Naya and E. Seoane. Amsterdam/Philadelphia, John Benjamins.

Dwyer, T. Ryle (1991). *De Valera: The Man and the Myths*. Dublin, Poolbeg Press.

Eliot, T. S. (1940). 'The Writer as Artist.' *The Listener*, 28 November: 773–4.

Empson, W. (1951). *The Structure of Complex Words*. London, Chatto and Windus.

Enciso, M. F. de and R. Barlow (1932). *A Brief Summe of Geographie*. London, Hakluyt Society.

Fowler, H. W. (1926). *A Dictionary of Modern English Usage*. Oxford, Clarendon Press.

—— and F. G. Fowler (1906). *The King's English*. Oxford, Clarendon Press.

Fowler, R. (1998). 'Robert Browning in the *Oxford English Dictionary*: A New Approach.' *Studies in Philology* 95: 333–50.

—— (2002). 'Virginia Woolf: Lexicographer.' *English Language Notes* 39: 54–70.

Furnivall, F. J. (1866). *Political, Religious, and Love Poems: From the Archbishop of Canterbury's Lambeth MS. no. 306, and Other Sources*. London, Early English Text Society, Trübner.

Ganz, P. F. (1973). *Jacob Grimm's Conception of German Studies*. Oxford, Clarendon Press.

Ghosh, J. C. and E. G. Withycombe (1935). *Annals of English Literature, 1475–1925: The Principal Publications of Each Year Together with an Alphabetical Index of Authors with Their Works*. 2nd edn, revised R. W. Chapman, 1961. Oxford, Clarendon Press.

Gilliver, P. (1999). 'Specialized Lexis in the *Oxford English Dictionary*', in *Fachsprachen Languages for Special Purposes*, ed. L. Hoffmann, H. Kalverkämper and H. E. Wiegand. Berlin and New York, Walter de Gruyter. 2: 1676–84.

—— (2004). '"That Brownest of Brown Studies": The Work of the Editors and In-House Staff of the *Oxford English Dictionary* in 1903.' *Dictionaries: Journal of the Dictionary Society of North America* 25: 44–64.

——, J. Marshall, and E. Weiner (2006). *The Ring of Words: Tolkien and the Oxford English Dictionary*. Oxford, Oxford University Press.

Goffin, R. C. (1934). 'Some Notes on Indian English.' Society for Pure English Tract 41. Oxford, Clarendon Press: 20–32.

Gray, D. (1991). 'Norman Davis, 1913–1989.' *Proceedings of the British Academy* 80: 261–73.

Green, J. (1997). *Chasing the Sun: Dictionary-Makers and the Dictionaries They Made*. London, Pimlico.

Haffenden, J. (1983). *W. H. Auden: The Critical Heritage*. London, Routledge & Kegan Paul.

Harris, R. (1982). 'The History Men.' *Times Literary Supplement*, 3 September: 935–6.

Harrison, B., ed. (1994). *The Twentieth Century*. (*The History of the University of Oxford*, ed. T. H. Aston, vol. 8.) Oxford, Clarendon Press.

Heilbron, J. L. (1998). *Geometry Civilized: History, Culture, and Technique*. Oxford, Clarendon Press.

Hill, G. (1989). 'Common Weal, Common Woe.' *Times Literary Supplement*, 21–27 April: 411–14.

Hinsley, F. H. and A. Stripp (1993). *Codebreakers: The Inside Story of Bletchley Park*. Oxford, Oxford University Press.

Hitchings, H. (2005). *Dr Johnson's Dictionary: The Extraordinary Story of the Book that Defined the World*. London, Murray.

Hoare, M. R. and V. Salmon (2000). 'The Vocabulary of Science in the *OED*', in *Lexicography and the OED*, ed. L. Mugglestone. Oxford, Oxford University Press: 156–71.

Horwill, H. W. (1935). *A Dictionary of Modern American Usage*. Oxford, Clarendon Press.

Hüllen, W. (2005). *A History of Roget's Thesaurus: Origins, Development, and Design*. Oxford, Oxford University Press.

Hutton, C. (1815). *A Philosophical and Mathematical Dictionary*. 2 vols. London.

Jack, R. J. et al., eds (1983). *The Poetical Works of Robert Browning*. 9 vols. Oxford, Clarendon Press.

James, C. (1977). 'Quote Me.' *New Statesman*, 18 March: 356–7.

Johnson, S. (1958–). *The Yale Edition of the Works of Samuel Johnson*. 18 vols. New Haven, CT, Yale University Press.

Jones, A. (1996). *Powers of the Press: Newspapers, Power and the Public in Nineteenth-Century England*. Aldershot, Scolar.

Ker, N. (1972). 'Kenneth Sisam, 1887–1971.' *Proceedings of the British Academy* 58: 409–28.

Kermode, F., ed. (1975). *Selected Prose of T. S. Eliot*. London, Faber and Faber.

Knowles, E. (1990). 'Dr Minor and the English Dictionary.' *Dictionaries: Journal of the Dictionary Society of North America* 12: 27–42.

—— (2000). 'Making the *OED*: Readers and Editors: A Critical Survey', in *Lexicography and the OED*, ed. L. Mugglestone. Oxford, Oxford University Press: 22–39.

Korn, E. (1989). 'Miracles of Miniaturization.' *Times Literary Supplement*, 13–19 January: 34.

Korshin, P. (1974). 'Johnson and the Renaissance Dictionary.' *Journal of the History of Ideas* 35: 300–12.

Landau, S. (2001). *Dictionaries: The Art and Craft of Lexicography*. 2nd edn. Cambridge University Press.

Langley, S. (1870). *Concordance to the Works of Alfred Tennyson*. London.

Laski, M. (1961). *Ecstasy: A Study of Some Secular and Religious Experiences*, London, Cresset Press.

—— (1968a). 'Reading for *OED*.' *Times Literary Supplement*, 11 January: 37–9.

—— (1968b). 'Words I–VII'. *Times Literary Supplement*, 1 February: 115; 7 March: 237; 11 April: 377; 30 May: 559; 1 August: 822; 5 September: 952; 31 October: 1232.

—— (1971). 'Words from *The Times*.' *Times Literary Supplement*, 2 April: 403.

Loane, G. G. (1920). *A Thousand and One Notes on 'A New English Dictionary'*. Surbiton, Philpott.

—— (1932). 'A Thousand and Two Notes on *A New English Dictionary*.' *Transactions of the Philological Society* 1925–30: 38–199.

Low, J. W. (1952). *Plane Table Mapping*. New York, Harper.

Lynch, J. and A. McDermott (2005). *Anniversary Essays on Johnson's 'Dictionary'*. Cambridge, Cambridge University Press.

McCarthy, W. (2004). 'Barbauld, Anna Letitia (1743–1825)', in *Oxford Dictionary of National Biography*. Oxford, Oxford University Press.

Macaulay, R. (1935). *Personal Pleasures*. London, Gollancz.

McConchie, R. W. (1997). *Lexicography and Physicke: The Record of Sixteenth-Century English Medical Terminology*. Oxford: Clarendon Press.

McDermott, A. (2005). 'Johnson the Prescriptivist?: The Case for the Defense,' in *Anniversary Essays on Johnson's Dictionary*, ed. J. Lynch and A. McDermott. Cambridge, Cambridge University Press: 113–28.

McMorris, J. (2000). 'OED Sections and Parts', in *Lexicography and the OED*, ed. L. Mugglestone. Oxford, Oxford University Press: 228–31.

—— (2001). *The Warden of English: The Life of H. W. Fowler*. Oxford, Oxford University Press.

Marsden, J. H. (1859). [Review of Trench's *On Some Deficiencies* and the Philological Society's *Proposal*.] *Edinburgh Review* 109: 365–86.

Marsh, G. P. (1860). *Lectures on the English Language*. New York.

Mathews, Mitford M. (1985). 'George Watson and the *Dictionary of American English*.' *Dictionaries: Journal of the Dictionary Society of North America* 7: 214–24.

Meech, S. B. and H. E. Allen, eds (1940). *The Book of Margery Kempe*. London, Early English Text Society, Oxford University Press.

Micklethwait, D. (2000). *Noah Webster and the American Dictionary*. Jefferson, NC, and London, McFarland.

Mitford, N. and A. S. C. Ross (1956). *Noblesse Oblige: An Enquiry into the Identifiable Characteristics of the English Aristocracy*. London, Hamilton.

Moon, G. W. (1865). *The Dean's English*. London.

Moore, B. (2001). *Who's Centric Now? The Present State of Post-Colonial Englishes*. South Melbourne, Oxford University Press.

Morpurgo-Davies, A. (1998). *Nineteenth-Century Linguistics*. London, Longman.

Morris, W. (1895). *Child Christopher and Goldilind the Fair*. 2 vols. Hammersmith, Kelmscott Press.

Morton, H. C. (1994). *The Story of Webster's Third: Philip Gove's Controversial Dictionary and its Critics*. Cambridge, Cambridge University Press.

Mugglestone, L. (2000a). 'Labels Reconsidered: Objectivity and the *OED*.' *Dictionaries: Journal of the Dictionary Society of North America* 21: 22–37.

—— (2000b). 'The Standard of Usage in the *OED*', in *Lexicography and the OED*, ed. L. Mugglestone. Oxford, Oxford University Press: 189–206.

—— (2000c). *Lexicography and the OED: Pioneers in the Untrodden Forest*. Oxford, Oxford University Press.

—— (2005). *Lost for Words: The Hidden History of the Oxford English Dictionary*. New Haven, CT, and London, Yale University Press.

Munro, J. J. (1911). *Frederick James Furnivall: A Volume of Personal Record*. London and New York, Frowde.

Murray, J. A. H. (1879). 'Eighth Annual Address of the President to the Philological Society.' *Transactions of the Philological Society* 1877–79: 561–621.

—— (1879–80). *An Appeal to the English-Speaking and English-Reading Public in Great Britain, America, and the Colonies*. Oxford, Clarendon Press. Available at <http://www.oed.com/archive/appeal-1879–04/>.

—— (1880–81a). 'Ninth Annual Address of the President to the Philological Society.' *Transactions of the Philological Society*: 117–74.

—— (1880–81b). 'Report on the Dictionary of the Philological Society.' *Transactions of the Philological Society*: 260–69.

—— (1882–84). 'Thirteenth Address of the President to the Philological Society.' *Transactions of the Philological Society*: 501–31.

—— (1884). 'General Explanations', in *A New English Dictionary on Historical Principles: Part 1: A–Ant*: xvii–xxiv.

—— (1885–87). 'Monthly Abstract of Proceedings.' *Transactions of the Philological Society*: ix–x.

—— (1900). *The Evolution of English Lexicography*. Oxford, Clarendon Press. Available at <http://dictionary.oed.com/archive/paper-romanes/>.

Murray, K. M. E. (1977). *Caught in the Web of Words: James A. H. Murray and the Oxford English Dictionary*. New Haven, CT, and London, Yale University Press.

Nevalainen, T. (1999). 'Early Modern English Lexis and Semantics', in *1476–1776*, ed. R. Lass (*The Cambridge History of the English Language*, ed. R. Hogg, vol. III). Cambridge, Cambridge University Press: 332–458.

Neve, J. (1887). *A Concordance to the Poetical Works of William Cowper*. London.

Newlyn, L. (2000). *Reading, Writing, and Romanticism: The Anxiety of Reception*. Oxford, Oxford University Press.

O'Gorman, F. and K. Turner (2004). *The Victorians and the Eighteenth Century: Reassessing the Tradition*. Burlington, VT, Ashgate.

Ogilvie, S. (2004). 'From "Outlandish Words" to "World English": the legitimization of global varieties of English in the *Oxford English Dictionary*,' in *Proceedings of the Eleventh Euralex International Congress, Euralex 2004*, ed. G. Williams and S. Vessier. Vol 2. Lorient, France, Université de Bretagne-Sud: 651–658.

Onions, C. T. (1923). '[Obituary of Henry Bradley].' *English Association Bulletin* 49: 22–3.

—— (1928a). 'How the Dictionary Is Made.' *The Periodical* 13 (143): 15–17. Available at <http://oed.hertford.ox.ac.uk/main/content/view/ 235/287/>.

—— (1928b). 'Report on the Society's Dictionary.' *Transactions of the Philological Society*: 1–5.

Osborn, E. B. (1933). 'Our Noble English.' *Times Literary Supplement*, 16 November: 781–2. [Review of Murray (1933)].

Osselton, N. (2000). 'Murray and his European Counterparts', in *Lexicography and the OED*, ed. L. Mugglestone. Oxford, Oxford University Press: 59–76.

—— (2007). 'Alphabet Fatigue and Compiling Consistency in Early English Dictionaries', in *Words and Dictionaries from the British Isles*, ed. J. Considine and G. Iammartino. Cambridge: 81–90.

The Oxford Dictionary: A Brief Account (1916). Oxford, Oxford University Press.

Oxford English Dictionary, 1884–1928: Speeches Delivered in the Goldsmiths' Hall, 6 June 1928 (1928). Oxford, Clarendon Press.

Pearsall, D. (1998). 'Frederick James Furnivall (1825–1910)', in *Medieval Scholarship: Biographical Studies on the Formation of a Discipline*, ed. H. Damico. New York, Garland. Vol. 2: 125–38.

Pijnenburg, W. and F. de Tollenaere, eds (1980). *Proceedings of the Second International Round Table Conference on Historical Lexicography*. Dordrecht, Holland, and Cinnaminson, NJ, Foris Publications.

Proposal for a Publication of a New English Dictionary by the Philological Society (1859). London, Trübner. Available at <http://oed.hertford.ox. ac.uk/main/content/ view/141/308/>.

Pyles, T. (1949). 'Innocuous Linguistic Decorum: A Semantic Byway.' *Modern Language Notes* 64: 1–2.

Quirk, R. (1982). *Style and Communication in the English Language*. London, Arnold.

Raymond, D. (1987). *Dispatches from the Front: The Prefaces to the Oxford English Dictionary*. Waterloo, Ontario, UW Centre for the New Oxford English Dictionary, University of Waterloo.

Reddick, A. H. (1990). *The Making of Johnson's Dictionary, 1746–1773*. Cambridge, Cambridge University Press.

Reeve, H. (1889). '[Review of *Encyclopædia Britannica, DNB*, and *NED*].' *Edinburgh Review* 169: 328–50.

[Review of 1933 Supplement] (1934). *Notes & Queries* 166: 51–4.

Rosen, C. (1975). 'Public and Private', in *W. H. Auden: A Tribute*, ed. S. Spender. London, Weidenfeld and Nicolson: 218–19.

Ross, A. S. C. (1934). '[Review of *OED* Supplement of 1933].' *Neuphilologische Mitteilungen* 35: 128–32.

—— (1954). 'Linguistic Class-Indicators in Present-Day English.' *Neuphilologische Mitteilungen* 55: 20–56.

Rossetti, D. G. (1881). *Ballads and Sonnets*. London.

Routh, G. (1965). *Occupation and Pay in Great Britain, 1906–60*. Cambridge, Cambridge University Press.

Rudd, N. (2005), trans. with introd. *The Satires of Horace and Persius*. London, Penguin.

Samuels, M. H. (1988). 'A Supplement to *OED*: Se–Z.' *Notes & Queries* 30: 483–7.

Schäfer, J. (1980). *Documentation in the O.E.D.: Shakespeare and Nashe as Test Cases*. Oxford, Clarendon Press; New York, Oxford University Press.

Schlegel, F. von (1818). *Lectures on the History of Literature: Ancient and Modern*. Edinburgh, Blackwood.

Schmidt, A. (1874). *Shakespeare-Lexicon, a Complete Dictionary of All the English Words, Phrases and Constructions in the Works of the Poet*. Berlin.

Schreyer, R. (2000). 'Illustrations of Authority: Quotations in Samuel Johnson's *Dictionary of the English Language*.' *Lexicographica* 16: 58–103.

Silva, P. (2000). 'Sense and Definition in the *OED*', in *Lexicography and the OED: Pioneers in the Untrodden Forest*, ed. L. Mugglestone. Oxford, Oxford University Press: 77–95.

—— (2005). 'Johnson and the *OED*.' *International Journal of Lexicography* 18: 231–42.

Simone, R. (1997). 'The Early Modern Period', in *History of Linguistics*, ed. G. C. Lepschy. London, Longman. Vol. 3: 149–236.

Simpson, J. (1994). 'Call for Research Materials for the *Oxford English Dictionary*.' *Review of English Studies* 45: 399–400.

—— (2001). 'Queen's English and People's English', in *Who's Centric Now?: The Present State of Post-Colonial Englishes*, ed. B. Moore. South Melbourne, Oxford University Press: 269–83.

—— (2004). 'The *OED* and Collaborative Research into the History of English.' *Anglia* 122: 185–208.

——, Edmund Weiner and Philip Durkin (2004). 'The *Oxford English Dictionary* Today.' *Transactions of the Philological Society* 102: 335–81.

Sisam, K. and J. R. R. Tolkien (1921). *Fourteenth-Century Verse and Prose*. Oxford, Clarendon Press.

Sisam, P. J. (1993). *Roots and Branches: The Story of the Sisam Family*. Marlow, Sisam.

Sledd, J. and W. R. Ebbitt (1962). *Dictionaries and that Dictionary: A Casebook on the Aims of Lexicographers and the Targets of Reviewers*. Chicago, Foresman.

St Clair, W. (2004). *The Reading Nation in the Romantic Period*. Cambridge, Cambridge University Press.

Stanley, E. G. (1990). 'The Oxford English Dictionary and Supplement: The Integrated Edition of 1989.' *Review of English Studies* 61: 76–88.

Starnes, D. T. and G. E. Noyes (1991). *The English Dictionary from Cawdrey to Johnson, 1604–1755*. Amsterdam, Benjamins.

Stein, G. (1983). 'Review of *A Supplement to the OED*, Vol. 3.' *Anglia* 101: 468–75.

—— (1997). *John Palsgrave as Renaissance Linguist: A Pioneer in Vernacular Language Description*. Oxford, Clarendon Press.

Strang, B. (1974). 'Review of Second Supplement.' *Notes & Queries* 219: 2–13.

—— (1977). 'Review of Second Supplement, Vol. 2.' *Notes & Queries* 22: 388–99.

Sutcliffe, P. H. (1978). *The Oxford University Press: An Informal History*. Oxford, Clarendon Press.

Sutherland, K. (2005). *Jane Austen's Textual Lives: From Aeschylus to Bollywood.* Oxford, Oxford University Press.

Swinburne, A. C. (1868). *William Blake: A Critical Essay.* London, John Camden Hotten.

Taylor, D. (1993). *Hardy's Literary Language and Victorian Philology.* Oxford, Clarendon Press; New York, Oxford University Press.

—— (1998). 'Thomas Hardy and Thomas Gray: The Poet's Currency.' *English Literary History* 65: 451–77.

Thackeray, W. M. (1848). *Vanity Fair: A Novel without a Hero.* London, Bradbury and Evans.

Tollenaere, F. de (1971). 'La Table Ronde des dictionnaires historiques.' *Cahiers de Lexicologie* 19: 116–28.

Toynbee, P. J. and L. Whibley, eds (1935). *Correspondence of Thomas Gray.* 3 vols. Oxford, Clarendon Press.

Trench, R. C. (1858). *On the Study of Words: Six Lectures, Addressed (Originally) to the Pupils at the Diocesan Training School, Winchester.* [8th edn.] London, Parker.

—— (1859). *English: Past and Present: 5 Lectures.* [4th edn.] London.

—— (1860 (1857)). *On Some Deficiencies in Our English Dictionaries.* London, Parker. Available at http://www.oed.com/archive/paper-deficiencies/.

Utz, R. J. (2002). *Chaucer and the Discourse of German Philology: A History of Reception and an Annotated Bibliography of Studies, 1793–1948.* Turnhout, Brepols.

Warburton, Y. (1986). 'Finding the Right Words: An Account of Research for the Supplements to the *Oxford English Dictionary*.' *Dictionaries: Journal of the Dictionary Society of North America* 8: 94–111.

Webb, D. (2006). *Inflation: The Value of the Pound 1750–2005.* Research Paper 06/09. 13 February 2006. Economic Policy and Statistics Section, House of Commons Library. <http://www.parliament.uk/commons/lib/ research/rp2006/rp06–009.pdf> [accessed 2 March 2007].

Weiner, E. S. C. (1985). 'The New Oxford English Dictionary.' *Journal of English Linguistics* 18: 1–13.

—— (1987). 'The New *OED* and World English.' *English Today* 11: 31–4.

—— (1990). 'The Federation of English', in *The State of the Language*, ed. C. Ricks and L. Michaels. London and Boston, Faber and Faber: 492–502.

—— (1994). 'Local History and Lexicography.' *The Local Historian* 24: 164–73.

—— (1997). 'The Use of Non-Literary Manuscript Texts for the Study of Dialect Lexis', in *Englishes Around the World: Studies in Honour of Manfred Görlach*, ed. E. W. Schneider. Amsterdam and Philadelphia, Benjamins: 235–53.

—— (2000a). 'The Language of Probate Inventories', in *When Death Do Us Part: Understanding and Interpreting the Probate Records of Early Modern England*, ed. T. Arkell, N. Evans and N. Goose. Oxford, Leopard's Head Press: 255–67.

—— (2000b). 'Medieval Multilingualism and the Revision of the *OED*', in *Multilingualism in Later Medieval Britain*, ed. D. A. Trotter. Woodbridge, Brewer: 169–74.

—— (2007). 'The Electronic *OED*', in *Oxford History of English Lexicography*, ed. A. P. Cowie. Oxford, Oxford University Press.

Whitney, W. D. (1867). *Language and the Study of Language: Twelve Studies on the Principles of Linguistic Science.* London, Trübner.

Wierzbicka, A. (2006). *English: Meaning and Culture.* Oxford and New York, Oxford University Press.

Williams, R. (1976). *Keywords: A Vocabulary of Culture and Society.* [London], Fontana.

Willinsky, J. (1994). *Empire of Words: The Reign of the OED.* Princeton, NJ, Princeton University Press.

Winchester, S. (1998). *The Surgeon of Crowthorne*. London, Viking Penguin.

—— (2003). *The Meaning of Everything: The Story of the Oxford English Dictionary*. Oxford, Oxford University Press.

Woodfall, W. (1773). '[Review of Barbauld's *Poems*].' *Monthly Review* 48: 54–9, 113–17.

Wyllie, J. M. (1958). *Vision of Truth*. Oxford, J. M. Wyllie.

—— (1961). 'Sir William Craigie, 1867–1957.' *Proceedings of the British Academy* 47: 273–91.

—— (1965). *The Oxford Dictionary Slanders: The Greatest Scandal in the Whole History of Scholarship*, Barras, Guernsey, Wyllie.

Ziman, J. (1963). 'The College System at Oxford and Cambridge.' *Minerva* 1: 191–208.

Index of Words

INDEX